Virginia Woolf's Unwritten

Virginia Woolf's Unwritten Histories explores the interrelatedness of Woolf's modernism, feminism and her understanding of history as a site of knowledge and a writing practice that enabled her to negotiate her heritage, to find her place among the moderns as a female artist and intellectual, and to elaborate her poetics of the "new": not as radical rupture but as the result of a process of unwriting and rewriting "traditional" historiographical orthodoxies. Its central argument is that unless we comprehend the genealogy of Woolf's historical thought and the complexity of its lineage, we cannot fully grasp the innovative thrust of her attempt to "think back through our mothers." Bringing together canonical texts such as *Orlando* (1928), *A Room of One's Own* (1929), *Three Guineas* (1938) or *Between the Acts* (1941) and under-researched ones – among which stand Woolf's essays on historians and reviews of history books and her pieces on literary history and nineteenth-century women's literature – this book argues that Woolf's textual "conversations" with nineteenth-century writers, historians and critics, many of which remain unexplored, are interwoven with her historiographical poiesis and constitute the groundwork for her alternative histories and literary histories: "unwritten," open-textured, unacademic and polemical counter-narratives that keep track of the past and engage politically with the future.

Anne Besnault is Senior Lecturer at the University of Rouen and the Vice president of the French Virginia Woolf Society (SEW). In 1997, she defended her Ph.D. dissertation "The Short Stories by Katherine Mansfield, Virginia Woolf and Elizabeth Bowen" at the University of Paris III-Sorbonne Nouvelle and obtained first class honours. She is the author of *Katherine Mansfield: La voix du Moment* (1997), and co-editor of *Construire le sujet. Textes réunis et édités par Anne Besnault-Levita, Natalie Depraz et Rolf Wintermeyer* (2014) and *Beyond the Victorian/Modernist Divide: Remapping the Turn-of-the-Century Break in Literature and the Visual Arts* (Routledge, 2018).

Among the Victorians and Modernists
Edited by Dennis Denisoff

This series publishes monographs and essay collections on literature, art, and culture in the context of the diverse aesthetic, political, social, technological and scientific innovations that arose among the Victorians and Modernists. Viable topics include, but are not limited to, artistic and cultural debates and movements; influential figures and communities; and agitations and developments regarding subjects such as animals, commodification, decadence, degeneracy, democracy, desire, ecology, gender, nationalism, the paranormal, performance, public art, sex, socialism, spiritualities, transnationalism and the urban. Studies that address continuities between the Victorians and Modernists are welcome. Work on recent responses to the periods such as Neo-Victorian novels, graphic novels and film will also be considered.

Music and Myth in Modern Literature
Josh Torabi

Materiality in Modernist Short Fiction
Lived Things
Laura Oulanne

Virginia Woolf's Unwritten Histories
Conversations with the Nineteenth Century
Anne Besnault

Illegitimate Freedom
Informality in Modernist Literature, 1900–1940
Gaurav Majumdar

For more information about this series, please visit: www.routledge.com/ Among-the-Victorians-and-Modernists/book-series/ASHSER4035

Virginia Woolf's Unwritten Histories

Conversations with the Nineteenth Century

Anne Besnault

Routledge
Taylor & Francis Group

NEW YORK AND LONDON

First published 2022
by Routledge
605 Third Avenue, New York, NY 10158

and by Routledge
2 Park Square, Milton Park, Abingdon, Oxon OX14 4RN

Routledge is an imprint of the Taylor & Francis Group, an informa business

Library of Congress Cataloging-in-Publication Data
Names: Besnault, Anne, author.
Title: Virginia Woolf's unwritten histories : conversations with the nineteenth century / Anne Besnault.
Description: New York, NY : Routledge, 2022. |
Series: Among the Victorians and Modernists |
Includes bibliographical references and index.
Identifiers: LCCN 2021020311 (print) | LCCN 2021020312 (ebook) |
ISBN 9780367354961 (hardback) | ISBN 9781032113715 (paperback) |
ISBN 9780429331787 (ebook)
Subjects: LCSH: Woolf, Virginia, 1882–1941–Criticism and interpretation. | LCGFT: Literary criticism.
Classification: LCC PR6045.O72 Z5543 2022 (print) |
LCC PR6045.O72 (ebook) | DDC 823/.912–dc23
LC record available at https://lccn.loc.gov/2021020311
LC ebook record available at https://lccn.loc.gov/2021020312

ISBN: 978-0-367-35496-1 (hbk)
ISBN: 978-1-032-11371-5 (pbk)
ISBN: 978-0-429-33178-7 (ebk)

DOI: 10.4324/9780429331787

Typeset in Sabon
by Newgen Publishing UK

Contents

    Nineteenth-Century Counter-Narratives   207

    Bibliography   233
    Index   252

Acknowledgements

Like many critical projects, this book took a long time writing: its orientation was regularly redefined along the years as I came to see the question of Woolf's unwritten histories through the lens of different approaches. My ideas took shape a few years ago, when I first read Melba Cuddy-Keane's *Virginia Woolf, the Intellectual, and the Public Sphere*. Woolf suddenly became alive, in a different way: a "pedagogic," complex figure, intervening in the public debates of her time, engaged in endless conversations with her predecessors and contemporaries in order to shape the future. With Michael Bentley and Laura Marcus, Melba Cuddy-Keane accepted to deliver a keynote at the conference that my friend and colleague Anne-Florence Gillard-Estrada and I organised at the University of Rouen in March 2014: "Beyond the Victorian/Modernist Divide." This was an extraordinary moment of exchange: my historian friends reminded me that "to understand is to historicise" – thank you so much Myriam, Geraldine and Michael – while my brilliant colleagues of the Woolf community stimulated my research on Woolf's singular modernity.

I owe a debt of gratitude to Professor Catherine Bernard for her generous guidance and unwavering support: she saw in me, before I was able to do so, the apprentice Victorian scholar that I needed to become, with my own heritage to negotiate. Woolf's parodic preface to *Orlando* could have served as a model here since – but without an ounce of irony – I also have many thanks to render to my editors (thank you so much Bryony Reece for your kindness and patience), and to the dear friends who have been in support of this project and of its author in so many ways and over the years: among them, Myriam Boussahba-Bravard, Florence Cabaret, Charlotte Coffin, Claire Joubert, Isabelle Gadoin, Géraldine Vaughan and my colleagues in the English Department of the University of Rouen. With my students, they are one of the reasons why I love my work so much.

My warmest thanks to my brilliant friend Louise Rosen for reading me until the last minute, and for pointing at the French in my English with grace, wit and invaluable competence.

viii   *Acknowledgements*

I would also like to thank my family and Philippe for their love and encouragements: you are all a source of deep, endless joy.

To my mother, who passed on to me her passion for English Literature and encouraged me to read Katherine Mansfield and Virginia Woolf when I was 20, my deepest gratitude.

This book is for her, my grandmothers and my three amazing daughters.

Abbreviations

AR	*A Room of One's Own*. 1929.
AWE	*A Woman's Essays*. Edited By Rachel Bowlby. 1992.
BA	*Between the Acts*. 1941.
CRI	*The Common Reader I*. 1925.
CRII	*The Common Reader II*. 1932.
CSF	*The Complete Shorter Fiction of Virginia Woolf*. Edited by Joanne Trautmann Banks. 1989.
D	*The Diary of Virginia Woolf*. 5 vols. Edited by Anne Olivier Bell. 1977–1984.
E	*The Essays of Virginia Woolf*. 6. Vols. Edited by Andrew McNeillie.1986–2011.
F	*Flush*. 1933.
JR	*Jacob's Room*. 1922.
L	*The Letters of Virginia Woolf*. 6 Vols. Edited by Nigel Nicolson and Joanne Trautmann. 1975–1980.
MB	*Moments of Being: Unpublished Autobiographical Writings*.
MD	*Mrs Dalloway*. 1925.
ND	*Night and Day*. 1919.
NFRR	"Notes For Reading at Random." 1979 (1940).
O	*Orlando*. 1928.
PA	*A Passionate Apprentice: The Early Journals, 1897–1909.* 1990.
	Edited by Mitchell A. Leaska. 1990.
TG	*Three Guineas*. 1938.
TL	*To the Lighthouse*. 1927.
TW	*The Waves*. 1931.
TY	*The Years*. 1937.
VO	*The Voyage Out*. 1915.

Introduction

We need to know the writing of the past, know it differently than we have ever known it;

not to pass on a tradition but to break its hold over us.[1]

The Past into the Present

Whether they were understood as the voice of filial rebellion, or as the result of a whole generation's impression that, after the war, the whole "fabric" of "life" was "shaken from top to bottom" (*E IV* 238), some of Woolf's most famous pronouncements have long led critics to take her at her word. If indeed "the mid-Victorian world [...] is the last that we of the present moment wish to see resuscitated" (*E II* 27) and "we are sharply cut off from our predecessors" (*E IV* 238), then the myth of modernism as a moment of radical change is one to which Woolf definitely subscribed and contributed. Recently, however, Victorian and Modernist scholars have joined efforts to remap the turn-of-the-century, replacing the "break theory" narrative with complicated versions of the "divide."[2] In parallel, Woolf's position regarding the Edwardians, the Victorians and the nineteenth century in general has become a rich terrain for scholarship, almost a battlefield reminding us of previous stimulating debates.[3] During the 1960s and the 1970s, second-wave feminist critics usually cast Virginia Woolf as an opponent to patriarchy, while the following generations found it harder to agree on the scope of her political engagement.[4] A decade later, when modernism was generally discussed in its relationship to postmodernism and the avant-garde, interpretations of Woolf as a highbrow aesthete competed with more radical views of her character and art.[5] Today, researchers agree that something needs to be retrieved in Woolf's oeuvre which critical approaches focusing on the modernist injunction to "make it new" have lost over time. Her theories of the modern have become indissociable from the act of looking back, leading scholars to follow new paths of criticism while reinterpreting old dichotomies. As they engage in fruitful conversations about Woolf's grasp of history, literary history and tradition as heritage – sometimes

DOI: 10.4324/9780429331787-1

reaching the unexpected conclusion that the former icon of high modernism is in fact a "traditionalist" or a "post-Victorian" – the past in Woolf's life and works emerges as a place of artistic negotiation and theoretical ambivalence.[6]

In 1980, Perry Meisel was among the first to "reverse the current political trend in Woolf scholarship" that he identified in his preface to *The Absent Father: Virginia Woolf and Walter Pater* (Meisel xv). Proving Woolf to be a "witting disciple of Pater" although "a veiled and secret one," Meisel suggested somewhat provocatively that Pater's influence on her work as fiction writer and critic was long unrecorded by modernist and feminist researchers because of his "misogynist" personality and because of the 1970s disaffection for questions of literary filiation (xii–xiii). Meisel's aim was, therefore, to recover what lay behind Woolf's significant repression and the manifest silence of scholars. In the following decade, critics increasingly recognised the influence of Woolf's predecessors on her work, viewing her modernist originality as "inscribed [...] in her rescripting of the past" (Spiropoulou 1). In *The Victorian Heritage of Virginia Woolf*, Janis M. Paul thus argued that "the external world is Woolf's personal Victorian past transformed into the material of fiction," her aim in life and art being to transcend the separation "between the world of the self and the world of the other" (Paul 1987: 4). Paul meant to demonstrate how Woolf's "innovativeness is everywhere counterbalanced by a strong traditional identification" (5). Ambivalence is the key term here: it characterises Woolf's character, her choice of genres and themes, her method and her manner of writing. For Paul, Woolf was torn "between society and individuality, between language and silence, between past and present, between traditionalism and experimentation, between externality and internality—in summary, between Victorianism and Modernism" (ibid. 7). Read by Paul, Woolf becomes a "transitional figure" who, like Joyce and Eliot, manifests in her fiction and essays "the pain and the exhilaration of the break with the past" (ibid. 46).

In the 1990s, Alison Booth and Gillian Beer, among others, continued to explore Woolf's ambivalent relation to the Victorians and to literary history, offering feminist versions of what Steve Ellis would later call "a complicated affair" (Ellis 2007: 2).[7] According to Booth in *Greatness Engendered*, George Eliot, rather than Walter Pater, was Woolf's "most substantial literary inheritance" (Booth 1992: 3). To establish a genealogical connection between the two novelists, she studies their "equivocal" way of addressing the question of womanhood and the problem of greatness for the woman writer, showing how both Eliot and Woolf inscribed themselves in a similarly ambivalent feminist "revision" of literary history (3). In *Virginia Woolf: The Common Ground*, Beer's interest lies more in the ways Woolf "persistently rewrote the Victorians in her novels" using parody and pastiche, conjuring up and measuring "the verbal traces of the past" (Beer 1996: 96). Her attention to rhetorical figures and writing manners points to the unavoidable fictionality of Woolf's vision of the past as history: for Beer, it is an imagined Victorian England that Woolf's writing "sustains, disperses, dispels, restores, interrupts" (ibid. 94).

In the first decade of this century, then, at least four major works were published that dwell extensively on the subject of Woolf's "retrospective susceptibilities" (Ellis 8). Two of these books address the question of Woolf's critical and fictional exploration of literary history, with many insightful comments on her special relationship with her nineteenth-century predecessors. Using an intertextual approach, Jane de Gay's *Virginia Woolf's Novels and the Literary Past* (2006) focuses on Woolf's major novels and explains how she drew upon the literary past as an "empowering model for herself as a woman writer," an influence and a major theme on her "route towards innovation" (de Gay 1–2). In *Virginia Woolf, Modernity and History*, Angeliki Spiropoulou chooses approximately the same corpus to show how Woolf's work was "deeply implicated in the historical actuality of modernity." Her main thesis is that Woolf's philosophy of history is similar to Walter Benjamin's pragmatic and deontological approach in the way "it is concerned not only with what happened but also with what did *not* happen, with suppressed aspects and unrealized potentialities of the past" (Spiropoulou 2010: 2–3).[8] Steve Ellis's *Virginia Woolf and the Victorians* and Emily Blair's *Virginia Woolf and the Nineteenth-Century Domestic Novel*, both published in 2007, exclusively treat Woolf's intricate relationships with her nineteenth-century predecessors, interpreting those relationships in the light of Woolf's interest in literary history. Emily Blair's book is a feminist study of female influence. It brings into play Elizabeth Gaskell and Margaret Oliphant to show how Woolf's appreciation of the "four great women writers" and her apparent dismissal of "minor" female novelists "recall dismissive masculinist associations of the feminine and the domestic, yet [...] also reverse nineteenth-century canonical criteria that valued the domestic life of the woman writer" (Blair 2007: 13). For Blair, Woolf's search for proper female predecessors is "revisionist"; yet it requires a critical reassessment of her views on literary history, nineteenth-century domesticity, and on the possibility of a female-centred modernist aesthetic. Steve Ellis's work is not a study of influence and does not situate itself in the tradition of feminist scholarship. Ellis understands Woolf's "Victorian retrospect" in terms of heritage, but he also analyses it as an "idea" that she needed, with that of the modern, in order "to structure her sense of history" and to negotiate the sense of "loss and gain" that the shift from nineteenth century to modern culture suggested to her (Ellis 6–8).

The critical approaches underlying the books mentioned in this brief account are varied, their conclusions depending in part on the corpus of texts that they examine. Jane de Gay analyses Woolf's nineteenth-century retrospect in terms of literary influence and heritage; Gabrielle McIntire,

Linden Peach and Angeliki Spiropoulou consider Woolf's revisionist historiographical counter-narratives from the vantage point of recent theoretical or philosophical approaches – Bergson, Foucault and Walter
Benjamin, among others. Paul's and Ellis's angle of analysis is mainly
thematic, and their commentaries are grounded in Woolf's major novels.
Situated within the diversified territory of the new modernist studies (a
territory marked, among other things, by a constant revision of the modernist canon, the refusal of dogmatism and a relatively recent embrace of
the historical "turn"),[9] the authors of these works, however, all acknowledge the importance of history in Woolf's training, as well as her long-
standing desire, regularly alluded to in her diaries and letters, to write a
history book. Some have studied the "diversity" and "plurality" of her
historical thought as it emerges from her fictions and essays.[10] This scholarship has also benefitted from the work on Woolf's essays which has
helped counter the image of Woolf as an uncommitted aesthete by enabling a complex critical persona to emerge out of a long unexplored corpus
of texts.[11] "Tearing down the fantasy of high modernism" (Ross S. 2009:
12), the research on which I build partakes in the general critical reassessment of the crucial transition between the nineteenth- and the twentieth
century. That Woolf was both an heiress and an innovator whose artistic
and political stance derived "from her reading and remaking of the literary past" (Fernald 2006: 2) now appears to be common knowledge,
although Woolf herself would have probably suggested that we need to
define the words "tradition" and "innovation."[12]

Despite the ground covered so far, a few essential questions thus still
arise whenever we choose to explore Woolf's understanding of history
as a site of knowledge and a writing practice that fuelled both her modernism and her feminism. Even if she intended these questions to remain
partially unsolved and reinterpreted ongoingly, they still prompt us to use
some of the critical tools that she modelled for us as we strive towards
"some definitive," although necessarily impossible, "verdict."[13] One of
those questions concerns Woolf's antithetical, or at least ambiguous, relationship with her predecessors, a relationship that appears as a sign of the
times in "How It Strikes a Contemporary": "No age can have been more
rich than ours in writers determined to give expression to the differences
which separate them from the past and not to the resemblances that
connect them with it" (*E IV* 238). Such a sentence can, again, lead to
various interpretations. As Woolf's anti-Edwardian stance is no longer
confused with a denigration of the Victorians, her Victorian retrospect
has been analysed as the intersection of the repressed, of a hidden traditionalism, of innovativeness, or of an essential ambivalence. If, however,
we read Woolf in context, as the "historicist" she herself was (Whitworth
2013: 5), while piecing together the scattered parts of her histories and
literary histories, Woolf's dialogues with the past appear as the site of an
evolving process of artistic and political negotiations that take us to a
new understanding beyond ambivalence and contradiction.

Another crucial question concerns Woolf's interpretation of past historical models and her construction of new ones. Reassessing Virginia Woolf's feminist contribution to literary history in *Writing Women's Literary History*, Margaret Ezell asserts that Woolf was certainly "a great novelist, but not a great historian" (Ezell 1996: 4), while Melba Cuddy-Keane later on persuades us that Woolf's "experiential approach" and "multiple versionings of history" prove her to be "a radical modernist." (Cuddy-Keane 1997: 60–61). Last but not least, Booth, Beer, Blair and other critics writing in the tradition of feminist scholarship reach diverging conclusions on Woolf's "vexed dualism and essentialism," (Booth 1992: 3), on her vision of womanhood her reshaping of a female canon or on the problematic inscription of a female voice in her writings. This genealogy of feminist approaches has been crucial to our understanding of Woolf's gendering of history, without exhausting her conception of history as a field of knowledge and a laboratory of the modern: how we "make" history and literary history through a back-and-forth exercise that constantly straddles the past, the present and the future is one the chief features of Woolf's practice as a critic and a historiographer. In this exercise, the nineteenth century evidently occupies centre stage.[14]

It is my belief that there are obvious difficulties in our understanding of Woolf's relationship with the nineteenth century, seen from the double angle of historiography and gender. The first of them, I would argue, resides in the temptation to homogenise Woolf's varied discursive tactics and formalist choices to recover a unified cultural and ideological stance. In the words of Natania Rosenfeld, Woolf's project is a "projection perpetually in progress and perpetually yearning and straining, both in subject and in form, towards the other side" (Rosenfeld 2000: 6). In the process, this project embraces both inconclusiveness and contradictoriness in the sense of a resort to non-exclusive alternatives.[15] But Woolf's method also implies that there is no truth outside the necessary historicisation of the speaking subjects and their discourses. As the narrator of *A Room of One's Own* suggests in her address to Mary Carmichael as the character (an allegory of the future female writer) sees "a piece of strange food—knowledge, adventure, art" coming her way: she "has to devise some entirely new combination of her resources, so highly developed for other purposes, so as to absorb the new into the old without disturbing the infinitely intricate and elaborate balance of the whole" (*AR* 64). The second difficulty, therefore, consists in paying attention to this "elaborate and intricate balance" by building bridges between Woolf's modernism as "a proposition about language" (Williams 1996: 5), her feminism as a major political thrust and her historical thought as inseparable from a promise of innovation. The Woolf that emerges from such a study, therefore, is neither an icon of feminism nor an ethereal figure of high modernism. Her modernity does not rely on the "desire to wipe out whatever came earlier, in the hope of reaching at last a point of origin that marks a new departure" (de Man 1983: 148). She writes "as a woman" while situating herself within a lineage of mostly male interlocutors; meanwhile, her identity as a female critic and fiction writer is "performed and actualized over time" (Felski 1995: 21) according to a coherent agenda that nonetheless involves a shift of focus according to circumstances. Both an insider and an outsider, she can envision the past with nostalgia or acridity, as the site of ideologies and prescriptive exhortations that need deconstructing and, simultaneously, as the place where to seek the "facts," "truths" and "evidences" of an enduring patriarchal system. Similarly, Woolf frequently reminds us of both "the effect of tradition and of the lack of tradition upon the mind of a writer" (*AR* 29). She sees how history as a discipline and a writing practice has long implied her foremothers' and her own exclusion, yet her own literary histories rewrite the traditional canon more than they propose a different one. As "life itself" and the allegorical, multifaceted characters of "Mrs Brown" in "Character in Fiction" (*E III* 420–438), or of Orlando when he/she anticipates the judgement of Nick Greene, Woolf cannot but escape the dreaded grasp of the imperfect critic.

Conversation as Negotiation

"It was distressing, it was bewildering, it was humiliating. Truth had run through my fingers. Every drop had escaped" (*AR* 24). What new insights, then, could a book entitled *Woolf's Unwritten Histories: Conversations with the Nineteenth Century* add to the debate? My aim here is to propose a renewed vision of Woolf as a historiographer, a critic and a female "intellectual activis[t]" (Cuddy-Keane 2003: 196) – this changing, pragmatic and self-reflexive figure who "think[s] back through [her] mothers" (*AR* 57) while negotiating her own presence among her male predecessors and contemporaries. Bringing together canonical texts such as *Orlando* (1928), *A Room of One's Own* (1929), *Three Guineas* (1938) or *Between the Acts* (1941) and under-researched ones – among which stand Woolf's essays on historians and reviews of history books, her pieces on literary history and nineteenth-century women's literature – I argue that Woolf's textual "conversations" with nineteenth-century writers, historians and critics, many of which remain unexplored, are interwoven with her historiographical poiesis and constitute the groundwork for her alternative literary histories: bringing the past into being to illuminate the present becomes, in Woolf's writing, an artistic and political commitment to the future, to the advent of "this book which we see on the horizon" (*E IV* 435). As a site of apprenticeship and a truth-claiming discipline, history thus enabled Woolf to transcend the weight of her Victorian heritage, to find her place among the moderns as a female artist and intellectual and to elaborate her poetics of the "new": not as a radical rupture but as the result of a process of unwriting and rewriting "traditional" historiographical orthodoxies. As a writing practice exhibiting the process of its own making up and exclusions, history remained, throughout Woolf's career, both a cultural and political battlefield and the fruitful laboratory of her feminist poetics as a fiction writer, critic and literary historian. In the course of my investigation, therefore, I hope to verify some of the arguments and hypotheses inspired both by the rich field of Woolfian studies, and by Woolf's own method as a critic and historiographer.

The first hypothesis that I would like to put forward is that the nineteenth and twentieth centuries offer an ideological and literary continuum of questions, if not of answers, about the writing of history, historiography, and the literary codings of female experience.[16] This continuum, I suggest, does not merely relate the modernist age to the turn-of-the-century as some scholars of the fin-de-siècle or the "New Woman" literature have maintained.[17] Woolf's ambivalences and anxieties about heritage, gender and discourse have indeed subterranean connections with the political question of the place of women in the literary and historiographical traditions of the early and middle nineteenth century. Unless we comprehend the genealogy of Woolf's thought on these subjects and the complexity of its lineage, we cannot fully grasp the innovative thrust of her attempt to reconfigure the present and prefigure the future as a time and place of emancipation.

I borrow the formulation of my second postulate from Karen Chase's (1989) essay on "Propriety, Madness and Independence in Feminist Literary History" where she reasserts "the deep intimacy between nineteenth-century fiction and the feminist critic, and more particularly the tie between the study of nineteenth-century women writers and the elaboration of a feminist critical theory" (Chase 11). Along with numerous feminist scholars, I consider that Woolf's aesthetic agenda is also a political one and that her endeavour to "think back" to the past is an essential contribution to the history and theory of both modernism and women's literature. However, the question is not to decide whether Woolf was a failed historian or a postmodernist one. Although constantly fascinated by the subject, Woolf's intention was not to write the kind of comprehensive and objective history of women's literature Margaret Ezell is implicitly referring to in her introduction. Woolf's revisionist histories are, I would argue, "unwritten" histories that echo the "Unwritten Novel" of Minnie Marsh's life in Woolf's famous short story, or Katharine Hilbery's biography of her grandfather in *Night and Day*. They remain "unwritten" because of the weight of tradition and of "illustrious names" – "perhaps the conclusiveness of a great ancestor is a little discouraging to those who run the risk of comparison with him" – because of the amount of "close-written manuscripts" and "papers" that accumulate "without much furthering one's task" (*ND* 34; 35). They also remain unwritten as the result of a need to find new modes and genres of expressions that necessarily "unwrite" previous texts, an experience Orlando discovers with his poem "The Oak Tree."[18] If Woolf's "histories" have never been written in the form of an academic historical book, it is because they belong to "this difficult region, where the unfinished, the unfulfilled, the unwritten, the unreturned" enable a utopian "construction of the present" from which "the future emerge[s]" – or could emerge – "more splendid than ever" (*ND* 534). By questioning and unwriting nineteenth- and early twentieth-century historiography, they offer alternative genealogies of Woolf's own. These genealogies entail a "practice of meaning," to borrow Michel de Certeau's expression in *The Writing of History* (de Certeau 1988a: 4) aimed at present and future intelligibility; they also anticipate the French historian's conception of reading as "poaching" in *The Practice of Everyday Life* (1988b). Relying on the common reader's background, motives and emotions, as well as her own, Woolf proposes to take him across foreign territories and to empower him into a process of co-creation out of the usual patterns of social influences. To assess the critical value of these counter-narratives, I, therefore, propose to draw attention to their diversity while recognising their coherence in the context of Woolf's predecessors' and contemporaries' varied approaches to history and historiography. How might a feminist's rewriting of history revise what gets remembered, and what should be discarded or rewritten to diminish the burden of heritage and to open the path towards emancipation is a question that Woolf asked continually throughout her career.

This study also takes its bearings from the idea that Woolf's quest for "Mrs Brown"[19] – the poetical and political allegory of the unrecorded in history and literature – cannot be separated from her need to reshape old literary forms. "Genres," Vincent B. Leitch explains in *Cultural Criticism, Literary Theory, Poststructuralism* (1992), are "sociohistorical discursive constructs partaking in regimes of reason, they are open to productive genealogical inquiry attentive to literary conventions and cultural practices as well as institutional and ideological matters" (Leitch 67). I suspect Virginia Woolf would have agreed: to her, "genres" were indeed historical and cultural productions acting as the useful depositories of literary tradition; she conceived them as the site of intense writing and reading negotiations with critical rules, hierarchies and judgements. However, Woolf approached generic categories in opposing ways. On the one hand, she "forced [her]self to break every mould & find a fresh form of being, that is of expression, for everything she felt and thought" (*D IV* 233); on the other, she considered that Georgian literature suffered "from having no code of manners which writers and readers accept as a prelude to the more exciting intercourse of friendship" and, therefore, lacked the common ground Woolf wanted to establish between writer and reader in the hope it would help bridge the perceived division between the artist and her audience (*E III* 434).[20] Quite logically, critical interpretations of Woolf's way of seeking an alternative female sentence within or without a male literary tradition diverge. For Lyn Pykett in *Engendering Fictions* (1995), Woolf's novels subvert "what she sees as conventional masculine forms e.g., literary history, realist fiction, biography and the essay and creates new gender- and genre-bending ones" (Pykett x). Emily Blair

thinks somewhat differently: she does not analyse Woolf's "story of reno-
vation," as Pykett names it, in terms of "rupture and the abandonment
of tradition" (Pykett 97), but as the result of a more ambivalent position
towards turn-of-the-century dominant discourses and shifting ideologies.

A similar question could be raised concerning Woolf's exploration
of the different modes of historical writing: as the daughter of Leslie
Stephen, she was asked to read extensively "Victorian Lives," biographical essays and what she would later call "historians' histories" (*E III*
3) – those books in several volumes that the heroines of *The Voyage
Out* and *Night and Day* see as the embodiment of patriarchal knowledge and as the proof of their own invisibility as women. Yet, far from
moving away from biography and the essay in her critical practice, Woolf
used these traditional writing "kinds" or "classes," as she called them,
as irreplaceable literary forms enabling her to understand past and present experiences "by looking at the picture of the lives of others" (*TG*
92). Alongside her more experimental fictions, they became locations for
her historiographical and theoretical reconfigurations. To examine the
explicit and implicit "conversations" with nineteenth-century and early
twentieth-century historians, critics and fiction writers that shape those
reconfigurations and counter-narratives, we thus need to bring together
an apparently hybrid and eclectic corpus of texts that are usually read
separately and never materialised into a "real historical work" (*L I*
202),[21] and yet that contribute to re-establish Woolf's place among the
male, high-modernist critics of her generation.[22]

I do not use the word "conversation" here as a euphemistic way of
alluding to critical quarrels. The conversation I am hoping to engage in
with Woolf's writings, reviewed texts and critics is first and foremost a
tribute to her own method of reading and creating, a method that she herself evokes in her diaries, essays and fictions. Woolf's idea, if not theory,
of conversation as the necessary "intercourse" in which the "writers
of England and the readers of England" "must be forever engaged" (*E
III* 499), as a mode of criticism inherited from Samuel Johnson – yet
the only one "worth having at present"[23] – and as the proper tone and
style for an essayist, or as the "turn and turn about method" (*D II* 247),
has led critics such as Leïla Brosnan, Melba Cuddy-Keane, Beth Carole
Rosenberg or Christine Reynier to analyse her essays and fictions along
new lines of interpretation. Often using Mikhail Bakhtin's dialogism to
examine the relationship between the Woolfian text and its "common
reader," those scholars mostly agree on the aesthetic, political and ethical effects of the conversational trope as redefined by Woolf. Woolf's
"dialogic" method thus implies a problematised utterance, "situated
readers" undergoing "repeated positionings," along with the recognition
of literary communication as a historically situated process related to its
material context and, in the case of literature, to previously produced
statements. Inevitably, then, we need a pragmatic approach to interpret Woolf's works, one that "operate[s] a metaphorical extension from

speech act to text, from linguistic interlocution to textual interpretation," as the French philosopher of language Jean-Jacques Lecercle explains in *Interpretation as Pragmatics* (1999: 34); one that also moves beyond Bakhtinian dialogism when it does not take into consideration the effects of the cultural politics of Woolf's time vis-à-vis her position as a female intellectual.[24] We also want to remember the variety of her interlocutors and the different communities of readers whom she addressed as she wrote for the *TLS*, *Academy & Literature*, *The Nation & Athenaeum*, but also for the middlebrow readership of *The Atlantic* or *Vogue*, along with the specific formats – lectures, reviews, essays and fictions – she had to adapt to. Analysed through the lens of the numerous "influences" – a pervading word in her essays – that she responded to, Woolf's contradictory impulses are bound to be cast in different terms. This is the reason why I would like to add to the Woolfian notion and practice of conversation the idea of negotiation. As a reader, a writer, and a cultural innovator, Woolf constantly needed to negotiate with past cultural traditions and her Victorian heritage. This process of negotiation appears to have been at times joyful – in *Orlando* – or more painful, as in *Three Guineas*. It was inspired by a belief in the possibility of persuasion and mutual argument while never evading necessary conflicts and confrontations. In the words of Adrienne Rich again, whose *On Lies, Secrets and Silences* (1979) acknowledges Woolf as a foremother,

> "revision" is for "us" (women) an act of looking back, of seeing with fresh eyes, of entering an old text from a new critical direction—[...] more than a chapter in cultural history: it is an act of survival. Until we can understand the assumptions in which we are drenched we cannot know ourselves.
>
> (Rich 35)

Virginia Woolf's theory of conversation thus teaches me a critical method. This method is grafted on a continuous dialogue with my own predecessors and contemporaries while expanding different strains of study. It brings together texts that are often read separately and interprets Woolf's conversations with the nineteenth century in a more pragmatic and less dogmatic way. It thus aims at recovering her implicit dialogues with personal and institutional interlocutors. It weaves close readings with source readings, historicised studies with comparative studies, the tools of feminist criticism and the more traditional approaches of formalism and genre studies. As a result, *Virginia Woolf's Unwritten Histories* moves the discussion of Woolf's historical thought and historiographical practice beyond the myth of the Victorian and Modernist break by complicating the critical assessment of her inheritance and legacy; it offers a historicist vision of this heritage by uncovering the archaeology of Woolf's historical thinking and writing; it demonstrates that Woolf's conception and feminist practice of literary history are indissociable from her vision of revisions of inherited historiographical patterns; it takes into account the complexity of Woolf's subject-position by refusing to interpret her texts as functioning unproblematically within a cultural power system. Finally, this book wishes to show how Woolf's conception and practice of history and literary history are sustained by a vital impulse towards a utopian future.

Unwritten Histories

In Part I of this book, I show how Woolf's use of the terms "historian" and "history" refers us to a succession of debates which cannot simply be ascribed to past traditions or to present modernity. Instead, Woolf's historical thought forces us to retrace and remap pre-existing clusters of historiographical discourses that she recasts in her own terms. To understand Woolf's "new historiography," we, therefore, need to have a clear idea of what "tradition" meant for her. But we also need to acknowledge how her pursuit of history was a reading and writing practice that evolved in time. This part, therefore, explores how Woolf's deep knowledge of history's official narratives pervades her production as a literary critic and fiction writer; it explains how her early desire to write a history book gradually became a need to "unwrite" and "rewrite" historians' histories and why her use of notions such as "truth," "fact," "change," "continuity" or "age" refers both to established historiographical concepts and to renovated critical tools. Part I also proposes to narrate the different phases of Woolf's historical thought and how they reflect both her traditional training in history and the emergence of persisting, more heterodox interrogations. From 1905 and her first review to the 1930s and the menacing shadows of rising fascism and the war to come, Woolf's conception of the past as history and of history as a written text was influenced, of course, by her own reality, along with the changing historical and cultural circumstances. As an "apprentice" historian imagining that she would, one day, produce a real historical work, her task was to negotiate the heritage handed down by her father; as a young reviewer and critic having taught English History at Morley College, she needed to transform the weight of this heritage into a learning opportunity. Later on, her apprenticeship transformed into a writing practice aimed at making sense of both the past and the present, a laboratory for her conception of the "obscure" and the "unwritten" in history and literature, and the very matter of her interventions in the cultural politics of the time.

Chapter 1 examines the nineteenth- and early-twentieth-century historians' histories that Woolf inherited and how the knowledge of their embedded discourses challenges the usual representations of her position vis-à-vis tradition. In this chapter, I uncover the similarities between Woolf's protagonists in *The Voyage Out*, *Night and Day* and *Jacob's Room*, and a generation of young women – and male students – faced with prescribed history books that most of the time leave them power-less as readers, autonomous subjects or as members of their social circle. I go on to consider the reasons why Woolf nonetheless actively engaged in conversations with the dominant discourse of nineteenth-century and early-twentieth-century historiography – a crowded and heteroge-neous field of knowledge. Inspired by Michael Bentley's historiograph-ical research, I then disentangle the reconstructed master-narrative of nineteenth-century historical thought encapsulated in the label "whig his-toriography" from its more complex version; my aim here is to recover Woolf's own, apparently less heterogenous, conception of "historians' histories" and the political strategy that underlies it.

Chapters 2 and 3 focus on the evolution of Woolf's historical thought as her reading experiences became articulated in her writing over the first decades of the twentieth century. In Chapter 2, I examine Woolf's reviews and essays on historical books between 1906 and 1919 and the way these texts testify to her romantic historiographical heritage – a subject rarely addressed, if at all. As I study these essays and reviews alongside Carlyle's and Macaulay's writings on history, I unearth affinities between Woolf's constant interest in the readability and representability of history as a written text and the romantic historians' attempts to capture some evocative immediacy of the past into the present. In Chapter 3, I move to Woolf's feminist dialogue with History and historiography in *Orlando* and *A Room of One's Own*, in a cultural context when innovation – the "new" – became an injunction for both modernist historians and mod-ernist literature. As Woolf more clearly engaged with a creative poetic and political practice, she continued to fracture past and present historio-graphical discourses along with their hegemonic pretensions. Keeping the tracks of Victorian and Modernist historiographical models that she pitted against one another, she resemioticised some of the historian's chief tools and concepts – among them biography, time and change – thanks to an empowering unwriting and rewriting practice.

Chapter 4 begins by considering how Woolf's generation experienced, from the 1930s onwards, the accelerated pace of history in the making. At the time when the question became "are we to believe that history has betrayed us?" (Bloch 1954: 5) and "what can art do for politics?," Woolf's historical writings were placed under the sign of urgency and pol-itical intervention, while her aspirations for a better future were sustained by a democratic vision of history. Examining first this specific context and how Woolf envisioned putting art and words into action, I explore Woolf's move towards the exploration of history in the "raw" and in the present, along with the question of historical distance. I then draw on Woolf's historiographical work in "Why Art To-Day Follows Politics," "Thoughts on Peace in an Air Raid," *The Years*, *Between the Acts* and *Three Guineas* to show how she prompted her readers to acknowledge her contemporaries' crisis in historical consciousness, to envision the chaos to come while resisting communal passivity. The last subsection of this chapter engages with the question of historical causality as embedded in Woolf's scorching critique of Victorian patriarchy.

Part II of this book builds on the discussions and critical tools of the earlier chapters and closely examines the interconnectedness of Woolf's conception of literary history and her grasp of historiography. The aim is again to situate Woolf within tradition – here examined as past and present conceptions of literary history – in order to assess her singular modernity. The chosen methodology follows Woolf's own approach to reading and writing as it first places her critical practice in dialogue with nineteenth- and twentieth-century practitioners of literary history. The conversations Woolf engages in, in her essays and reviews, with the nineteenth- and twentieth-century illustrious and less eminent figures of the literary world are primarily considered as the site of various strategies – resistance strategies, conflict strategies, creative strategies – out of which emerges an image of Woolf as a literary critic and a female intellectual that contrasts with the usual, and even recent, definitions of her journalistic, non-theoretical essayism.

My aim in Chapter 5 is to reconcile Woolf, the modernist critic – still considered one who never produced any major contribution in the history of criticism – with Woolf, the historiographer and foremother of feminist literary history. To do so, I begin by disentangling the threads of her legacy as a reviewer, essayist and critic, those threads being themselves woven into the evolution of literary history and general history in the nineteenth- and twentieth centuries. I then examine several of Woolf's critical essays to assess the specificity of her practice as a critic and a historiographer. This practice, I argue, is both framed by a specific context – here the construction of the story of English literature at the end of the nineteenth century – and the result of a strategy consisting in breaking down illusory boundaries (between practices, periods, literary categories) and redrawing new affiliations. In a context when most of her contemporaries had abandoned literary history to university lecturers and scholars, I seek to shed light, in Chapter 6, on Woolf's alternative forms of literary history. Looking at her historiographical and critical work on the genre of the essay, then at "Phases of Fiction" and "Anon," I suggest that these unwritten literary histories – in the double sense of incompletion and absence of closure – are anchored in the pragmatics of experience and interlocution while resulting from the fruitful tension between the learning and unlearning of pre-existing models of literary knowledge.

Chapters 7 and 8 of this book stem from the arguments exposed in the preceding ones. Chapter 7 begins with an assessment of Woolf's feminist legacy in the light of her "contradictoriness." This leads me to probe the "woman question" as Woolf inherited it, addressed it and transformed it. The nature of this transformation gains in clarity as I compare some of Woolf's reviews and essays on women and fiction with George Lewes's (1852) essay "The Lady Novelist" and E.M. Forster's (1910) lecture on "the Feminine Note in Fiction." I suggest here that while Woolf eschewed the reductive terms of nineteenth-century dominant discourses on the gender binary, she never detached her process of conceptualisation (of women and fiction) from the complex and historicised "embodiment" of sexual difference. I finally show how this double thrust towards embodiment and theorisation is enacted by Woolf's gendered allegories of "Fiction as a Lady": satirically unwriting and rewriting a whole genealogy of critical discourses on the feminisation of the novel and mass culture, Woolf denounces the epistemological violence on which they rely, returning the performative value of this violence against the patriarchal system that gave birth to it. Chapter 8 examines how Woolf wrote her nineteenth-century foremothers into complex counter-narratives. I begin by looking at Woolf's (1922) review "Jane Austen Practising" which I read alongside Lewes's (1859) essay "Jane Austen." Framed in the context of Austen's Victorian reception, I suggest that Woolf's own dialogue with the novelist is typical of her critical and historiographical "pattern of inquiry," one that musters the counter-mechanisms that she developed as a female artist, critic and historiographer. From there, I move to the assessment of Woolf, herself, practising in *Room of One's Own*, before turning to the unwritten story of how she thought back through her mothers.

Notes

1 Adrienne Rich, "When We Dead Awaken: Writing as Re-Vision," in *On Lies, Secrets, and Silence*, New York: Norton (1979: 35).

2 On this subject, see *Late Victorian into Modern* (eds. Laura Marcus, Michèle Mendelsohn and Kirsten E. Shepherd-Barr, 2016); *Reconnecting Aestheticism and Modernism: Continuities, Revisions, Speculations* (eds. Bénédicte Coste, Catherine Delyfer and Christine Reynier, 2017) and *Beyond the Victorian/ Modernist Divide* (eds. Anne Besnault-Levita and Anne-Florence Gillard-Estrada, 2018).

3 In *Modernism, Memory and Desire: T.S. Eliot and Virginia Woolf*, Gabrielle McIntire evokes the recent "battle about modernism's relation to the past" (2008: 4–5).

4 See Toril Moi's discussion, in *Sexual/Textual Politics: Feminist Literary Theory* of Elaine Showalter's "negative feminist response to Woolf" in *A Literature of Their Own* (Moi 1985: 1–18), and her critique of Jane Marcus's vision of Woolf as a "guerrilla fighter in a Victorian skirt" in "Thinking back through our mothers" (Marcus 1981: 1).

5 For representative arguments about this question, see Peter Bürger (*Theory of the Avant-Garde*, 1984); Andreas Huyssen (*After the Great Divide: Modernism, Mass Culture, Postmodernism*, 1986); Raymond Williams (*The Politics of Modernism: Against the New Conformists*, 1996).

6 Steve Ellis's way of summarising the 1990s debates, in *Virginia Woolf and the Victorians* (2007), concerning Woolf's relation with the past and with her Victorian heritage is symptomatic of the thought-provoking critical disputes on the subject. Ellis deplores that a critic such as Ann Banfield (*The Phantom Table* 2007) should be "unable to resist the lure of Woolf's 'December 1910' as definitive watershed" (Ellis 2007: 5), but he does not agree either when

other studies (he mentions Jane de Gay's) see Woolf's Victorian retrospect as "a form of traditionalism" (Ellis note 19; 182–183). "Post-Victorian" is for him the "apt designation" to express "the blend of conservatism and radicalism that informed [Woolf's] outlook" (Ellis 9).

7 Ellis is referring here to Woolf's "affiliation with and dissent from" her forefathers, as well as her "affiliation with and dissent from her modern present" (Ellis 2).

8 See also Jane Lilenfeld's "Introduction: Virginia Woolf and Literary History" in *Virginia Woolf and Literary History, Woolf Studies Annual 9* (2003: 85–116).

9 According to Andrew John Miller in "Fables of Progression: Modernism, Modernity, Narrative" (2009), this embrace – what he calls "the intellectually conservative turn toward history and away from theory that, by the early 1990s, set the dominant tone for modernist studies" – came long after New Historicism "had expanded in other fields or periods of research" (Miller 2009: 177–178).

10 See Linden Peach's *Virginia Woolf and New Historicism* (2000), and Melba Cuddy-Keane's "Virginia Woolf and the Varieties of Historicist Experience" (1997).

11 As most of my contemporary peers, I am much indebted to the work of Beth Carole Rosenberg (*Virginia Woolf and Samuel Johnson: Common Readers*, 1995); Gillian Beer (*Virginia Woolf and The Common Ground*, 1996); Elena Gualtieri (*Virginia Woolf's Essays: Sketching the Past*, 2000); Beth Rosenberg and Jeanne Dubino (*Virginia Woolf and the Essay*, 1997); Melba Cuddy-Keane (*Virginia Woolf, the Intellectual, and the Public Sphere*, 2003); Katerina Koutsantoni (*Virginia Woolf's Common Reader*, 2009); Randi Saloman (*Woolf's Essayism*, 2012). I would also like to acknowledge the recent work by French specialists on the subject of Woolf and the essay: Catherine Bernard (*Woolf as Reader/Woolf as Critic or, The Art of Reading in the Present*, 2011); Christine Reynier (*Virginia Woolf's Good Housekeeping Essays*, 2018) and Caroline Pollentier (*L'invention de la communauté: esthétique et politique de l'ordinaire dans les essais de Virginia Woolf*. Ph.D. Thesis, 2011).

12 See also the important contributions assembled by Carol M. Kaplan and Ann B. Simpson in *Seeing Double: Revisioning Edwardian and Modernist Literature* (1996); Andrea Zemgulys (*Modernism and the Locations of Literary Heritage*, 2008); Gabrielle McIntire (*Modernism, Memory and Desire*, 2008).

13 The irony of Woolf's words as she comments W.L. Courtney's book in her 1905 review of *The Feminine Note in Fiction* will be given further attention in Chapter 7: "Virginia Woolf, Fiction, and the 'Woman Question'."

14 On this subject, see Christine Ross's introduction to *The Past is the Present; It's the Future Too: The Temporal Turn in Contemporary Art* (2012), and her pages on the "contemporary experiences of temporal passing" that attempt to free "the three categories of time (past, present, and future)," to complicate "their connection" and to "activate the past into the present" by allowing it "to condition the future in that very process" (Ross 1–17; 5). On paradoxical time and the back-and-forth movement that constitutes cultural memory, see also Georges Didi-Huberman in *The Surviving Image: Phantoms of Time and Time of Phantoms* (2018 [2002]), Angeliki Spiropoulou on Woolf and

Walter Benjamin (2010) and Herbert Grabes's edition of *Literature, Literary History, and Cultural Memory* (2005).

15 Woolf's "contradictoriness" has recently been studied from different angles by the contributors of *Contradictory Woolf: Selected Papers from the Twenty-First International Conference on Virginia Woolf* (eds. Derek Ryan and Stella Bolaki, 2012).

16 John R. Reed's comprehensive study of the Victorian self in *Victorian Will* (1989) shows how, from the early-nineteenth-century to late-Victorian fiction, "Victorians faced apparently contradictory recommendations of asserting and suppressing the self, contradictions that they embodied in fictional characterisations and narrative strategies" (Reed 15–16).

17 See, for example, Jane Eldridge Miller in *Rebel Women: Feminism, Modernism and the Edwardian Novel* (1994).

18 On "The Oak Tree" and Woolf's art of the palimpsest in *Orlando*, see Chapter 3 of this book.

19 See "Character in Fiction" (*E III* 420–438).

20 On Woolf and "friendship," also see this essential excerpt from her essay on "Montaigne":

> We must dread any eccentricity or refinement which cuts us off from our fellow-beings. Blessed are those who chat easily with their neighbours about their sport or their buildings or their quarrels, and honestly enjoy the talk of carpenters and gardeners. To communicate is our chief business; society and friendship our chief delights; and reading, not to acquire knowledge, not to earn a living, but to extend our intercourse beyond our own time and province.
>
> (*E* 76)

21 In this letter to Violet Dickinson dated July 1905, Woolf writes, a few hours before the visit of the English historian Frederic Maitland (with whom she collaborated when he wrote the life of his friend and mentor Leslie Stephen):

> Do you feel convinced I can write? I am going to produce a real historical work this summer; for which I have solidly read and annotated 4 volumes of medieval English. Fred Maitland was here this afternoon. There is a man I respect. He would read 4 volumes to write two words, and think nothing of it.
>
> (*L I* 244)

22 On the assessment of Woolf as a "journalistic" critic having a lesser influence on the following generations than T.S. Eliot or F.R. Leavis, see Stephan Collini (2019) and Chapter 5 in this book.

23 The quotation is extracted from "George Moore":

> The only criticism worth having at present is that which is spoken, not written – spoken over wineglasses and coffee cups late at night, flashed out on the spur of the moment by people passing who have not time to finish their sentences, let alone consider the dues of editors or the feelings of friends.
>
> (*E IV* 260)

24 See, for example, Koutsantoni's analysis of Woolf's Bakhtinian "co-operative, dialogic pact between writer and reader" in her essays in *Virginia Woolf's "Common Reader"* (2009: 148). Lecercle's interpretation of dialogue is more

agonistic and reminds us, as it relies on the French Marxist Philosopher Louis Althusser's concept of "interpellation," that:

> meaning is the product of a dialogue between two texts, the interpreted text and the interpretation that reads it [...] and the subjects involved, the author and the reader, are not free but assujettis in Althusserian parlance—in other words that they are effects of the structure.

(76–82)

I argue in this book that as a daughter of an educated man, as a modernist artist and a female writer Woolf was confronted to forms of interpellation that she needed to negotiate.

Part I

"Historians' Histories" and Woolf's New Historiography

1 Prescribed Books and the Possibilities of Knowledge

Making Sense of Tradition

I read some history: it is suddenly all alive,
branching forwards & backwards & connected with
every kind of thing that seemed entirely remote before.[1]

Those "Long Histories in Many Volumes"

As the daughter of a Victorian "educated man," Virginia Woolf had an extensive grounding in biography and history. In her article about Leslie Stephen's influence on Woolf (1998), Katherine Hill remarks, "this education, stemming as it did from Stephen's beliefs about the interrelations of biography, history and literature was crucial in shaping her approach to literary criticism and her theorizing about the development of literary genres" (Hill 353). In 1897, the year when she began Greek and History classes at King's College, London, Virginia dipped into the lives of Coleridge, Mary Russell Mitford and Henry Fawcett. She records in her diary how her father "gave" or "lent" her Mandell Creighton's *Queen Elizabeth* (1896), some Charles Oman,[2] some Titus Livius, Macaulay's *History of England* (5 vols., 1848–1861), Thomas Carlyle's *French Revolution* (1837) and *Cromwell* (1845), Thomas Arnold's *The History of Rome* (5 vols., 1840–1843), Froude's *History of England From the Fall of Wolsey to the Defeat of the Spanish Armada* (12 vols., 1856–1870). In the following decade, she buried herself in other major titles from Stephen's library such as Carlyle's *The French Revolution* (3 vols., 1834–1837) and *History of Friedrich II of Prussia* (12 vols., 1858–1865), Edward A. Freeman's *History of the Norman Conquest* (6 vols., 1876), J.R. Green's *Conquest of England* (1883), J.B. Bury's *History of Greece to the Death of Alexander the Great* (2 vols., 1900–1902) or Edith Sichel's *Catherine de' Medici and the French Reformation* (1905).[3]

The weight of this Victorian heritage and education and how it "provided [Woolf] with a breadth and depth of knowledge typically reserved for university-bound men like her brothers" (Westman 1998: 3) has often received critical attention.[4] The place of history in the formative years of a young female subject is also a recurring motif in *The*

DOI: 10.4324/9780429331787-3

Voyage Out and, to a lesser extent, in *Night and Day*, Woolf's two novels of apprenticeship. For Rachel Vinrace and Cassandra Otway, to read Gibbon or Macaulay is an ordeal, a way of testing their capacity to submit to, or resist, the cultural and ideological demands of patriarchy: "'About Gibbon,' [Hirst] continued. 'D'you think you'll be able to appreciate him? He's the test, of course'" (*VO* 172). The two characters are quite different from each other, but both experience the difficulty of expressing a personality under the pressure of educated men. Although these educated men entertain a friendly or even loving relationship with the young "untrained" women,[5] their will to "educate" them is symptomatic of a form of pompous and patronising arrogance: the history books they recommend are the paradigms of a culture steeped in tradition that the young heroines do not yet possess and which they can definitely not acquire "by tea-time," as Katharine is very well aware in *Night and Day* (*ND* 452). To discover St John Hirst reading "Gibbon's *History of the Decline and Fall of Rome* by candle-light" in the ninth chapter of the *Voyage Out* and to visualise this quintessentially Cambridge man "knock[ing] the ash automatically, now and again, from his cigarette and turn[ing] the page, while a whole procession of splendid sentences entered his capacious brow and went marching through his brain in order" is to enter the world of patriarchal culture and university education from which women are excluded (*VO* 116). The reason for this exclusion, Woolf suggests, is that the "masculine acquirements" of their fathers and masters induce girls "to take a very modest view of [their] own power": as Hirst self-righteously explains to Rachel, to "reach the age of twenty-four without reading Gibbon" makes one wonder whether women's lack of mind is due to their "lack of training" or "to native incapacity" (*VO* 172). Even when the young heroine wants to comply and show her good will, she feels belittled, unable to understand the amused reaction of another paternal figure telling her that she should give up on "the ten big volumes" of Gibbon's history and read "Plato" instead, and "Sophocles, Swift [...] Balzac [...] Wordsworth and Coleridge, Pope, Johnson, Addison, Wordsworth, Shelley, Keats. One thing [leading] to another." But then, "'what's the use of reading if you don't read Greek?'" Rachel's uncle, Ridley Ambrose, asks her. "'After all, if you read Greek, you need never read anything else, pure waste of time—pure waste of time'" (*VO* 192). Before they become appropriated in a lonely room, far from the judgmental look of male elders who want to impress their tastes and cultural language on still hesitant female subjects, the books Rachel or Cassandra "must" read – "'Must you read Macaulay's History, Cassandra?' Katharine asked, with a stretch of her arms" (*ND* 452) – in order "to know things thoroughly" (*ND* 369) understandably provoke a series of negative reactions. The "prescribed volumes" are "dropped" down, their authors are cursed in a most "unwomanly" manner – "Damn Lord Macaulay" (*ND* 452; 453) – and the "not formed" young women (*ND* 338) naturally prove reluctant to "settle" into their reading, "looking ruefully at the dull red cover" of books (*ND* 452) that they finally consent to read, although they make them "horribly, oh infernally, damnably bored!" (*VO* 239).

Strikingly enough, a similar impression of boredom characterises *Jacob's Room*, Woolf's third Bildungsroman, where a generation of young men can enjoy the privileges of college education. First standing "in sheer confidence and pleasure" at the thought of being about to "receive this gift from the past" – "a sense of old buildings and time; himself the inheritor" – Jacob will remain untransformed by his Cambridge educators and prescribed readings (*JR* 57). As history is knocking at the door, its written text has ironically prepared none of the students as to what comes next. Jacob's reading room is a male territory where Carlyle is a "prize" and sits on the shelves next to "Lives of the Duke of Wellington, [...]; Spinoza; the works of Dickens; the *Faery Queen*; a Greek dictionary with the petals of poppies pressed to silk between the pages; all the Elizabethans." The Carlylean question "Does History consist of the Biographies of Great Men?" remains unanswered (*JR* 48–49). Travelling to Italy and Greece, Jacob plans to write "an essay upon civilisation. A comparison between the ancients and the moderns [...] – something in the style of Gibbon," but never does (*JR* 186). Evan Williams, whom he meets in Athens, has "the political history of England at his finger-ends" but realises that compared with "Chatham, Pitt, Burke, and Charles James Fox," he "ha[s] accomplished nothing" (*JR* 197). In the end, "Macaulay, Hobbes, Gibbon", this "conglomeration of knowledge" (*JR* 147) shaping the young educated men's personalities, does not prevent them from leading meaningless lives, or from being sent to their deaths.

In *The Voyage Out*, *Night and Day* and *Jacob's Room*, historians are not yet the butt of Woolf's irony, as they will be in *Orlando*, where they are described as forming a vague, satirised category of learned men who in general fail to provide an account of the truth. But the knowledge they have produce questions of the readability of written historical texts and on their transmission; history's capacity to illuminate the present is challenged, and the discipline is shown to be the site of a distinct imposition of gender. For male characters, to read history books is to feel empowered, "masterly" (*JR* 57), and to be put in the apparently comfortable position of "inheritors." Conversely, for the female characters of Woolf's early novels and later fiction, the transmission of historical knowledge is one of the tools of an education and learning process that most of the time leaves them powerless as readers, autonomous subjects or as members of their social circle. In *Mrs Dalloway*, Doris Kilman, the German tutor of Elizabeth Dalloway, can read and teach history; her "knowledge of modern history [is] thorough in the extreme" (*MD* 106); but she is and will remain an outsider, the image of the bitter spinster. In the first chapter of *The Years*, "1880," Kitty's tutor Lucy Craddock is in awe of Dr Andrews – nicknamed old Chuffy – "the greatest historian of his time" and author of "The Constitutional History of England" (*TY* 63–64), but Lucy's knowledge and passion do not enable her to realise her full potential as an academic woman: she is "sneered at" by Dons (*TY* 67) and remains an impoverished scholar and little-respected spinster. As a novelist, Woolf does not seem ready to make peace with history as a discipline, a branch of knowledge and a record of the past until *Between the Acts*; as if "The Outline of History" Lucy Swithin refers to – a loose reference to H.G. Wells' 1919 book of the same name which sold one and a half million copies in Great Britain – represented a form of history-writing that could finally bridge the gap between the past and the present while opening a door onto the future.

And yet, for these young heroines, sometimes an encounter does take place. In *The Voyage Out*, Mrs Thornbury suddenly recalls how her "dear" father "was always quoting [*The Decline and Fall of the Roman Empire*] at us, with the result that we resolved never to read a line. [...] A very wonderful book, I know." Mrs Flushing suddenly thinks of how "We used to lie in bed and read Gibbon—about the massacres of the Christians, I remember—when we were supposed to be asleep," and "Gibbon the historian" is unexpectedly "connect[ed] with some of the happiest hours of [her] life" (*VO* 225). Rachel discovers the more mature pleasure of the historian's craftsmanship: "With a feeling that to open and read would certainly be a surprising experience," a page is turned and read; the magic of Gibbon's words operates, "so vivid and so beautiful—Arabia Felix—Aethiopia" that they seem "to drive roads back to the very beginning of the world, on either side of which the populations of all times and countries stood in avenues." A sense of "excitement at the possibilities of knowledge now open[s]" before the young female reader and replaces her earlier sense of duty and helplessness (*VO* 196). Reading history becomes an experience with words, sentences and the oral transmission of a narrative that suddenly alleviates the weight of the "great big book, in double columns" (ibid.). As many of her early heroines deprived of a university education, yet aspiring to please a father, a brother or a lover, Woolf's approach to history was first "an act of reading," as Angeliki Spiropoulou (2010: 44) suggests. But unlike these same heroines, Woolf transformed her encounter with history as a woman reader into an act of writing, driven by the need to answer the very questions raised in her fiction by the books of Gibbon, Macaulay and other "historians' histories" – those "long histories in many volumes" that one "must" read (*JR* 55): what is it that makes history readable, intelligible and so "suddenly alive" that it branches "forwards backwards" and becomes "connected with every kind of thing that seemed entirely remote before"? (PA 178)

"I Want to Write a History"

Several critics have reported how Woolf's personal engagement with the written texts of history gradually gave way to a desire to "write history one of these days." In 1905, she was already describing herself as a "journalist who wants to read history" (*L I* 190). In July of the same year, just after having sent the *Academy* "Famous Women of Wit and Beauty," she wrote to Violet Dickinson: "Do you feel convinced I can write? I am going to produce a real historical work this summer; for which I have solidly read and annotated four volumes of medieval English" (*L I* 202). From the expression of this early vocation to the posthumous publication of "Anon" and "The Reader," we now have a clear picture of Woolf's projects and achievements involving her acquaintance with history. In 1904 – the year her father died and she decided to help F.W. Maitland with his Life of Leslie Stephen – her apprenticeship began to serve her new projects, first as a reviewer for *The Guardian, The Times Literary Supplement, The Academy* and *The National Review*, then as a lecturer for women at Morley College.[6] Published in 1906, her early short fiction, "The Journal of Mistress Joan Martyn," anticipates *Orlando* by exploring the possibility of an alternative history, spoken in the first person by a middle-aged female historian. In 1915, Woolf mentions reading Dostoevsky's *The Idiot*, Michelet and Walter Scott, and "plodding through the dreary middle ages" – an experience which leads her to contemplate the idea of writing "one day [...] a book of 'Eccentrics': Mrs Grote will later be one. Lady Hester Stanhope. Margaret Fuller. Duchess of Newcastle. Aunt Julia?" (*D I* 23). In 1928, wondering what to write next after *Orlando* she confesses:

> Well but Orlando was the outcome of a perfectly definite, indeed overmastering impulse. I want fun. I want fantasy. I want (& this was serious) to give things their caricature value. And still this mood hangs about me. I want to write a history, say of Newnham or the woman's movement, in the same vein. The vein is deep in me—at least sparkling, urgent.
>
> (*D III* 203)

A year later, she would remember with pleasure how her father made her read Hakluyt:

> He must have been 65; I 15 or 16; & why I don't know, but I became enraptured, though not exactly interested, but the sight of the large yellow page entranced me. [...] I was then writing a long picturesque essay upon the Christian religion, I think; called Religio Laici, I believe proving that man has need of a God; but the God was described in process of change; & I also wrote a history of Women; & a history of my own family—all very longwinded & El[izabeth]than in style.
>
> (*D III* 271)[7]

Many of those projects never materialised or were not fully executed: in the end, Woolf did not write the "real historical work" she had once planned to complete (*L I* 202). Was it because once she had paid her tribute to the looming figures of her parents she was free to forget about teaching history – in 1905, when she gave a class at Morley for working men and women, both the college and she herself were unhappy with the outcome of her lectures on English History "from the beginning" – and to write an academic history book? (*PA* 1992: 255).[8] Or was it because she discovered that her true purpose was not so much to write history as to unwrite and rewrite "traditional" historiographical discourses and orthodoxies? At any rate, history remained, throughout Woolf's career, a site of apprenticeship, a cultural and political battlefield and the fruitful laboratory of her feminist poetics as a fiction writer, critic and literary historian. Woolf's conversations with the past, and more particularly with nineteenth-century historiography, are interwoven with her poetics as poiesis – the creative bringing into being of the past into the present and an engagement with the future. They constitute the groundwork for her alternative literary histories. Nineteenth-century historiography is not, however, the homogeneous tradition that many Woolf scholars claim as her inheritance. This is why this study begins with the exploration of the nineteenth- and early-twentieth-century historiographical discourses Woolf engaged with, the heterogeneity and diversity of which prompt us to revise such categories as "historians' histories," "traditional historiography" or "traditional historicism."

For a researcher in Victorian studies, there is nothing surprising about the influence of history on a literary career: the importance of this discipline in nineteenth-century scholarly discussions has long been established. In his book on *The Victorian Critic and the Idea of History*, Peter Allen Dale explains how, from the 1820s in England onwards, a "new preoccupation with history [took] vigorous hold on the national mind" and set up historical process "not as in itself a sufficient explanation of experience but as the most likely venue to such an explanation. Not through physics and metaphysics could one best discover the meaning of life, but through history" (Dale 1977: 2; 4).[9] Although it was a long time before this renewed interest took the form of a speculative system, as the British historian and professor of metaphysical philosophy R.G. Collingwood was to deplore in the 1930s, from the mid-1820s onwards history was assigned a new "mission": "to exhibit the evolution of humanity, and to form thereby a social science."[10] The eighteenth century had seen the birth in Europe of the historical method and of philosophies of history and was concerned, in England at least, with growing divisions between antiquarians on the one hand, and enlightened historians such as David Hume and Edward Gibbon on the other. A century later, the historical-mindedness of the Victorian historian, whether Tory or Whig, implied views on the past and on its meaning for the present that were to influence deeply nineteenth- and early-twentieth-century literary historiography and poetics. As Ted Underwood (2013: 84; 95) shows, from the 1830s onwards, "the model of historical cultivation for English literary history was one that insisted on the useful continuity of past and pre-sent," on "the connections between stages of development" and on a deep sense of "national self-consciousness," to give but one example. However, all Victorian historians cannot be affiliated with what Herbert Butterfield called in 1931 "The Whig Interpretation of History." The whole purpose of Michael Bentley's *Modernizing England's Past* is thus to study another category of historians that he names "modernist," and whose achievements since 1870 are bound to have had a different type of influence on the literary world.

The influence of history and its models on modernist literature was long minimised if not denied. Although "Bloomsbury was born and bred Victorian" (Rosenbaum 2003: 21) and some of its eminent members wrote historical books – among them, Lytton Strachey's *Eminent Victorians* (1918) and E.M. Forster's *Alexandria, a History and a Guide* (1922) – the myth of the modernists' ignorance or rejection of history was revised only when revaluations of modernism itself took place in the 1990s.[11] Today, deep historicism is not merely at the core of the New Modernist Studies; it is in tune with the recent interest in the larger issue of the modernists' relation to the past. But the discussion is rarely set in terms that clearly expose the complexity and evolution of the debate regarding historical thought that the modernists inherited from their predecessors.[12] In the case of the recent research on Woolf's "historicism" (Peach 2000: 2), for example, critics generally have two main goals: to decide whether Woolf was closer to the moderns or her Victorian ancestors (or torn between the two), or to explore the way she anticipated later philosophies of his-tory. Again, her ambivalence regarding her Victorian heritage is pointed at, the question of her theoretical positioning is answered in various and sometimes opposing ways, but the heterogeneity of the historiographical traditions she inherited and responded to is rarely examined.

Typically, Hotho-Jackson explained in 1991 that because of her "Bergsonian presentism" and her reliance on a "self-reflexive conscious-ness of history" in *Orlando* and *Between the Acts*, Woolf's place is at first sight "with the moderns" (Hotho-Jackson 296).[13] But this demonstration soon moves beyond false evidence to show that "Woolf's approach to history displays a combination of a modern view of history and a trad-itional concept of history as story and particularly as English story" that led her to reject contemporary historiography "not because she found a radical new approach to history but [...] because she favoured an even more conventional approach" (297). Among Hotho-Jackson's arguments supporting Woolf's traditionalism are her debt to her father and his vision of history as a "large-scale map," her "sentimentalism," her vision of his-tory as having a "consoling power" and "escapist function," her belief in the working of "the spirit of the age" (298–299), her "purism as regards the combining of fact and fiction," her Victorian "appreciation of prime source links" (305) and her vision of English history as "almost automat-ically [...] consecutive" (308).

Six years later, Melba Cuddy-Keane's conclusions on the same subject are quite different. In "Virginia Woolf and the Varieties of Historicist Experience," she argues that Woolf's writing of history is the "subversive method" of a "radical modernist" resulting from a "pluralistic and experiential" approach that contrasts both with her Victorian predecessors and the "globalizing systems" of some of her modernist contemporaries (Cuddy-Keane 1997: 60–61; 66). To support this view, Cuddy-Keane puts forward Woolf's vision of the historian as a "historicized fallible reader" and of history as the product of a "dialogical relationship between the historical text and the historian's understanding." She also emphasizes Woolf's interest in "unpublished and non-canonical works" and her focus on "the common man's" and the "common woman's perspective" (61–64). However, Cuddy-Keane is careful to avoid the risk of "reading [Woolf] too much through the lens of what historicist thinking is later to become and thus inscribing her not in her time but rather before (ahead of) her time, that is in our time" (62). Thus, if Woolf is "bold" in the way she develops "effective modes for writing alternative histories" in the form of dialogic fictions and dialogues, Cuddy-Keane suggests that her "historicism" is not devoid of any nineteenth-century influence, with references, for example, to "Carlyle's defense of the history of common life," "Macaulay's extension of English history into such aspects of daily life (drinking, eating, popular culture)" and "Leslie Stephen's elements of radicalism" (63).[14]

Written in 1998, Karin E. Westman's "The Character in the House: Virginia Woolf in Dialogue with History's Audience" proposes a less balanced view of Woolf's historical thought than Cuddy-Keane's or Linden Peach's (2000) a decade later.[15] Westman studies some of Woolf's essays and reviews (among which *A Room of One's Own*, "Anon" and "The Reader") and the short fiction entitled "The Journal of Mistress Joan Martyn" to show that their author's "dialogic historiography" anticipates the work of Michel Foucault, Dominick LaCapra (a reference that she shares with Cuddy-Keane) and Michel de Certeau. For Westman (1998: 2), the Bakhtinian "dialogic narrative which will in turn become [Woolf's] method for the writing of fiction [...] recovers what established histories often elide: the embodied voice necessary for the constitution of character"; its success "hinges on the audience's active relationship to the discursive representation of embodied experience." It is this "emphasis on embodied exchange between writer and reader," Westman explains, that both differentiates Woolf's "dialogic theory from those of other intellectual historians" and identifies her "feminist materialist goals."[16]

Although the theoretical underpinnings of their analysis might be different, Westman and other researchers in the same field such as Fernald (1994), Peach (2000), McIntire (2008) and Spiropoulou (2010) share a vision of Woolf as a cultural and political innovator. Whether she is shown to anticipate Foucault or Benjamin, Woolf is cast as a "feminist historian, the first, with its contradictions, differences, différance, obscurity" (McIntire 2008: 190) or at any rate as a writer committed to challenge "the barbarisms of history, the threats presented by her historical actuality, and the omissions of tradition with a view to an alternative future" (Spiropoulou 2010: 58).[17] As the subsequent pages will suggest, the references to Foucault and de Certeau in these works are enlightening. One can follow Cuddy-Keane (1997: 66) when she insists on the need to acknowledge the heterogeneity and diversity of the historiographical approaches that were available to Woolf in her time, or when she concludes that it is specifically Woolf's way of writing history that is "her most distinguished characteristic as a historiographer"; it is persuasive that the manner in which Woolf explores and writes history rests on a renewed dialogue with "history's and literature's audiences" (Westman), and that overall, Woolf's historical thought is deeply critical of traditional historiography and more contemporary philosophical abstractions or systems. But the perspective I adopt here is different. First, the subject is not "the relationship between history and historicity in Woolf's fiction" (Peach 2000: 6) but the interconnectedness of her historical thought and her literary historiography as it appears in her reviews, essays and fictions. Second, the thrust is towards Woolf's conception of historiography as "written history and the writing of history," not Woolf's "historicism" if the word means a situated philosophy and discourse, and more precisely "the attempt, found esp. among German historians since about 1850, to view all social and cultural phenomena, all categories, truths, and values, as relative and historically determined." (OED) Above all, under scrutiny here is a coherent speculative system anticipating future theories rather than the historical knowledge Woolf inherited, used and challenged in order to write her own histories of nineteenth-century women's literature.

In this respect, Woolf's twenty-first-century readers are faced with the same kinds of difficulties her young heroines encounter: the field of her historical readings and writings is as crowded as the field of recent literary criticism of her historical thought. On first examination, it seems almost impossible to understand it "thoroughly" and to resolve the contradictions most of the critics mentioned earlier have underlined without always explaining them. The question here is no longer whether we see Woolf as a belated Victorian or as a radical innovator but the way her historical thinking prompts us to complicate the heritage constituted by the "historians' histories" that she read and that have often become, in the critics' eye, synonymous with a homogeneous tradition, itself built on a rather monolithic apprehension of Victorian art and culture.

A Complex Heritage

Indeed, the discourse of historiography was far less "closed" or homogeneous in the nineteenth and early-twentieth centuries than some scholarly views on "whig" or Victorian historical thought have made it appear. Similarly, Woolf's numerous attacks on the historical writings of traditional historians – in *Orlando* and *A Room of One's Own* for example – build up to a less easily identifiable position when we consider the essays, reviews and early fictions, where the recurring references to the eighteenth- and nineteenth-century historians, belonging to the tradition of the gentleman literary scholar (Gibbon, Carlyle, Macaulay, Froude), are contrasted with the absence of Victorian scientific historians, like Henry Thomas Buckle or of philosopher-historians such as R.G. Collingwood.[18] This would seem to support the view of Woolf as a traditionalist unable to escape the weight of her father's training. But the complexity of the tradition and legacy of nineteenth-century historical thinking, together with Woolf's ability to transmute inherited historiographical debates into renovated concepts and tools, both contradict this appreciation.

In his introduction to the fifth chapter of his *Companion to Historiography*, Michael Bentley states that

> the story [of Western historiography since the Enlightenment] cannot be read [...] as a single narrative. It is better seen as a series of overlapping (and often contradictory) moods and doctrines whose interactions we must heed and explain if the account is to go beyond a roll of honour or the flat description of forgotten books.
>
> (Bentley 1997: 395)

The same can be said about English historiography since the Enlightenment. However, the "single narrative" Bentley alludes to is often considered to be the "traditional historiography" inherited by the moderns and with which they all supposedly strived to part. Whenever Woolf's critics use the words "conventional," "traditional" or "Victorian" interchangeably in discussing her views on nineteenth-century historical thought, they, therefore, convene this single narrative in a way that needs to be challenged. Indeed, while the simplified and questionable narrative Bentley is referring to usually distinguishes three periods and three types of historians, each of them the embodiment of a different view of history as a discipline and practice, the second version of this history of historical thought through the eighteenth, nineteenth and twentieth centuries appears to be more subtle and less linear. It calls into question the notion of post-determined historiographical "ages" and thresholds while revealing a genealogy of historiographical discourses that provide alternative insights into Woolf's apparently ambivalent position with regards to tradition.[19]

In the "single" narrative, the two pivotal moments correspond to a turn of century. In the years after 1800, the leap of England and the rest of Europe into what is now seen as a renewed historical consciousness has been attributed to varied factors. Among them, one could place the reactions against the French Revolution as a symbolical fracture, the need for the reading public to make sense of a changing society and for historians to restore an organic continuity with the English past.[20] A century later, John Bagnell Bury's (1903) Inaugural Lecture delivered in the Divinity School at Cambridge and his statement that "history is a science, no less and no more" constitutes a second epistemological break (Bury 3–4). According to Molly Westerman (2008), with the influence of fin-de-siècle philosophies of history, the rise of professionalism in literature and literary criticism, and the rise of scientific protocols in the historians' practice, "the historical tradition of the Victorian gentleman-scholar came under increasingly powerful attack [...]" (Westerman 15). Thomas William Heyck (1982) explains that while

> History in the world of the men of letters like Macaulay was a coherent operation with procedures and critical standards consistent with its functions and those of other forms of literature [...], the different social and cultural functions of academic historians like Bury, Stubbs and Maitland towards the end of the century required different procedures and standards as well as institutional settings.
>
> (Heyck 122)

Of course, the First World War was another essential factor for change, triggering new perspectives on history. The Victorian historians came to be seen as gentlemen whose values had not prevented so many young men from being killed. History became "not only a substantive burden imposed upon the present by the past in the form of outmoded institutions, ideas and values, but also the way of looking at the world which gives to these outmoded forms their specious authority" (White 2010: 39).[21]

In this linear version of the evolution of English historiography, the eighteenth-century historian is clearly different from his nineteenth-century counterpart, himself radically distinct from the twentieth-century scientific version of the profession. Philippa Levine (1986: 71) has described the practice of eighteenth-century antiquarians as one characterised by "collection and classification on a descriptive basis, regardless of chronology and embracing both text and artifact," a "promiscuous mix of sources," the "use of both literary and material evidence" and "the constant abjuration of anything removed from the purely factual." During this first grand age of scholarly research, the historical study of "antiquities" resulted in the massive production of excavated artefacts and of rarely classified documents, numerous collections of coins and ancient manuscripts and findings published in periodicals or heavy volumes. For many years, antiquarians were seen as passionate amateurs without a proper method, and doubt was cast on their authority as historians by the next generation.[22]

By contrast, authority and methodology became key concepts in the nineteenth century, even if Victorian historians "acquired the apparatus of the modern professional academic world" later than in France and Germany for cultural reasons. Levine explains that the "collective instinct" of the antiquarian was then replaced by "a new faith in the text" and in "archival research" (Levine 86–87). From the 1830s onwards, the opening of government archives and diplomatic documents to scholars in European capitals provided historians with a new and powerful tool: for the first time, they could base their texts on official papers and primary sources, not merely on their predecessors' authority. Because of the nature of the documents, this "new" history concentrated on state-systems and political matters, a trait which met wide-ranging popular concern regarding the ideas of nationality, law and constitutional convention. In an age of deep change, England and other countries developed pride in their past, a veneration for their cultural traditions and languages, a better awareness of what they had lost and of their collective purpose. In this respect, history became a didactic or ideological form, while nineteenth-century historians tended to see themselves as part of a self-conscious community whose purpose was to promote an ideal vision of their country, and to celebrate the past and the present through a tribute to political tradition and stability. According to Levine, in Great Britain at least, and until the last decade of the nineteenth-century, "it was inevitable that such views would produce a strongly teleological reading of history" leading to "the fusion of process and progress" (Levine 86). The same idea can be found in Heyck's account of Victorian historical thought. The Victorians "needed a particular history," Heyck explains, one that "provided support and political advice by celebrating the evolution of the proudest elements of nineteenth-century English life—the rule of law, the supremacy of parliament, and the liberty of the individual" (Heyck 1982: 123).

In this attempt to rationalise the past and interpret the present through the uncovering of recurring historical patterns, we may detect the influence of Auguste Comte's positivism which, from the 1840s onwards, encouraged an analogy between the study of the past and natural sciences. The main idea was to approach the past though the needs of the present – what Heyck calls the "present-mindedness" of the "Whiggish" historians (Heyck 123) – and to achieve generalisations and laws.[23] The search for significant patterns became common practice. In Carlyle's terms: "by revealing the recurring pattern or necessary direction of human affairs this study of history became, in fact, the study of the future. [...] Only he who understands what has been, can know what should be and will be" (1833: 169). One of those significant patterns became predominant around 1849: according to Bentley (1997: 440), with John Mitchell Kemble's account of *The Saxons in England*, the history of England "assumed a particular shape" based on a continuity thesis:

'England' emerged from the Teutonic migrants from Northern Germany; it was confirmed in the events of the Norman invasion, sullied by the Angevins, rescued by the barons. Then [...] the way was open for the factious wars of the fifteenth century, The Tudor tyranny and the rescue-bid of William III.

In his famous *The Whig Interpretation of History* (1931), Herbert Butterfield was one of the first to lament some of the strong tendencies of what he contributed to unify as the whig historians' legacy.[24] Exposing what he calls the "fallacies" of the whig interpretation of history, Butterfield overtly criticises "the study of the past with direct and perpetual reference to the present" (11), the theory of "the abridgement of history" (24) that leads to a false sense of continuity between the past and the present, the superimposed idea of a "scheme of general history" leading to the "obvious idea of progress" (12), the simplistic doctrines of "evolution" and "proof of providence" (23), "the belief in an unfolding logic in history, a logic which is on the side of the whigs and makes them appear as co-operators with progress itself" (42), the "misconceived quest for origins" (43) and "the passionate desire to come to a judgment of values" (64).

Michael Bentley begins his own account with a statement echoing Butterfield's views:

> The whig history of England was a Bad Thing, most modern historians would agree. It worked, they might say, simply as a form of English literature and supplied uplift and emotional satisfaction rather than a careful and scholarly account of evidence.
>
> (Bentley 2006: 5)

But the whole purpose of Bentley's "Prelude: After the Whigs" is to take some distance with this "single" version of nineteenth-century historiography the story. The whig historians, he explains, were not all "Whigs": they "formed an interlocking dynasty of authors with perhaps Henry Hallam and Thomas Babington Macaulay at one end of their period of dominance and William Stubbs, J.R. Green and E.A. Freeman at the other end"; their "narratives of the past share a few characteristics but are more varied than expected"; above all, the whig historians "did not die" after 1914 and the First World War (Bentley 2006: 6–7). Consequently, the idea of a "whig interpretation of history" should be understood as a post-determined myth, a "plausible and suggestive story" (Bentley 2006: 6) reproduced when the post-whigs were retrospectively given a unified identity as "modernists" by the postmodernists. And yet he stresses the need to analyse the various ingredients of this "story" to explain what the moderns consciously fought against and unconsciously reproduced. However, we also need to be aware of this single narrative in order to understand what Woolf's critics refer to when they speak of "a nineteenth-century model of narrative historiography" (Ezell 1996: 22). Contrasting with the nineteenth-century idea of the "apprentice-historical" scholar, his biased reading of "facts," his present-mindedness leading to anachronism and finalism,[25] the reformist historians of the late nineteenth century and the inter-war period (F.W. Maitland, J.B. Bury, E.A. Freeman, J.R. Tanner, J.R. Seeley) saw themselves as professionals who investigated "sources" and "documents" with "objectivity," criticised the Whigs' focus on constitutional history, politics and the Lives of great men, and did not confuse history with story. The Whigs' manner of writing which often combined facts embellished by imagination and was seen, by Macaulay (1828b: 196) and others, as "a compound of poetry and philosophy [...] impress[ing] general truths on the mind by a vivid representation of particular characters and incidents" also came under attack. The past needed to be examined in its minutest or detailed facts, but its reporting had to be radically purged of all fictional devices, even to the risk of losing the power of "whig" chronological narratives, "that pompous conventional romancing of which all serious men are tired" according to Seeley. Seeley's tone here and in the rest of his lectures may sound arrogant and spiteful; yet it reflects the "spirit of the age" and the conviction that history had entered a new era:

> It seems not generally known how much the study of history has been transformed in late years. Those charges of untrustworthiness, of pompous and hollow conventionality [...] are in the main groundless now. History has been in great part rewritten; in great part it is now true, and lies before science as a mass of materials out of which a political doctrine may be deduced. It is not now pompous and solemn, but it is thoroughly serious, much more serious than ever.
>
> (Seeley 1883: 173–175)

Of course, there exist unchallenged facts to reassure the post-whigs in their difference. At the turn of the new century, the change from "history as literature" to "history as science" was accompanied and supported by the new methodological standards the academic world had adopted along with the establishment of learned journals, the inauguration in 1900 of the International Congress of the Historical Sciences, and the foundation of the Historical Association in 1906. The new demands of a new audience, expecting history to focus on the people rather than their rulers, led to a social and economic history and, for the first time, women such as Kate Norgate, Mary Bateson, Caroline Skeel or Eileen Power took up academic careers in history.[26] Then came the tragedy of the First World War and its own set of interrogations and doubts. The past had to be reclaimed in a different way; a new world and a new culture demanded a new history. But, however useful, this "single narrative" is misleading for two reasons: first, because it leaves aside the obvious differences between historians of the same generation, and because it masks a series of continuities that link historians of different generations. In this respect, Bentley's pages where he deconstructs the meta-narrative he was careful to recount echo Ernst Cassirer's reasoning many years before in *The*

Problem of Knowledge: Philosophy, Science and History since Hegel: "It is a mistake to believe," the German philosopher explained

> that historical thinking as such was discovered, and its specific value to knowledge first realised by Herder and romanticism. The Enlightenment, generally discounted as unhistorical, was not only familiar with this manner of thinking but made use of it as one of the chief measures in the battle for its own ideals.
>
> (Cassirer 1950: 217)[27]

Cassirer, Bentley, Heyck and Blaas thus share a preoccupation with the myriad similarities and differences characterising mainstream historical thought over the last three centuries. As we read their work, new distinctions and new genealogies emerge. First, the figures of the "traditional" historian multiply. In the eighteenth century, the antiquarian had a rival in the figure of the "enlightened historian" – David Hume or Edward Gibbon – who took to history after having established his reputation as a man of letters. In the nineteenth century, a fissure emerges between the early whigs (e.g., Froude) and the late whigs such as E.A. Freeman or J.R. Green; another between "the Romantics" (Carlyle and Macaulay) and the whigs (the two types being found within the same generation), and yet another between the late whigs and the modernists: in the late nineteenth century, "the simple-mindedness of early whigs disturbed the later ones who wanted to mix a whig temperament with an awareness of science that their century had made *de rigueur*" (Bentley 2006: 6). Sometimes, one particular historian appears in different categories so that, in the end, we understand why the expressions "traditional" or "nineteenth-century" have come to replace more problematic labels. As Bentley (2006: 92–93) remarks, "Many 'whig' historians would not have recognised themselves as whigs" and a "particular weakness of Butterfield's paradigm, after all, is that it includes just about everybody, once we have left out Carlyle, who fits no one's model." At the same time, connections and overlapping ideas that remained obscured in the single narrative emerge to challenge the linearity of its retrospectively determined phases. New divides can be drawn depending on the historian's position in recurring debates, some of which seem to have attracted Woolf's attention, while others did not.[28]

Here, we may draw a parallel between the confusion induced by the use of labels and classification in more or less recent historiographies, and Woolf's refusal to use them in *Orlando*, *A Room of One's Own* and *Three Guineas*, three texts supposedly based on her "rejection of Victorian meta-narratives" (de Gay 2006: 147). In *Orlando*, there is a "Victorian age" and "Victorian literature," but no "Victorian," or "whig" historian. Instead, we find "historians," in the generic sense: "a historian"; "the historian." There are "nineteenth-century novels" and "nineteenth-century novelists" in *A Room*, but no "nineteenth-century historians" or histories. "Biography" can be a "Victorian" discipline or a "Victorian" genre in *Three Guineas*, but "history" is never envisioned through a specifically nineteenth-century lens. What the critics mean when they mention Woolf's relationship with "traditional" historiography's interests is, therefore, as vague as Woolf's own use of signifiers.[29] In *Orlando*, the "puzzled" historian faced with "a hole in the manuscript big enough to put your finger" could clearly be an eighteenth-century antiquarian, a mid-Victorian whig or a late nineteenth-century reformist (*O* 115): the only thing that is quite certain is that he is a male historian. In *Three Guineas*, the historians – who "are of course mainly concerned with war and politics; but sometimes throw light upon human nature" – could belong to any of the representative figures mentioned earlier (*TG* 273). The same might be said of "the historian," in *A Room*, "who records not opinions but facts" (39). Should we see him as a figure whose characteristics depend on the varying historical contexts he evolves in, or as a more palimpsestic, multilayered composition?

Woolf's use of the word "tradition" in those texts is not based on the expected opposition between old and new trends of thought. In *A Room*, a "tradition" of their own is what women writers "lack" and urgently need to forge (31). In *Three Guineas*, "tradition" is synonymous with patriarchal ideology; it is "that ancestral memory which lies behind the present moment" and excludes women from the public sphere: "the exclusion of women has remained the traditional attitude" (*TG* 308). Like "sex," "education" and "values," tradition is what "trains" and "influences" men and women differently and prompts the latter to be "not merely critical but creative" (*TG* 126; 234). Of course, one reason Woolf rarely contextualises "tradition" when she tackles the subject of historiography might be that she opposes it implicitly to her own, in-the-making, historical thought. In this respect, she anticipates Michel Foucault who contrasted "traditional history" with Nietzsche's "wirkliche Historie" ("effective history") as genealogy (Foucault 1984: 76–100). As Molly Westerman remarks when commenting upon "Nietzsche, Genealogy, History," Foucault's critique "encompasses several traditions of historiography" premised upon similar "enlightenment assumptions" (Westerman 2008: 28). However, this explanation is not sufficient. Whenever Woolf uses the term "historian" or "history," she refers to a succession of debates that cannot simply be ascribed to the past as synonymous with tradition or to the present as embodying modernity. Instead, Woolf's historical thought obliges us to retrace and remap pre-existing clusters of historiographical discourses which she recast in her own terms. To understand why she keeps referring to Gibbon, the Romantics Macaulay and Carlyle,[30] and Froude but seems to ignore a great many others (the other whigs, the reformists, the modernists, the first women historians), or why she picks up old, or rather timeless debates – on the continuity between history and literature, on the conception of history as art or science, on the reading and writing of history or on the institutional settings of history – we need to have a clear idea of what "tradition" meant to Woolf, her predecessors, her followers and to the contemporary critics reconstructing it. But we also need to be aware of how her pursuit of history as an exercise in reading and writing evolved over time.

Notes

1 Virginia Woolf (*PA* 178).
2 Charles W.C. Oman (1860–1946), military historian and author, before 1897, of *The Art of War in the Middle Ages* (1885), *A History of Greece From the Earliest Times to the Death of Alexander the Great* (1888), *The Story of the Byzantine Empire* (1892), *A History of England* (1895).
3 See *The Passionate Apprentice* (105–269) and Edward Bishop's *A Virginia Woolf Chronology* (1–2).
4 Also see Hill (1998), Hotho-Jackson (1991) and Westerman (2008).
5 The male figures concerned with Rachel Vinrace's education in *The Voyage Out* are her father, her uncle Ridley Ambrose, her lover Terence Hewet and his friend St John Hirst. In *Night and Day*, when William Rodney realises that he is in love with Katharine Hilbery's cousin Cassandra, he decides that "with his training and accomplishments, he could be of service to her" (*VO* 293).
6 See *Letters*, vol. 1, 180.
7 See also Katherine Hill's "Virginia Woolf and Leslie Stephen: History and Literary Revolution" (Hill 351–355).
8 On this question, see Hermione Lee (1997: 222–224).
9 See also Ernst Cassirer (1950): "It is a widespread and constantly recurring belief that the nineteenth century was not only a 'historical' century but that precisely this feature is what distinguishes it from all earlier periods" (Cassirer 217).
10 G.E. Lewes, "State of Historical Science in France," *British and Foreign Review* 31 (1844). Quoted by Dale (4).
11 On the myth of "ahistorical modernism," see, among others, Paul de Man's definition, in *Blindness and Insight* (1983), of modernity as a "desire to wipe out whatever came earlier, in the hope of reaching at last a point of origin that marks a new departure" (de Man 148), or Hayden White on the modern writers' "hostility towards history" in "The Burden of History" (White 1992: 28; 31). For a brief outline of similar arguments, see Astradur Eysteinsson's (1990: 8–49) chapter on the "Paradigms of Modernism" in *The Concept of Modernism* or Gabrielle McIntire's Introduction to *Modernism, Memory and Desire* (1–9). For more recent revisions of the myth, see also Blakeney-Williams (2002).
12 Michael Bentley's (2006) book on English Historiography (*Modernizing England's Past. English Historiography in the Age of Modernism, 1870–1970*) is one of the few exceptions.
13 In this respect, Hotho-Jackson goes one step further than Katherine Hill who was among the first in 1981 to look for a continuity between Woolf's historical thinking and her father's. Attributing this continuity to an "identification between father and child" (Hill 1998: 352) and to Leslie's plans for Woolf to be an essayist or a fiction writer, Hill provided a list of Woolf's readings as Leslie's daughter (Macaulay, Froude, Carlyle, Arnold) before turning to the

"common critical assumptions shared by" the two of them in Woolf's "How Should One read a Book" and "The Leaning Tower," and in Stephen's "The Study of Literature."

14 When Cuddy-Keane evokes Woolf's "varieties of historicist experiences," she does not refer to German "Historismus" but to Woolf's historical understanding and thinking. Besides, according to Charles R. Bambach (1995), the term historicism "does not become accepted until it reaches the end of its vital phase in the years after the Great War in Germany" (Bambach 4, note 5). See also Friedrich Meinecke (1972).

15 Linden Peach's subject in *Virginia Woolf* is "as much history in the work of Virginia Woolf as Woolf's work in history" (1).

16 Westman's references are to Michel Foucault's (1984) "Nietzsche, Genealogy, History"; Michel de Certeau's *The Writing of History* (1988a) and *Heterologies* (1989); Dominick LaCapra's *Rethinking Intellectual History* (1985) and *History, Politics and the Novel* (1987).

17 On Woolf, history and Foucault, see Peach (2000), Cuddy-Keane (1997) and Westerman (2008). On Woolf and Benjamin, see Spiropoulou (2010).

18 Buckle, Henry Thomas (1821–1862), English historian, author of *History of Civilization in England* (1857–1861). Neither Collingwood, nor Buckle is mentioned in Woolf's essays, diaries or letters.

19 Infer those two versions from my reading of Bentley (1997, 2006), Butterfield (1965), Cassirer (1950), Heyck (1982), Levine (1986), Westerman (2008) and White (2010).

20 See Levine (1986: 84)

> The identification of past events with current structures and their use as justification for and explanation of those structures, was a means of establishing not just a common consensus but a sense of both individual and collective purpose. Historians sought an organic continuity with the English past wherein present conditions could claim to be not just the only logical but the best outcome of a revered and celebrated past.

21 On this subject, see also Butterfield, (1931: 3–4).

22 See Rosemary Sweet (2004: xiii–xxi).

23 Buckle's *History of Civilisation in England* (1857–1865: 5 vols.) is considered a representative work of this trend. So was Hippolyte Taine's *Les Origines de la France contemporaine,* published between 1875 and 1893.

24 It must be noted that in this short but landmark study, Herbert Butterfield only gives the names of two "whig" historians – Thomas Babington Macaulay and Lord Acton – explaining that "the whig interpretation of history is not merely the property of whigs and it is much more subtle than mental bias; it lies in a trick of organisation, an unexamined habit of mind that any historian might fall into" (Butterfield 1931: 30).

25 See Blaas's (1978: 15) definition of finalism as "a form of interpretation strongly oriented towards the present".

26 Norgate, Kate (1853–1935), English historian, author of *England under the Angevin Kings* (2 vols., 1887), *John Lackland* (1902), *The Minority of Henry the Third* (1912), *Richard the Lion Heart* (1924). Bateson, Mary (1865–1906), historian and suffragist, attended Newnham from 1884 to 1887, taking a first class in the historical tripos at Cambridge in 1887 and winning the historical essay prize at Newnham for a dissertation, "Monastic civilisation in the

fens." Skeel, Caroline Anne James (1872–1951), English historian, entered Girton College, Cambridge, in 1891 (classics and history), was elected in 1921 to the council of the Royal Historical Society, author of "The influence of the writings of John Fortescue" (published in *Transactions of the Royal Historical Society*, 1916) and other historical essays. Power [*married name* Postan], Eileen Edna Power (1889–1940), English economic historian, went to Girton College, Cambridge, from 1907 to 1910, on a Clothworkers' scholarship, and took a first in both parts of the historical tripos, became director of studies in history at Girton in 1913, author of *Medieval English Nunneries* (1922).

27 Cassirer here refers to the German philosopher of the Enlightenment John Gottfried Herder (1744–1803).

28 See Bentley (1997: 411) on the school of "history as a social science" (Taine, Fustel de Coulanges, Gabriel Monod, Henry Thomas Buckle) and history as a "human discipline [...] quite foreign to the laboratory and the scientific journal": here he mentions Macaulay, Carlyle, Michelet; also see Hotho-Jackson on history as art (Macaulay, Trevelyan) and history as science (Hotho-Jackson 294).

29 See, for instance, Hotho-Jackson (1991: 294–296); Louise Blakeney-Williams in *Modernism and the Ideology of History* (2002: 6–7).

30 Categorised by Bentley as a Romantic, Macaulay is called a "nineteenth-century Whig" by Virginia Woolf herself in her 1937 essay on Gibbon (*E VI* 84), but it is unclear whether she refers to his political allegiance or historical thought. J.B. Bury, to take another example, is a transitional figure, in between the late whig, and the pre-modernist.

2 History's Readability
Woolf and Romantic Historiography

An Apprentice Historian

The story of Woolf's evolving historical thought remains unwritten: some of its aspects have been addressed before, but it has rarely been considered a learning process involving a constantly renewed dialogue with "tradition" and with what Woolf labelled "historians' histories" (*E III* 3). When she was young, the books by Carlyle, Macaulay, Froude or Thomas Arnold prescribed by her father led Woolf to think that she was "surfeited in history" but also "eligible for the first B.A. degree if the ladies succeed" (*PA* 87). The text books recommended for the English and Continental history lectures she attended at King's College Ladies' Department in 1898 and 1899 familiarised her with the politically liberal and more scientific approaches to history of Samuel Rawson Gardiner and E.A. Freeman. At Morley College, where she held a voluntary teaching post in January 1905 and was asked by her working-class students to "lecture steadily at English History [...] from the beginning" (*PA* 255), she seems to have encouraged a coherent and linear study of English history, while worrying that her female students might feel disempowered by grand narratives that could exclude personal narratives and everyday life. From 1906, when she published "The Journal of Mistress Joan Martyn" and her first review on a historical biography in *Academy & Literature*, until 1919, Woolf's pursuit of history thus reflects both her orthodox historiographical training and the emergence of persisting, more "heterodox" interrogations.[1] As an apprentice historian imagining that she could soon "produce a real historical work" (*L I* 202), her task was to negotiate an all-male heritage; as a young reviewer and critic, constrained by her editors to comment on books she had not chosen to read and by her public "to say what was agreeable,"[2] she needed to transform this constraint into an opportunity, which she clearly did, as a teacher, fiction writer and essayist, using, in this capacity, "unpromising material to carve out her ideas" or "making the very most of the good material" (Lee 1997: 216). As a matter of fact, between 1906 and 1919, one of Woolf's major – and yet underrated – interventions in the field took the form of an active rereading of history from the standpoint of a writer and

DOI: 10.4324/9780429331787-4

literary journalist preoccupied with history's ability, depending on the methodology, to either empower or disempower the reader; to make the past present and the present intelligible, or, on the contrary, to obscure the connections between past, present and future.

Between 1906 and 1937, Woolf wrote at least 12 reviews of historical books, mostly for the *TLS*, one signed article on Jules Auguste Lair's *Louise de La Vallière et la jeunesse de Louis XIV* for the "Book on the Table" series of the *Cornhill Magazine* ("Louise de La Vallière") and one unsigned leading article for the centenary of Edward Gibbon: "The Historian and 'The Gibbon'." She composed 11 of those reviews before 1919 and before fiction, poetry, criticism and biography became her favourite subjects as a reviewer and essayist. Except for Froude's *English Seamen in the Sixteenth Century* and the five volumes of Hakluyt's *Voyages, Travels and Discoveries of the English World*, the books Woolf was given to review were all recent ones. None were the work of contemporary historians, nor did any of the reviewed books become important. Thus, while Woolf might have read G.M. Trevelyan, J.R. Tanner, F.W. Tanner, R.G. Collingwood, Lewis Namier or John Holland Rose,[3] she never refers to them in the texts studied.[4] Woolf's reputation as a fiction writer interested in historical thought and biography, her position outside the prestigious institutions where specialists of history flourished, along with the little liberty she had, at the beginning of her journalistic career, to choose among the miscellaneous books she was sent to review by Margaret Lyttleton, Reginald Smith or Bruce Richmond probably explain why the books she mainly commented upon were historical biographies or memoirs written by men of letters like Professor Walter Raleigh, more or less popular fiction writers such as Edith Cuthell or D. Bridgman Metchim, and female biographers. Interestingly, though, the works examined in the following pages also bear testimony to the enduring popularity of such hybrid genres as historical biography and memoir and to Woolf's taste for them. More importantly, those rarely examined texts offer new insights into Woolf's critical method and relation to past historiographical debates. That this method relies largely on "a shifting and problematizing of historical terminology" is something that Marie-Louise Gättens (1995: 33) has already emphasised in her study of Woolf's political strategies in *Three Guineas*. However, it remains to be examined how this terminology, together with the debates it contributes to resemioticise, is clearly indebted to romantic historicism.

Romantic historiography first emerged in resistance to the Enlightenment's rationalism and as an attempt to "transcend the world of flat, nomological reportage and to produce a history that was creative and alive and the reverse of value-free." The Romantics "chose to make history learn from literature and to function in the same way" in order "to keep a reader reading" (Bentley 1997: 412). Bentley quotes the famous passage in Macaulay's essay on "History" where the author of *The History of England* regrets that his contemporaries should practise "the art of controversy" but "miserably neglect the art of narration, the art of interesting the affections and presenting pictures to the imagination" (Macaulay 1828a: 188). So, Carlyle "turned history into a rival for the three-decker novel" while for Michelet and other romantic historians, social history needed to be developed even if it was still considered to be, in Carlyle's words, "the essence of innumerable biographies" (Bentley 1997: 413–414). Ann Rigney uses the term "romantic historicism" to "designate broadly the historical culture of [the early nineteenth century] and the convergence of influences by which it was characterised." At the core of this historical culture, Rigney sees "a radicalized awareness of the alterity of the past and of the historicity of experience" (Rigney 2001: 7). She shows how the historical works of Macaulay, Carlyle and Michelet, among others, together with the historical romances of Sir Walter Scott, were characterised by the elaboration of "an alternative history" whose chief legacy is "the idea that there is a possible disjunction between relevance and representability," a legacy born out of the realisation by romantic historians that "history should no longer focus on dramatic, narratable events deemed of national importance" (Rigney 2001: 96–97). From that moment on, the question of history's methodology, and notably of its "rivalry with fiction," became "thematized" in historical writing (98). On the one hand, the idea that "history should attempt to get as close as possible to the everyday past as it was *experienced* by contemporaries" led historians to conceive of its writing as enabling "the latter-day public could vividly imagine the experience"; on the other hand, Rigney explains, such notions as the "unknowability" of everyday life and its "unintelligibility" kept haunting romantic historians. Strikingly enough, what she calls "the imperfection" of history as discourse – its contradictory impulses, its "hybridity" (Rigney 2001: 26; 2) and its silences – retrospectively echoes some of Woolf's abiding preoccupations. Read alongside the famous essays of Carlyle and Macaulay on history, Woolf's reviews and essays on historical works map the trajectories of earlier historiographical arguments: Woolf's "romanticism," as we shall see, is an intervention in, and disruption of, a dominant tradition whereby she recovers and recasts the question of history's readability and representability in her own terms. To look at this heritage provides new insights into Woolf's conception of key notions such as "truth," "fact," "fiction," "imagination" and "the unrecorded," all related to the central question of the past's intelligibility, readability and representability. It also enables us to address the issue of Woolf's apparent paradoxical stance *vis-à-vis* history as a legacy: she needed to free herself from looming actual and symbolic parents and transformed this legacy into a cultural and political terrain of investigation, one that made her discover tools, debates and writing practices that she would continue to share with her "common readers." In this respect, the reviews and essays I am about to discuss do not result from a filial rebellion that would place Woolf outside or against a monolithic tradition. They rather invite us to consider new filiations of historians – from Gibbon, Macaulay and Michelet to Raphael Samuel and others – for whom history could not and cannot be an enclosed discipline, nor "an esoteric form of knowledge" (Samuel 2012: 3).

The Romantic Heritage

In 1906, Woolf reviewed *Wilhelmina Margravine of Bayreuth* by Edith E. Cuthell (1905), English author of novels, biographies, children's books and short stories set in India. The book was a historical biography based, among other sources, on documents found in the Royal Secret State Archives and Family Archives in Berlin – among them Wilhelmina's memoirs – and tells the story of the Princess Royal, from her "parentage," "birth" and "christening" to her death in 1758. Woolf's "The Sister of Frederic the Great," which appears in *Academy & Literature*, consists mostly of a summary of the life recounted by Cuthell and offers almost no critical comments on her achievements as a writer. The reviewer simply declares the book to be "full of interesting materials" although the method of its author "is at times too crude and colloquial to be altogether pleasing" (*E I* 91; 87); Woolf mentions Carlyle's *History of Friedrich II of Prussia* and Sainte-Beuve's *Causeries du lundi* – two works in which the Princess and her letters and memoirs are mentioned – in a way that shows her obvious knowledge of them. Woolf's text does not display the critical faculties that characterise her later reviews and essays on history and historiography: at this stage, she prefers to quote the usual authorities on the subject rather than foreground her opinion. We might want to consider, however, a few apparently anecdotal expressions, such as those that appear in the last sentence of the review's first paragraph: "Miss Cuthell [...] has given us a picturesque and readable account of a woman who is invariably interesting." Indeed, the whole point of Woolf's review is to justify this comment by focusing on the "picturesqueness" of Cuthell's historical biography, in other words, on the details of Wilhelmina's life and character that make her life and times easy to imagine for a reader. She recounts the story chronologically, focusing on the "intrigues" (88) and on the portraits, based on facts, of the Royal Princess and of the characters that surround her. Woolf's critical method here is not highly refined; her review calls to mind Macaulay's (1828a: 160) defence of "portrait-painting" as he comments on Thucydides's art in his historiographical essay on Greek and Roman history: "we could mention portraits [...] which condense into one point of time, and exhibit, at a single glance, the whole history of turbid and eventful lives – [...] in which every wrinkle is a comment on some important transaction." For the romantic historians and Woolf, the "delineation of character" and "the details which constitute the charm of biography" (Macaulay 1828a: 169; 189), ought to accompany the "faithfully recorded facts" that, alone, cannot make history "interesting" (*E I* 90).

Another Wilhelmine is the historical personage who inspired Marie Hay's biography *A German Pompadour. Being the extraordinary History of Wilhelmine von Grävenitz, Landhofsmeisterin of Winterberg. A narrative of the eighteenth century* published in 1906 and reviewed by Woolf the same year. In "Sweetness – Long Drawn Out," Woolf again appropriates the debate on history and fiction inherited from her predecessors. That Marie Hay (Baroness Hindenburg)[5] should have begun her literary career as a writer of historical romances and fictional biographies might explain why Woolf devotes a long paragraph to Hay's methodology and more particularly to "her compromise between history and fiction": "[Miss Hay's] is always guiding herself by authentic facts, and her emotions are regulated by the documents at her side" (Woolf alludes here to Hay's use of "official archives" and "acts") but "she may indulge [her imagination] to such an extent that the reader does not know when he is reading history and when he is reading fiction." As a result, the book is a "composite production, where the truth has the vagueness of fiction and the fiction is diluted with fact" (*E I* 118). The word "composite" interestingly calls forth Macaulay's pages on the historian and the historical novelist where the words "compound" and "composition" refer to a desirable sharing of "duties" and achievements between the two: "History," Macaulay explains, should ideally be "a compound of poetry and philosophy," a "perfect amalgamation" of such "hostile" elements as "the imagination and the reason," to express "general truths on the mind by a vivid representation of particular characters and incidents." Because this amalgamation is difficult to achieve, it has finally been abandoned, so that "Good histories, in the proper sense of the word, we have not. But we have good historical romances, and good historical essays" (Macaulay 1828b: 196). However, the same Macaulay would have agreed with Woolf that whenever the frontiers between reason and imagination or facts and fiction are partially blurred, a historian does not write a good history. Speaking of the "romantic historian Herodotus" he thus writes:

> The fictions are so much like the facts, and the facts so much like the fictions, that, with respect to many most interesting particulars, our belief is neither given nor withheld, but remains in an uneasy and interminable state of abeyance. We know that there is truth; but we cannot exactly decide where it lies.
>
> (Macaulay 1828a: 155)

In those sentences, as in Woolf's review, is implicitly enclosed one of the most crucial questions raised by romantic historicism: how to reclaim for history the forms and materials of literature and still tell the historical truth. Of course, the answer to this question depends on how each historian defines "truth." For modernist historians, the scientific truth of ascertained facts was the only truth: it could not be manipulated by imagination or personal point of view. As for Woolf, she would go on exploring the epistemological issue of truth in general, and factual truth in particular, with not only increased awareness, but also with the suspicion that to fiercely believe in the "Truth and nothing but the Truth" (*O* 129) was the best way never to find it.

The next history book that she reviewed was her own choice, Andrew McNeillie suggests (*E I* 220). It appeared in October 1908 as a signed article in "The Book on the Table" series of *Cornhill Magazine* and was based on *Louise de La Vallière et la jeunesse de Louis XIV*, by Jules Auguste Lair, the French archivist and palaeographer. Lair published his biography in France in 1887 and it was translated into English in 1908. Entitled "Louise de La Vallière," Woolf's review focuses this time on the fascinating destiny of "the daughter of an ancient, though scarcely noble house" who became the maid of honour of Princess Henrietta, the King's brother's wife, and later on, Louis XIV's mistress (*E I* 215). She does not comment here on the author's skills as a historian, nor on his method: nothing on the sources he uses – memoirs, letters, photographs, paintings and history books – and no remark either on his art of narrative. Woolf's technique consists in writing a short version of the book she has read to try and justify why it deserves to be read. In his "avant-propos," Lair presents his work as both a "history" and a "story": "this history, or to take a less pretentious word, this story, began in the small castle of Bures, right in the middle of the Vallée de Chevreuse."[6] Woolf's interest lies here in the singularity of one woman's destiny: not the life of an eccentric or obscure character but of a woman whose "fate" "took place when she was but sixteen, in the spring of 1661" and whose "splendid moment" of exultation – when she went from maid of honour to "Louis's mistress" – she knew to be "a passing one" (*E I* 216; 219). Strikingly enough, her reading of Lair's historical biography foregrounds her own lively art of storytelling, the importance she attaches to details, moments of crisis, character presentation and language. In the wake of Macaulay (1828a: 188), she is attentive to the author's "art of narration, the art of interesting the affections and presenting pictures to the imagination," implicitly agreeing with the idea "that a writer may produce these effects without violating truth," a fact that is "sufficiently proved by many excellent biographical works." Woolf also indirectly pays a tribute to the importance, for the Romantics, of "historical personality" and "the luminous moment of action" (Bentley 1997: 414): she clearly invites her readers to "conceive the untried vigour of men of 20 and of women of 18, set free from all constraint, and inspired by love and fine weather" to "imagine" what happened "when the sun rose, on a cloudless summer morning, and promised brilliant hours till dusk, and then a warm summer night among the trees" (*E I* 219). She manages to "invest," as Macaulay recommended, "with the reality of human flesh and blood beings whom we are too much inclined to consider as personified qualities in an allegory" (Macaulay 1828b: 196), while acknowledging that "the instruction derived from history" should "be received by the imagination as well as by the reason. It would not merely be traced on the mind, but branded into it" (Macaulay 1828a: 195).

For the Romantics, imagination was indeed one of the necessary tools to bridge the gap between past and present. The fruitful links and tensions that Woolf discovers here between historical representation and a presentation of facts that interlaces the threads of narration, character presentation and visual theatricality bring to mind Woolf's acknowledgment, in "a Sketch of the Past," that "scene-making" was her "natural way of marking the past" – with one scene "always com[ing] to the top; arranged; represenive," enabling her to "disentangle" and sum up "a knot out of innumerable threads" (*MB* 145). Far from being merely a "literary device" (ibid.), however, the aim of this way to "bring before us" the experiences and lives of the past (*E I* 217) is not to restore an ideological continuity with the present but rather to bridge the otherness of the past to make it intelligible. As Woolf would explain in *Three Guineas*, in the famous passage about the photographs of dead children sent by the Spanish Government in 1986:

> But besides these pictures of other people's lives and minds – these biographies and histories – there are also other pictures – pictures of actual facts; photographs. Photographs, of course, are not arguments addressed to the reason; they are simply statements of fact addressed to the eye. [...] But the eye is connected to the brain; the brain with the nervous message.

Thus understood, intelligibility and "simplicity" do not so much distort the truth of facts as they enable the reader to experience a sense of "fusion" within himself, along with feelings of inclusion and commonality (*TG* 95–96); without those feelings, the lessons that one can draw from history are bound to be incomplete.

In her 1909 review for the *TLS* of *Venice. Its Individual Growth from the Earliest Beginnings to the Fall of the Republic* by Italian art critic and historian Pompeo Molmenti (1852–1928), Woolf's analytical terminology again constantly refers us to the questions of history's representability and readability as the romantic historians raised them. Molmenti's book is presented as the

> history of the "individual growth" of the state, ignoring Venice's fortunes abroad and narrowing his gaze upon the nature of the constitution, and in particular, upon the customs and the characteristics of the people in all ranks and upon all occasions.

(*E I* 243)

It is this last aspect that clearly interests Woolf the most as she writes her own synthetic version of Molmenti's evocation of a political and social world "at the moment of [Venice's] fullest life" (243). After a short description of the contents of the book and the political situation of Venice in the eighteenth century, Woolf evokes the town's paradoxical energy. The "learning" of the historian, together with "the vivid way in which he presents his facts" (strikingly, the word "vivid" occurs seven times in Macaulay's first essay on history) allows the readers, she writes, "to gaze into streets and workshops and drawing-rooms, and with this insight into the temperament of the people we can understand more clearly their action abroad." Political history combines here with social history. Woolf appreciates the way the historian "gives the detail of each occasion" and enables his reader to "compose some picture which shall serve for many" (245). The pictures thus elaborated through a constant use of picturesque and sensorial details – "the people cloaked in gold and scarlet," the "women" and their "stiff robes of velvet, damask or brocade," "the blue sky and the faintest breeze" – all contribute to enable the reader to "imagine" or "conceive" the crowd and "the joy of life in Venice" during its Golden Age (245). Woolf's review of this "history of the 'individual growth' of the state" focusing on "the customs and characteristics of the people in all ranks and upon all occasions" is itself both a "story" (243) and a highly visual evocation. Her vocabulary constantly resorts to the semantic field of sight and colourful details since her review is concerned with historical facts and focused on what Venice had "to show" (247). This explains why she often refers to the historian's and the reader's "gaze[s]" and "impression[s]," thus using what Ann Rigney calls the "permeability of the border between historical writing and other forms of expression" (Rigney 2001: 6). But as she tries to revive Venice's past glory, Woolf is also mindful of "the alterity of the past and of the historicity of experience," which Rigney considers to be part of the essential legacy of romantic historicism (Rigney 2001: 6; 8). At the end of her review, she thus writes:

> The history of Venice in the eighteenth century has the fascination of extreme distinction and at the same time a curious unreality. The sounds and sights of the outer world are to be found here, but only in quaint echoes, as though, in passing through the waters, they had suffered some sea change.
>
> (*E I* 247)

Time has changed the colours of the painting and altered the spirit of the age, but Woolf also reminds us here that in spite of the historian's art of "making the past present," Carlyle (1830: 5) was right when he explained that "the current of human affairs [is] intricate, perplexed, unfathomable, even when seen into with our eyes, are their thousand-fold blending movements," so that "the true representing of it is easy or impossible." The continuity that Woolf restores here is, therefore, not the temporal and ideological continuity that characterised most nineteenth-century narratives of progress: it is rather the vestige of earlier historiographical debates on history's "imperfection," its readability and its writability. What the historian brings "before us" is a picture, a painting, a text, a mediated truth anchored in the empiricism of facts. As Woolf relishes the evocation of changing scenes and sense impressions, *Orlando* and *Flush* loom on the horizon.

With "The Girlhood of Queen Elizabeth," a 1909 review published in the *TLS* of *The Girlhood of Queen Elizabeth [1533–1603]. A Narrative in Contemporary Letters* by English journalist and historian of the British book trade Frank A. Mumby, Woolf leaves the domain of social and political history to return to historical biography. As she did in "The Sister of Frederic the Great" and "Louise de La Vallière," she summarises here the "story" of a female historical "personage" (*E I* 321–322). She quotes Mumby (1909: xvii) several times and appears to agree with his view that private letters shed a "fierce" light "upon human character and motives," "social life and custom" and "the habit of mind of bygone generations." Thus, Woolf asserts in her introductory paragraph that "If we can arrive at some knowledge of [Elizabeth's] nature and of the circumstances that formed it, we shall read our history with a greater understanding" (320). Woolf displays her debt to romantic historicism in the very structure of her review – an inverted mirror image of Macaulay's "general rule" according to which "history begins in novel and ends in essay" (1828a: 154). She begins by presenting her views on some nineteenth-century historiographical questions; in Part II of the review, she proceeds to narrate the essential moments of Elizabeth's youth and the interest of the book under study. Her general opinions are, therefore, foregrounded, although her reference to an authority such as Froude to introduce the subject of sovereignty as a universal one might sound like a self-protective strategy: "There is a memorable passage at the end of Froude's History, in which, before summing up the qualities of the great Queen and delivering judgement, he bids us consider what it is to be a sovereign." Woolf does not expand here on Froude's prejudiced views on Elizabeth and is rather interested in the Carlylean "challenge of living in history, shared by all generations, ancient, medieval and modern," to take up Ciaran Brady's (2013: 230) words in his intellectual biography of James Anthony Froude. She writes: "Human nature when set upon a throne seems unable to sustain the enormous enlargement" (*E I* 319). To Woolf, Mumby's historical narrative enables us to look beyond the "spectacle of royalty" into "the mind of one of the great actors" of history; we can then better understand the struggle of "the normal human being" hidden "beneath the superhuman burden laid upon it by its fellows" (319). "Human character," as Woolf would explain a few years later, is shown to be an essential vantage point from which to examine changes in "religion, conduct, politics and literature" (*E III* 422). In this sense, therefore, "History is the essence of innumerable Biographies" (Carlyle 1830: 5). But if eighteenth-century "historians ha[d], almost without exception, confined themselves to the public transactions of states, and ha[d] left to the negligent administration of writers of fiction a province at least equally extensive and valuable" (Macaulay 1824: 80), history is not fiction. Woolf also acknowledges here, as in most of her other reviews, the specificity of a discipline looking for its own truth. She is aware of its methodology, and for example, of the "difficulties" that a "student of early documents" such as private letters encounters: "With their formalities and encumbrances, the very language they write is different from ours; they have a thousand inducements to tell lies, nor can they always tell the truth if they wish it." However, these documents are "original matter out of which history is fashioned before us" (320). Picking up all historians' preoccupation with truth, Woolf contests in those paragraphs the dominant post-romantic historiographical discourse that refuted the works of the previous generation for their lack of documentation and primary sources – a critique that her writing of *Orlando* would later explore in more satirical terms. She is aware that while some novelistic techniques like narration and description might bring the past "before us," primary sources speak a language of their own and require some form of translation and mediation implying the possibility of error. The first part of Woolf's review thus reads as a discussion embedded in earlier debates that it complicates; at the same time, Woolf is mapping here the trajectory for further historiographical and epistemological conversations.

Published in 1910 in the *TLS*, "Modes and Manners of the Nineteenth Century" is composed in a way that gradually becomes Woolf's method in her essays and reviews on historical books. It begins with general theoretical considerations, continues with the presentation of the reviewed book and ends on a final appreciation of the examined work and its achievements.[7] From the start, however, Woolf's style contrasts with the amiable tone of her previous reviews, as if she was already enacting the fundamental changes that she would later bring to the fore in her writings on modern fiction and human character: "When one has read no history for a time the sad-coloured volumes are really surprising. That so much energy should have been wasted in the effort to believe in something spectral fills one with pity." As she evokes "wars and ministries and legislation," those narratives of "unexampled prosperity and unbridled corruption tumbling the nation headlong to decay," she anticipates the expression "historians' histories" (*E III* 3) by depicting the actors and narrators of past history as "gentlemen in tall hats in the Forties who wished to dignify mankind" (*E I* 330–331). Anger, if not spite, is perceptible as Woolf sets to contrast the "three volumes" of the reviewed book, "thin and green, with innumerable coloured pictures and a fair type," and the thick volumes written by male mid-Victorian historians. Whether what has since been called the whig historical method was based on facts or not is a question that appears irrelevant to the reviewer who uses the verbs to "invent" and to "believe" to undermine the very idea of historical truth. Military histories or constitutional history, national narratives of progress insisting on the superiority of English culture and empire but failing to document it are said to finally compose a sad "mausoleum" of useless "delusion[s]" (331). Conversely, a history of manners, which would "endeavour to relate the history of the people" (Macaulay 1848: 2), looks back to the Romantics' attempts to write a history of "men and women in the mass" and to read the "trivial" alongside the so-called essential (E I: 241) in order to recover some of the material conditions of the multitudes whose lives as they were lived are so rarely recorded. But it also anticipates later works such as G.M. Trevelyan *English Social History* in 1943, along with historians whose work, from the 1930s onwards – the French *Annales* historians, E.H. Carr, Raphael Samuel, Ivan Jablonka, to name but a few – raised the question of history as a form of social knowledge linked with material culture.

At any rate, Woolf's tone in the first lines of her review is authoritative and falsely impersonal: "one" can only feel "pity." The reason for this uncensored anger appears in the next line: "Our point of view they ignore entirely: we have never felt the pressure of a single law; our passions and despairs have nothing to do with trade; our virtues and vices flourish under all governments impartially." "We," Woolf goes on, have been led to believe in the "machine they describe"; but "they" have not understood "the heart if it." In the end, "we are left out, and history, in our opinion, lacks an eye" (331). Woolf's use of the first-person plural is highly significant: the "sad-coloured volumes" never bridge the gap between "we," the common people, and "they" – "the clever, honest, interesting young men" whose educated minds have elevated "to a very high tower from which the human race appeared to them like rats and mice squirming on the flat" (*VO* 231). "We," Woolf explains, have a body, a heart and contradictory emotions; "they" are interested in laws, trades and governments. The metaphor of "the machine" and "the heart" anticipates Woolf's opposition between the "materialists" and the "spiritualists" in "Modern Novels": the historians that Woolf targets fail to "come closer to life" (*E III* 33); they "ignore" and "leave out" what, perhaps, "they cannot understand" (*E I* 331). Macaulay's (1828a: 190) "noiseless revolutions," "the changes of manners and morals, the transition of communities from poverty to wealth, from knowledge to ignorance, from ferocity to humanity" that "are not achieved by armies, or enacted by senates" are not explicitly mentioned here but seem to be implied. Because the three volumes of *Modes and Manners of the Nineteenth Century* "are thin and green, with innumerable coloured pictures and fair type," and because they deal with "how we feel and dress," the author of the review opens them with "unusual hope" (*E I* 331).

Karin Westman explains how Woolf's presentation of Fischel and von Boehn's book leads us to expect, from this moment on, "a different reading experience," not the encounter with "a tomb of the dead," but with "the lives of those who once lived." Yet, she goes on, "modes and manners" turn out not to be enough, since they cannot provide the "heart" that Woolf desires history to relate within its pages (Westman 13): "the history is not a history of ourselves, but of our disguises." As a matter of fact, Woolf concludes that "the poets and the novelists are the only proper people from whom we cannot hide" (*E I* 334). According to Westman, "even though it describes a social world which a textbook history might omit," a history of modes and manners is likely to remain "on the side of [...] narrow materialism" and to miss "the characters behind the facade" (Westman 13).[8] To Westman, Woolf here anticipates de Certeau and LaCapra by insisting on "the inevitable similarity between fiction and history by acknowledging the constitutive role of the historian's imagination in recreating the scenes of past experience" (ibid. 5). But Westman fails to mention that if neither Macaulay nor Carlyle used the word "emotion" in their seminal essays on history, they at least evoked "the passions" of the mind (Macaulay 1828a: 194), the uselessness of historical representations "divested of all individuality" and the historical "personifications" that are "not men" (Macaulay 1824: 70). In that sense again, Woolf's discourse is embedded in a male historiographical genealogy that she re-examines. But far from anticipating a form of post-structural history whereby the past is only a subjective discursive construction, she enables the reader to relive an experience in a way that borrows from romantic historiography. Also to be noted is how Woolf, by mentioning Carlyle's talent of "making the smaller ridicule the greater," reminds us of the growing interest, at the turn of the nineteenth century, in a cultural history encompassing the history of manners. "Manners as we call them" (*E I* 331) were already enlarging the boundaries of history when Voltaire published his "Essay on Manners" in 1754. The word recurs in Macaulay's historiographical essay and even becomes a central notion when he explains that

> by observing the manners of surrounding nations, by studying their literature, by comparing it with that of his own country and of the ancient republics, [the speculator] is enabled to correct those errors into which the most acute men must fall when they reason from a single species to a genus. He learns to distinguish what is local from what is universal: what is transitory from what is eternal.
>
> (Macaulay 1828a: 185)

Without dismissing this principle, Woolf nonetheless wonders what "manners," when they mean "clothes," have to say about "character" and "thought" (331). The whole point of Woolf's analysis here is to try and answer this question by making sense of the history of modes and manners under review. "Such a history," Woolf concludes, "is not a history of ourselves" and "the poets and novelists are the only people from whom we cannot hide" (334): a statement that, again, she would validate in *Orlando*, in which clothes and fashion are key ingredients in her exploration of cultural change. In this sense, then, Westman is right; but Woolf's rekindling of the rivalry between fiction and history is not the only way she participates in the ongoing historiographical debates.

Even more compellingly, her text is the site of an original reappropriation and transformation of the notion of the "spirit of the age" as the essence of what a "proper" historian should capture. The despised historians alluded to in Woolf's introductory paragraph believed in something "spectral." But what of this other "spirit" that supposedly manifests itself in "dress"? Because it "represents some part of man picturesquely" and might, therefore, "lend [...] itself happily to the satirist," this spirit, "like a shadow, [...] walks beside the truth and apes it." This is why, Woolf suggests, "the temptation to hook [dress and manners] together" might lead in the end to "the most airy conjectures" (331). This allegory of dress as an individual spirit embodying the spirit of an age enables Woolf to engage in a conversation with both her contemporaries and predecessors. In her introduction to the book under review, Grace Rhys writes that "to European dress and its changes, we must look not for the charm and interest of primitive custom and feeling, but for the large expression of a social history common to all men" (Fischel and Von Boehn 1909: vi). This view might remind us of Macaulay's (1828a: 192) statement that "the perfect historian is he in whose work the character and spirit of an age is exhibited in miniature." Similarly, Woolf's "spirit" brings with it Hazlitt's "spirit of the age," Ernst Moritz Arndt's *Der Geist der Zeit* and John Stuart Mill's use of the expression in his 1831 series of essays.[9] If Mill feigned to ignore those sources – "the 'spirit of the age' is in some measure a novel expression" (Mill 1831: 20) – Woolf seems to be playing with them: her review is haunted by a spirit returning from the past, wearing multiple guises and carrying with it an invariable idea: that "Mankind are then divided, into those who are still what they were, and those who have changed: into the men of the present age, and the men of the past" (Mill ibid.).[10]

That Woolf should have been interested in the notion of "change" is no surprise: in "Mr Bennett and Mrs Brown," change is a radical and dated fact. In *Orlando*, however, Woolf keeps questioning the value and efficiency, for historians and biographers, of such notions as change, periodisation and the spirit of the age, as I shall demonstrate (Chapter 4). In "Modes and Manners of the Nineteenth Century," those questions are linked, again, to an interrogation of the value of social history. The "spirit" Woolf personifies in her review is indeed mischievous and elusive:

> Now the skirt begins to grow, until it trails for six feet upon the ground; suddenly the spirit leaps to the throat, and creates a gigantic ruff there, while the skirt shrinks to the knees; next it enters the hair [...]; next the arms are attacked; they imitate Chinese pagodas; [...] Suddenly, without warning, the entire fabric is pricked; the spirit

moves the empress Eugénie one night (January 1859) to reject her crinoline. In an instant, the skirts of Europe melt away.

(333)

As in an accelerated cartoon, periods and fashions succeed one another as if by magic. The spirit of each age becomes an inexplicable force – "The democratic spirit required felt hats that drooped; in 1848 they dissolved about the ears" (333) – until Woolf wonders: "Are we truly in the grip of a spirit that makes us dance to its measure, or can it be laid without recourse to magic?" The message delivered by the author of the reviewed book is "not clear." First because, dress, furniture and manners can be explained by "a dozen different aims"; then, because "manners," Woolf thinks, is too "vague" a term and "people's behaviour is the roughest guide to what they mean" (334). Fischel and Von Boehn's work is, therefore, promising: it does not ignore "how we feel and dress" (331). But it does not manage to account, perhaps because fashion "comes from without" (333), for change and character: "only great artists, giving their minds to nothing else, represent their age" (334). By using explicit and implicit intertextuality, caricature and allegory, Woolf's review becomes a palimpsestic text indirectly exploring her vision of dress, manners, change and historical truth. As such, it clearly anticipates the historiographical questions she raises in *Orlando* while placing the primary text she is reviewing in dialogue with a genealogy of debates of which she constantly trails a trace.

The year 1910 was the year of the death of Edward VII, the first post-Impressionist exhibition in London, of Woolf's half-hearted involvement in the Votes for Women Campaign and of the Dreadnought Hoax.[11] More importantly, it was the year Woolf assertively declared to be the time when "human character changed," although critics have often forgotten to quote Woolf's next sentence: "The change was not sudden and definite like that" (*E III* 421–422). Woolf's turn-of-century consciousness has now been a matter of debate for a few decades. However, we might want to agree that "a change there was" (*E III* 422), characterised by an increased tension, among the Edwardians, between the "conservatives and the dissenters," and on a more personal level, the need to combine, as in the "Dreadnought Hoax" different forms of subversion: "ridicule of empire, [...] mockery of bureaucratic procedures, cross-dressing and sexual ambiguity" (Lee 1997: 282–283). The professional consequences for Woolf of this new subversiveness are not immediately clear. First, because she wrote very few reviews and essays between the end of 1910 and 1913 (only seven according to McNeillie's edition of *The Essays*)[12]; and then because the writing of *The Voyage Out* occupied most of her time. However, her critical work after 1910 clearly shows that her apprenticeship as a reviewer had ended. As McNeillie and others have remarked, "her command of the medium is complete," Woolf feels more "liberty to write as she pleases" and less obligation to "celebrate [...] her subject at length and in depth" (*E I* xv). One of the characteristics of her reviews and essays on historical books after 1910 is the ironical tone of their opening paragraphs.

In 1916, Woolf's "Queen Adelaide" begins with a quotation from the reviewed book – *The Life and Times of Queen Adelaide* (1915), by Mary F. Sandars – followed by a scathing comment:

> "I request not to be dissected nor embalmed, and desire to give as little trouble as possible," wrote Queen Adelaide characteristically when she was considering the disposition of her dead body; and all the industry of Mrs Sandars has not been able to violate the privacy of her spirit.

That the reviewer "cannot boldly affirm, after reading 298 pages about her, that she never existed" is not Sandars' fault, Woolf explains: "the Queen is dumb" and the imagination of her biographer could not make her alive. "We" never actually "meet her," nor do we "hear more than the murmur of her voice" (*E II* 19). The first duty of a historian, or biographer, Woolf implies here, is to find an riveting subject. If Mrs Sandars has managed to "produce the Queen for us" (19) – an expression that reminds us Macaulay's (1828b: 196) view that part of the duties of the historian is "to call up our ancestors before us" – this is not enough: the rest of the review regretfully concentrates on the "dreary" scenes of what appears to have been a meaningless life (21). Woolf's frustration, however, is revealing: as a reader, she needed the Queen's "voice" to be recovered, and we know how the notion of "voice" would always be deeply connected with her vision of subjectivity and presentation of character.

Also reviewed by Woolf in 1916, *Social Life in England: 1750–1850* is the printed version of eight Lowell lectures delivered by historian Frederick J. Foakes in Boston that same year. This time, Woolf finds the subject inspiring: the century pictured by Jackson was indeed, she writes in her introduction, "a momentous one in our social history." However, the first lines of Woolf's review – "Social Life in England" – raise the question of the book's "misleading" title and cover which seem "to promise something more solid than we have here" (*E II* 64). What the assembled lectures lack, Woolf explains, is "some grouping or emphasis which would bring a general theory to our attention." The book is "readable," "but the reader slips from one picture to another, and is left for the most part to make up his mind as to the kind of world they illustrate for himself" (65). The lecturer is not "altogether sure of his own opinion," does not provide any "guidance" to his readers, gives very few "dates and details" and "advanc[es] only the most temperate opinions [...], supporting them almost invariably by the authority of others" (65). To qualify a rather harsh appreciation, Woolf provides some excuses for these failings: the audience is American, so that, in the end, "what Dr

Foakes Jackson has given us, oddly enough, is not a picture of ourselves, but a picture of a cultivated American audience" (66). Many historiographical issues are being reshuffled here, notably the tension between historical facts and unifying theories. In his historiographical essay, Macaulay had already insisted on this tension and the way it might lead the work of a historian to be out of balance. On the one hand, he wrote,

> in fiction, the principles are given, to find the facts: in history, the facts are given, to find the principles; and the writer who does not explain the phenomena as well as state them, performs only one half of his office.

On the other hand,

> the best historians of later times have been seduced from truth, not by their imagination, but by their reason. They far excel their predecessors in the art of deducing general principles from facts. But unhappily they have fallen into the error of distorting facts to suit general principles.
>
> (Macaulay 1828a: 163; 185)

Obviously, Foakes Jackson fell in the first of these two traps, at least according to Woolf.

Another essential issue broached by this review is that of a history's readability, a notion depending on the book's materiality and length along with its ability to make sense for a contemporary audience. In his review of Hallam's *The Constitutional History of England, from the Accession of Henry VII to the Death of George II* for the *Edinburgh Review*, Macaulay (1828b: 198) was already perfectly aware of history's changing readership and of the necessity to address the proper audience with the proper language and method: "[Mr Hallam's] work is designed for readers who are already acquainted with the ordinary books on English history, and who can therefore unriddle these little enigmas without difficulty." As for Carlyle, in his 1845 introduction to *Cromwell's Letters and Speeches* he deplored that the history of the Civil War was inaccessible to his generation since "extrinsically, the documents and records of it, scattered waste and shoreless chaos, are not legible." Because those documents have not been properly edited, they have remained "unread," "as if non-existent" (Carlyle 1845: 4). In Woolf's review, an awareness of her audience is conveyed by the recurring use of the pronoun "we" which progressively builds up the image of an ordinary contemporary reader. It is the same "we" that can be found in her critical essays on modernity, and as such, it differs greatly from the "we" used by Carlyle and Macaulay when they refer to themselves as representatives of the learned reader or when they want to stress their personal opinions; Woolf's "we," as Katerina Koutsantoni very clearly explains in *Virginia Woolf's Common Reader*, is an "inclusive 'we', including both the writer-speaker and the reader-hearer"; it involves "both the writer and the reader in the same activity" (Koutsantoni 2009: 60). Woolf's review, therefore, ends on an ironical sentence underlining Dr Foakes Jacksons' failure to understand English life: "the best way to lead [the American audience] across the desert of the lecture hour is to bring them a pocket of sweetmeats and produce them one after the other until the minutes are consumed" (*E II* 66). But beneath sarcasm – Woolf's distrust of, and even disdain for, the American world is a recurring feature of her essays[13] – lies a sharp critique: "we," as readers and historical subjects, have been excluded from the historical, national and social panorama of the book under examination.

Woolf's subsequent reviews on historical books resort to this inclusive use of "we" as a key ingredient of their rhetorical strategy and theoretical assumptions. Thus, the reason she enjoyed reading Lady Newton's *The House of Lyme. From its Foundation to the End of the Eighteenth Century*, a book she reviewed for the *TLS* in March 1917 ("The House of Lyme"), is not its protagonists: as Woolf explains in a letter, "the truth was that the Legh's were almost invariably stupid – which accounts, I suppose, for their centuries of life on the same spot" (*L II* 147). However, "we are still under the spell of Lady Newton's narrative, and her gifts, unfortunately, are by no means common ones." Because of Lady Newton's "skillful arrangement," "freshness of feeling which imparts a most delightful naturalness to her story," "we are able for the moment to forget the substantial veil of the present to gaze upon the lives which have receded from us but have not disappeared" (*E II* 97). Woolf's appreciation relies once more on the reappropriation of a "romantic" conception of historical writing: the historian is here, first and foremost, an artist who accommodates the tools of fiction to "open the door" (here a "private door") onto the past and lead the reader through it. Lady Newton has for her characters a form of empathy – "She writes of them as if she had known them" – that she shares with the reader, thus enabling him to look through the door and free the "ghosts" and "spirits" that were locked behind. On first examination, this implicit association of the House of Lyme with a gothic castle harbouring many secrets in the form of "Old letters" seems to undermine the potential grandeur of a history here transformed into popular romance (96–97). Under this light, Woolf's assertion, at the beginning of her review, that "the production of such works by the people who inherit such houses should be made compulsory by Act of Parliament" sounds ironical (96). By proceeding to discuss the value of Lady Newton's sources as private documents and by acknowledging her role as their essential "interpreter" (97), Woolf emphasises, however, the articulation between serious historical writing and enjoyable reading. Just as the gothic as a genre has an indisputable place in literary history, the door "thrown open at many generations of the family of Legh" is a door opened at "much of the history of England" (97). In her own terms, Woolf envisions this history as defined by a landscape, a dwelling place and the succession of generations "in the same spot," "for something like five centuries" (98). This apparently uneventful "continuity" is evoked in letters that "drown the drums and trumpets of history with a deeper and subtler music of their own" (99). The House of Lyme functioned as a social microcosm employing "eighty or a hundred people," and entertaining a "floating population consisting of visitors from the great families of the neighbourhood"; its story, therefore, is the social history of a "self-sufficient community highly organised in each of its departments" (99). Woolf invites the reader to alter his/her views on what may define a historical event; to focus on slow changes and transformations affecting housing, domestic life, manners and speech. There is essential knowledge in the evocation of this "under current" of society which Macaulay contrasted with the upper current embodied by armies, senates and statesmen (Macaulay 1828a: 190), an undercurrent that "flows steadily on, unruffled by the storms which agitate the surface" (Macaulay 1824: 80). Woolf's review ends, noticeably, on a nostalgic note as she contrasts the image of a "sanctuary for the lovely wreckage of the past" with her contemporary world, "bent on ruin and oblivion" (100). This nostalgia could be explained by the feeling of threat and rupture provoked by First World War. Woolf's emphasis on continuity here, however, is not the post-revolutionary celebration of a regretted past: Woolf's work is always one that uncovers illusory breaking points and sheds light on unrecorded, non-teleological continuities.

In 1918, Woolf published two reviews on historical books, very different in tone and scope. One, entitled "A View of the Russian Revolution," appeared in the *TLS* and is dated December 19, 1918. It discusses *Petrograd. The City of Trouble 1914–1918,* published by Meribel Buchanan, daughter of the British Ambassador at St Petersburg (1910–1918) with a foreword by Hugh Walpole. Woolf is here clearly less admiring of the book than she is of the Russian writers (Dostoevsky, Chekhov, Turgenev and Tolstoy) whose novels were the subject of at least seven reviews between 1917 and 1919. Disagreeing with Walpole that Miss Buchanan's "account of Petrograd in the last four years" manages to give the world "a sense of the *atmosphere* of Russia under the shock and terror" of the Revolution, she explains that the author's method is defective since it "rest[s] wholly upon shrewd and personal observation" (*E II* 338). Miss Buchanan provides "a vague outline of events," confuses "gossips" with "fact" and writes in a "purely descriptive" way. The question is not so much that she is not a professional historian, but that she relies on "intuition" to elucidate "politics" (339). Woolf's disparaging comments suggest that to be a direct observer of historical events does not make one a historian; not all diaries and testimonies have historical value.

Woolf's appreciation of Richard Hakluyt and James Anthony Froude as historians is, of course, very different.[14] Her 1918 review in the *TLS* based on *Hakluyt's Collection of the Early Voyages, Travels and Discoveries of the English Nation* and Froude's *English Seamen in the Sixteenth Century* (1895) has the same title – "Trafficks and Discoveries" – as her 1906 review for the *Speaker* of Walter Raleigh's introduction to the last volume of Hakluyt's *The Principal Navigations*. In her 1906 review, Woolf paid a tribute both to Hakluyt's work and Professor Raleigh's "luminous and authoritative comment" (*E I* 123). The interest of Raleigh's preface, she explains, is to prevent the reader from being "gloriously confused with the medley of rich names and places, of spices and precious stones, of strange lands of monsters" provided by the author (120). Professor Raleigh's editorial work has fortunately helped the reader "see the whole pageant in its proper proportions" (121). Whatever "romantic ambiguity" there was in Hakluyt's five volumes, he has managed to suggest how it was "founded on hard truth." Thus, Hakluyt's "romanticism" is first linked with the absence, in the original text, of "map or index or editorial footnote" that would have pointed the way and enabled the reader to stop "groping in the dark" (121). But the second occurrence of the adjective "romantic" is associated with Hakluyt's "little landscapes" described with a "sober and veracious eye": those "perilous woods," the "strange thunder of waters" that transform the "story" into a "tale" that "reads like some colored opium dream" (122). Woolf's use of romantic clichés in those expressions and in others – she evokes "the opulence of the imagination [...] yielding treasures of another sort" and "the air of unsophisticated simplicity" that the sailors' direct testimonies convey – goes along with a more interesting vision of history as a hybrid model of discourse. Hakluyt's combination of "story," "tale," "pageant" and "lists of 'commodities'" composes a "chapter of English history," she explains, that "enlightens our knowledge of the men and their adventure." This history is all the more valuable in that it pays attention to words – those, "authentic," of the sailors, and the historians, whose "material glitter" is a potential source of "intoxication," dream and truth at the same time (121–122). In this 1906 review, in which the term "pageant" immediately calls to mind *Between the Acts* and the demystification of the history it represents, Woolf's debt to romantic historiography was enriched by a more personal reflexion on the way the historian's art is always encapsulated in his poetic use of "sentence."

That the historical method sketched out here should help make history in general more readable is the statement with which Woolf begins "Trafficks and Discoveries" in 1918:

> Most people have only time to ask whether history is readable, not to seek further whether it is true. But in one sense the most readable histories are also the most true, in so far as their vivid and spirited qualities arise from the force with which the historian himself has believed in his narrative; and perhaps no one can write with fire and conviction unless he has got hold of some form of the truth.
>
> (*E II* 329)

The ideas discussed in this text are in keeping with her 1906 review and her subsequent reflections, some of which may appear illogical to many professional historians. As she states that "the most readable histories are also the most true," Woolf argues the romantic case that history should be accessible and readable as a novel while addressing her own vision of the "common reader." She praises the "beauty of phrase" in the reported speech of Hakluyt's seamen, and her description of the works under study suggests that she conceives historical truth as poetic, and not merely factual and expository: in Froude's history, she explains, "nothing is lacking that poet, novelist, or historian could desire" (329). However, by insisting from the outset on the needs and concerns of the reader, Woolf maps the trajectory of earlier arguments while offering a new way to articulate the debate on the writing and reading of history.

Her paradoxical and slightly provocative opening statement is meant first to introduce James Anthony Froude, Regius Professor of Modern History at Oxford in the 1890s, as "among the most readable of historians." Woolf could not have ignored that Carlyle's disciple and biographer, often labelled a whig historian, was among the first to work mainly with archival sources while rejecting the claim that history could be a science: Froude did not write as a specialist but as a widely read man of letters who also published fiction.[15] This vision of history partly inherited from the Romantics was apparently why E.A. Freeman had tried for two decades to discredit Froude's reputation as a historian.[16] Woolf, on the contrary, felt in tune with this method. An example of Froude's prose extracted from his 1893–1894 lectures on *English Seamen in the Sixteenth Century* might help us understand why she considers that his account "tells itself rather than is told." In the following lines evoking the exploration of the North-West passage under Henri VIII's patronage, "the knots of the narrative dissolve in his fingers as he touches them" and each historical figure "stand out as clear-cut in feature and as inevitably placed as if Froude spun the story from his own imagination" (*E II* 329):

> They apparently relied on Providence to take care of them, for they made little other preparation. They reached New-Foundland, but their stores ran out, and their ships went on shore. In the land of fish they did not know how to use line and bait. They fed on roots and bilberries, and picked fish bones out of the ospreys' nests. At last they began to eat one another—careless of Master Hore, who told them they would go to unquenchable fire.
>
> (Froude 1895: 9–10)

But beyond the tribute paid to a controversial Victorian figure, Woolf's gesture to the historian's audience also picks up the Romantics' preoccupation with truth. For Macaulay, history could not "be perfectly and absolutely" true since "to be perfectly and absolutely true, it ought to record [...] all the things done and all the words uttered during the time of which it treats." Truth, therefore, was the truth of facts that a historian could "narrate without inventing"; it was necessarily partial but "nearly produce[d] the effect of the whole" (Macaulay 1828a: 159–160). It had to be "authenticated by sufficient testimony" but also needed to be given, "by judicious selection, rejection, and arrangement," "those attractions which have been usurped by fiction" (ibid. 191). Woolf's own definition of historical truth does not contradict this approach, but she complicates the terms of the debate by equating history's truth with its readability while linking the readability of any historical work with the historian's "belief" in his own narrative, the "sense of conviction" with which "he shapes" it. For the sake of the reader's needs, the historian's authority is here recovered, not on account of his historical method, but because his subject position is acknowledged, and his convictions, "prejudices and opinions" allow him to convey to his readers "some form of the truth" (*E II* 329). This "truth" is, therefore, the result of a "shaping process" that depends on "the vantage-ground of the historian." Thus, Woolf explains, if Froude's seamen lose "something of the humanity which we discern in them obscurely engaged with their forgotten comrades" in Hakluyt's version of their story, they also gain in "richness, depth and variety" by being "studied in the rough" (330). Curiously, Woolf's appraisal of the work of major historians such as Gibbon or Froude does not dwell on the underlying vision of what they should teach, the "moral foundations" (Froude 1867: 21) that they need to reveal, or the direction of human affairs that enables the study of the future. She does not look for "truth" as an abstraction of facts or an absolute. While acknowledging, like the Romantics, the difficulty historians may have defining it, she sees it as dependent on the "point of view" that makes it readable.

Strikingly, a very short review of *Our Own History of the War: From a South London View*, by British author D. Bridgman Metchim, ironically plays with the meaning and value of the word "view" and takes issue with the author's method, although it differs from many of his predecessors'.[17] The opening statement of "The War From the Street" is clearly provocative: "Mr Metchim has discovered the very important truth that the history of the war is not and never will be written from our point of view" (*E III* 3). The butt of Woolf's irony is first the "cynical" and "sluggish" opinion, accepted by traditional historians and their audience that "history as it is written" will never resemble "history as it is lived." "We," therefore, should not complain "if we are fobbed off once more with historians' histories." On first examination, Metchim's book seems to offer a way out of this dilemma by describing the Great War from the perspective of an ordinary citizen – "we," in his text, or "you" when he chooses to directly address the reader as an involved citizen. But who exactly "we" and "you" designate is the question raised by Woolf's critique of Metchim's project:

Mr Metchim here records the history of the war as it appeared to a gentleman living in South London so far as the body is concerned, but populating the whole of England spiritually, constituting, in fact, that anonymous monster of the Man in the Street.

(3)

The comic contrast displayed here points to the paradox, if not aporia, underlying such a challenge. Mr Metchim, Woolf suggests, cannot be an individual body inhabited by the mind of whole England; therefore, he cannot claim to speak for us – "we" in the text – and write history as it has been "lived" by everybody (3). The "man in the street" is indeed no individual; he remains a "vast, featureless, almost shapeless jelly of human stuff taking the reflection of the things that individuals do." Thus, "we" and "you" mask the reality of essential divisions: between Metchim's body – "his own experience as a flesh and blood human being" – and the "spirit" of the citizens he claims he stands for; between "they, the individuals, the generals, the statesmen, the people with names, [who] proclaim war" (*E III* 3) and "you," who in a passive and "muddled way reflect what they do in blurred pictures half obliterating each other" (4). The unity of the civilian viewpoint on the war implied in the title of Metchim's book is here undermined by Woolf's remarkably confusing use of pronouns throughout the text. Woolf considers the unity artificial and misleading, reconstructed by the historian. In fact, Metchim's "you" sounds to Woolf as a rhetorical device which never coincides with her own sense of "we."

In the second half of the essay, the "you" which Metchim addresses as a homogenous social group becomes a dispersed, fragmented entity without agency. The recurring use of the passive voice in Woolf's review suggests an "interpellated" you, in Althusser's sense of linguistic interpellation, no longer a singular, individual "you," but a "subject" preceded and hailed by language and the forces of ideology:

> you get somehow broken off and turned into soldiers and sent to France, [...]. Soon your mind, if one may distinguish one part of the jelly from another, has had certain inscription scored upon it so repeatedly that believes that has originated them.

And how can "you begin to have violent opinions of your own" since "for four years and more you are nothing but a vast receptacle for the rumours of other people's opinion and deeds." At the end of her review, Woolf subtly complicates the reference of this haunting "you" whose profound "conviction," she explains, is that "nothing is ever going to touch you" (4). In this respect, and as Karen L. Levenback suggests in *Virginia Woolf and the Great War*, Woolf's text seems to be in line with these words in her diary: "most people have grasped neither war nor peace" (*D I* 215). But if "you" is also "we," then the subject who refuses to be touched can also be Metchim himself. Woolf's conclusion, therefore, is both somewhat melodramatic and ambivalent: "you" – Metchim's persona as a historian, as well as the reconstructed "you" of citizens having shared a similar experience of the war – "are not us": "and therefore the history, is, as it is always fated to be, not ours" (*E III* 4). Although Levenback's understanding of the problematic meaning of "you" remains unsure, her introductory remarks on how Woolf actually "lived through the Great War," was aware of the chasm between its reality and representation, but was nonetheless long considered the "passive bystander" that she describes, are persuasive (Levenback 1999: 1–2). Not only was Metchim's historical account unlikely to make the horrors of the war comprehensible, it also unconsciously aroused a feeling of exclusion that was to haunt Woolf in the following years, anchoring the question of the "proper stuff" of history in a more personal story.[18]

In the meantime, Woolf reacted to the forces of exclusion by diving into her heritage and embarking on a conversation that reconfigured its continuities and overlaps. Her method here was one that she would continue to adopt: to expose prior judgements and discourses, to learn and unlearn from the past, recall its lessons, while always exhibiting the making of this process within the self-reflexive framework of the essay. In this respect, Woolf's grasp of history is related to her own historicity as an experiencing subject, to her claimed position as a marginalised female intellectual asking for more visibility and, above all, to a critical method that she would keep practising, with various agendas, for the rest of her life. This method anticipates Michel de Certeau's (1988b: 67) non-professional or "common" "poaching" reading practice: it results from socially constructed relationships between the acts of reading and writing; as it undermines the perpetuation of dominant forms and values, it allows the reader to travel in foreign territories, to think and imagine in spite of, and against, a literary elite, and to remain in an empowered position of creative production, the creative production of an "active" reader who has learnt to "try the accepted forms," to "*discard* the unfit, to create others" as Woolf will suggest one year later in "Men and Women" (*E III* 195).

In this respect, romantic historiography became for Woolf, during these years, this inherited yet foreign territory approached from her "here" and "now," through an act of looking back that tracked forms of intelligibility whereby history could be read as the history of lives as they were lived. She gradually turned her own impressions as a reader into a political narrative that wove together fragments of official and unofficial history, reconfiguring the romantic interest in history's new audiences, in its silences, in the tension between single biographies and collectivities and between necessary objectivity and the value of creative imagination. Doing so, she began questioning the claim to knowledge of "historians' histories" together with their assumption that this knowledge "filters downwards" (Samuel 4). Then, in a strikingly "untimely" way, she also blurred the boundaries that modernist historians were so keen on establishing between their discipline and literature. At this period of her life, the review and essay as genres gave Woolf the opportunity to explore and invent what Ivan Jablonka calls the "new rules" and "new operators of textuality" in that they enable the "I" critic or historian to

> tell [...] the story of the investigation as well as its 'results,' going back and forth between the past and the present to which we belong, using emotions as a tool for better understanding, placing the cursor at the right spot between distance and empathy, choosing the right words and allowing for the languages that the investigator usually does not share with the people (living or dead) that he encounters.
>
> (Jablonka 2018: viii)

At a time when the divide between popular histories and academic historical work was beginning to widen, when economic and social history had not begun their future modern emergence, and above all when the Great War changed the world and its perception of history, Woolf continued to read the Romantics: Carlyle, not for his love of heroic leaders but because of his pictorial style that made the past unforgettable; Macaulay for his "endeavour to relate the history of the people as well as the history of the government" (Macaulay 1848: 2) along with his art of "interesting the affections, and presenting pictures to the imagination" (Macaulay 1828a: 188); but also Jules Michelet, whose avowed aim was to speak for the masses, to listen for "words that were never spoken" and to "make the silences of history speak."[19]

Notes

1 On this subject, see Clara Jones (2017: 17–64).
2 Quoted by Christina Froula from Woolf's *Published Manuscripts Notes* (Froula 2007: 217). On this subject, see also Jeanne Dubino (1997: 25–40).
3 R.G. Collingwood is mainly known as a philosopher, but he published *Roman Britain* in 1923; Lewis Namier's *The Structure of Politics at the Accession of George III* in 1929; John Holland Rose's *The Life of Napoleon*, vol. I, in 1910; *William Pitt and the Great War* in 1911 and *The Development of the European Nations* in 1915.
4 While most of the renowned nineteenth-century historians (J.B. Bury, Thomas Carlyle, E.A. Freeman, J.A. Froude, S.R. Gardiner, J.R. Green, T.B. Macaulay, J.R. Seeley) are referenced at least once in the indexes of Woolf's volumes of essays, those more contemporary names are not mentioned there, nor in Woolf's notebooks.
5 See *The Winter Queen*, being the unhappy history of Elizabeth Stuart, electress palatine, queen of Bohemia; a romance (1910) and *Madame Dame Dianne de Poytiers*: la grande seneschale de Normandie Duchesse de Valentinois: a monograph (1900).

6 "Cette histoire, ou pour prendre un mot moins prétentieux, ce récit a été commencé dans le petit château de Bures, en pleine vallée de Chevreuse" (Lair ii). *My translation.*

7 *Modes and Manners of the Nineteenth Century. As Represented in the Pictures and Engravings of the Time: 1790–1817*, by German Historian of culture Max Ulrich von Boehn (1860–1932) and German art historian Dr Oskar Fischel (1870–1939).

8 At this moment in her essay, Westman is commenting upon Woolf's "sweeping criticism of a popular historical method" exemplified by Ellen G. Hill's *Maria Edgeworth and Her Circle in the Days of Buonaparte and Bourbon. With Numerous Illustrations* (1909) and quotes from Woolf's first paragraph:

> The past has an immense charm of its own; and if one can show how people lived a hundred years ago—one means by that, how they powdered their hair, and drove in yellow chariots, and passed Lord Byron in the street—one need not trouble oneself with minds and emotions.
>
> (*E I* 315)

9 See William Hazlitt, *The Spirit of the Age; or, Contemporary Portraits* (1825); in the December 1, 1916 issue of *The Examiner* (759), Hazlitt mentions the German patriotic author (1769–1860) from which the term probably originates.

10 On this subject, see also Gertrude Himmelfarb's introduction to *The Spirit of the Age: Victorian Essays* (Himmelfarb 1–17), and notably how she mentions David Hume's own use of the expression "Of Refinements and the Arts," in his *Essays* (1741–1742); see (Hume 1904: 275).

11 This hoax is, according to Hermione Lee, "the best-known and most sensational of all 'Bloomsbury's' public exploits." On February 7, 1910, Adrian Stephen, Horace de Vere Cole, Duncan Grant, Anthony Buxton, Guy Ridley and Virginia Stephen disguised as the Sultan of Zanzibar, the Emperor of Abyssinia and their suit, fooled the British Navy at Weymouth and managed to be welcomed on board the Dreadnought by Admiral William May and the Stephens' cousin, Commander William Fisher (Lee 1997: 282–283).

12 The legacy of 2500 pounds from her aunt Caroline Emilia Stephen is obviously another explanation for her slowing-down input as a critic.

13 On Woolf's vexed relationship with the Americans, see Andrew McNeillie, "Woolf's America" (2001: 2).

14 Although Hakluyt was first and foremost a geographer (1553–1616), his *Principal Navigations, Voyages and Discoveries of the English Nation* (first published in one volume in 1589 and later reprinted as *Hakluyt's Collection of the Early Voyages, Travels and Discoveries of the English Nation*, 5 vols., 1809–1812) is a documentary history of the Elizabethan expeditions overseas, combining historical, diplomatic, economic papers and maps in order to establish British right to sovereignty at sea.

15 On Froude's conception of history as no science, see James A. Froude (1867: 1–25), "The Science of History," *Short Studies on Great Subjects*, 2nd ed., London: Longmans, Green and Co.

16 On this subject, see Julia Markus's biography, *James Anthony Froude: The Last Undiscovered Great Victorian* (2005: 45–82).

17 Very little is known of D. Bridgman Metchim, author of only another book, *Atlantis, Book of Angels* in 1903.

18 The expression the "proper stuff of" is borrowed from Woolf's famous quotation in "Modern Fiction": " 'The proper stuff of fiction' does not exist; everything is the proper stuff of fiction; whatever one honestly thinks, whatever one honestly feels" (*E III* 36).

19 Quoted in Bentley (2005: 35). Edward Bishop indicates in his *Chronology* that Woolf reads a volume of Michelet's *Histoire de France* on December 9, 1914, 4 months after Britain declared war on Germany, and a "later volume" on February 14 (Bishop 1989: 30–31). She returned to Michelet in January 1928, January 1939, and a few months before her death in September 1940 (Bishop 111; 204; 215).

3 Rewriting History
Contexts for Change

Is it not the critic's duty to tell us, or to guess at least, where we are going?[1]

New Departures

For Woolf's generation, the end of the First World War definitively turned a page in history. As Jean-Michel Rabaté suggests in *1922: Literature, Culture, Politics* (2015), the 4 years that led to the apex of high modernism were needed to

> take stock of the universal catastrophe, to assess what had changed in Europe and the world, and to see whether the promise of the new that was so prevalent in 1913 would lead to a new order or to a new chaos.

The new, indeed, appeared as "really new, and the old more notably old" (Rabaté 2015: 1). The perception of a necessary break with the past – the "radical change in religion, conduct, politics and literature" that Woolf dated back to 1910 in her famous 1924 essay "Character in Fiction" (*E III* 422) – implied both a reconsidering of the whole social and cultural system, and a new sense of direction. Each time, therefore, Woolf would attempt an evaluative description of her "age," one of "crisis" as she frequently stated, she would seek to understand what was and what could no longer be while looking towards the future. In the two decades that led to the Second World War, she thus spared no effort to "reconstruct a habitable dwelling-place" from the "ruins and splinters" of still-resisting "tumbled mansion[s]" (*E III* 388). To do so, she kept unwriting the past and rewriting the present, experimenting different tools and writing modes as both a critic and an artist. However, while she became more than impatient with the weight of her Victorian heritage and of dominant patriarchal discourses, she also understood that one does not contribute to change by erasing the past but rather by clarifying it to create the contexts for change.

DOI: 10.4324/9780429331787-5

Interestingly, in 1919 Woolf moved with Leonard to what was to become their country home for the rest of their lives – Monk's House, in Rodmell, a Sussex village bathed in a sense of Englishness and historical continuity that Woolf found more and more engaging as the years went by.[2] Whether in Rodmell or London (the Woolfs moved into 52 Tavistock Square in March 1924), she not only experienced phases of illness and phases of intense writing, fits of anxiety, but also a new sense of her legitimacy as a writer. Early in 1920, Woolf wrote about the feeling of exhilaration that her experiments in the short story form had given her: she had "stumbled" on a "new form for a new novel. Suppose one thing should open out another [...]. [C]onceive mark on the wall, K[ew]. G[ardens]. & unwritten novel taking hands & dancing in unity" (*D II* 13–14). The "immense possibilities" that she had conceived of led to the publication of *Monday or Tuesday* in 1921, *Jacob's Room* in 1922, *Mrs Dalloway* in 1925, soon followed by *To the Lighthouse* (1927) and *Orlando* (1928). She had found her own voice, as an entry of her diary dated July 26, 1922, suggests: "there's no doubt in my mind that I have found out to begin (at 40) to say something in my own voice; & that interests me so that I think I can go ahead without any praise" (*D II* 186). As a reviewer and essayist, Woolf had also realised that she could no longer write "like a woman writing well," "refined and cordial": reacting to critic Arthur Bingham Walkley's "attack" on her unsigned 1920 *TLS* review of the *Letters of Henry James* – the critic had hinted that she was a "sentimental Lady friend" – she took "a vow [she]'d say what [she] thought, & say it in [her] own way" (*D II* 29–30). Spurred by the blame, she, therefore, asked the *Times Literary Supplement* to write leading articles and reviews on subjects of her choice. Prior to 1919, she had signed only 12 out of her 254 contributions to *Academy and Literature*, *Cornhill Magazine*, the *Guardian*, the *National Review*, the *Speaker* and the *TLS*, 3 among which were essays in literary criticism; her reviews then represented 90% of her production, and literature was the subject discussed in only 25% of them. After 1919, Woolf signed 60% of her contributions to the *Times*, *Nation and Athenaeum*, *Criterion*, *Vogue*, the *Daily Herald*, the *New Republic*, the *New York Post Literary Review* and, from 1924 onwards, to the *Atlantic Monthly* or the *Saturday Review of Literature*. Of her critical writing, 45% was now concerned with literature and literary history. Between 1919 and 1925, she also contributed her major essays on modern literature – "On Re-reading Novels," "Mr Bennett and Mrs Brown," "Character in Fiction" – and revised others such as "The Modern Essay," "Modern Fiction" and "How It Strikes a Contemporary" for the publication of *CR I*.[3]

As a reviewer and essayist, fiction clearly became Woolf's priority. In the interwar years, Woolf read, or re-read, Cervantes, Madame de La Fayette, Bunyan, Defoe, Samuel Richardson, Radcliffe, Sterne, Jane Austen, Dickens, Gaskell, Hardy, Forster, H.G. Wells, Bennett, Galsworthy, Gissing, Dorothy Richardson, Melville, Henry James,

Katherine Mansfield, D.H. Lawrence, Joyce, Giraudoux, Proust, Tolstoï, Dostoevsky and Chekhov. She also read about the lives of Samuel Johnson, Lord Byron, Walpole, Tennyson, Henry James, Dorothy Osborne, Benjamin Constant, Tolstoï, and probably a few more. Biography as a genre also remained a central preoccupation. Fuelled by the Memoir club,[4] this renewed interest in life-writing found an outlet in her reviews of the letters, memoirs, diaries or biographies of Samuel Butler, Olive Schreiner, Mary Russell Mitford, Thomas Hardy, George Eliot, George Gissing, Mrs Humphry Ward, Molly MacCarthy, among others. In *The Bloomsbury Group Memoir Club*, S.P. Rosenbaum (2014: 28) shows how the club members were "both impressed and bored" by nineteenth- and even eighteenth-century life-writing, how they "shunned the hopeful idealism, the reserve, the sentimentality, and the piety and agnosticism of many of these records." He also suggests that Woolf's return to the Edwardian past in the form of an anti-memoir in *Jacob's Room* was probably influenced by the "stimulus" of the Club's meetings. So was, he argues, *To the Lighthouse*, Woolf's second elegiac novel centring on pre- and post-war settings, loss, memories and a fragmented past brought into the present (Rosenbaum 2014: 122–125). In 1920, Woolf published "A Talk about Memoirs" in which two young girls, Ann and Judith, have a lively conversation about five volumes of aristocratic Victorian life writing, criticise "Mr Lytton Strachey" for "behaving disrespectfully to the great English art of biography" while being simultaneously ironical about "the parents and begetters of our race," their "cold" and "stiff" temperament," "unyielding authority" and passion for horses (*E III* 180–185). Seven years later, Woolf's signed essay "The New Biography" was published in the *NYHT*: her review of Harold Nicolson's "new attitude to biography" and "method of writing" in *Some People* was an occasion to praise a book which she saw as neither fiction – "because it has the substance, the reality of truth" – nor biography "because it has the freedom, the artistry of fiction" (*E IV* 475–476).[5] Woolf's long-lasting interest in biography thus shifted towards a theoretical reflection on its necessary rewriting: its late-nineteenth-century version needed further changes, as the author of *Orlando* would write to Vita Sackville West on October 9, 1927: "It sprung upon me how I could revolutionise biography in a night" (*L III* 429). Twelve years later in "The Art of Biography," she was to paint a telling modernist portrait of the biographer as a pioneer, going "ahead of the rest of us, like the miner's canary, testing the atmosphere, detecting falsity, unreality, and the presence of obsolete conventions," to give his readers "the creative fact; the fertile fact; the fact that suggests and engenders." As the creator of an immortal, androgynous, transgender character, and of Flush, Elizabeth Barrett Browning's Victorian dog, she had embodied this pioneer, working on that "high degree of tension" between imagination and facts "which gives us reality" (*E VI* 186–187).

The 1920s were also a period during which Woolf's commitment to the intellectual and political debates of her time took new forms. In July

1920, her signed article on "The Plumage Bill" and "sex antagonism" in the feminist weekly *Woman's Leader* announced a new phase in her activism as a writer. Her deep interest in the economic, political and cultural aspects of the woman question was made manifest in "Men and Women" (1918), "The Intellectual Status of Women" (1920) – her "counterblast" to Arnold Bennett's assertion of Women's intellectual inferiority in *Our Women: Chapters on the Sex-Discord*[6] – "Women and Fiction" (1929), "Women and Leisure" (1929) and "Memories of a Working Women's Guild" (1929). Her commitment to the women's cause also constituted one of the political subplots of her fictional work. In March 1928, the Representation of the People Act gave women the vote on the same terms as men, but the Women's Movement was now divided between the "new" feminists and the "old" feminists who believed, with Winifred Holtby, that "when liberty and equality of action and status for men and women have been obtained, then all other reforms, including the arrangements of domestic life [...] will concern sons and husbands as well as mothers and daughters."[7] In September 1928, Woolf signed a letter of protest with E.M. Forster in *N&A* against the banning of Radclyffe Hall's lesbian novel *The Well of Loneliness*: entitled "The New Censorship," the letter insisted that the novel "had obviously been suppressed because of the theme itself" and stated that "the subject of the book exists as a fact among many other facts in life" (*E V* 39).[8] In October of the same year, Woolf gave a second "Women and Fiction" paper at Cambridge, Girton College, asking "some brilliant student at Newnham or Girton," and her larger audience of readers to "add a supplement to history," and to call this alternative version "by some inconspicuous name so that women might figure there without impropriety" (*AR* 42–43).

Woolf's ironical tone here echoes her evocations, in her essays and fictions, of the Victorian age, a time when a woman like Orlando would never "cease [...] blushing till she had reached her country house" and "wrapped herself as well she could in a damask quilt which she snapped from her bed" (*O* 223). In the interwar years, Bloomsbury's anti-Victorianism was symptomatic of what Leonard Woolf called a feeling of "living in an era of incipient revolt [...] against a social system and code of conduct and morality, which, for convenience' sake, might be referred to as bourgeois Victorianism" (Rosenbaum 1995: 138). Three of the Bloomsbury members' deeply ironic books were published just after the First World War ended: Lytton Strachey's *Eminent Victorians* in 1918, Maynard Keynes' *The Economic Consequences of the Peace* in 1919 and Leonard Woolf's *Empire and Commerce in Africa* in 1920. Woolf's own attacks on the Victorians and Edwardians have been explored in all their dimensions. On a personal level, these attacks need to be understood in the context of Arnold Bennett's (1923) harsh criticism of Woolf's achievements in *Jacob's Room*.[9] Like some of his predecessors and contemporaries, Bennett indirectly helped Woolf to inscribe her own female subjectivity within a male writing tradition. But Woolf's vexed relations

with her literary forefathers her and critical assessment of what the Age
of Victoria and Edward VII had produced should also be examined in the
light of her conversations with some of her closest friends. Among them,
Lytton Strachey holds an essential place, especially if we consider the evolution of Woolf's historical thinking along those years. In 1909, Strachey
(1964: 13) had already explained, in an essay for *The Spectator*, that
"uninterpreted, truth is as useless as buried gold, and art is the great interpreter. It alone can unify a vast multitude of facts into a significant whole,
clarifying, accentuating, suppressing and lighting up the dark places of the
imagination." Published in 1918, *Eminent Victorians* came as a shock:
Strachey's iconoclastic book manifested a philosophy of historiography
that completely debunked the Victorians as well as their vision of history
and biography (2013).[10] In 1924, Strachey dedicated his *Queen Victoria*
to Woolf; their ongoing exchanges on the subjects of biography and history found an echo in "Character in Fiction" where Woolf praised his
"effort and strain of writing against the grain and current of the times"
(*E III* 435), and in "The New Biography" in which she portrayed him as
an "artist" rather than a traditional "chronicler" (*E IV* 475).

The relationship that Woolf enjoyed with Strachey involved both a sense
of rivalry and a deep friendship. His "gender-bending" life, his interest
in biography and history and his critique on simplistic notions of sexual
identity nourished their intimate and literary complicity. Strachey would
praise her "new prose style" and "new version of the sentence"; she would
urge him to "write plays—stories—anything to break the mould of the
early Victorians" (*D I* 277). She indeed shared his irreverence towards the
Victorians, if not his hatred of them. More importantly, when one reads
the letters exchanged between the two Bloomsbury artists and intellectuals
in the 1920s along with Woolf's diary, one becomes aware of their shared
interest, beyond biography, for historiography, even if Strachey's inclusion
of the personal, the biographical and the microscopic in his histories was
less sensitive to the social, economic and political forces than Woolf would
have wished. On April 15, 1921, she thus writes:

> I have been lying recumbent all day reading Carlyle, & now
> Macaulay, first to see if Carlyle wrote better than Lytton, then to see
> if Macaulay sells better. Carlyle (reminiscences) is more colloquial &
> scrappy than I remembered, but he has his merits.—more punch in
> his phrase than in Lytton's.
>
> (*D II* 210)

A few days later, a conversation during which Strachey mentioned his project to write on George IVth led her to think: "the worst about George IVth
is that no one mentions the facts I want. History must be written all over
again. It's all morality—& battles, I added" (*D II* 115). In this respect, and
although the book was dedicated to Vita Sackville West in recognition of
her importance in its conception,[11] *Orlando* was an answer to Strachey's

Eminent Victorians, and to his *Elizabeth and Essex: A Tragedy* published the same year as Woolf's mock biography. Before 1919, Woolf had used her experience as a reader and reviewer to reengage the conversation with her predecessors. In the interwar period, she used fiction and essay-writing to intervene within, and disrupt, dominant historiographical discourses, thus opening a new space for formal experimentation, critical inquiry and political propositions. History still appeared to her "the most fantastic concoctions of the human brain" (*L III* 453); but to rewrite it, it became urgent to change the tone and the method, and use, more than before, the satirical vein of fantasy that was "deep" in her.[12]

Modernism, Historiography and Novelty

Strikingly enough, most historians of the interwar period shared with Woolf and Strachey the idea that "history must be written all over again." Just as Bloomsbury was being anti-Edwardian and anti-Victorian, scholars and researchers were now implementing anti-whig methodologies more suitable to the scientific age they lived in, an age that could no longer be satisfied with the romantic vision of history as narrative and of historical time as inextricably related to the notion of *Zeitgeist*. In the academic world, historical enquiry continued to be inspired by Bury's (1903) pronouncement that history was "a science, no less, no more," and not just a commitment to "accuracy"; the pursuit of historical truth in the form of unchallengeable facts was grounded, more radically than ever before, in the belief that all forms of conjectures, subjectivity and bias could be erased by the right laboratory procedures. To find the proper "sources," to "ascertain" "finite and identifiable" facts – a method that was bound to turn into a "hunt for new material" and possibly the sometimes desperate search for "an unused piece of the past" (Bentley 2006: 1999) – constituted the main thrust of the scientific approach advocated in universities as well as in academic history journals and reviews. This call for change was naturally a condemnation of the Whigs and the Romantics, who, according to such modernists as F.W. Maitland, had an "unsatisfactory" approach to the nature of historical facts, sources and proofs, had no time for documentary verification and tended to "still arrange historic phenomena under periods, centuries, reigns, dynasties, while lacking a real rather than a temporal classification."[13] But this search for new subjects, and above all, for a scientific historical method that broke with the "mistakes" of the past, tended to abandon the nineteenth-century historians' own interest in addressing a wider audience. Specialisation and institutionalisation demanded a specific readership, one that was more scholarly than inclusive: Woolf's "common reader" was bound to feel "fobbed off once more with historians' histories" (*E III* 3).

The flourishing – when compared with the situation in France, Germany or Russia – of forms of social and economic history that the constitutional turn of English historiography had long maintained at the margins of the discipline was another key element in the interwar history of English historiography, also marked by the concomitant appearance, after 1918, of professional women historians such as Elizabeth Levett, Caroline Skeel, Lilian Knowles and Helen Cam. While Eileen Power's and R.H. Tawney's voices and books were associated with the London School of Economics, Lawrence and Barbara Hammond, like Beatrice and Sidney Webb before them, appeared as proponents of a "people's history" outside the academy.[14] Meanwhile, in the mid-1920s, British idealist thinkers such as R.G. Collingwood explained that "scientific truth" could not be the whole truth.[15] Again, this was a period when history as a discipline and field of research was a heterogeneous domain that could not be subsumed under a unifying label. Change there was, and to some extent, the change was radical: a contest between generations was taking place, one that Bourdieu (1993: 30; 60) would later call the strategy of "position-taking," inevitable for "young challengers" trying to distinguish themselves from established figures. But as Michael Bentley (2006: 111) recalls, these new historiographical trends went along with the persistence, or "ghostly resurgence," of a "moving whig paradigm," with its "various species of rolling stock," among which George Macaulay Trevelyan who happened to give lectures in English History at Morley, while Woolf was herself a teacher there.

A similar form of heterogeneity characterised literary modernism's desire for change: as Michael North reminds us in his chapter on "Aesthetic Modernism," the novelty that modernist writers were looking for in between the wars is a "problem" that they shared "with the science of the time" and that was inspired by its cohort of verbs such as to "invent," "discover" or "experiment" (North 2013: 157). When, in "Modern Fiction" (1919), Woolf describes the impressions received by the mind as "an incessant shower of innumerable atoms, composing in their sum what we might venture to call life itself," science is her chosen metaphor for the necessity of new developments in the arts (*E IV* 160). Before her, Walter Pater had spoken of the necessity of "curiously testing new opinions and courting new impressions," running each of these under the "microscope of thought" (Pater 1878: 221). Obviously, for many modernist historians and writers though, the resort to the category of the "new" was not merely a question of rhetoric: beyond the expected entwinement of discourses coming from different fields lay the idea that "change" required new tools and implied the more or less conscious reconstruction of a homogeneous and archaic past to break with. We are now well aware that the mapping of such a break was a strategy, if not a sheer illusion, just as we know how "novelty" took, for modernist writers, various forms and reflected diverging agendas.

A comparison of the appeals to the "new" made by the modernist writers and historians reveals how much those appeals, however different in their goals, were subtended by a view of the world as historical. In a recent book entitled *History in Times of Unprecedented Change*, historian Zoltán Boldizsár Simon explains that contrary to common belief, history is not concerned with the past. It is all about "novelty," about "that which looms on the horizon and which, in the present, is conceived of as new and different from whatever has been before" (Simon 2019: vii). Thus, for many modernist historians and writers, to account for a new world and a new world view was bound to mean to wipe out the past to enhance the clash between generations, and between the old and the new.[16] But it also meant, in the long run, to rely on the not so "novel" concepts of "revolution," "evolution" or "resurgence."[17] For Woolf, who addressed the question of the "modern" in ways that seem to acknowledge a gulf with the preceding era, at least in her major essays of the period, to "rewrite" history implied a process of unwriting that was far from being a form of erasure. Neither did it entail the "advent" of the modern "as if it were the return of something long exiled in the past," or the confusion of the idea of "rebirth" with that of "birth" (North 2013: 151). To be able to grasp what escaped present knowledge – a necessary precondition for envisioning the future – she needed, again and anew, to remember and acknowledge a heritage that for all its strategic reconstruction comprised at least one unavoidable truth: from the eighteenth century onwards, the Enlightenment project of civilisation and emancipation had excluded from its debates the voice of the obscure.

That Woolf rewrote history and literary history in a creatively re-gendering manner is common knowledge. Gabrielle McIntire, Melba Cuddy-Keane, Rachel Bowlby, Elena Gualtieri, Jane Lilenfield, Angeliki Spiropoulou, Sabine Hotho-Jackson, Molly Westerman, Linden Peach, among others, have illustrated this point in many ways. Although the approaches of these critics and the corpus of examined texts may vary, there appears to be among them a general agreement on the way Woolf's historical thought, over the course of what I have chosen to define as a second significant phase of Woolf's pursuit of history, implied the "enunciation of a process of differentiation, an act of separation from the past, a means of legitimating rebellion against hierarchical social structures and prevailing modes of thought" (Felski 1995: 13–14). In Woolf's case, however, this process of differentiation did not replace one hegemonic discourse by another, nor was it blind to gender questions and political issues.[18] Beyond its apparent homogenisation of "tradition" Woolf's new historiographical theory and practice as she conceived it rather implied the building of a self-reflexive framework that was inclusive: of traces of the past, of other possible discourses, of the "we" of the common reader, and above all, of what had been excluded from mainstream representations and histories. In *A Room of One's Own* and *Orlando: A Biography*, Woolf enacts with critical virtuosity such a framework: she displays, unwrites and rewrites past historiographical discourses, focuses on the highly modernist and modern notion of "change" and simultaneously suggests that "change" is part of a common understanding that is itself ever changing.

To unearth the assumptions and orthodoxies associated with those dominant models while capturing the experience of the past and present in an alternative discursive form, Woolf needed first to expose the failed authority of the male historian and its avatars – the male biographer, literary historian and man of letters – and, in the words of Elena Gualtieri, to construct her target as the "masculine, institutional perspective" that he, in a generic sense, embodied (Gualtieri 2000: 162). Like the historians he is generally associated with, the narrator-biographer in *Orlando* is a destabilised generic figure who has limited "powers" as far as the "truthful account[s]" of the facts are concerned; those facts that he generally reports in a discourse introduced by "the historians say" or the "historian suppose" sometimes leave him "puzzled" or "dull as ditch water" (*O* 115; 144). First situated as an omniscient, objective narrator, able to give the reader access to Orlando's inner thoughts, his narratorial authority is constantly undermined by Woolf's irony.[19] In *A Room of One's Own*, John Aubrey – the seventeenth-century antiquary and biographer whose posthumously published *Brief Lives* (1669–1696) is founded on the collection of notes and anecdotes that he wrote about his contemporaries – "hardly mentions" any woman, no doubt considering, Woolf suggests, that "she never writes her own life and scarcely keeps a diary" (*AR* 42). The type of historian "who records not opinions but facts" and whom he stands for is indeed part of a long tradition of male writers who have considered woman as "completely insignificant" and "absent from history" (*AR* 34). When he appears under the contemporary features of a respectable and celebrated figure of the academy – Professor Trevelyan, for example, whose acclaimed and widely-read *History of England* (1926) the narrator consults to understand "under what conditions women lived [...] in the time of Elizabeth" (*AR* 39) – the masculine and institutional perspective that he represents sees his discipline necessarily focusing on "The Cistercians and Sheep-farming [...] The Crusades [...] The University [...] The House of Commons [...] The Hundred Years' War [...] The Wars of the Roses [...] The Renaissance Scholars [...] The Dissolution of the Monasteries [...] Agrarian and Religious Strife [...] The Origin of English Sea-power [...] The Armada' and so on," with an "individual woman" mentioned occasionally, "an Elizabeth, or a Mary; a queen or a great lady" (ibid.). Whether anonymous or identified, a figure of the past or the present, a dependable or unreliable authority, this historian shares a knowledge of the past and a writing practice that reminds us that history is a mediated construct "buttressed by a political power," as Michel de Certeau explains. Its written text also "promotes a selection between what can be understood and what must be forgotten in order to obtain the representation of a present intelligibility." To Woolf, this "forgotten" dimension that Michel de Certeau calls the "repressed" of history (1988a: 4–6) and which I have chosen to call "the unwritten" obviously includes women – the Mrs Browns and Mrs Martyns of fiction, biography and history, the excluded "we" of Woolf's reviews of history books, the "girl behind the counter too" whose "true history" Woolf "would as soon [have] as the hundred and fiftieth life of Napoleon" (*AR* 84). As Beth Carol Rosenberg (2000: 76) explains, the rewritten history Woolf envisions in the 1920s is "not a history of existing eminent lives but a projected history of lack, of the missing and unaccounted for."

To recommence history from a present new perspective, Woolf also needed to further her critique of "traditional methods and historiographical principles," a critique which takes the form, in *Orlando*, of "a parodic pastiche of tropes of historical representation and historical events" (Spiropoulou 2010: 76). Thus, the biography's mock-academic format, its assaults on the so-called objectivity of the historian, its unorthodox choice of a subject and of the major events in his/her life, its explicit references to the inaccessibility of historical and biographical truth, together with its questioning of national history and identity through Orlando's marginal personality, all contributed to examine and question the various tools, methods and "normative limits" that, Dominick LaCapra explains, the professionalisation of the discipline then needed to "stabilize the movement of historical understanding" (2004: 2). It is precisely these tools, a product of male-dominated discourses that Woolf already turns "against themselves" in *Orlando* and *A Room* while re-examining former discipline parameters, which, brought together, offer new practices of meaning. Among these parameters and renewed historiographical emphases, fiction, imagination, the question of characters in history and their unstable identities, the place of biography and memory, as well as the inscription of an audience, have already been addressed in convincing ways while not being clearly correlated with Woolf's romantic heritage. By recovering narrative as an essential bridge between fact and fiction, by constantly interrogating the borderland between the two genres of discourse and using fiction as "a spider's web, attached lightly to life to all four corners" (*AR* 39), Woolf fought against the patterns of exclusion that the patriarchal machinery had set up. By creating Judith Shakespeare, she added a "supplement" to previous histories and retrieved the "facts [that] are so hard to come by" (*AR* 39; 44), letting her audience imagine the historical and social conditions of the production of an artistic genius. At the same time, she acknowledged the necessary role of the imagination – a debt to her romantic heritage – suggesting that the task of historians and biographers is to "reveal character" (*E I* 118–119) and give us access to memory and the workings of the mind, since both affect the construction of all individuals. In this respect, and more particularly in *Orlando*, Woolf's modernist writing, this foregrounding of a non-linear time and narrative that refuses totalising historical paradigms, is indissociable from the modernity of individual experience with its shifting rhythm, confusing overlaps, and "multiple, multi-temporal, multi-gendered subjectivity" (Spiropoulou 2010: 77).

Woolf's dialogue with the past and historiography in *Orlando* and *A Room of One's Own*, although it shared parallel objectives, relied on different strategies and tones. In *A Room*, the main subjects are women, fiction and the written or still unwritten text of literary history; Woolf's voice negotiates between rhetorical self-deprecation and feminine wit, between anger and conciliation as the narrator-essayist controls her irony and sometimes feigns detachment.[20] In *Orlando*, the question of literary history is embedded in the "grand historical picture" she had planned to write, itself grounded in "the memoirs of one's own times during people's lifetimes" (*D III* 161). The tone is playful, ironical and constantly parodic, but the voice is that of a bombastic male biographer-narrator, which might make us underestimate the complexity of Woolf's historiographical work: beyond her satire against what is generally referred to as historiographical "tradition" lies the work of a cultural innovator whose originality appears clearer when set against the context of the changes that have been evoked. This is why I disagree with Beth Carole Rosenberg's (2000: 1114) view that historicising Woolf's historiography "does not necessarily reveal the dimension of [her] work." First, because Woolf's modernity was grounded in a reshuffling of past and present historiographical discourses that implied a complex vision of tradition as a heterogeneous field, as I have previously shown. In this respect, Woolf's problematic narrators in *A Room* and *Orlando* also reflect the problematic "I" of a fluctuating enemy: the male "I" historian or biographer. Behind the apparent homogeneity of the speaker or the person addressed lies the heterogeneity of discourses and postures that needed unearthing. Then, because Woolf's historiographical approach entails the building of a self-reflexive framework that is always inclusive. In this sense, her flexibility as a thinker – the way she "poaches," unwrites and reconfigures – is not only the result of an enunciative strategy: it is a writing method that deconstructs the hegemonic potentialities of past and contemporary discourses by uncovering them and assessing their weight on the present to imagine new scenarios for the future. Seen in this light, Woolf's responses to "historians' histories" can be understood as the result of a radical feminist agenda rather than as the negotiation that characterised her modern reading, in her essays, of the Romantics. Unless of course we understand negotiation as a way for her to bring about a radically different vision and to write herself against, more than into, the male dominant tradition.

On first examination, Woolf's representation of past and present historiographical discourses, particularly in *Orlando*, seems indeed to blur the complexity of their differences, of their self-critical awareness and of their evolution in the interwar period. In this configuration, as in her essays on modern fiction, the heritage of the Victorians, Edwardians and Georgians appears to be reconstructed and to make room for a radically different discourse which does not need to mention the subtle differences between the generations or the late emergence of social history. At times, thus, it seems that Woolf's irony is directed at the definition of history, in J.B. Bury's words, as a "science, no less, no more" (Bury 1903: 7), a now-stable discipline requiring an insistence on empirical evidence, objectivity, timeless universal causal laws, the objective detachment of the historian from his subject and his repudiation of any ideological bias. Such features are clearly satirised in *Orlando* as a fantasy, so the Victorian traditionalism against which Woolf struggles in her fictional biography is clearly different from "the old envelops" that embarrassed Bury and his fellow modernist historians.[21] In other passages, however, she can mock the Whigs' or whiggish rejection of the Romantics' lack of documentation and their concentration on constitutional theory – "the constitution of England was altered and nobody knew it" (O 218). Constitutional history then becomes the symbol of this male hegemonic coherence that she had described, in *To The Lighthouse*, as the "admirable fabric of the masculine intelligence, which runs up and down, crossed this way and that, like iron-girders spanning the swaying fabric, upholding the world" (*TL* 123). If we follow this hypothesis, we might want to conclude that Woolf presents a political construction of historiographical tradition as essentially patriarchal – which would explain why she cannot refer, in *A Room* notably, to the new work of contemporary female historians. Unless we believe, along with Molly Westerman, that Woolf's aim, in *Orlando* this time, was not to "stabilize a shorthand caricature of Victorian historiography to be dismissed as absurdly outdated, hypocritical, and inadequate to historical reality," but to "accommodate ambivalence" with "narrative slipperiness and humour," since in the end, "both Victorian Grand-Narratives and the modernist stance share those enlightenment assumptions" (Westerman 2008: 35–86).

My vision of how Woolf writes history as a woman in *A Room*, and more particularly in *Orlando*, agrees with this hypothesis and pushes it further. As a matter of fact, what the contextualisation of her historical thought and historiographical practice brings to light is missed when we understand her alternative project simply in terms of a new quarrel of the ancients and the moderns, or if we consider that what she herself called "historians' histories" represents a monolithic truth and is not a strategic construct. First, by rejecting some of the historiographical shifts in the new historiographical discourses of her time while endorsing others, once more anticipating de Certeau's poaching reading practice, Woolf ironically mirrored the fake clarity and uniformity that many contemporary historians thought characterised their discipline and its methodology. On the other side of the looking glass lay a more obscure truth, marked by its overlaps, erasures and confusing perplexity: on one side, the belief in new beginnings tended to set aside essential questions such as those raised by the Romantics – questions that are still addressed today; on the other, this belief tended to ignore the possibility of new forms of authoritative discourses – what R.G. Collingwood (1924: 41) would call, in his 1924 *Speculum Mentis*, the claims of the major fields of knowledge, history included, to "give the absolute or ultimate truth concerning the nature of the universe." As the butt of Woolf's irony, *Orlando*'s narrator is a constant reminder that the "footprints of truth" are not "indelible" (*O* 63), and that the "ground of ascertained truth," if "firm," is always "narrow" (*O* 126). Read with and against this contemporary theoretical context, then, Woolf's ongoing interest in the notions of "truth," "fact," "events" and "imagination" – particularly in *Orlando* where those words appear frequently – is proof of her commitment to an epistemological conversation that was replaced, in the interwar years, by the modernist historians' belief that factuality "legislates for all forms of 'interpretation'" (Bentley 2006: 13): in that sense, she was both close to the Romantics and their awareness of the difficult "representability" of the past, and to the anti-Enlightenment trend of historicism that emerged in the nineteenth century and that, with Dilthey, Croce, Collingwood and their followers, has since rejected the equation between historical laws and the laws of science, between "events" having actually occurred in the past and recorded historical "facts."

Indeed, the third original component of Woolf's historiographical reflection that we might miss when not reading her in context is how much her method of looking back is a way of looking forward, and vice versa. That her feminist or alternative counter-narratives anticipate, Michel Foucault, Dominick LaCapra, Walter Benjamin, and more recently, such historians as David Carr (*Time, Narrative and History*, 1986), Hayden White (*The Fiction of Narrative*, 2010) and Alexander Macfie (*The Fiction of History*, 2015) who have reappraised the frontiers between history and fiction is undeniable.[22] But the extent to which what she anticipated was the fruit of her reading and rewriting of past and present historiographical traditions has been understated. In *Orlando* more than in any other Woolfian text of the interwar period, anteriority as a way of looking back is a process of dynamic counter-interpretation that takes the form of a dialectical palimpsestuous poetics: it is indeed in this intricate network of overlapping, and sometimes conflicting, layers of time, discourses and critical acts that the unthought and inconceivable can emerge.

Historical Time, Change and Woolf's Palimpsests in *Orlando*

As Sarah Dillon explains in her study of De Quincey, the palimpsest is an object, a metaphor and an epistemological tool that has been explored since the nineteenth century onwards to rethink "such key contemporary issues as the subject, time, history, culture, gender, sexuality, and the processes of reading and writing themselves" (Dillon 2005: 243). In his 1845 essay "Suspiria de Profundis," De Quincey (1998: 104) interpreted the inscription of texts or fragments of texts on an already layered written surface in terms of how "our deepest thoughts and feelings pass to us through perplexed combinations of concrete objects [...] in compound experiences incapable of being disentangled." Since then, the palimpsest has become a metaphorical and critical tool employed across disciplines such as literature, philosophy and the new science of psychology. In *Virginia Woolf and the Literary Past*, Jane de Gay characterises the Woolfian text as a "palimpsest of earlier writings," a "physical space in which past writers are present and active," the past being "made current by placing it at a *spatial* rather than temporal distance from the present" (de Gay 2006: 10). But beyond what de Gay calls Woolf's "comparative method" throughout her book, and the obvious presence of what Gérard Genette defined as the various forms of copresence of different texts – such as intertextuality, metatextuality or architextuality – in a same literary work, I am interested in the new relationality between disciplines and dimensions of time at the core of the Woolfian palimpsest. As *Orlando*'s reader learns about the life of a character whose composite experience integrates the personal and the collective, the past and the present, change and stability, the masculine and the feminine, he or she is invited to think synchronically and diachronically, to de-compartmentalise and reconfigure fields of knowledge and notional binaries. More "palimpsestuous" than "palimpsestic" in its dialectical dynamic,[23] Woolf's rewriting of biography and history goes here far beyond a satirical re-inscription within a male writing tradition: by making the underlying and the overlying texts of the palimpsest constantly visible, it resists any temptation to pit generic categories against one another or to purely erase the past to clear the horizon. Instead, it reconfigures common thoughts on time, continuity and change – subjects that historians, among other scholars, study all the time – to ponder the difference between fruitful permanence and impairing perpetuation, between what has been construed as unchangeable and what is in fact transformable.[24]

That "History [...] is the explanation of significant processes of change and instances of stasis" seems indeed a conviction that Woolf's scholar-biographer shares with his predecessors and contemporaries.[25] His "life" of Orlando thus follows a linear chronology, itself implicitly framed by an attempt to particularise and differentiate, to calibrate and judge what causes his character to evolve, according to the "spirit of the age." The word "change" appears at least 60 times in the novel and recurs at an accelerated pace from the moment Orlando becomes a woman. But just as historians have more than one way of building a chronology and selecting significant events, "there is more than one way of being concerned with change or more than one change to be concerned with" (Burke 1998: 1). Thus, the changes Woolf is mostly interested in are either mysterious and undocumented episodes – like Orlando's trances – or the kinds of alterations that are usually considered as non-events by biographers and historians: changes of mood and atmosphere, clothes, style (whether "style" refers to his/her costumes, writing or body language), manners and sensory impressions. Whenever change is perceptible and recordable, it concerns phenomena that are traditionally unaddressed: the presence of "yellow icebergs" replaced by a "covey of swans" (*O* 159), the colour of the "cabbages" and of the "light" penetrating one's domestic space (*O* 217), the painted signs in London or the speed of motor cars, to cite but a few. Other remarkable "events," such as Orlando's actual, yet surreal, change of sex, cannot be accounted for either by the biographer – "at great pains to prove (1) that Orlando had always been a woman, (2) that Orlando is at this moment a man" (*O* 133) – or by Orlando him/herself. Conversely, when it can be explained, or is of paramount importance according to historians, change is not immediately perceived and understood by the individual: not having yet "realized the invention of the steam engine," Orlando thus takes a seat "in a railway carriage [...] and had the rug arranged about her knees without giving a thought to that stupendous invention, which had (the historians say) completely changed the face of Europe in the past twenty years" (*O* 260). Even more noticeable, the assertion of change, whatever its nature, is often contradicted by its non-existence: when Orlando realises that in spite of a very long life "she had remained [...] fundamentally the same," she reflects "upon the eternity of all things" but finally writes: "she was so changed" (*O* 180). And yet, beyond those complex changes affecting one individual, one can sense what Woolf would later describe, in "A Sketch of the Past," as the "immense forces society brings to play upon each of us" – the "stream" of those "invisible presences," whether political, technological or ideological that shape, to some extent, personal identity and that so often hold women in place (*MB* 92). As to the idea of continuity in the sense of chronological linearity, it is a directing line that takes the reader through Orlando's and history's various "ages," but one with "holes," since historians and biographers can only do their "best to piece out a meagre summary from the charred fragments" that remain from the manuscripts and sources on which they rely (*O* 115). The endlessness of Orlando's life undermines both the conventions of "life writing," and the whig historians' sense of "finalism" without which a comprehensive interpretation of history (or of an individual's life) was deemed impossible. *Orlando*'s incipit and excipit are proof that inaugural beginnings and ruptures are contingently determined by the writer, although he tries to impose coherence on the unfolding flux of history and individual life. This capricious mutability of represented time undermines both the teleological approach of former "historians' histories" and the sequences of causes and effects on which they often relied.

Echoing the way Orlando "inclined herself naturally to the Elizabethan spirit, to the Restoration spirit, to the spirit of the eighteenth century, and had in consequence scarcely been aware of the change from one age to the other" (*O* 233), Woolf's use of chapters, chronology, reigns and dates (although there are very few of them) seems to "incline" itself to traditional periodisation while systematically challenging it: her text obliterates parts of the temporal boundaries, breaks and turning points that it keeps track of while adding new layers of time and alteration. Woolf's reflections on history, time and change take the reader in multiple directions and confuse him/her, her writing never resulting in one unified theoretical discourse: "What the future might bring, Heaven only knew. Change was incessant, and change perhaps would never cease" (O 168). Parody, pastiche and satire seem to prevail – the result of an empowering act of writing – more particularly in those scenes of change and abrupt discontinuity where Woolf undercuts the zeitgeist model of history writing. In Chapter I, the pages on the 1608 Great Frost are inspired by Thomas Dekker's account of the same event published that same year in the form of a dialogue: the hyperbolic treatment of this improbable yet verifiable episode juxtaposes tragic scenes of starvation, death, terror and bathetic petrification with the recording of James I's coronation and the brilliant "carnival" on the Thames, itself a Renaissance pageant debunking the grandeur of the English Court. Orlando's change of sex, under the reign of Charles II, is another highly theatrical and burlesque episode written as a pageant and a Masque scene where the Ladies of Purity, Modesty and Chastity bridge the gap between medieval morality plays and nineteenth-century patriarchal conduct books. For once, the change is radical – although "Orlando remained precisely as he had been" (O 133) – but so baffling that it renders the search for meaningful facts and philosophical explanations impossible. The character's transformation is first dramatic only in the spectators' eyes and appears to be less relevant to personal identity than clothing and cross-dressing throughout the story. As it has already been shown, the "performance" of gender, in Judith Butler's sense of the term, that is staged before, in and after this particular scene, conveys Woolf's utopian desire to escape conventional models of femininity and masculinity.[26] The approach is here again one of subversive reinscription – "to repeat and, through a radical proliferation of gender, to displace the very gender norms that enable the repetition itself" (Butler 1990: 189). It also involves a form of displacement, since Orlando's sex change takes place in Constantinople, a carnivalistic, bustling, oriental town propitious to the deregulation of gender norms.[27] In Chapter V, the transition from the eighteenth- to the nineteenth century is a parodic and satirical rewriting of John Ruskin's "The Storm-Cloud of the Nineteenth Century," a lecture delivered on February 4, 1884, at the London Institution, in which Ruskin used the image of the "storm-cloud" – a phenomenon documented in his personal diary – as the symptom of a world threatened by industrialisation.[28] Like Ruskin, who was a member of the Meteorological and Society and the Geological Society in the 1830s, and a shrewd observer of natural and urban environments, Woolf's mock-Victorian biographer observes the sweeping climate change and its "effects everywhere." Overblown classical references characterise the two texts but are deflated by comic contrasts: "Under this bruised and sullen canopy the green of the cabbages was less intense." Ruskin's "plague-cloud" and moral prophecy are gradually turned into an allegory of "damp" as the cause of the radical alteration of the very "constitution of England" (O 217–218). As he uses the conventions of

Zeitgeist history-writing, Woolf's biographer appears to agree with John Stuart Mill (1831: 20) that "the nineteenth century will be known to posterity as the era of one of the greatest revolutions of which history has preserved the remembrance, in the human mind, and in the whole constitution of human society." Soon, however, the word "constitution" no longer stands for political and cultural institutions, fundamental beliefs or values; instead, it designates a more prosaic change of "diet" announced in a comically dramatised parodic tone: "the muffin was invented and the crumpet" (O 218). There is no change, Woolf suggests, that is not an experience mediated by language and perspective, and, therefore, embedded in a written text itself referring to a cultural tradition. Woolf reiterates this point in an emphatic way in the last chapter of her mock biography. She introduces free indirect discourse in the pages covering the transition to the Edwardian age, offering us a dizzying Freudian vision of identity that leaves Orlando and her biographer dumbfounded as they try to make sense of "these selves of which we are built up, one on top of another, as plates [...] piled on a waiter's hand" (O 294). She ends by amusing us with a self-derisory pastiche of modernist interior monologues: "A snob am I? The garter in the hall? The leopards? My ancestors? Proud of them? Yes! Greedy, luxurious, vicious? Am I? (here a new self came in)" (O 296).

These passages are palimpsests in every sense of the word: as multi-layered documents, they bear the traces of partially erased inscriptions that they reactivate and transform; they blur the frontiers between history, literary history and biography while incorporating, assessing and reconfiguring the methodological tools and theoretical presuppositions of these disciplines: from the opening of the novel onwards, Orlando's life is embedded in issues of race, gender, Empire and nationalism, all of them entangled in prior historical or ideological discourses. In fact, the whole book rewrites in its own terms Carlyle's (1833: 8) definition of history as a "complex Manuscript, covered over with formless, inextricably entangled, unknown characters." Above all, it is a political tale of boundary crossings that poetically builds on the root metaphor of "The Oak tree" – an actual tree, a manuscript designed to be reused, a possible reference to John Locke's pages on change and the essence of identity in "Essay on Human Understanding,"[29] and a text whose "many lines" Orlando keeps "scratching out" from the inception of the story until its last episodes, as if "in the process of writing the poem would be completely unwritten" (O 108). To take up Coleridge's usage of the term in "The Wanderings of Cain" (1928), and De Quincey's in "Suspiria de Profundis," these pages and what they recount are composed of the "lines of the Palimpsest tablet" of individual and collective memory; they echo the "natural and mighty palimpsest [that] is the human brain."[30] Since they offer complicated versions of notions that are of interest to historians, biographers, philosophers and psychologists, such as time, sex, identity and memory, they enable the reader to assess the weight of conformity in dominant discourses, and to perceive the space left for cultural and political resistance.

If time is endless repetition, a cycle of fall and decline or a linear line with its predictable patterns and direction, then history will go on excluding what it has kept excluding from **its** perspective. Conversely, to "re-creat[e] the past in more flexible ways helps us better to imagine a future with multiple possibilities" (Cuddy-Keane 2018: 36). Time, in *Orlando*, thus includes both continuity and discontinuity, moments of being and non-being; it is a flux where each present moment potentially integrates the recaptured past together with an uncertain, anticipated future. While temporal gaps are inevitable and our lives are composed of "a thousand-odd, disconnected fragments, now bright, now dim, hanging and bobbing and dipping and flaunting," memory withholds in its multilayered, palimpsestic nature, the experiential quality of the past: it is a "seamstress" although a "capricious" one (*O* 75–76), sometimes providing an impression of continuity and unity, at other times, offering a more chaotic vision of the strata of the self and of the mind. In this version of time, and, therefore, of history – "the present is neither a moment of violent disruption, nor doomed to be forgotten in the past"; the future is not already familiar because it derives from the past. Both an "organic" and "abstract" notion, as French historian François Hartog explains (Hartog 2017: 16), time is also the most immediate and the most mediated experience, as so many passages of Woolf's mock biography suggest. This is not a reality that the "spirit of the age" and its periodisation can reveal; but it is a truth that those who saw, and still see, time as multilayered have envisioned, from St Augustine – for whom there existed in the soul "three times; a present of things past, a present of things present, and a present of things future"[31] – to Fernand Braudel's dialectics of duration grounded in the distinction between "geographical time," "social time" and "individual time" (Braudel 1980: 4). The events recorded in *Orlando* form the surface of what unfolds at a different speed according to specific "durées": the rhythms of an individual life, the span of a generation, the continuance of social and cultural traditions, the rapid pace of technological innovation, the ageless presence of an architectural monument. As Woolf suggests when she refers to the reign of Edward VII in "Mr Bennett and Mrs Brown," there are "ages" that seem to be "just breaking off from our own" (*E III* 385); but not all lived times are experienced "as a rupture, as a period of transition, in which the new and the unexpected continually happen[s]." In this, Woolf's historical thought differs from what many historians, according to Reinhart Koselleck, have defined as change since the second half of the eighteenth century (Koselleck 2004: 246). Instead, her palimpsestuous poetics in *Orlando* anticipates Hartog's definition of "regimes of historicity": a self-conscious way of "linking together past, present and future or of mixing these categories" that is bound to involve "the idea of degrees, of more or less, of mixtures and composites, and an always provisional and unstable equilibrium" (Hartog 2017: xv).

Woolf's palimpsests also preempt Michel Foucault's archaeological eye and genealogical perspective. Genealogy, Foucault (1984: 76; 86) explains, "operates on a field of entangled and confused parchments, on documents that have been scratched over and recopied many times"; contrary to "historians' histories," it does not "compose the finally reduced diversity of time into a totality fully closed upon itself," nor does it to refuse to seek events in "the most unpromising places, in what we tend to feel is without history." The task of the genealogist, therefore, is to make "visible of what was previously unseen" by "addressing oneself to a layer of material which had hitherto had no pertinence for history and which had not been recognised as having any moral, aesthetic, political or historical value" (Foucault 1980: 50–51); it is also to uncover "the various systems of subjection," the "endlessly repeated play of domination" (ibid. 85) that the multilayered, written text of traditional history tends to reveal even as it masks it. For this very reason, then – and here Woolf would have agreed with Raphael Samuel in *Theatres of Memory* – history cannot be the "prerogative of the historian"; truth will not be seized by his assumption that "knowledge filters downwards" as his "trained" mind bears on "an apparently disorderly assembly of materials." Rather, it is "a social form of knowledge; the work, in any instance, of a thousand hands," and as such it should not raise one historical genre at the expense of others, such as geography, biography, mythology, historical romance or popular memory (Samuel 2012: 5–8).

In *A Room of One's Own*, the tension between the repeated acknowledgment of patriarchy and the desire to escape it revolved, Christy Burns explains, "around the metaphor of being locked in and locked out of institutions" (Burns 1994: 347); in *Orlando*, it revolves around the question of being locked in and locked out of history. To open the path towards a more promising, if not utopian future, Woolf absorbs traditional historiographical scenarios and tools. By unmasking past and current creeds, she assesses the strength of the enemy, the space one has for resistance to social demands for conformity – how we may, at the same time, be "of" our age and remain ourselves – and the power of creative energy. Parody, satire and critical distance are part of this power in that they resist patriarchal perpetuation; so is imagination, which, in these two major texts of the 1920s, enables Woolf to add a "supplement" to history, by layering her "grand historical picture" of inheritance and change with the "granite" and "rainbow" of biography (*E IV* 473), and by sowing the seeds of a transnational, transgender and trans-genre history. "Only through history is history conquered," Paul de Man (1970: 391) explained as he commented upon the evolution of Nietzsche's thought on history and modernity. In Woolf's case, history is conquered through the joyful unwriting and rewriting of historians' histories, a process that is inseparable from a self-reflexive exploration of the past as "written" since, in the words of Ivan Jablonka claiming the heritage of Paul Veyne and Michel de Certeau, "history produces knowledge because it is literary, because it is carried out by means of a text, because it reveals, uncovers, unearths, explains, contradicts and proves; in other words, because it *writes what is true*" (Jablonka 2018: 7). To "conquer" history, however, implies more than critical reading and joyful rewriting. The negotiating of heritage – or, from a more overt feminist standpoint, the gendering of history – is a long journey. In *Orlando*, this allegorical journey takes more than four centuries and is an ongoing individual and collective process; it is filled with immutable obstacles and changing interrogations; it implies progress and backlashes, painful transformations and easier ones. But after all, and as Woolf herself would later write in "The Humane Art": "a self that goes on changing is a self that goes on living" (*E IV* 227).

Notes

1 The quotation comes Woolf's essay "Poetry, Fiction and the Future" (1927):

> For it is an age clearly when we are not fast anchored where we are; things are moving round us; we are moving ourselves. Is it not the critic's duty to tell us, or to guess at least, where we are going? Obviously the inquiry must narrow itself very strictly, but it might perhaps be possible in a short space to take one instance of dissatisfaction and difficulty, and, having examined into that, we might be the better able to guess the direction in which, when we have surmounted it, we shall go.
>
> (*E IV* 429)

2 The year 1919 was also the year when the Sex Disqualification Removal Act gave women access to all the professions.
3 I have calculated these numbers by hand, based on the six edited volumes of the *Essays of Virginia Woolf* (ed. Andrew McNeillie and Stuart N. Clarke).
4 The Memoir Club was founded in March 1920 by Molly MacCarthy to gather the "bloomsberries" – at the time Molly and Desmond MacCarthy, Quentin Bell, E.M. Forster, David Garnett, Vanessa Bell, Virginia and Leonard Woolf, Duncan Grant, Maynard and Lydia Keynes, Lytton Strachey and Roger Fry – around the project of promoting and writing autobiography.
5 Written by Vita Sackville-West's husband and published in 1927, *Some People* comprises nine portraits of fictionalised characters, including Nicolson himself, and offers a satiric amalgam of autobiography, fiction and memoir recording life in Edwardian England.
6 On this episode, see Woolf's diary (*D II* 69), Lee (1997: 286) and Gualtieri (200: 72).
7 According to Julia Briggs, this distinction was first drawn by activist and novelist Winifred Holtby (1898–1935) in a letter to the Yorkshire Post, reprinted in the feminist periodical *Time and Tide* of which she was director (on August 6, 1926, 714–715): The New Feminism emphasises the "woman's point of view," the Old Feminism believes in the primary importance of the human being. Holtby was also the first author of a critical study of Virginia Woolf in 1932, *Virginia Woolf, A Critical Memoir.* (see Briggs 2005: 460, note 23)
8 See "The 'Censorship' of Books" (*E V* 36–40).

9 Arnold Bennett's (1968: 87–88) essay "Is the Novel Decaying" was published in *Cassell's Weekly* in March 1923: it explained that Woolf's novel, although "packed and bursting with originality" and being "exquisitely written," failed because "the characters do not survive in the mind" and "the author has been obsessed by details of originality and cleverness."

10 On this subject, see Floriane Reviron-Piégay (2013).

11 Obviously, Sackville-West inspired Woolf's fictional writing on family history, gender roles, Sapphism and imaginary biographies.

12 See the diary entry dated November 7, 1928, where Woolf evokes the "aftermath" of *Orlando*, the need to write for her own "pleasure" and her "overmastering impulse" to have "fun," "fantasy" and to "write a history, say of Newnham or the womans movement, in the same vein" (*D III* 201–205).

13 Quoted in Roland G. Usher, *A Critical Study of the Historical Method of Samuel Rawson Gardiner* (1915: 147–148).

14 Tawney, Richard Henry (1880–1962), historian and political thinker, founder of the *Economic History Review* in 1926 and of its journal, *The Economic History Review*, which he co-edited with Eileen Power from 1927 and 1934; he is the author of two influential books between the wars: *The Acquisitive Society* (1921) and *Religion and the Rise of Capitalism* (1926). Barbara Hammond (1873–1961), wife of Lawrence Hammond (1872–1949), historian and journalist and co-author of the Labourer Trilogy – *The Village Labourer* (1911), *The Town Labourer* (1917), *The Skilled Labourer* (1919) – and of *The Rise of Modern Industry* (1925).

15 See Collingwood's Hegelian *Speculum Mentis* (1924).

16 On the conflict between literary modernity and history, see Paul de Man, "Literary History and Literary Modernity" (1970).

17 In his pages on the subject, North mentions, among others, the cultural resurgence of Italy for the futurists, the "primitivism" of D.H. Lawrence, and the rebirth of Gothic art in Apollinaire's appraisal of the new painting of the school of Paris (North 2013: 144–171).

18 In *The Gender of Modernity* (1995), Rita Felski explores the gendered myths of modernity while using a feminist approach to address the question of the modern experience of historicity. In her pages on "Modernist Aesthetics and Women's Modernity," she shows how the "traditions" of elitist formalism and New Criticism are "united in their largely uncritical reproduction of a masculine – and often masculinist – literary tradition" (Felski 1995: 22–29; 24).

19 On this question, see also Molly Westerman's dissertation: *Narrating Historians: Crises of Historical Authority in Twentieth-Century British Fiction*, Chapter II, "Acts of Inheritance: Virginia Woolf, Orlando and the Impossible Legacy of Victorian Historiography" (2008: 35–86).

20 On Woolf's controlled anger in *A Room*, see Alex Zwerdling's *Virginia Woolf and the Real World*, Chapter 9, (Zwerdling 1986: 243–270).

21 See how Bury defends the "dignity and authority" of history in the same excerpt from his "Inaugural Lecture" – delivered in Cambridge's Divinity School on January 26, 1903 – against "old traditions and associations":

> In the story of the nineteenth century, which has witnessed such far-reaching changes in the geography of thought and in the apparatus of research, no small nor isolated place belongs to the transformation and

expansion of history. That transformation, however, is not yet complete. Its principle is not yet universally or unreservedly acknowledged. It is rejected in many places, or ignored, or unrealised. Old envelopes still hang tenaciously round the renovated figure, and students of history are confused, embarrassed, and diverted by her old traditions and associations. It has not yet become superfluous to insist that history is a science, no less and no more; and some who admit it theoretically hesitate to enforce the consequences which it involves.

(Bury 6–7)

22 This issue has been recently discussed by Beverley Southgate in '*A New Type of History*': *Fictional Proposals for Dealing with the Past* (2015).

23 Where "palimpsestic" refers to the process of layering that produces a palimpsest, "palimpsestuous" describes the structure that one is presented with as a result of that process, and the subsequent reappearance of the "underlying script" (Dillon 5).

24 See, for example, Peter Burke, "Introduction: Concepts of Continuity and Change in History" (1998: 1–14).

25 The definition comes from Mark Hewitson in *History and Causality* (2014: 2).

26 On this subject, see Christy Burns, "Re-Dressing Feminist Identities" (1994: 342–364).

27 On Constantinople in *Orlando*, see David Roessel, "The Significance of Constantinople in Orlando" (1992: 398–416).

28 On *Orlando* and "Ruskinian change," see also Jane de Gay (2006: 141–143) and Max Saunders, *Self Impression: Life-Writing, Autobiografiction, and the Forms of Modern Literature* (2010: 448).

29 "In the state of living creatures, their identity depends not on a mass of the same particles, but on something else. For in them the variation of great parcels of matter alters not the identity; an oak, growing from a plant to a great tree, and then lopped, is still the same oak: and a colt, grown up to a horse, sometimes fat, sometimes lean, is all the while the same horse: though, in both these cases, there may be a manifest change of the parts; so that truly they are not either of them the same masses of matter, though there be truly one of them the same oak, and the other the same horse." John Locke, "Of Identity and Diversity" (1689) in *An Essay Concerning Human Understanding* (Locke 243).

30 See Coleridge, "The Wanderings of Cain": "I have in vain tried to recover the lines from the palimpsest tablet of my memory; [...]" (1921: 287); and De Quincey, in "Suspiria de Profundis":

What else than a natural and mighty palimpsest is the human brain? Such a palimpsest is my brain; such a palimpsest, O reader! is yours. Everlasting layers of ideas, images, feelings, have fallen upon your brain softly as light. Each succession has seemed to bury all that went before. And yet in reality not one has been extinguished. And if, in the vellum palimpsest, lying amongst the other diplomata of human archives or libraries, there is any thing fantastic or which moves to laughter, as oftentimes there is in the grotesque collisions of those successive themes, having no natural connexion, which by pure accident have consecutively occupied the roll, yet, in our own heaven-created palimpsest, the deep memorial palimpsest of the brain, there are not and cannot be such incoherencies.

(De Quincey 1998: 144)

31 See St Augustine's Confession on time and memory (Book XI, Chapter XX):

> What now is clear and plain is, that neither things to come nor past are.
> Nor is it properly said, "there be three times, past, present, and to come":
> yet perchance it might be properly said, "there be three times; a present
> of things past, a present of things present, and a present of things future."
> For these three do exist in some sort, in the soul, but otherwhere do I not
> see them; present of things past, memory; present of things present, sight;
> present of things future, expectation. If thus we be permitted to speak, I
> see three times, and I confess there are three. Let it be said too, "there be
> three times, past, present, and to come": in our incorrect way.
>
> (Augustine 1891: 239)

4 "Why?"

The 1930s and History in the Present

I hold that a writer should not in any circumstances or for any cause

surrender his duty to criticise and to enquire freely

into the soundness of any idea,

faith, doctrine, delivered to him by the mouth of authority[1]

Who Live Under the Shadow of a War...[2]

As Woolf finished her writing of *The Waves* in 1931, the belief in a promising future that Orlando's adventures might have led her readers to expect, along with a more general faith in human progress that many nineteenth- and early-twentieth-century historians shared, was slowly disintegrating under the menacing shadow of fascism. In her play-novel, she has her character, Louis, say,

> But listen [...] to the world moving through abysses of infinite space. It roars; the lighted strip of history is past and our Kings and Queens; we are gone; our civilisation; the Nile; and all our life. Our separate drops are dissolved; we are extinct, lost in the abysses of time, in the darkness.
>
> (*TW* 127)

The sense of an impending catastrophe began to loom over the work and lives of artists, thinkers and civilians in 1929. Immunity from the outer world, if wished for, was no longer possible. The Wall Street Crash signalled the beginning of the Great Depression, the hope of a stable European peace was shattered while Stalin, Mussolini and Hitler were wielding power and adulation: "fierce economic nationalism and cut-throat competition for the shrinking amount of world trade" was replacing "the atmosphere of confidence and détente that flourished in Europe after 1925" (Bell 138). In the federal elections of September 1930, 18.3% of German cast votes for the *National Sozialistische Deutsche Arbeiter Partei*; again, it took some time before everybody understood

DOI: 10.4324/9780429331787-6

who the pre-Führer was. In 1931, Wyndham Lewis wrote the first book published in Great Britain about Hitler: it described him as a "Man of Peace" whose anti-Semitism did not threaten the world (Lewis 4). That same year, Ramsay MacDonald formed a National Coalition to face the economic crisis, and what was referred to as his "betrayal" of the Labour Party he had helped found precipitated the secession of Oswald Mosley who, in the wake of this internal strife, created the British Union of Fascists a year later. Shortly after, Vita Sackville West's husband, Harold Nicolson, was recruited to edit the *New Party's* Journal. In May 1932, a deranged Russian fascist assassinated French President Paul Doumer. By 1933, Hitler was Chancellor of Germany and the English translation of *Mein Kampf* was widely available. After the Coup d'État by Austrian Nazis in February 1934, Woolf wrote to Quentin Bell: "Everybody here says this is the beginning of the end. We are to have Mosley within five years" (*L IV* 277). And it was, indeed, the beginning of the end: Mussolini invaded Ethiopia, then Abyssinia in October–December 1935; meanwhile, in England, George Lansbury's pacifist position in favour of unilateral disarmament was defeated at the 1935 Labour Conference Party in Brighton, the year the Nuremberg Laws against Jews were passed in Germany. "It's odd," Woolf wrote on March 13, "how near the guns have got to our private life again" (*D V* 17). Four months later, the Spanish Civil War broke out, and in November she received, from Spain, the package of photographs of dead children that would become a recurring motif in *Three Guineas*. With the pending out-break of the Second World War, every week and month brought their share of frightful news: the destruction of Guernica in April 1937; the German Anschluss with Austria and the beginning of German invasions over Europe in 1938; France's and Great Britain's declaration of war on Germany in September 1939; Germany's Invasion of Denmark and Norway in April 1940, Belgium and Holland in May; the fall of France in June; the beginning of the Battle of England in July; the bombing of the Woolfs' house in Mecklenburgh Square in September, six months before Woolf's suicide in March 1941.

This short chronology reminds us of the accelerated pace of history from 1930 to the daily raids raging over Woolf's contemporaries five years after George V's Silver Jubilee, on May 6, 1935. From March 1938 onwards, she felt overwhelmed by history's upheavals: "When the tiger, ie Hitler, has digested his dinner, he will pounce again" (*D V* 132). On May 15, 1940, she reports in her diary having "discussed" suicide with Leonard: "if Hitler lands. Jews beaten up. What point in waiting? Better to shut the garage doors. This is a sensible, rather matter-of-fact talk" (*D V* 284). As a backup option, they had obtained from Adrian Stephen a lethal dose of morphine. One month later, she anticipated that there would never be a "27th June 1941" (*D V* 299), and when, in October, she addressed her "Thoughts on Peace in an Air Raid" to the "huntsmen who are up in America, to the men and women whose sleep has not yet been broken by the machine-gun fire," the rhythm of her sentences echoed the relentlessness of the experienced violence:

> A bomb drops. All the windows rattle. The anti-aircraft guns are getting active. Up there on the hill under a net tagged with strips of green and brown stuff to imitate the hues of autumn leaves guns are concealed. Now they all fire at once.
>
> (E VI 243)

Whether or not Woolf knew by then that she was, with Leonard, among the 2820 names on Hitler's Black Book of British residents and European exiles to be arrested upon the planned invasion of Great Britain does not change the horrendous truth: death and destruction were imminent, "the future shadowed their present, like the sun coming through the many-veined transparent vine leaf; a criss-cross of lines making no pattern" (BA 103).

It appears, therefore, quite surprising that given this factual reality and Woolf's response to it, she should have often been described as "withdrawn" from the outside world. While she continued to be crowned by some as the "Queen of the High brows" (Bennett 1929: 258), this was a phase of her life when she could no longer accept any form of labelling, or vision of her as the epitome of the uncommitted aesthete. To understand how her work and standpoint might have been mistakenly assessed, it is important to turn rapidly to the "1930s" as a reconstructed object of cultural analysis. There is obviously good reason for the use of traditional periodisation to refer to this "post-war to pre-war" time. But just as modernism is no longer seen as a homogenous, clearly delineated moment of British and American culture, the decade that led to global conflict can no longer be labelled under the "Auden generation." As Alice Wood, among others, convincingly explains, Samuel Hynes's 1976 study of Auden's contemporaries – Cecil Day Lewis, Louis MacNeice, Stephen Spender, Christopher Isherwood, Graham Greene, John Lehmann, George Orwell among them – emphasised oppositions that critics now dispute while minimising the role of contemporary women writers and less established authors: not all of them were male, middleclass and university educated. Similarly, the idea that art in the 1920s was characterised by high-modernist aesthetic autonomy, whereas the 1930s were all about new forms of realism and political commitment, has come under close scrutiny. Clearly, the 1930s were an age of increasing anxiety and doubts. However, reactions to the ever-present threats were undeniably complex, varied and beyond the binary simplicity of opposition. First, as Valentine Cunningham explains, the 1930s contained at least "three literary generations," with "Auden and his coterie" in the middle, Eliot, Joyce, Forster, Lewis and Woolf on one side, the "immediate inheritors of the Auden generation" on the other (Cunningham 1998: 21–22); then although a conflict between generations was actually taking place – one that, from Woolf's perspective, was opposing the "Leaning Tower" of "middle-class birth and expensive education" (*E VI* 267) to the "ivory tower" where some members of the other faction thought she dwelled – there was no easy, definitive response to the debates and conflicts that entered the lives and consciousness of artists, writers and intellectuals. Art, indeed, became an increasingly politicised arena with its factions and affinities, but also with its complex networks of affiliations and antagonisms. At a time when trauma was reactivated and "Things f[e]ll apart" again,[3] the differing and sometimes purely personal responses – active militancy, political critique or distraction – evolved over time, blurring the frontiers between aestheticism and realism, patriotism and pacifism, idealism and pragmatism. Today, critics and literary historians see the so-called divide between outmoded high-modernist writers and politically committed younger ones as a convenient myth.

The reception of Woolf's work from the 1930s onwards and until the 1990s is symptomatic of the way this myth was constructed. At the end of the 1920s, Woolf's literary reputation as a high-modernist fiction writer and critic was at its peak. In 1931, *The Waves* proved a commercial success and most reviewers saw in it a major literary achievement. But Arnold Bennett was not the only one among her contemporaries to have some reservations. In the first critical study devoted to Woolf's novels, Winifred Holtby (1932: 201) thus explained that the author's range was "limited" and "her contact with life delicate and profound rather than comprehensive." In a context when the question of the congruence between art and politics became critical, Woolf's talent for exploring the inner world of human experience was seen as lacking political and social substance.[4] The publication of *CR II* reinforced the idea that her goal was not to explore the complex political and cultural reality since this second collection of her critical essays was read mostly in connection with the earlier volume. Nor did critics see how the issues of race, gender, patriarchy and Empire in *Flush* anticipated *Three Guineas*. And because her output of journalistic essays drastically diminished in the period – from 117 essays between 1925 and 1930 to 50 articles in the 10 years before her death (Wood 2015: 11) – the extent of her involvement in the cultural and political debates of her time remained undervalued for quite some time. Even after the publication of *The Years* in 1937, Woolf continued to be "caged," as she herself angrily noticed,[5] as a representative of experimental modernism or a foil to the younger generation of politically active and socially committed authors. Fortunately, the recent critical remapping and revaluation of Woolf's writing before and after the publication of *A Room of One's Own* has undercut this vision of a writer engrossed in solipsism and withdrawn from the world of current affairs. In the wake of Linden Peach, Merry Pawlowski, Melba Cuddy-Keane and Christine Reynier, among others, Alice Wood has shown how "the close relationship between formal and political radicalism in Woolf's early and late work undermines the integrity of viewing her oeuvre in two distinct phases, the modernist 1920s and the socially engaged 1930s" (Wood 3). Like many writers across the generations, she was constantly in conversation with the world outside, striving to find new artistic responses to the painful movements of history "in the raw" (*TG* 92), eager to document the contemporary facts, articles, theoretical discourses and testimonies that nourished the current debates on British and European politics, pacifism, patriotism, anti-Semitism, militarism and the role of women in the public sphere. To read her personal "chronology" and diaries between 1929 and 1941 offers many samples of this engagement while bringing to the fore the potent correspondence between her "war within and the war without"[6] as she kept struggling to find "the right relationship" between her "self" and "the world of other people."[7]

On first examination, a sense of loss haunts those pages: the death of many friends, relatives and well-known interlocutors added to the anxiety aroused by external circumstances. D.H. Lawrence died in March 1930, Arnold Bennett one year later, Lytton Strachey in January 1932. Dora Carrington committed suicide in March 1932, George Moore died in 1933; and then Roger Fry (September 1934), Francis Birrell (January 1935), Julian Bell (July 1937) – he had just joined the International Brigade against Franco – Lady Ottoline Morrell (1938) and James Joyce, two months before her own death. Woolf's world slowly became peopled with ghosts "knocking at the door" (*D IV* 275), recalling other ghosts and dramatically announcing a collapsing world. Each loss meant one response less to her own writing, as if "the thinking stuff were a web that were fertilized by other people [...] thinking it too" (*D IV* 193). Strachey's death thus gave Woolf the feeling that it was "like having the globe of the future perpetually smashed [...] a sense of something spent, gone" (*D IV* 64–65). She was counting on his reaction to *The Waves* and deeply missed their conversations, just as she had cruelly felt Katherine Mansfield's absence. After the loss of Roger Fry, she again felt "dazed: very wooden" (*D IV* 242). The present was overwhelming, the recent past seemed far long gone.

Woolf's anxiety about her literary output and status as an intellectual was another of her wars within. Such a preoccupation was not entirely new; what was new, however, was the intensity with which the world outside accompanied and disrupted her artistic battles. Between the recurring bouts of illness – the worst of them since 1913 occurring in 1935 as she was writing the biography of Roger Fry and revising the proofs of *The Years* – and the flourishing projects, she had moments when she wanted to feel safer and to absent herself temporarily from the public scene: "To be immune, means to exist apart from rubs, shocks, suffering; to be beyond the range of darts; to have enough to live on without courting flattery, success; [...]" (*D IV* 116). But most of the time, the outer world broke what she called the "dam" between the hard-fought-for inner peace she needed to write, and the everyday as a revelation of history (*D IV* 346). The newspapers, the radio – whose broadcast programs abolished the frontier between private homes and the external reality – the visits of those who were trying, in their own way, to bridge the gap between art and politics, or who wondered whether writing could enact a mode of resistance, all participated in creating a collective experience that encouraged her to explore new ideas and new artistic forms. Her dispute with the Young Poets in 1933 is a chief example of the way Woolf was challenged into getting out of her "cage," as Hermione Lee explains: "The very word 'new' was the signature tune of the writers who were now coming through the door of Tavistock Square and changing the tone of the Hogarth Press. It was essential for her to be in touch with their thoughts" (Lee 1997: 608–609). Among them, John Lehmann – who was to become the Press's partner-manager – Stephen Spender, and her nephew Julian Bell were those whose ideas she valued the most. Old Bloomsbury, it appears, disliked this group of young, leftist and successful writers who were highly critical of British politics and of their high-modernist predecessors. Woolf herself was often irritated by this new Oxford generation of male artists who counted no women amongst them. Their choice of a scapegoat – the "bourgeois, middle-class family from which [they] sprung," she wrote in "The Leaning Tower" (*E VI* 269) – their need to engage with working-class writing, their desire to find new literary forms that would encapsulate their views on the present, together with their "longing" to be "human," "closer to their kind" (273) both bothered and stimulated her. So did their youth, courage, self-confidence and outspoken anger. They offered perspectives on the congruence of art and politics that fuelled her thoughts and work during the whole decade, and although she remained suspicious of "the curious bastard language in which so much of this leaning-tower prose and poetry [was] written" (272), she shared with those who, like her, lived "under the shadows of war," the urgent need to find answers to Stephen Spender's question: "What can I do that matters?"

"How to put art and words in action?" (*E VI* 242) became one of the essential subjects that Woolf discussed with the friends and interlocutors who contributed to the sometimes exhausting, at other times thrilling, debates she engaged in with many of her contemporaries. Lehmann, Spender, Julian Bell, Eliot, Huxley, Isherwood, David Cecil, Desmond MacCarthy, H.G. Wells or G.B. Shaw had, again, one feature in common: they were men. As such, they were less inclined to address the urgent issues of fascism, totalitarianism, socialism and pacifism from the perspective of women's oppression. On the contrary, composer Ethel Smyth, who had joined the Women's Social and Political Union in 1910, shared Woolf's concern with the issue of patriarchy; she also had forceful ideas on the necessary mingling of the historical, the political and the aesthetic. She was 72 and a great admirer of *A Room of One's Own* when she met Woolf for the first time. Smyth was a musician, a writer and a bold militant, both more eccentric and radical than Woolf's other female friends. Woolf was inspired by her friend's personal experience of struggle within the codes of conventional femininity, fatherly authority and what Smyth herself called the "Inner Circle" of "University men, rich music patrons, Heads of Colleges" and "publishing houses."[8] The story of their relationship and of Woolf's shifts between fascination and exasperation has been well documented. On the one hand, Smyth stood for what Woolf was not: elderly, plain-spoken and fiercely patriotic. Her approach to women's emancipation had always been energetically militant: she had served two months in Holloway Prison with Emmeline Pankhurst, had written "The March of the Women" suffragist anthem and was indomitable. On the other hand, Smyth had done for music what Woolf was trying to do with literature: being of "the race of pioneers, among the ice-breakers, the window smashers," she "made a way for those who come after her" (E V 637). As the very opposite of the Angel in the house, she inspired the characters of Rose in The Years and Miss La Trobe in Between the Acts and probably helped Woolf to come to terms with her "ladylike" writing posture. It is, therefore, not surprising that her friendship and association with this formidable woman should have led her, on January 21, 1931 to talk about women's professions and sexuality on the platform of the London and National Society for Women's Service (L&NSWS), a feminist association that had grown out of the moderate wing of the women's suffrage movement.[9] She went there with Ethel whose witty performance seems to have overshadowed her own. But the typed draft and holograph versions of Woolf's talk suggest that her speech kept "knocking on the door of her mind," its meanings finding reverberations in The Pargiters,[10] her 1935 essay "On Being Despised," and in Three Guineas (Lee 602).

Other suffrage activists and feminist intellectuals were part of Woolf's circle in the 1930s and shared her thoughts on the interactions between community and subjectivity, art and patriarchy. Among her contemporary "mothers" and "sisters" were the Strachey women – Jane, her daughters Philippa and Pernel, and their sister-in-law, Ray – whose close relationship with Woolf influenced her views on women's artistic and political emancipation in A Room of One's Own, "The Plumage Bill" and "The Intellectual Status of Women," as well as in two of her early short fictions: "A Woman's College from Outside" and "A Society of Women."[11] Woolf had written Jane Strachey's memorial in The Nation and Athenaeum in 1928; and as Principal of Newnham College, it was Pernel Strachey who had invited her to talk of "women and fiction" in Cambridge. In A Room, Ray Strachey's The Cause (1928) is the book mentioned when the narrator raises the issue of the financing of women's college.[12] Woolf was to quote Ray's feminist history of the women's movement again, this time explicitly, along with her 1935 survey on "Careers and Openings for Women" in Three Guineas when she argues for the economic relevance of women's work. Although they have different forms and objectives, The Cause and Woolf's 1937 pacifist pamphlet rely on a similar use of "facts," "evidence and material" (Ray 5). As to

Philippa, she invited Woolf and Smyth to speak on "Music and literature" to the audience of L&NSWS young women. Her *Memorandum on
the Position of English Women in Relation to that of English Men* (1935)
also appears in Woolf's bibliographical references in *Three Guineas*.
Woolf's relationship with the Strachey women is thus symptomatic of
this "cross-generational feminism" that Kathlyn Holland mentions in
her article on the subject (Holland 2013: 87). It also invites us to have
a closer look at the network of late nineteenth- and twentieth-century
women intellectuals and activists whose work she had read, thought
about, but had rarely paid a tribute to until then.[13] While she had always
denounced the silencing of women's voices, paradoxically and perhaps
intentionally, it was the discourses of her male interlocutors and rivals
that as an essayist and a critic she kept responding to, and, therefore,
emphasised. In this respect, the 1930s marked a new start as she more
explicitly honoured the work and achievements of her foremothers and
female contemporaries.

In this period bound in its historical moment, the "non-joiner" that
Woolf said she preferred to be "joined in" many times. In 1932, she
became a member of the London National Society for Women's Service
and signed up for the cause of the Women's Service Library. She regularly
attended the Annual Conferences of the Labour Party; raised money,
in April 1935, to help finance the project of an anti-Fascist exhibition
in reaction against the "Exhibition of the Fascist Revolution" held in
Rome between 1932 and 1934; supported the Artist's International
Association in defence of Culture in October 1936 and wrote "Why
Art Today Follows Politics" at their request.[14] She attended the meeting
organised by the National Joint Committee for Spanish Relief in June
1937 and raised money for the Refugees Society by selling the manuscript of *Three Guineas* in February 1939. Just as he was by her side
during the trip to Germany she had organised in April 1935 – a few days'
expedition on their way to Rome whose burlesque climactic moment
was their driving through a reception organised by Goering in Bonn[15] –
Leonard Woolf proved, during those years, a close intellectual partner as
well as a challenging "culturally Other" (Rosenfeld 2000: 10). His life-
long socialism, his engagement with colonial issues and for international
peace, his experience in political and documentary journalism together
with his interwar idealism stimulated Woolf's cultural criticism.[16] In
1930, Leonard Woolf founded *The Political Quarterly* with Professor
William Robson, a Centre-Left journal in which he expressed his views
on the labour movement, foreign policy and the need for international
disarmament; in 1931, he was appointed chairman of the New Fabian
Research Bureau and Committee for International Affairs, published
the first volume of *After the Deluge* – an essay on "communal psychology" – and commissioned the Hogarth Letters series on current issues
with his wife and John Lehmann. Published in 1933, his introduction to
The Intelligent Man's Guide for the Prevention of War was an answer

to Mussolini's vision of pacifism as a doctrine "born of a renunciation of the struggle and an act of cowardice in the face of sacrifice": his conviction that "if [the intelligent man] wants to prevent war, war can be prevented" (Woolf L. 7; 10) obviously anticipated Woolf's own thesis in *Three Guineas*. A parallel can also be established between the satirical impulse at work in her anti-fascist pamphlet and her husband's *Quack, Quack!* (1935), an essay on autocracy, intellectual dishonesty and the brutal quackery of modern totalitarianism. "Outsiders together" – "she privileged by her background, but excluded from centers by her gender, he privileged by gender and marginalized through background" (Rosenfeld 2000: 4), Virginia and Leonard took risks as writers and intellectuals. Two distinct sensibilities nourished their awareness that power politics determine social relations and artistic expression; but they both imagined new cultural plots as alternatives to the dominant thinking. Commenting on *Between the Acts* and *The War for Peace*, two different projects written the same year, Rosenfeld points out their common "antiauthoritarianism" and "anti*authorial*ism": "both books posit an open-endedness, a plot whose outcome is decided, democratically, by others" (ibid. 13). It is thus quite moving to read Woolf's comment in a letter to Lady Cecil, a few days before her death, upon Leonard's fervent defence of pacifism in *The War for Peace*: "the only kind of thing worth writing now" (*L VI* 483).

After Munich, nobody in Europe could remain withdrawn from the horrendous reality of the present. "All slipping consciously into a pit," Woolf felt in September 1938 (*D V* 170). The "crisis," E.M. Forster (1939: 889) wrote in "The 1939 State," had become "a habit, almost a joke"; the period was bound to its historical moment, and the "I" of each and every one could no longer feel isolated from the "we" of threatened nations and communities. This awareness pervades most of Woolf's works in the period. Of course, one might choose to focus on those essays or quotations from her diaries and letters where she seems to be engrossed in the depiction of "an insubstantial self without a world" (Zwerdling 1986: 12); one might also argue that she kept using the present as a "platform to stand upon," as she herself explains in her 1939 autobiographical essay "Sketch of the Past" (*MB* 87), from which to view the past and find a refuge. But this hypothesis obviously does not hold. First because, as suggested before, from 1932 onwards, Woolf spent much time reading the newspapers, collecting documents and scraps of the present by amassing manifestos, memoirs and cuttings from the Press to explore, and respond to, contemporary social and political events. Thus, in *Three Guineas*, Woolf cites 95 books – mostly biographies, memoirs and literary texts—to support her argument: among them, 54 were published in the 1930s and 37 in between 1935 and 1938. Throughout the 1930s, her mind and writing focused on the interface between past and present history as a laboratory of power relationships and patriarchal violence. The question was no longer how, as the daughter of a Victorian gentleman, to negotiate with one's heritage, but how this heritage conditions the implacable reality of its perpetuation. What then had become "worth writing" needed to enact a form of cultural resistance to all types of injunction. As an artist and intellectual, Woolf had consolidated her place in a genealogy of highbrow experimental writers: more than ever, she now needed her voice and words to reveal the traumatic afterlives of patriarchal and historical violence: the present required change, this time in the sense of political intervention.

The Past, the Present and Historical Distance

"Like so many people nowadays," Woolf confessed in 1934, "I am pestered with questions." Woolf's "whys" keep recurring in her work of the period: "Churches, public houses, parliaments, shops, loud-speakers, motor cars, the drone of an aeroplane in the clouds, and men and women, all inspire questions" (*E VI* 30–31). There are more than a hundred "whys" in *The Years* that raise questions about individual intentions and human motives. They often remain unanswered at a time when everybody was aching for answers. In fact, just as many historians would try for decades to search for the causes of the Second World War, Woolf felt the pressing need, during this period, to answer as many of those "whys" as possible: "Why lecture?"; "Why does one do it?" (*TY* 351); "Why are not females permitted to study physics, divinity, astronomy, etc., etc. [...]?" (*TG* 157), and of course: "Why fight?" (*TG* 92). But as always, the "why" of things, and more particularly of the history unfolding before her eyes, was bound to come with a "how?": "how in your opinion are we to prevent war?" (*TG* 89); how to "make ideas effective" and "fire them off?" when all "the idea makers who are in a position to make ideas effective are men" (*E VI* 242). This acute awareness of the necessity to find "effective" alternative modes of recording and narrating "history in the making" spurred Woolf's political creativity in the 1930s. At a moment when art and politics appeared as unlikely to disjoin as the remembered past and the current moment, her various projects took what Thomas Davis (2016: 1) calls the "outward turn" of "late modernism": a "form of attention" given to "the temporalities, spaces, surface appearances, textures, and rhythms of everyday life—and [to] the disorder in the world-system that pushed the locus." "The historian to-day," Woolf explains in her 1936 famous essay on art and politics, is

> writing not about Greece and Rome in the past, but about Germany and Spain in the present; the biographer is writing lives of Hitler and Mussolini, not of Henry the Eighth and Charles Lamb; the poet introduces Communism and fascism into his lyrics; the novelist turns from the private lives of his characters to their social surroundings and their political opinions.
>
> (*E VI* 75)

Because it constantly interrupted the flow of daily lives, like the voice of Hitler on the radio and the sounds of aircrafts in the night, the "here and now" evoked in these lines came as an attack against entrenched habits and thoughts; it compromised the policies of appeasement, redoubled the fear of repetition and above all, Rebecca West would later explain, was experienced as an

> event which affects one so that it tests one, and one tests it. It calls one to take account of it, to pass judgment on it, to modify one's philosophy in the light of the added knowledge it has brought one.[17]

Many writers of Woolf's generation, including herself, were driven by the necessity to "test" their everyday reality, struggling with its representation in that it implied both an understanding of current affairs and a reading of "the old and the new side by side" (*E VI* 398). To do so, they used their personal experiences as observers, readers and common citizens to remember, document and make sense of "history in the present," convinced that "the past is not dead, it is not even past."[18] The literature of the 1930s thus often blurred the usual boundaries between "memory" and a form of realism conveyed by the author or narrator as "witness." In her study of *Men and Women of the 1930s*, Janet Montefiore evokes the generic hybridity of George Orwell's *Homage to Catalonia* (1936), Christopher Isherwood's *Goodbye to Berlin* (1939) and Louis MacNeice's *Autumn Journal* (1939). To this short list, one must add the war memoirs of Storm Jameson (*Europe to Let* – 1940) and Naomi Mitchison (*Vienna Diary* – 1934); the historical novels of Vera Brittain (*A Honourable Estate: A Novel of Transition* – 1936) and Vita Sackville-West (*The Edwardians* – 1930); the feminist dystopias of Naomi Mitchison (*We Have Been Warned* – 1935), Katharine Burdekin (*Swastika Night* – 1934), Storm Jameson (*In the Second Year* – 1936) and Phyllis Bottome (*The Mortal Storm* – 1937); and, obviously, Woolf's *The Years*, *Between the Acts* and *Three Guineas*.[19] All these authors struggled with "history's necessity and impossibility," and with the "formal mechanics" of its representation and narration (O'Malley xiv–xv). Explicitly or implicitly, they tackled historiographical and epistemological issues: while the conception of "History as the Understanding of the Present" was not new, the idea of writing accounts of "history in the making," or of "histories of the present" appeared, by definition, unorthodox.[20] For women artists, however, there was additional complexity to this challenge. They experienced a form of "revived hostility to feminism"[21] with the return of a traditional celebration of the domestic sphere – a celebration that was all the more threatening since fascism's ideological vision of motherhood endorsed it – and therefore conceived history as "a battleground of their own": a new form of tyranny added to the existing ones on the "home" front. At the very moment when, once again, they were bound to be silenced for having no potential influence on the unfolding of the present, they needed to find a way to say what they knew they would hardly be allowed to say. And yet, "through the lens of the social documents that shaped their experience," they created "historical fiction that perform[ed] the act of historical interpretation," Phyllis Lassner argues in *British Women Writers of World War II* (1998: 21). Woolf was, therefore, not alone in this "struggle" with "history's necessity and impossibility." I would argue, however, that far beyond its feminism and aestheticism, what makes her work in the 1930s unique is the way Woolf constantly refused the modalities of authority and power that she found so often attached to history and exposed her tools and interrogations as an artist and historiographer – a process which, this time, sought to reveal the truths of the present by digging into the past.

The first of these historiographical issues was concerned with the essential question of sources: what kind of material should document which kind of present reality? Woolf's goal in *The Years* was

> to give the whole of present society—nothing less: facts as well as the vision. And to combine them both. And there are to be a million of ideas but no preaching—history, politics, feminism, art, literature— in short a summing up of all I know, feel, laugh at, despise, like, admire hate & so on.
>
> (*D IV* 151–152)

Many scholars have described the intense search for sources in the fields of history, economics, politics, education, the law, international relations and women's emancipation that nourished her work in the 1930s. From 1927 on, Woolf began amassing cuttings from newspapers, manifestos and memoirs for what would become her three war scrapbooks. Alice Wood recounts how a visit of Huxley and his wife Maria to Tavistock Square on February 16, 1931, made her feel intimidated by their active militancy, and "painfully aware of her comparative lack of public commentary on current affairs" (Wood 35): "They are going to the Sex Congress at Moscow, have been in India, will go to America, speak French, visit celebrities—while here I live like a weevil in a biscuit" (*D IV* 11). When commissioned to write "Six Articles on London Life" by the popular, middlebrow magazine *Good Housekeeping* in 1931,[22] Woolf, therefore, used the occasion and the format for cultural analysis: taking up the "humble tradition" of "the guidebook" and of the "ethnographic exploration" while moving it far beyond the expectations associated with the genre (Reynier 2018: 4), she bore witness to, and questioned, the contemporary function of institutions such as the Church and Parliament, the patriarchal value attached to architecture and national monuments, the mechanisms of capitalist free trade and consumerism, the production and consumption of commodities, the contrast between wealth and poverty, and the place that women occupy in the city she guides her reader through.

In *The Years*, Woolf's documentary impulses echo her diary entry of December 19, 1932, where she evokes her fascination for the external world and its accessible factuality:

> This one, however, releases such a torrent of fact as I did not know I had in me. I must have been observing & collecting these 20 years—since Jacob's Room anyhow. Such a wealth of things seen present themselves that I can't choose even—hence 60,000 words all about one paragraph. Of course this is external: but there's a good deal of gold—more than I'd thought—in externality.
>
> (*D IV* 133)

Woolf's family-chronicle addresses the subjects that her *Good Housekeeping* articles had explored within the format of the cultural and political essay: the patriarchal power of British institutions, class inequalities, gender discriminations, urban poverty, "the oppressive structures of modern bourgeois culture both in the private and the public sphere" (Spiropoulou 2010: 117). In her novel, Woolf narrates everyday life as a concept that "acquires specificity and coherence within an articulated network of political, economic, and social life" (Davis 2008: 5). Keeping the actions of great men and major historical events at the margins of the story, she foregrounds the minutiae of individual lives as the characters try to make sense of their present situation, torn between the historical and the personal.

During the years that led her to the publication of *Three Guineas*, Woolf immersed herself in "that marvellous, perpetually renewed, and as yet largely untapped aid to the understanding of human motives which is provided in our age by biography and autobiography. Also there is the daily paper, history in the raw" (*TG* 92). The lives, memoirs and letters of her contemporaries and elders, the records of "the public life which is history," the "annals" of "public bodies," the "figures" of "poverty" supplied by *The Times* newspaper (*TG* 112; 115), the reports issued by consultative committees, the testimonies of British civil servants and Whitaker's *Almanack* for the year 1937 compose Woolf's personal archive of references that Anna Snaith retrieves in the bibliography added to the 2015 edition. For *Between the Acts*, Woolf returned to her "journalistic scrapbooking" (Wood 124) and incorporated news reports in her fiction.[23] Directed towards the suspended moment between peace and war, Woolf's play-novel is anchored in the contemporary: "The hands of the clock had stopped at the present moment. It was now. Ourselves" (*BA* 167). Its first draft, *Pointz Hall*, was written on April 2, 1938, less than a month after Germany had invaded Austria (*D V* 129) and the third Moscow Trial had taken place, two combined facts that on March 12, she wrote, had put their "thorn into [her] morning" (*D V* 129). The novel's composition also "saw the end of the Spanish Civil War and Franco's triumph with the final fall of Madrid" (Wood 113), the mass arrival

of Jewish and intellectual refugees to Britain and France from Central
Europe, Germany's invasion of Poland, the Battle of Britain in 1940, the
destruction of the Woolf's house. The "queer sense of suspense" evoked
in a diary entry dated February 8, 1940 – "War surrounding our island"
(*D V* 265) – pervades the world of the novel and of Miss La Trobe's
pageant. But of course, the present in *Between the Acts* also lurks in the
silences of the text: in the unofficial histories and personal stories that
come about "between the acts" of the representation of English national
and cultural history, and in the interruptions that force the spectators of
the pageant to renegotiate their experience of reality, time, fragmented
selves and community.

Woolf had thus started her own "mass observation project" around 1929
(Snaith 2015: xxvii). Like the team of investigators, observers and writers
involved in this social research organisation founded in 1937 by an anthropologist (Tom Harrisson), a painter and film-maker (Humphrey Jennings)
and a *Daily Mirror* journalist (Charles Madge), she studied the everyday
lives of ordinary people in Britain before Kingsley Martin invited her to
review a Mass Observation survey on account of her work in *The Years*.[24]
Thomas Davis (2008: 77) explains that "Mass-Observation" conceived
itself as "a revolutionary group that would not produce facts about the
masses, but allow the masses to produce facts about their everyday lives
by submitting diaries, answering questionnaires and surveys, and bearing
witness to the daily doings of English life." Perhaps because she did not
have the experience of combat, was not considered to be radical enough,
or because she was a woman, Harrisson never mentioned Woolf in his
"Why Not War Writers" manifesto published in October 1941, a text in
which the founder of the MOP regrets that very few books were written
on the war by British writers.[25] And yet, as many other eyewitnesses of
events forced upon them, she turned potential powerlessness into active
archival work, building her own "anthropology of ourselves" in order
"to get written down the unwritten laws and to make the invisible forces
visible" (Madge and Harrisson 1938: 8). Used in a letter to *The New
Statesman* where the Mass Observation project was launched, the phrase
"anthropology of ourselves" finds striking echoes in *The Years*, where the
feeling that "we do not know ourselves, ordinary people" is a haunting
one: "If they want to reform the world, [North] thought, why not begin
there, at the centre, with themselves?" (*TY* 385). The same idea recurs
in *Three Guineas*, where Woolf calls upon her readers in similar terms:
"Let us never cease from thinking—what is this 'civilization' in which we
find ourselves?" (*TG* 145). It appears again in *Between the Acts*, when
the spectators of the pageant read on the programme "The present time.
Ourselves" and wonder: "But what could she know about ourselves? The
Elizabethans yes; the Victorians, perhaps; but ourselves; sitting here on a
June day in 1939—it was ridiculous" (*BA* 160).

In this respect, Woolf's investigation of the afterlife of history as it
merges in the present echoes other literary works of the 1930s. However,

this investigation also stretches out her exploration of the multilayered nature of contemporary reality in the 1920s while anticipating later forms of history writing. First, in so far as it records and analyses facts, news, current events and affairs, Woolf's enquiry into the historical patterns of everyday life is typical of the methods that the school of "historians of the present" have chosen to explore scientifically since the 1950s.[26] In the practice of scholars such as François Bédarida, Henri Rousso, Robert Frank and François Hartog, among others – a practice whose "pitfalls" are linked to the tension between "knowledge and experience, distance and proximity, objectivity and subjectivity, researcher and witness" – the time frame of the present can be identified with "contemporaneity": a "present marked by the weight, sometimes the burden, of the past, a present open as well to the possibilities, even the uncertainties of the future" (Rousso 2016: 3–4). The politics of knowledge underlying such "an anthropology of ourselves," with its focus on what we know and how we know it, also anticipates the archival turn of the 1990s, an epistemological shift that continues to probe into what counts as reliable historical evidence and pays attention to the inherent omissions, gaps and exclusions of any constructed corpus of sources. Woolf's valorisation, notably in *Three Guineas*, of letters, diaries, memoirs, private papers and photographs is perfectly in line with this body of historiographical reflections, and with Raphael Samuel's contention "that history is not the prerogative of the historian, nor even, as postmodernism contends, a historian's 'invention'. It is, rather, a social form of knowledge; the work, in any given instance, of a thousand different hands" (Samuel 2012: 10). In a similar dialectical movement, Woolf's appraisal of the everyday as "a place where contemporary history becomes legible, made visible for analysis, scrutiny, and, sometimes, bewilderment" (Davis 2008: 4) builds on the emergence of social history and forms of micro-history in the late nineteenth century while anticipating the work of Michel de Certeau, Henri Lefebvre, Walter Benjamin and others. To uncover the material reality of the everyday (here in its "contemporaneous" dimension) proved indeed an essential tool for the recuperation of the unrecorded "lives of the obscure," women in particular. To understand how "we, ourselves" experience history in the present then became a foundational practice whereby she could politically recast the notions of commonality and community. Woolf's conception and representation of the present also resonate with her project to write history as it is "lived," as she had explained in her 1919 essay "The War from the Street": a history that proves close to the bone of phenomenological experience – the present being captured in an instant, in its physical embodiment and material circumstances.

To demonstrate how some patterns of the past "repeat themselves," "like a gramophone whose needle has stuck, is grinding out with intolerable unanimity" (*TG* 140; 214), Woolf needed to explore a "present continuous" (Spiropoulou 2010: 121) grounded in historical awareness as self-awareness; but she also needed to establish valid, objective connections between the unfolding present and what gave form to it beforehand. Consequently, the second issue she and her contemporaries faced was the historiographical question of "historical distance," in the sense, first, of "the distance that separates the historian from the specific past under description," then of the "sense of temporality constructed by every historical account as it positions its readers in relation to the past" (Phillips 2000: 31–32). Woolf knew that "when the present presses so close that you can feel nothing else," then the clarity that comes from the experience of a present "backed from the past" is at risk (*MB* 108). She had formerly argued that readers and critics almost always "agree about the old," but disagree "about the new" (*E III* 353). The assumption shared by most nineteenth-century historians that an objective recording of the past requests temporal remoteness, might explain why Woolf's opening statement in "Why Art To-Day Follows Politics" was partly inaccurate. In the 1930s, examples of biographies and literary works focusing on topical subjects were abundant. As to the corpus of contemporary history books, the bibliographical references from the catalogues of the French and British National Libraries tell otherwise. Between 1930 and 1949, around 30 books on Hitler, only 8 on Mussolini, were published in Europe and the United States. The few British historians who published on the subject of the coming war and its major protagonists were, or had been, journalists, had a Jewish background or occupied international functions. Henry Wickham Steed, who was among the first to express alarm about Hitler's intentions in the 1930s, had started his career as a foreign correspondent for *The Times*. In 1934, he published *Hitler Whence and Whither* and *The Meaning of Hitlerism, Our War Aims* in 1939. "Who Hitler is," also published in 1939, is a pamphlet written by Robert C.K. Ensor, British intellectual, writer and journalist. Lewis Bernstein Namier's Polish-Jewish background and Zionist commitment might have influenced the two highly critical essays published, respectively, in 1933 and 1935 on the rise of Hitlerism in *The Manchester Guardian*.[27] Hugh Redwald Trevor-Roper, whose famous *The Last Days of Hitler* was only published in 1947, was a specialist of early modern Britain before he was assigned as a British intelligence officer in 1945 to investigate the circumstances of Hitler's death in Nazi Germany. Edward H. Carr was a diplomat, a journalist and a specialist in international relations, and above all, a historian supporting the idea of history as progress when he published *The Twenty Years' Crisis* in July 1939: the book exposed his "appeasement" theory grounded in his analysis of the First World War and its aftermath. In the course of the same decade, a number of historical books on The Great War were published in Britain; only a few in Spain or Germany.[28] Interestingly enough, and according to Lucy Dawidowicz, the British perspective on the Second World War from the 1940s onwards remained marked by the astonishing "minimal attention" it gave to German anti-Semitism and to the destruction of the Jews.[29] My research indicates that medieval history, economic history, foreign policy and international relations were the main areas of historical enquiry in the 1930s, and that no women historians published on the subject, except for Elizabeth Wiskemann, an English journalist and historian of Anglo-German ancestry who wrote a study of Europe after the Munich Agreement – *An Undeclared War* – in 1939.[30] Whatever their experience or field of expertise, for the historians of the period, to write "histories of the present" meant to run the risk of returning to a pre-Rankean period when "contemporary history was thought to be the best history" (Ash 2009: xiv). As to the few female scholars of the profession, they had rarely been trained in modern history and tended to avert their gaze from what seemed a male field of knowledge. Married to a leftist Jew and haunted by the multifaceted threat of violence and domination, Woolf, however, did not see the gender gap or the scholarly questions of methodology as immovable barriers: to engage in a renewed conversation on "the conditions of possibility" of reading the past and making sense of the present enabled her to continue her exploration of the battlefields of history as a woman, an artist and a cultural innovator.

Besides, she was well aware that historical distance is an intrinsic part of all historical accounts; often seen as a standard or a norm, it varies over the centuries and according to historical genres as a vantage point resulting from political, ideological and emotional choices. The notion has its own history, Mark Salber Phillips explains: from the time of Thucydides, when to be a participant in the recorded events was considered an advantage, well into the eighteenth century, when the dignity of the discipline started to be associated with a form of aloofness distinct from the "evocative closeness" of biographies and memoirs (Phillips 2000: 36). As shown in Chapter 2 of this book, romantic historiography returned to a valued sense of present immediacy: Carlyle (1832: 4) wanted to gain "some acquaintance with our fellow creatures, though dead and vanished, yet dear to us" while Macaulay "posed the dilemma as a problem of genre" since he saw "modern historical understanding as having suffered a division between the distanciating rationality of analytical historians and the evocative power of the historical novel" (Phillips 2000: 43). Then came the "Whigs" and the modernists with their condemnation of the former generation's presentism along with their conception of temporal distance – with the studied object – as an essential academic requirement. Woolf knew, as her work in the 1920s manifests, that if history requires source materials which are bound to depend on first witnesses, there is no such thing as an objective standpoint; she understood that any historical record bears the marks of a situated historian and a specific agenda. But because understanding the "present" from a nonconformist and female-constructed standpoint was more vital than ever, she needed to probe again into the question of "vision" – her choice of word – and perspective:

not to question the validity of all truths in the name of relativity, but out of a political compulsion to build a less patriarchal transaction with reality.

In "Why Art To-Day Follows Politics," expressions such as "close touch" and "angle of vision" refer to these very notions of "distance" and specific standpoint (*E VI* 75). In "The Historian and the Gibbon," Woolf begins by underlining how the historian's choice of a "distant," "safe" and "extensive" subject in *The Decline and Fall* led him to adopt an "attitude, a style" and a particular stance "since he was not dealing with his own times and contemporary questions": "we seem, at least, as we read him raised above the tumult and the chaos into a clear and rational air" (*E VI* 82; 84). The "Leaning Tower" is another metaphor of a writer's "station" and constructed "vision" (E VI 266) linked to the multiple "influences" – the word keeps recurring in the essay – that have built his sense of belonging and perspective. Aware of her own standpoint, Woolf begins her polemical essay on the generation of the "young poets" by staging embedded gazes in the concrete temporality of her observation: the gaze of the essayist looking at the writers he examines, "glancing over" the "shifting surface" of a "large expanse of print," and the gaze of those very writers as they keep their eyes "fixed [...] upon a certain object" (ibid. 259; 262). In this analysis of the social construction of a vantage point, Woolf takes the risk of making a provisional "theory" based on facts, experience and the comparison between the nineteenth-century writer "seated in front of human life [...]; and looking at it through their eyes" (262), and the "group which began to write about 1925" (267). As she unfolds her argument, she keeps returning to the visual metaphor of constructed "distance": "must [the next generation] too be a leaning-tower generation—an oblique, sidelong, self-centred, squinting, self-conscious generation with a foot in two worlds?" (274). Whatever the partiality of her judgement on her contemporaries in this essay, Woolf's assessment of the temporal, affective and sociological distance that influences a writer's apprehension of reality, whether past or present, did not lead her to adopt a prescriptive view of the notion. That is because she was not a historian, one might argue, and historians, Mark Phillips explains, "build their disciplinary claims on prescriptive understandings of distance." But Phillips (2013a: 4) also reminds us that although the legacy of nineteenth-century historicism involves a conception of historical distance that relies on the dialectics of "alterity" – the necessary detachment that enables the historian to better grasp the reality of the past – and "insight" as the indispensable ingredients of the discipline's authority, historical representation has always involved a wider range of "distance-positions" related to a "multiplicity of engagements, including formal structure and vocabulary, affective impact, moral and ideological interpellation, and underlying intelligibility." The "heuristic" of distance that he proposes is "relational" rather than didactic; it dissolves the usual binaries of "now" and "then," objectivity and subjectivity, while combining the notions of "form," "affect," "summoning" and "understanding" (Phillips 2013b: 6).

As her critical approach to "historians' histories" has shown, Woolf did not believe that time ensures objectivity, nor that it prevents prejudices and the imposition of "grand narratives" as forms of ideological dominant discourses.[31] Conversely, to play with historical distance and points of view enabled her to read unofficial histories alongside official history while looking at the way this very distance shapes our experience and representation of reality. In this respect, *The Years*, *Three Guineas* and *Between the Acts* clearly belong to different genre traditions and "structures of representation"; they imply diverse modes of "rhetorical address" and "emotional experiences"; they call for "reflection," "action" and "engagement" in distinct ways (Phillips 2013b: 6). They also enact Woolf's late modernist "outward turn." But above all, they are written from the standpoint of a woman asking a question that no historians' histories were asking at the time: "How might a feminist representation of history revise what it gets remembered and what does not get reenacted?" (Wiley 1995: 3–4). In *The Years*, Woolf's entwining of the facts of history and biography within the visionary art of the fiction writer refers us to her "granite and rainbow" metaphor. According to Diana Wallace, this combination also invites us to look at the emerging tradition of "Women Writers and the Historical Novel in the Thirties": feeling the urge, in between the wars, to recapture their past as a "prehistory of the present," artists like Rose Macaulay, Vera Brittain, Vita Sackville-West or Naomi Mitchison broke the convention established by Walter Scott in his *Waverley* novels and explored, with a feminist agenda, what George Lukács called in *The Historical Novel* (1962) "the present as history" or "self-experienced history" (Lukács 1962: 83–84). This "structure of representation" allowed Woolf to elaborate links between the private sphere of personal and domestic lives and the institutional structures of patriarchy; to retrieve the facts and details of ordinary daily lives within the larger patterns of public life; to expose the tyranny of the Victorian family, the silencing of women and their curbed development; to satirise the history of the Empire. As Hermione Lee suggests, the novel "rewrote her earlier works" in a more subversive, "generalized and decentred way" since the lives described are "case histories" and obvious "products of a political system" (Lee 1997: 637–638). Focused on an ongoing present, the perception of which is constantly questioned – "But what is this moment; and what are we?" (*TY* 317) – Woolf's "novel-essay" combines close-up effects and the broader perspective of multiple voices and viewpoints, a historiographical technique that shatters the sense of a coherent, collective experience. Woolf's art of mediation here conveys the ideas of fragmentation and powerlessness while offering a multi-perspective conception of history that opens the path for new possibilities: not the promise of progress, but the potential power of a yet-ungraspable vision: " 'Look here' [...] [Peggy] began. She wanted to express something that she felt to be very important; about a world in which people were whole, in which people were free" (*TY* 370). Woolf's radical voice, the voice that she used in her diary from 1932 onwards and that led her to write "I have enough powder to blow up St Paul" (*D IV* 77), is hardly ever heard in *The Years*; it is dispersed rather than embodied by one character or one speaker. Faced with the relentless unfolding of historical and ideological conflicts, whether imperial, national, economic or sexual, her characters sometimes feel extreme anger: but this inward or outward rage appears to be drowned in a sense of unfulfilled yearnings and impossible emancipation. And yet, the novel continues to engage our thoughts through the very "failure" that mirrors the debacle of patriarchal politics and culture. As she summons her reader's critical attention, Woolf reveals to them the recurring and alienating patterns of life and history, from the Victorian age to their symptomatic present-day realities.

Belonging both to the traditions of pamphlets and letter writing, a combination that conflates the masculine and the feminine in terms of literary genres, *Three Guineas* has a complex and empowering "structure of representation." The "emotional experience" at the core of its writing brings to mind the inter-chapters of *The Pargiters* that Woolf had abandoned in *The Years*: "With a great boiling up, it splashed over everything that affected her: not just the patriarchal home and 'infantilism' of male society, not just the education and employment of women, but the establishment, the media, the church, psychiatry, science, dress" (Lee 1997: 680–681). In *Three Guineas*, indeed, Woolf's affective distance with her studied objects might appear minimal and, therefore, questionable; her vantage point as "the daughter of an educated gentleman," limited; her rhetorical strategy can also be perceived as a form of self-posturing. As a pacifist pamphlet, it has been considered politically inadequate, irrational or irrelevant; as a feminist argument, readers have found it class-bound, uselessly aggressive, unreasonable. Except for Naomi Black in 2004, very few scholars have read it in the cultural context of its conception or tried to appreciate the political relevance of Woolf's "Credo" (*D V* 169) beyond its biases and potential blind spots. And yet the radical achievement of *Three Guineas* lies precisely in the unique combination of the text's unapologetic standpoint, objective resort to facts, and clear historiographical approach. Obviously, Woolf needed to find a strategy that would provoke her readers' response by turning them into accomplices while trying not to alienate her male audience completely. She, therefore, abandoned the potential, more aggressive titles for her project – "On Being Despised" and "Why Men are Like That" – together with some of her more subversive arguments, like her comparison between St Paul and Hitler, and between priests and dictators (Lee 681). But she also braved her utmost fear, which was to be misread, or not read at all, and definitely renounced the comfortable position of the observer and highbrow aesthete for whom "politics are best avoided. [...]—all politics be damned" (*L V* 436).[32] One may judge Woolf's historiographical method in *Three Guineas* empirical and contingent; her "metahistorical and pancultural construction of fascism as well as essentialist theories that women are only passive war victims" can be debated (Lassner 4). Paradoxically, it is because "Woolf would not let her opponents, or those who think differently, live in peace," and because she actually believed in the possibility of change and in "living, living [...] differently, differently" (*TY* 371) that the history she interprets is still relevant today. "Self-pity and victimhood" have nothing to do with it.[33]

In *Between the Acts*, Woolf does not use the "politics of affect" that, in *Three Guineas*, was meant to address a non-partisan, yet politically involved readership. David McWhirter argues that the perspective adopted in this novel is both "abstract and empathetic" (McWhirter 1988: 807). According to Alice Wood, Woolf's anti-nationalistic pageant relies on an "oblique feminist-pacifist commentary on the past, present and potential future of English culture" (Wood 2015: 126; 103). Gillian Beer sees the book as a "mischievous and playful work" that explores England "how it came to be as she explored it in *Three Guineas*, patriarchal, imperialist and class-ridden" (Beer 125; 147). Situated in June 1939 – at this place, again, where "contemporary history becomes legible, made visible for analysis, scrutiny, and, sometimes, bewilderment" (Davis 2008: 4) – the novel presents the past from the vantage point of the present in a clear retrospective mode that differs from the previous two works. Bridging the gap between fiction and cultural commentary, narrative and drama, the text holds a mirror to the audience of the play and to Woolf's readers, prompting them to see themselves as they are in a moment that derives from the past, and as members of a community that wishes to forget the wider national and international contexts:

> *Look at ourselves, ladies and gentlemen! Then at the wall; and ask how's this wall, the great wall, which we call, perhaps miscall, civilisation, to be built by* (here the mirrors flicked and flashed) *orts, scraps and fragments like ourselves.*
>
> (TY 169)

Another response not only to the political climate of the times but also to the accusations of individualism directed at Woolf by her contemporaries, *Between the Acts* asks both audience and readers to imagine themselves acting a part and to finally speak against fascism. In her chapter on Woolf's last "historical narrative," Angeliki Spiropoulou has shown how her response to "turbulent contemporaneity" takes the form of a "critical historiography" that introduces the temporal modes of a "primeval, originary time," "timeless repetition," and cultural historicity to "question modernity's self-image of being the most advanced and progressive of ages" (Spiropoulou 2010: 140–143). She has also described the Benjaminian constellations between the now and then, the historical and the cultural that characterise Woolf's historiographical approach in her posthumously published novel. Closer to *The Years* because of its nostalgic mood, more temperate than *Three Guineas*, *Between the Acts* stages history as an "event" and a "spectacle" that offer their witnesses and spectators a past and present narrative to make sense of. The unfolding present and looming future being entwined in, and interrogated by, the chronicling of British cultural history, the audience's sense of identity and capacity to break off from inherited values and traditions is constantly exposed. Striving to move beyond the binaries of community and diversity, fragmentation and unity, isolation and belonging, discordance and harmony, Woolf's play-drama examines history from multiple distances and standpoints: the prehistoric past, British national history, the communal, national and international experiences of the "then" and "now." Each of these perspectives is displayed as culturally constructed, but never for the sake of an anticipated postmodernist emphasis on the essential instability of all facts and truths. In this respect, if *Between the Acts* is "an intensely self-reflexive work" (Wood 2015: 125), it also enacts, in its aesthetic, political and historiographical exploration, Miss La Trobe's undertaking: beyond the "play," its "performance," the failed "ruling" of its unfolding – these three words and their meanings being announced by the novel's title – the novel tests the author's and the playwright's capacity to "make [us] see," to make us change and to make us "act," even when we do not fully "grasp [...] the meaning" (*BA* 88; 180).

History and Causality

To "act" as a committed artist and intellectual, Woolf opened new regimes of history and historicity. As other women writers of her generation, she kept questioning "ongoing approaches to the cultural politics of war" and engendered "new forms of resistance" by testing "the ideological and aesthetic grounds of traditional genre definitions" (Lassner 1–2). As such, *The Years*, *Three Guineas* and *Between the Acts* build on her previous work, sharing a similar preoccupation with history as a field of knowledge, a "practice of meaning" and an "act of writing" (de Certeau 1988a: 6). Grounded in what Catherine Bernard calls a "critical empiricism of the here and now,"[34] Woolf's enquiry into the present times anticipates, again, some of the epistemological shifts or "turns" that have characterised historical thinking since the 1950s, and the renewed debates on narrative, memory, biography, material culture and gender studies that followed. Christine Reynier, Anna Snaith, Caroline Pollentier and Melba Cuddy-Keane, among others, have addressed the democratic, anti-imperialist and utopian dimensions of her political perspective over the period. In the wake of these important contributions, I would like to focus now on the rarely addressed connection between Woolf's frequent resort to why- and how-questions in the 1930s and the notion of historical causation. "The great historian," H.E. Carr explained in 1961, "– or perhaps I should say more broadly, the great thinker – is the man who asks the question, Why?, about new things or in new contexts." Confronted with a "list of causes of his own compiling," he establishes some hierarchy of causes which would fix their relation to one another, perhaps to decide which cause, or which category of causes, should be regarded [...] as the ultimate cause, the cause of all causes. This is his interpretation of his theme; the historian is known by the causes which he invokes. [...] Every historical argument revolves round the question of the priority of causes.

(Carr 83; 86)

Driven by her deeply anchored belief that "we cannot understand the present if we isolate it from the past" (*TP* 8), looking for the traces of history's afterlife and "didactic force" (Reynier 2018: 147),[35] Woolf kept being haunted by a "cause" – her feminist and pacifist agenda – and by her own reflection on "causality," a reflection that saw progress more as a utopian possibility than as an anchored belief.[36] This clearly appears in *The Years*, as was suggested earlier, and in *Three Guineas*, where the recurring use of the question, "why?" is echoed, this time, by the repeated occurrences of "because" and of expressions such as "the reasons why" or "for such reasons." Woolf's "causes" are well known, and she made them clear, understanding that

the relation of the historian to his causes has the same dual and recip-rocal character as the relation of the historian to his facts. The causes determine his interpretation of the historical process, and his inter-pretation determines his selection and marshalling of the causes.

(Carr 1961: 98)

But she also provides clear access to the tools she uses. In "Why Art To-Day Follows Politics," Woolf's method to answer the questions asked first implies the search for definitions: "we must try to define the relations of the artist to society" where "no such definition has ever been made." It also requires a reference to contexts (historical, economic and social), together with the use of ascertained facts and the search for explanatory "reasons" (*E VI* 75–79). In "Thoughts on Peace in an Air Raid," one of the questions raised is "What is it that prevents us [from being free]?" "Hitler!" comes as an easy explanation. But unchecked assumptions often miss the point, and the "cry with one voice" of "loudspeakers" can speak the undemocratic language of propaganda. Woolf, therefore, tests the theory first by "dra[gging it] into consciousness," then by offering her own explanation: "the desire for aggression; the desire to dominate and enslave." She does not stop here. The next step of her investigation is to listen to other "voices": the inner voice of present experience; the thoughts triggered off by this very experience in "the chambers of the brain"; the voice of breaking news and politicians; then the voice of a "young Englishman who fought in the last war" and whose testimony undercuts the current thinkers' belief "that by writing 'Disarmament' on a sheet of paper at a conference table they will have done all that is needful." Woolf also gives voice to the male soldier's instincts: "ancient instincts, instincts fostered and cherished by education and tradition." She does not dismiss the voices fed by "the emotion of fear and of hate" but counterbalances them by "the memory of other Augusts," which gives way to "more positive, reviving, healing and creative" thoughts: the kind of thoughts that enable the essayist to "act" by sending her "fragmentary notes to those," in America, who will "rethink them generously and charitably, perhaps shape them in something serviceable" (*E VI* 242–245). Woolf's interpretations are thus always inscribed within the framework of a conversation that takes into account her own historicity while refining and recasting the terms of the discussion. Similarly, Woolf's commitment to "the cause of peace" and "the cause of equality" in *Three Guineas* leans on a constant search for the evidence, proofs and reasoned facts susceptible to determine "the causes" that lead to war. And while the genre of the pamphlet determines its polemic tone, Woolf's thesis implies the dialogic structure that characterises her practice of the essay.

Obviously, the "knowledge" required to reach such an understanding of "causes" expands beyond the usual boundaries of historical analysis in the early twentieth century: in the course of her argument, Woolf gathers "political," "economic," "cultural," "racial," "psychological," "material," "physiological" and even "theological" factors, as well as data related to "sex" and "class" which she does not organise according to a coherent and linear time sequence.[37] What she presents as "causes," "reasons" and "explanations" would probably be dismissed by many scholars in the name of their discipline's definition of historical causation. The logic of cause and effects was indeed seen as depending either on the individual actions of "great men," or, from the late nineteenth century onwards, on "those general principles which govern the order of events" (Buckle 1857: 7). Contrary to most historians who wrote on the "origins of the Second World War," whether retrospectively or, more rarely, at the time of the impending conflict, Woolf's search for the forces which lay behind the change to come or already taking place do not include any of the two major theories developed in history books from the 1930s to the 1960s.[38] For the proponents of the "thirty-year war" thesis, the humiliation of the Germans, the instability of the peace settlement and "instability of Europe after 1919 rendered the outbreak of another war almost inevitable"; for the advocates of the "Hitler Thesis," among them British Historian G.P. Gooch,[39] there would have been no war without the "great depression and its dreadful consequence, the advent of Hitler," explains historian P.M.H. Bell (2007: 40; 51–52). Thus, in *Three Guineas*, Woolf does not address such subjects as diplomatic relationships, strategic alliances, military technology, armament race, the expansionism of Germany and Italy and other combined reasons. Not because she ignored all these factors but because, according to her, the origin of this war and of all forms of enslavement was patriarchal tyranny. As many "daughters of educated men who were called, to their resentment, 'feminists'," she wanted to show "that the tyrannies and servilities" of the public world "are the tyrannies and servilities" of the private world (*TG* 215). She also felt that she was uncovering and combatting a structure of power whose increased manifestations in the Victorian age would lead Michel Foucault (1990: 1–14) to speak of "We, 'Other Victorians'" in his introduction to the first volume of *The History of Sexuality*. In this respect, it might be tempting to compare Woolf's patriarchal hypothesis with Foucault's "repressive hypothesis" in terms of approach: both writers focus on the way a particular discourse acquires a status of knowledge; both enact a critical history that refuses the imposition of philosophical, meta-historical theories; both are interested in narratives of power and power-lessness themselves located in places usually ignored by historians such as images, instincts, emotions or consciousness. To that extent, Foucault's "prisons" are Woolf's "family homes." Whatever the forms it takes, Woolf's patriarchy, however, is not only a discursive object in a history of knowledge. She indeed examines domestic tyranny, political dictator-ship and imperialism within a history where "facts" matter: the "fact of education," the "fact of property," the "fact of that difference" between the sexes, all those facts "we are confronted with" and which, "whether we like them or not, we must face" (*TG* 138). Woolf's act of historical interpretation in the 1930s is thus grounded in a disruptive methodology, both empirical and epistemological, which uncovers the unwritten laws of legacy to envision the desire to "live differently" (*TG* 239).

Woolf's empiricism is manifest in the way she represents and records, in their own time sequencing, the lived experiences of her forebears and contemporaries. It can be seen in her observation of the minutiae of everyday life, in the way she makes her readers familiar with the sen-sory material of past and present realities, all combined with her fre-quent reliance on "history in the raw." It is rendered effective by her use of diverging and complementary viewpoints, by the inversion of the hierarchies of senses in *Flush*, by the play on diverse forms of historical distance in her essays and other novels. Woolf's empirical approach is obviously political. Anchored in her experience and readings as a woman, her inductive mode of reasoning and study of the repeated patterns of tyranny enabled her to find in the "atmosphere" of the private sphere the causes of oppression in the public sphere: "Atmosphere," she explains, "is one of the most powerful, partly because it is one of the most impalp-able, of the enemies with which the daughters of educated men have to fight" (*TG* 135). The obliterated history of patriarchal domination and the forgotten narratives of the reality of the home front are inferred from the specific cases, data and sources that Woolf wants to make visible to all. But Woolf's balanced empiricism is also, in itself, an epistemo-logical tool[40]: it relates back to eighteenth-century historiography with its emphasis on observation, and inductive method of reasoning. However, it challenges the Whigs' and the modernists' conceptions of historical archives characterised by the usual rejection of "secondary" sources such as personal memoirs or accounts written after the event under observation. As *Orlando* had suggested to its readers, the facts of history cannot be "pure"; they are always mediated by a historian who calls on them. Besides, as Woolf was well aware, the very historians who had insisted on the factuality of truth and the "pure" truth of facts had excluded women, as witnesses and agents, from the realm of written historical events.

Encapsulated in "Thoughts on Peace in an Air Raid," the epistemological value of Woolf's historiographical approach relies on three other major tools which guarantee its political and ethical dimensions: definition, contextualisation and conversation. The definitional work Woolf proposes consists in unpacking the "echoes," "memories," and "associations" of words in order to grasp the "many-sided" truth "they try to catch" (*E VI* 95). In the case of historical causation, she makes the task of the critic difficult: if she knew anything about the concept, she never mentioned it, in the same way as she had kept covering the traces of the process that led her to unwrite and rewrite historical traditions. On first examination, the terms that she uses in connection with the idea of causality – among them "reason," "explanation," "influence" and "cause" – are interchangeable. In *Three Guineas*, Woolf's argument appears to build on an ideological study of women's "influence" – or lack of – and of men's "force" in the sense of power, and not on a "historical" sequence of cause and effects. Thus again, her conception of causality seems inseparable from her "cause" and from the "number of causes that you [men] are championing" and that she challenges (*TG* 141). On closer examination, though, the haunting repetition of the words mentioned earlier is an act of writing that uncovers the unwritten laws of causality while arming her readers against the incapacity to break from the past. Woolf's use of the notion of "influence" is here a case in point. In *Three Guineas*, the noun and verb recur so often – 78 times – that one might want to consider understanding Woolf's anti-war pamphlet as a study in "influence" as in that it conditions, or prevents, the possibilities of change. This study begins with an ironic, almost Foucauldian "enquiry" concerned with women's "influence" as what should allow women to help prevent the war. But since rank, class, money, uniforms, property, university education and professions are the only proven "influences," Woolf reminds her addressee and readers, and since women have long been denied access to the power related to these "influences," how could they contemplate the idea of influencing anyone, men in particular? Woolf's enquiry then becomes a short history of women's slow, impeded emancipation, followed by a study of the weight of "memory and tradition" (*TG* 102) as the conscious and unconscious "forces" – the word is used in a polysemic way throughout *The Years* and *Three Guineas* – that perpetuate the structures of domination. In the course of her polemic argumentation, Woolf thus turns the language of patriarchy against itself. The "only weapon" against the war, she establishes, is an "independent opinion" and "the freedom from unreal loyalties" (*TG* 102; 159); real "power" is not "the power of medals, symbols, orders and even, it would seem, of decorated ink-pots to hypnotize the human mind" but "the power to change and the power to grow" (*TG* 190); the real "enemies" are not other nations, but the more "impalpable" and "unconscious" forces that defeat the aspirations to liberty.

To put to the test the ideas behind the use of words without pinning them down to one meaning, to understand their history and the contexts of their utterance are indispensable instruments of political awareness. If a man is educated as his father and his grandfather were, Woolf explains, and if he succeeds in his profession, then the words

> 'For God and Empire' will very likely be written, like the address on a dog-collar, round [his] neck. And if words have meaning, as words perhaps should have meaning, [he] will have to accept that meaning and do what [he] can to enforce it.
>
> (*TG* 152)

Literary craftsmanship, obviously, forbids any form of propaganda, especially if it takes into account historical contexts and historicity. Woolf's references to time and space contexts in her essays and fictions of the period is insistent. Her sense of her own position as "the daughter of a Victorian gentleman" has attracted criticism more than it has shed light on her method and ethics. The aim of the interrelation that she establishes between the present and the past, and in particular the Victorian age, enables her to further a deep understanding of both ages and to propose a guide to action grounded in the observation of repeated patterns. For this very reason, the "causes" that she supports and the particular type of "causality" she is interested in also need to be read in the context of the 1930s. Woolf indeed shared with Vera Brittain, Storm Jameson, Naomi Mitchison, Phyllis Bottome and other women writers of the period the wish to become agents of change; her analysis of the correspondences between the war within (at home) and the war without also finds striking echoes in their work; the certainty that "they had been warned" and that most historians, politicians and intellectuals had refused to listen is another common feature.[41] So is the eloquent reluctance, if not silence, with which the cultural work of these women has been considered: and yet, it might be argued that the question they raised in their own terms – how have we become what we are? – is still a valid reflection on historical causality.

"What is the use of history?" Marc Bloch remembers his son asking at the beginning of *The Historian's Craft*.[42] Before answering the question, the French *Annales* historian apologises for "the circumstances of [his] present life," not long after June 1940, "for the impossibility of reaching any large library, and the loss of [his] own books." In a context when the question had become "Are we to believe that history has betrayed us?," he explains that beyond its "entertainment value," history has a deeply "pragmatic" use: to "aid us live better," to "direct our actions" and to offer "guidance." Woolf's historical writing in the 1930s was grounded in the same urgent need and mission; it also shared Bloch's belief in the historian's "ability to promote action" (Bloch 1954: 3; 5–9). Her goal, in this respect, might have been unrealistic, or at best utopian. The war was not prevented, other wars are waged all other the world, and the patriarchal structures of power have not been dismantled. But at least her aspirations for a better future were sustained by a democratic vision of history: "without any statues or heroes but where traces of everyone feature" (Reynier 2018: 150). The democratic ethic of this vision relied on what I call the third epistemological pillar of her historiographical method: the interchange of ideas and texts that the aesthetic structure of her writing made possible. This "unending dialogue between the present and the past" that "evolves with the progressive emergence of new goals" (Carr 26; 119) is at the core of a political process of reinvention. As Melba Cuddy-Keane has convincingly shown,

> when Woolf focuses on recreating a historical context, her underlying [purpose] is comparative. She seeks out differences and commonalities between past and present to stimulate a contextual understanding of the past and to heighten her readers' awareness of their present positionalities. Paradoxically perhaps, she also suggests a transhistorical world that can be grasped as a collective whole.
>
> (Cuddy-Keane 2003: 151)

In the 1930s, these interactions and conversations took the form of "a shock therapy" that expectedly unleashed violent reactions. Interpellated as the "daughter of a Victorian gentleman," as the "Queen of highbrows," as a woman, who according to H.G. Wells and many other men, did not visibly participate in any "woman's movement to resist the practical obliteration of their freedom by Fascists or Nazis'" (*TG* 127), Woolf answered back, in the name of her struggling sisters and of all "the obscure." Using the power of her thoughts and words, she prompted her readers to acknowledge the crisis in historical consciousness, to envision the chaos to come while resisting communal passivity; she urged them, in fact, to continuously ask "why?"

Notes

1 Storm Jameson, *Civil Journey* (1939: 13).
2 Stephen Spender, untitled poem, 1933: "Who live under the shadow of a war / What can I do that matters / My pen stops, and my laughter, dancing, stops / Or ride to a gap" (Spender 1955: 21).
3 The reference is to W.B. Yeats' "Second Coming" (1921).
4 On this subject, see Majumdar and McLaurin, *Virginia Woolf: The Critical Heritage* (2003).

5 The reference is here to Woolf's answer to Harold Nicolson's description of her work, and of Joyce's, Lawrence's and Eliot's in a BBC radio broadcast: "Lord—how tired I am of being caged" (*L IV* 402).

6 Barbara Lounsberry (2018): *Virginia Woolf: The War Without, The War Within: Her Final Diaries & the Diaries She Read.*

7 The reference is to her signed essay "A Letter to a Young Poet," published in July 1932 in the *Yale Review* (*E V* 315).

8 See Ethel Smyth, *Female Pipings in Eden* (1933: 17).

9 See "Speech to the London and National Society for Women's Service" (*E V* 635–648).

10 On January 20, 1935, Woolf writes in her diary:

> I have this moment, while having my bath, conceived an entire new book— a sequel to A Room of One's Own—about the sexual life of women: to be called Professions for Women perhaps—Lord how exciting! This sprang out of my paper to be read on Wednesday to Pippa's society.
>
> (*D IV* 6)

See also Naomi Black (2004: 54–58).

11 The Strachey family, females and males, were very involved in the campaign for the Suffrage; Ray was the secretary of Millicent Garrett Fawcett.

12 See note 2, Chapter 1, in *A Room* (*AR* 16).

13 Anna Snaith's 2015 edition of *Three Guineas* and complete bibliography of the works cited in the essay are here revealing.

14 This Intellectual Liberty Group was the British Wing of the French, anti-Fascist "Comité de Vigilance."

15 On this episode, see Bishop (1989: 175) and Lee (1997: 678–679).

16 On this subject, see Peter Wilson (2003).

17 Rebecca West, "The Event and Its Image" (1962), quoted in O'Malley (2015: x).

18 A quote from William Faulkner's *Requiem for a Nun* (1951) serving as the epigram of Raphael Samuel's preface in *Theatres of Memory* (Samuel 2012: vii).

19 For more references, see *The Cambridge Companion to the British Literature of the 1930s* (Smith 2019).

20 Influenced by German historicism and advocating a rapprochement of philosophy and history, R.G. Collingwood wrote, after 1933, an undated manuscript entitled "History as the Understanding of the Present" in which he stated that "The ultimate aim of history is not to know the past but to understand the present" (Collingwood 1934: 140). According to Timothy Garton Ash, the phrase "history of the present" was "coined by the veteran American diplomat and historian George Kennan in a review of [his] book about Central Europe in the 1980s, *The Uses of Adversity*," as the description of Ash's project combining "the crafts of historian and journalist" (Ash 2009: xiv).

21 Vera Brittain, *The Honourable Estate* (1936), quoted in Lassner (1998: 13).

22 These articles ("The Docks of London," "Oxford Street Tide," "Great Men's Houses," "Abbeys and Cathedrals," "This is the House of Commons" and "Portrait of a Londoner") were published between December 1931 and December 1932. In *Virginia Woolf's Good Housekeeping Essays* (2018),

Christine Reynier reassesses their cultural, intermedial and aesthetic value in the context of the 1930s and of Woolf's modernist and democratic practice of the essay.

23 The main historical allusions to present facts are: the mention of Prime Minister of France Daladier "pegging down the franc," the rape of a young girl by three English soldiers, the allusion to the Jewish refugees. On this subject, see Wood (2015: 125–126).

24 Woolf declined the invitation of the editor of the *New Statesman*, being engrossed in the writing of *Three Guineas* (*L VI* 172).

25 Quoted in Lassner (1998: 1).

26 In France, the Institut d'Histoire du Temps Présent was founded in 1978 by François Bédarida.

27 Lewis Namier, "Pathological Nationalism" (21–26), and "Germany: Arms and Aims" (27–35), *In The Margin of History* (1939).

28 In the same period of time, G.M. Macaulay published *England Under Queen Anne* (3 vols., 1930–1934) and *The English Revolution, 1688–1698* (1938); R.G. Collingwood, *Roman Britain and the English Settlements* (1936), Herbert Butterfield, *The Whig Interpretation of History* (1931), a short biography of Napoleon (1939) and *The Statecraft of Machiavelli* (1940).

29 In *The Holocaust and the Historians* (1997), Dawidowicz mentions the historians of modern Germany Allan Bullock (1914–2004), A.J.P. Taylor (1906–1990) and H.R. Trevor Roger (1914–2003); she also evokes Woolf's diplomat and historian friend Harold Nicolson, in whose attitude "snobbery and anti-Semitism" were not unusually "coupled" (Dawidowicz 31–32).

30 In her chapter on women's history and historiography between 1900 and 2000, (2001), Billie Melman provides several elements of explanations for what can be seen as a contrast between the number of women writing about their experiences of the present and the few scholarly historical works on the subjects of women as a group, or on women in the interwar years. In spite of the emergence of professional women's history around the turn of the century and the rising interest in economic and social history, Melman explains that until the 1950s "modern history was highly gendered in its selection and use of documents, privileging of subjects and even in the construction of the identity of the historian" (Melman 2001: 16). Among those subjects were constitutional history, legal history and high diplomacy, fields related to the emergence of the nation-sate from which women were excluded. Women historians in the 1920s and 1930s often specialised in medieval history – Helen Cam is a renowned example here – or in economic history, and yet, they hardly ever published on the subject of women as a group, except for British economic and social historian Ivy Pinchbeck in *Women Workers and the Industrial Revolution, 1750–1850* (1930).

31 On history and "scientific objectivity" since the nineteenth century, see Georg Iggers, *Historiography in the Twentieth Century: From Scientific Objectivity to the Postmodern Challenge* (2005).

32 In this letter to Julian Bell, dated October 25, 1935, Woolf recounts how

> Janie [Bussy] brought M. Walter round here, imploring us intellectuals to stand by the French anti-fascists. And now Charles Mauron wants us to go to a conference in Paris. And then there will be the general Election.

> But I gather that politics are best avoided; and in any case my views are likely to be inaccurate and perhaps partial—all politics be damned.

François Walter was editor of the French journal *Vigilance*.

33 The words come from a violent attack on *Three Guineas* in one of the most feminist newspapers of the English Press – "Blame it on Bloomsbury" – dated August 17, 2002, which English Cultural critic Theodore Dalrymple concludes by explaining that

> Had Woolf survived to our time, however, she would at least have had the satisfaction of observing that her cast of mind – shallow, dishonest, resentful, envious, snobbish, self-absorbed, trivial, philistine, and ultimately brutal – had triumphed among the elites of the western world.
>
> (www.theguardian.com/books/2002/aug/17/classics. highereducation. [Accessed June 2, 2020])

34 Catherine Bernard, to be published.

35 On Woolf's vision of history as "trace" (or "survival of the past in the present"), see Christine Reynier's chapter in *Virginia Woolf's Good Housekeeping Essays*, "Constructing History as Trace," and her reference to Paul Ricœur, Marc Bloch and Jacques Rancière:

> Such history would recognize those that French philosopher Guillaume le Blanc calls the 'invisible' ones in *L'Invisibilité sociale*. It would be democratic and in keeping with the 'democratic helter skelter [...] of the street' (303), 'the humdrum democratic disorder of the hurrying street' (304) evoked in the essay; rather than being monolithic, it would allow for a plurality of voices – those we hear in her last novel, *Between the Acts*.
>
> (Reynier 2018: 147–150; 149)

36 Edward Hallett Carr's belief in a historically determined progress differs from Woolf's vision. "Man is capable of profiting (not that he necessarily profits) by the experience of his predecessors," Carr wrote, so that "progress in history, unlike evolution in nature, rests on the transmission of acquired assets" (Carr 1961: 117). It is precisely these "acquired assets," when underpinned by patriarchal culture, that Woolf aimed at deconstructing for change to happen.

37 These eight adjectives are used in Woolf's text.

38 On this subject, see P.M.H. Bell's, "On War and the Causes of War," in *The Origins of the Second World War in Europe* (2007: 12–23).

39 See G.P. Gooch, "The coming of the war," *Contemporary Review*, July 9, 1940.

40 In *Empiricism and History*, Stephen Davies explains that contrary to general thought, empiricism is not an intuitive method of research but a "doctrine of epistemology" that has been shared by historians "for the last 200 years at least," although this doctrine has long "remained undertheorized" (Davies 2003: 1).

41 On Naomi Mitchison's censored *We Have Been Warned* (1935), Vera Brittain's historical novel *The Honourable Estate* (1936), Phyllis Bottome's anti-Fascist novel *The Mortal Storm* (1937) and Storm Jameson's *No Victory for the Soldier*, a modernist novel on the Spanish Civil War (as James Hill – 1938),

see Phyllis Lassner's *British Women Writers of World War II: Battlegrounds of Their Own* (1998).

42 The English translation of French Historian Marc Bloch's *Apologie pour l'histoire ou Métier d'historien* (1949), written between 1940 and 1943, was published in 1954. With Lucien Febvre, Bloch was a founder of the Annales School of French Social History. Born to an Alsatian Jewish family, he joined the French Resistance in 1942, and was captured and shot by the Germans in 1944. In 1934, Bloch was invited to speak at the London School of Economics where he met historians Eileen Power and R.H. Tawney. Before the 1960s, English historiography tended to discard the method of the "Annalistes," their focus on the diversity of human experience, and the way they used the insights of other social sciences. Although E.H. Carr was not an Annales historian, some of his pronouncements testify to the links between his "new history" and theirs. In *What is History*, he thus explains:

> since the preoccupation with economic and social ends represents a broader and more advanced stage in human development than the pre-occupation with political and constitutional ends, so the economic and social interpretation of history may be said to represent a more advanced stage in history than the exclusively political interpretation. The old inter-pretation is not rejected, but is both included and superseded in the new.
>
> (Carr 1961: 120)

Part II

Virginia Woolf's Unwritten Literary Histories

5   The Critic as Historiographer
Blurring Illusory Boundaries

I […] describe myself as a journalist who wants to read history.[1]

Just as Woolf was aware of the literary condition of history, she knew that literature was bound to a field of historical conversations. In her case, therefore, to distinguish the critic from the historiographer is as "fatal" as the "distinction" she refused to make between life and literature.[2] And yet, while her interest in the history of literature started at an early age and never faltered, and in spite of the recent scholarship on Woolf's historical thinking, little has been written on Virginia Woolf's conception and practice of literary history. Twenty years after Beth Carole Rosenberg expressed her surprise at this neglect, the situation has changed only marginally.[3] Several explanations can be offered. First, Woolf never wrote a full-length literary history. Working outside the academy, she was never asked, and probably would not have wanted, to produce a manual or textbook in the wake of Sir Walter Raleigh, George Saintsbury and Hugh Walker. She conceived the two volumes of *CR* as collections of revised and reprinted essays organised chronologically but was uncertain about its "main line" (*D II* 61); she planned "Phases of Fiction" as a "book" of criticism – "something to do with prose & poetry in novels" (*D III* 50) – but it was finally published in the *Bookman* as a signed essay in three installments, which inevitably blurred its diachronic dimension. As to Woolf's project to write a "history of English literature" (*D III* 297), it resulted in the two unfinished chapters edited by Brenda Silver in 1979: "Anon" and "The Reader." In addition, some of Woolf's observations on the amateur reader that she claimed to be when compared with the admirable examples of "writer-critics" in the shadow of whom she stood – "The Dryden, the Johnson, the Coleridge, the Arnold" (*E IV* 235) – have often been taken at face value.[4] Maria DiBattista's rather dismissive chapter on Woolf in the *Cambridge History of Literary Criticism*, for example, seems to rely on the confusion between Woolf's statements and the actual value of her contribution: "[Woolf's] criticism, as she openly confessed, was of the grosser sort, adulterated by personal likings and aversions, alloyed by doubts and perplexities" (DiBattista 2000: 122).

DOI: 10.4324/9780429331787-8

Only with the emergence of feminist criticism in the 1970s did Woolf acquire the status of a literary historian. However, critics have mostly attached her "revisionist," or "counter-literary histories," to one or several canonical texts – *A Room of One's Own*, *Orlando* or *Between the Acts* – to one literary period, for example, the Renaissance, to one specific genre, or to the influence of particular writers such as George Eliot or Walter Pater.[5] In the 1990s, when scholars began to explore Woolf's corpus of essays extensively, they addressed questions of literary history in discrete ways without trying to reach a more encompassing vision of Woolf's take on literary history. Melba Cuddy-Keane's "Woolf and the Variety of Historicist Experiences" is still a short but valuable exception.[6] In other words, the substantial, yet fragmented, aspect of Woolf's critical output as an essayist, along with the apparent absence of any clear theoretical line, may have hindered any attempt at synthesis.

Thus, for someone as eminent in the field as Stefan Collini, Woolf belongs with John Middleton Murry, Desmond MacCarthy, Cyril Connolly, Rebecca West and V.S. Pritchett to the category of "journalist criticism," not to the generation of "prominent literary critics" that includes T.S. Eliot, F.R. Leavis, William Empson and I.A. Richards (Collini 2019: 1). The issue here is not gender, since Collini writes a chapter on Queenie Leavis, but of status: Woolf, he implies, simply did not influence the following generations of literary critics in a meaningful way.[7] Last but not least, one can explain the relatively few studies devoted to Woolf as a literary historian by the fact that contrary to "literary criticism," "literary history" has come under attack since the late nineteenth century from various angles and for different reasons. In the course of the twentieth century, Collini states,

> literary history in its scholarly forms has come to seem like the eternal poor relation, an inescapably boring, subordinate activity. It lacks the allure of literary criticism [...] but it also lacks the reach and power of what in the first half of the twentieth century was usually referred to as 'general history'—what its advocates are sometimes prone to think of as 'real history'—or what in disciplinary terms is just classed as 'History'.
>
> (Collini 13)

Published in 1992, *Is Literary History Possible?* grounds itself in the same observation. In his introduction, David Perkins (1992: 1–7) retraces the history of a discipline that used to enjoy "popularity and unquestionable prestige" until the 1890s when it was contested for its "inadequate and reductive" conception of literature first by fin-de-siècle critics such as Edmond Scherer, then by the Russian Formalists and the early twentieth-century New Critics. With the flourishing of social, cultural, institutional, regional or national histories in the last decades of the twentieth century, along with the emancipation of formerly marginalised voices and communities, literary history, he explains, has now regained its former central position in literary studies although it is shaped by various schools of criticism – "hermeneutic philosophy, [...] cultural anthropology, sociology, communications theory, and cultural semiotics." And yet, Perkins, who is one of the few theoreticians in the field, writes a book in which he keeps wondering whether the "discipline can be intellectually respectable" (12).

Given this context, to look at Woolf as a literary historian means to reconcile, or at least to reassess, two apparently conflicting approaches to her work. As a critic, she has long been, and is probably still now, considered dispensable for modernist scholarship; however, her feminist readers and commentators think of her as the indispensable foremother of a female revisionist tradition that she herself created. The premises of the first view used to be that her critical work was too "impressionist" – not theoretical enough – to have had the equivalent imprint on English criticism as her renowned male contemporaries'.[8] The proponents of the second view see her as a radical innovator, one who Margaret Ezell finds dangerously prescriptive when she evokes the "evolutionary pattern of female authorship proposed by Virginia Woolf in *A Room of One's Own*" later on adopted by Showalter, Moers, Gilbert and Gubar, and others (Ezell 1996: 22). The figure of the "literary historian" as it evolved from the eighteenth century onwards adds another difficulty to any appraisal of Woolf's contribution. Like historians, literary historians before the 1920s were mostly male academics: the idea of Woolf as a "literary historian" is bound to come with an insistence, again, on her vexed relationship with her forefathers and with the institution of English studies – one that gives little room for an assessment of her singular modernity as a critic and historiographer. This question echoes the conundrum that has already been explored: Woolf's commitment to speak as a woman while situating herself in a male tradition that she constantly engages with is an inescapable fact. That she herself became a point of departure for a female tradition of literary criticism is another. A third essential fact is that she always refused to be "caged" in any of the categories that some of her male contemporaries claimed for themselves – "the critic," "the Professor" or the "literary historian" – by adopting the posture of the outsider. At any rate, Woolf, again, makes the task of the "common" reader more difficult. Her work requires from him or her to be her "fellow worker" and "accomplice" (*E IV* 390), to piece the "orts, scraps and fragments" together (*BA* 169), compare and contextualise, before any form of judgement is passed – a method that she herself advocates in "How Should One read A Book" (*E IV* 390–400). In the end, one may want to argue that Woolf resisted both theory as the "new," essential tool of literary criticism, and literary history as an academic discipline, an assumption that could reduce her own "creative criticism" to a series of unrelated essays and counter-discourses.

Before any attempt at a conclusion, however, and because Woolf saw heritage and history as sites of either dangerous reverence or potential empowerment, we need to disentangle the threads of her legacy as a reader, reviewer and essayist – one who kept alluding to the "centralising influence" of the writer-critics of the past as opposed to the lack of "giant[s] of fabulous dimensions" in her own age (*E IV* 235–236). Those threads are themselves woven into the evolution of general history in the nineteenth- and twentieth centuries. In that respect at least, Woolf anticipates Wellek, Perkins and Collini's shared conviction that historiography, literary history and literary criticism are intertwined fields of knowledge, and that there is no particular moment that is not already historical. Woolf never makes the case of these interactions explicit in her essays. And yet, at the very moment when specialisation and polarisation seemed to prevail, these interactions and tensions are precisely what she invites us to examine and make sense of. As a reader trained in history, she learned how to "move across the lands" of her predecessors and contemporaries, "poaching" from them as an act of anti-conformism and reappropriation (de Certeau 1988b: 174); as an essayist and fiction writer, she questioned dominant discourses while constantly blurring common historical and cultural contrasts between the past and the present; as a committed intellectual, she lay the groundwork for new generations and the books she saw on the horizon by assessing both pragmatically and politically the past as a legacy and the present as an unfolding history. The goal of the following chapters is, therefore, threefold: to examine Woolf's hereditary position in English letters from the lens of her place as a reader; to explore her immersion in the literary past as "her treck to a better literature" (Zemgulys 2008 Chapter 6).[9] Above all, I propose a picture of Woolf as a critic and historiographer that reads in context the apparent contradictions of its subject: coherent but multifarious, pragmatic and utopian, feminist yet interested in other genealogies than female literary families, "cut off from [her] predecessors" yet feeling estranged from her contemporaries, reinventing cultural continuities while being intent on the necessities of change.

Two Histories

What was left then of literary history in its Victorian guises when Joel Spingarn, the spokesman of a whole generation of English and American scholars and critics, expressed scepticism on the subject in a lecture delivered at Columbia University in 1910:

> We have done with all the old Rules. [...] We have done with genres, or literary kinds [...]. We have done with the comic, the tragic, the sublime, and an army of vague abstractions of their kind. [...] We have done with the race, the time, and the environment of a poet's work as an element of criticism. To study these phases of a work of art is to treat it as a historic or social document, and the result is a

contribution to the history of culture and civilization, with only a
subsidiary interest in the history of art?

(Spingarn 1911: 20–31)[10]

In the early twentieth century, the consensus among critics seems to have
been that the continuity between the nascent eighteenth-century tradition of literary historical writing and its established form in the nineteenth century was broken. The rise and fall of literary history from its
beginnings in the eighteenth century to its replacement by criticism and
theory in the early decades of the twentieth century is a story that echoes
the evolution of history with regards to the organisation of knowledge
over the same period – one that takes us from a random form of empiricism, through the rise of professionalisation, and towards the modernist
and scientific "turn" described in Chapter 1 of this book.

In Britain, the last decades of the Age of Enlightenment had seen the
growth of English literary history as a "slow process" which was only
possible when "biography and criticism coalesced, and when, under
the influence of political historiography, the narrative form began to
be used" (Wellek 1941: 1).[11] In the mid-eighteenth century, literary history addressed a multiple and heterogenous readership, in a variety of
forms – from antiquarian research to literary lives, collective biographies,
poetry series, anthologies and memoirs – and its creative effervescence
was nourished by debates on the interrelations between literature, social
development, and cultural heritage.[12] A commonly shared narrative of
these beginnings tells us that this diversity of agendas, modes of writing
and forms of dissension gave way to a more unified conception of
British literary history from 1800 onwards, as more restrictive attitudes
to an audience that gradually welcomed inexperienced readers accompanied the gradual division of literature into specific fields of knowledge.
According to April London, the "formative conditions" of this transition
at the turn of the nineteenth century comprise the end of a patronage
culture, the emergence of professional authorship, the commodification
of literature and the rising anxieties concerning its reception. As a result,
literary history lost part of its power as a "regenerative form" enabling
the "cultivation of opinion" and an "enhanced access to the literary past"
(London 2010: 5–6).

The diminishing prestige of literary history after 1810 might sound
paradoxical if we recall that the nineteenth century was the time
of the dominion of history as an academic discipline and of "historical mindedness" as a form of cultural obsession with the past. As it
weaves the threads of general history's and literary history's unfolding,
David Perkins's account of the Victorian age confirms the idea of a shift
from disorganised proliferation in the eighteenth century to increasing
order and homogeneity under the authority of new personalities with
new convictions. He thus explains that in the 1780s, three fundamental

assumptions characterised literary history: "that literary works are formed by their historical context; that change in literature takes place developmentally; and that this change is the unfolding of an idea, principle, or suprapersonal entity" such as genres, the "spirit of an age," the characteristics of a race, region, people or nation as expressed in its literature – just as "nations, religions and classes" were suprapersonal entities in general history. "As a synthesis of history and criticism," he adds, "literary history seemed more powerful, for some purposes, than either discipline" (Perkins 1992: 1–3). Most literary historians, therefore, conceived their histories of literature in developmental terms with few turning points or new beginnings. Chronology, periodisation, "shapes" or types – today "genres" – became essential features of those narratives which expressed concise visions of artists and their work according to a shared system of standards and conventions. Beyond national specificities, Perkins argues, these characteristic features were common across Europe as Taine's *History of English Literature* (1863), Francesco de Sanctis's *History of Literature* (1870–1871) and George Saintsbury's *Short History of English Literature* (1898) attest (Perkins ibid.).

Focusing on Britain, Stefan Collini takes a more psychological and ideological angle when he examines the stability of literary history as discipline and genre in the mid-nineteenth century. British "confidence" and "pride in ancestry," he suggests, explain the "celebratory mode" of Victorian literary history which "replicated and confirmed the Whig story as narrated by the 'general' historians" (Collini 2019: 4). This was indeed a time when men of letters and Victorian "sages" had a large readership and were not yet replaced by professional scholars. They wrote full-length studies, textbooks, surveys, reviews in various periodicals and believed in the humanistic aspect of culture. Their relationship to their educated audience was more important than any school of criticism or methodological argument. Their belief in the purpose and progress of history led them to trace the spiritual, moral and intellectual influence of the past as it was being transformed by what they saw as a beneficial continuing change. At that time, there were few debates, if any, on the difference between literary criticism and history, and no expression of surprise when gentlemen scholars or writers such as George Henry Lewes, Leslie Stephen, Andrew Lang or Edmund Gosse – to name a few – addressed subjects other than literature.

The humanistic mission ascribed to the study of the literary past began to be questioned in the 1880s, when Britain was still plunged in what had prompted Matthew Arnold to write *Culture and Anarchy* in 1869, three years after the Hyde Park riots. In those times of social and political unrest, Arnold's conviction that the cultivation of human perfection through the arts and that a state-administered system of education would encourage free-thinking and national unity sounded like an act of faith. What Linda Dowling calls "the tradition of Whig aesthetics," this "polis of the mind or spirit where people become, through the experience of art, literature and ideas, the better selves that had before lain underdeveloped due to the accidents of social circumstances," came under attack or was at least threatened by contrary impulses (Dowling 1996 2–3). The individualism and libertarianism that Arnold had tried to counter by turning to a new politics of culture was reaffirmed, in different ways, by the Aesthetic Movement and its attempts to move away from politics and from a long tradition of social criticism. Walter Pater's anti-Victorian brand of aestheticism in his *Studies in the Renaissance*, and Oscar Wilde's provocative aphorisms – "No artist has ethical sympathies" and "All art is quite useless" are a few famous examples – made it clear that for the proponents of Art for Art's Sake the chief function of criticism was no longer to follow Matthew Arnold and "try books as to the influence which they are calculated to have upon the general culture of single nations or of the world at large" (Arnold 1862: 41).

Other changes and forms of polarisation marked the fin-de-siècle period. The new antagonism between the professional scholar and the "amateur" critic, itself the result of the recent academic professionalism, is one of them. From the 1880s onwards, the "twin process of professionalization and specialization," Josephine M. Guy and Ian Small explain, gradually removed cultural authority from the figure of the Victorian sage, while literary criticism was assigned a lesser role in educated debates (Guy and Small 1993: 379). As the scientific paradigm informed all fields of knowledge, cultural and scientific expertise became associated with formal procedures and normative standards of analysis and evaluation. For literary critics and scholars, this meant, for example, a mandatory reliance on literary facts – among them biographical evidence and bibliographical data – as opposed to subjective opinions. The first consequence of this new organisation of knowledge was the prestige ascribed to academic professionals at the expense of "amateur" critics. Whether in science or in humanities, authority came to rest on scientific guidance more than on the individual aesthetic judgement of writer-critics and men of letters. Literary scholars shared their work and expertise in specialist academic journals or during university lectures, more particularly in the new scholarly forms – systematic and comprehensive – of literary histories mapped according to subject areas and periods, or of anthologies built on canon formation.[13] Those scholarly works also solidified the idea that professional research, education and university training provided the best introduction to judgements on literary value. There lay the "truths" that readers had previously looked for in the enlightened judgement of one individual critic.[14]

The process of professionalisation and specialisation resulted in another form of polarisation. Literary history and criticism began to lose their concern for the general public as the Victorian readership became larger and more diversified, leading to a deepening of the divide between high and popular culture. Conversely, common readers no longer turned to literary critics to form an opinion on cultural and social issues. At the turn of the century, though, "amateur" critics – whether practising writers, nonacademic journalists or men of letters – still existed: many of them tried to belie Algernon's satirical remark addressed to Jack in *The Importance of Being Earnest*: "literary criticism is not your forte my dear fellow. Don't try it. You should leave that to people who haven't been at a University" (Wilde 1965: 35). In the wake of Matthew Arnold, Leslie Stephen or George Saintsbury, they did not think that "criticism must be of all things 'scientific'," nor that "generalisations" and "laws" are possible in literature; they still believed in the moral foundations of all literary judgements and in literature's cohesive function (Saintsbury 1896a: xii–xiii).

As they introduce the seventh volume of *The Cambridge History of Literary Criticism*, Louis Menand and Lawrence Rainey evoke the double requirement that continued to characterise literary criticism and literary history in the first decades of the twentieth century: on the one hand, "a professionalising economy and an intellectual culture obsessed with the promise of pure science pushed the university towards a research mission and a vocational mission in the decades around the turn of the century"; on the other, a growing number of "common" readers began to look for experts to help them discriminate among the available books and art-istic products (Menand and Rainey 2000: 10). On first examination, and perhaps for this very reason, the 1910s saw a widening of the divisions mentioned earlier: whether among men of letters and professors; between academic readers and a wider audience; between general culture and a professionalised university, last but not least, between literary history and literary theory. Inside and outside the academic arena, the time had definitely come for new critical practices centring more narrowly on the distinctive character of literary language: like "modernist" history, mod-ernist criticism thus found "new methodologies geared to a scientific age" (Bentley 2005: 119).

The story of the emergence and development of literary theory and the New Criticism in the first half of the twentieth century on the other side of the Atlantic has been told many times. Anyone interested in the status of literary history at the time Woolf was writing needs to take this into account, along with its different versions in America and Britain. Often seen as an ideological battle opposing literary criticism to more traditional historical scholarship, what Morris Dickstein describes as "machinery for the production of close readings" was, he argues, never institutionalised in England as it was in the United States. Among the reasons for this contrasted diffusion and influence, Dickstein mentions the long, rich history of British literary journalism, the role of the critic as a guardian of literary value, the slower growth of higher education "with its need for a new mass pedagogy," along with the nation's "more ingrained, more conservative sense of the past" (Dickstein 1992: 131). Nonetheless, one can see how T.S. Eliot's influence on F.R. Leavis and

I.A. Richards derived from his own anti-impressionistic, rigorous and "formalist" method departing both from journalistic amateurism and Victorian historicism. To return to Spingarn's manifesto, it appears, therefore, that the 1920s indeed marked the end of the "logical absurdity" of literary history "when its data are not organically related but cut up in sections"; of the "theory of style" which has nothing to do with the artistic "expression"; of the "standards of ethics" used to test literature and, obviously, of the "evolution of literature" and its corollaries: periodisation, classification, theories of continuity and changes (Spingarn 1911: 21–32). Likewise, the relationship between the canon of national literature and the "spirit of the age" was largely dismissed: if history was contingent and no enlightened personality could embody authority, then literary criticism could no longer claim access to the social and cultural significance of a work of art. At a moment when the notions of discontinuity and "contrast" between periods, audiences and areas of knowledge dominated both the fields of history and literary studies, the threads between those two disciplines paradoxically appear to have been broken.[15] Strikingly, though, Woolf's essays in criticism prove otherwise. In fact, they rather corroborate Collini's thesis that "even the supposedly 'purest' or more formalist versions of literary criticism always, in practice, depended upon and secreted various types of historical understanding" (Collini 2019: 23).

"A Great Critic is the Rarest of Beings"[16]

Compared to the evolution of "general history" over the same period, the short narrative of literary history from its emergence to its marginalisation as a praised form of literary criticism and replacement by literary "theory" is not surprising. Along with the shifts in Britain's politics of knowledge and education, the transformations of material culture and readership constitute the backdrop to these intertwined stories which, when told as such, tend to foreground a teleological unfolding, expected turning points, a series of increased polarisations and divisions, and, for the sake of clarity, a homogenised version of each different age. Thus, British "romantic" writer-critics such as Coleridge or Carlyle – often mentioned by Woolf – do not appear to form a specific category in the nineteenth-century chapter. Similarly, this synthetic account does not take into consideration the evolving role of "reviewers" as critics – a subject that Woolf addressed in her 1939 essay on "Reviewing" (*E VI* 195–209). Another characteristic here is the absence of women contributors to English historiography prior to the 1920s: Clara Reeves's *The Progress of Romance* or Charlotte Stopes's *Shakespeare's Warwickshire Contemporaries* 1907, to give a few examples, do not appear in Wellek's or Perkins's works. Like Woolf after them, women historiographers were neither academics, nor literary historians in the traditional sense of the word; feminist scholars have just begun to recover and examine their historical biographies, fictions and amateur works of criticism.[17] Woolf's knowledge of this timeline, of its specific terminology, historiographical exclusions and unobserved overlaps appears in her reviews and essays, always incidentally, a cogent indication that we might want to look, again, for a more thickly layered approach to her exploration of past legacy and present influences.

Read in the light of this linear narrative, Virginia Woolf appears to belong neither to her age nor to the past. At first glance, her conception of the role of the critic, who, she kept asserting, needs to address both the "common reader" and the contemporary writer, bears no direct affinities with eighteenth-century empiricism and antiquarianism, nor does it seem to have been influenced by whig cultural historicism. As to literary "theory" and the "New Criticism" in its various modalities, she did not hesitate to dismiss its methods – "every work of art can be taken to pieces, and those pieces can be named and numbered, divided and sub-divided, and given their order of precedence, like the internal organs of a frog" – and refuse its "wonder-pills" (*E III* 43–45). Woolf's deep frustration with both literary history as an academic discipline and contemporary literary criticism is a recurring feature of her essays. Many begin with a dire assessment of a present situation characterised by the absence of models and the loss of proper guidance: "our age is meagre on the verge of destitution," she asserts in "How It Strikes a Contemporary. [...] There is no name which dominates the rest, no master in whose workshop the young are proud to serve apprenticeship" (*E IV* 236). As she reviews the works of critics and scholars, Woolf usually acknowledges the difficulties they are faced with and their efforts to offer a "rule, a discipline" to "the great republic of readers." But their failure, in fact the failure of almost all critics after Matthew Arnold, is the unmistakable reflection of a chaotic, "barren and exhausted age" that finds reassurance in an idealised past, or in the false remedies of the present (*E IV* 235; 237).[18] In such a context, a true critic, according to Woolf, should manifest those few essential qualities that she keeps emphasising: the "courage" to face his contemporaries (*E II* 256) and voice his opinions, a form of authority that refuses arrogance and literary doctrines, a "love of books" manifested in the generous "support" of artists (*E II* 67); last but not least, the humble acceptance that the aim can only be to "frame tentative outlines of belief, always shifting and modifying their terms as we read" to provide "material" for the "great critic to build with when he comes" (*E II* 324).

That such a figure is nowhere to be found is a fact that Woolf regrets, always with deep concern, sometimes using a form of delightful irony or more cruel sarcasm. A reviewer cannot be a "great" critic – or at least a valuable one – because the

> review has become an expression of individual opinion, given without any attempt to refer to 'eternal standards' by a man who is in a hurry;

who is pressed for time; [...] who is bothered by the knowledge that he is not fulfilling his task; who is doubtful what that task is.

It is, therefore, "a public duty to abolish" him, Woolf concludes (*E VI* 198–199). Her perspective is less severe when she speaks of the value of "men of letters" in the tradition of the gentleman scholar or the writer-critic: according to the personalities whose work she comments upon, her judgement is more nuanced. Very few in this loose category, however, meet her entire approval. Arthur Symons, whose stimulating criticism is grounded in his "love of books" and the belief that "art is undoubtedly a part of life as bread, or air" (*E II* 68–69) is one of them.[19] George Moore is another: when he speaks about others' books, he lights up their "pages" and "faces" partially, but so "warmly and brightly" that those pages, along with "the engrossed and ardent countenance of the writer himself," appear to us clearly, suddenly made vividly present in a manner that recalls romantic historiographers (*E III* 119).[20] In the previous generations, Woolf explains, nobody could compete with Coleridge or Arnold. Nineteenth-century men of letters like Alfred Ainger were often interested in "ethical rather than aesthetic" ideas; they were tempted to "use [their] knowledge of a man's life to interpret his work" (*E I* 83; 85).[21] In Patmore's case, "judgements upon doctrines set beyond the reach of accident and temperament" replaced "impressionist criticism." But Patmore "was content to state his principle and shut the door," some of his "oracular" statements remaining barren for lack of real discussion (*E III* 310–311).[22] Others, like William Ernest Henley, proved that they hardly differed from their eighteenth-century predecessors especially when their method consisted in relying on "biography, psychology, and criticism all squeezed together" (*E III* 285).[23] As to professors and scholars of Walter Raleigh's generation, at best, they touched their subject "with life," discarding "those convenient but indigestible little pellets which between them have made the history of literature about as interesting as Bradshaw" (*E II* 73).[24] At worst, the "adventure of creation [was] unknown" to them. This, she explains, "is because their task was not to br[reak] down barriers," so that their "tightly academic books" never went "outside the critical fence" (*E IV* 343–344).[25] Fortunately, if there were traces of the "pedagogue" in Saintsbury or in Raleigh – who, at least, plotted fiction's "family history with scrupulous skill" (*E IV* 457) – there was not "any trace of the dictator" about them (*E V* 145).

What Woolf often saw as misplaced arrogance and superiority – her representation of Clayton Hamilton as a vociferating "professor on a platform exhorting the peasants" to come up and buy a "diagram" or his "long Latin words" to cure their "disease" is one of her most remarkable caricatures (*E III* 43) – obviously disgruntled her for personal and ideological reasons.[26] When faced with new systematic approaches to literature, she was deeply suspicious: she did not agree with F.R. Leavis's vision of cultural authority as located in the university, called *Scrutiny* a "prigs

[sic] manual" since all "they" could do was "to schoolmaster" (*D V* 165), and although she valued T.S. Eliot's work, the "common readers" she addressed were not part of his favoured "university Extension audience" of student critics.[27] This scepticism could turn into a feeling of deep threat whenever she saw how cultural dogmas and political doctrines could be interrelated. Published in 1930, her signed review of Augustine Birrell's *Collected Essays* thus resorts to the polemical idea of "dictatorship" in a way that anticipates her criticism of lecturing in "Why?" four years later and her fulmination against university tutors, lecturers and examiners in "All About Books" (1931): their "method, of course, produces an erudite and eugenic offspring" (*E V* 223). With Birrell, however, Woolf pays tribute to a man who has none of the flaws of his generation's critics and scholars:

> There is little talk in Mr Birrell's pages of schools and influences and origins and developments and how style grew out of another; no new theory of poetry is advanced; no key to aesthetics warranted to unlock all doors is forged.
>
> (*E V* 143)[28]

Birrell is no "philosophic critic" but he did not fill his pages with "airy flimsy gossip"; his essays convey an "elastic and humane quality" that avoids any form of superiority, or arrogance; he "eschews aesthetic criticism" but has a "taste" and a "code of his own." In fact, Birrell's main "weakness," which is first to "exclude whole tracts of literature" and then to "neither illumine the present nor acknowledge the future" (*E V* 146–147), is almost endearing when set against Clayton Hamilton's "industrious band" who "see far off upon the horizon a circle of superior enlightenment" (*E III* 45), or against the almost military "uniformity" of the academic study of English literature, in which "one age follows another; and one influence cancels another; and one style is derived from another; and one phrase is better than another" (*E V* 222).

As additional reviews gave her the opportunity to test other critics' methods and her own response to them, Woolf sheds light, in "Augustine Birrell's Essays," on the merits she valued the most as a reader and writer of literary criticism: a love of books; a strong personality and point of view; a way of turning books into people and of making their authors appear in "the flesh" (*E V* 148). Another common feature of this corpus of meta-critical texts is the way they confirm, although less overtly, Woolf's perfect understanding of labels and categories as the result of the institutional and cultural rivalries that she distanced herself from: the belletrists who lack the courage of their opinions and the doctrinaires whose literary rules we tend to accept "without thinking" (*E III* 310); the "critics of the cuttlefish school who suffuse their pages with the many-coloured ink of their own impressions" and the "scientist" who "taps the page and proves it hard" with "a handy little hammer" (*E IV* 302). As we read through her essays in criticism, the contemporary critics, professors and men of letters whose work she examines turn into a multifarious yet recurring figure resembling their historian counterparts: whatever their status and "methods," they are educated men, rarely geniuses – geniuses, Woolf seems to think, all belonged to the previous generation – and their efforts to come to terms with a changing audience and competing critical approaches are laudable. But most of the time, their critical methods are self-defeating.

There is something entertaining in this observation, and we can imagine that, at times, Woolf herself chose to be entertained rather than perplexed or annoyed. Because she had none of the academic credentials of her subjects under study, we might also want to accuse her, as some of her contemporaries did, of bad faith, elitism, "self-indulgent" release of "sex hostility"[29] or simply of engaging in a conversation that allowed her to make room for her own voice while posturing as the "outsider" that she was to some extent, and yet was not. But although we need to address these issues, to give them prominence at this stage of the discussion would ignore a few important facts. As a reviewer and an essayist, Woolf indeed engaged in conversations with her mostly male predecessors and con-temporaries; however, when the critic happened to be a woman, she was not more generous. In "Hearts of Controversy" (1917), she praises Alice Meynell's talent but condemns her for making the audience "so conscious of their stupidity" (*E II* 176).[30] Second, Woolf's models, as suggested before, are male nineteenth-century poets and writers: gender becomes an issue when it is prescribed by institutions and organised cultural power, or when "authority" becomes a form of imposed "reverence" transforming readers and writers into "followers" deprived of their individual "wild voice" (*E V* 221). In short, there is bound to be at least one Nick Greene in each generation, but not all male critics are Nick Greenes.[31] More importantly, to consider that Woolf's criticism was being primarily an opposition strategy prevents us from situating her both in her time and ahead of it, and, therefore, from re-establishing her singular place in a genealogy of modernist critics who renewed the conversation between history, culture and literature.

Woolf's commitment to the cultural debates of her time but ambiva-lent engagement with her contemporaries form a crucial component of her singularity. On the one hand, her essays in criticism are obsessed with her present situation. The more she acknowledges the "trivialities" of a chaotic "age of endeavour" and the "imperfections" of modern lit-erature, the stronger she believes in the need "to cherish" the "burning ground of the moment" rather than "the safe tranquillity of the past" (*E IV* 237–238). But because "we are not fast anchored and things are moving around us," she deplores in "Poetry, Fiction and the future" that "the greater number of critics turn their backs upon the present and look steadily into the past" instead of looking into the future and "tell us where we are going" (*E IV* 428–429). On the other hand, she often turns to the past herself to condemn "her time," pitting "one century against another" to find the "comparison [...] overwhelmingly against us" (*E IV* 237). Contemporary writers, she thinks, have ceased to "believe" in life and in literature: "They cannot make a world because they are not free of other human beings. They cannot tell stories, because they do not believe that stories are true. They cannot generalise" (*E IV* 240). As to contemporary critics, their "influence" cannot "penetrate beyond our day to that not very distant future which it pleases us to call immortality" (*E IV* 236).

This ambivalence is particularly striking each time Woolf examines, with insatiable curiosity, twentieth-century examples of literary theory. In "Henley's Criticism," she explains that "there are times when we would sweep aside all biography and all psychology for the sake of a single song or a single page expounded and analysed phrase by phrase" (*E III* 286). Yet, in the same review, she opposes the critical authority of Carlyle in *Boswell*, or of Macaulay's *Warren Hastings*, to the "freak-ishness of contemporary criticism" (*E III* 287). Testing Percy Lubbock's controversial *Craft of Fiction* in an essay on the new editions of Jane Austen's, the Brontës' and George Meredith's novels, she agrees with the author that "the criticism of fiction is in its infancy" – therefore, "names have to be found and methods defined for the first time" (*E III* 339) – but she also believes that his concept of "form," borrowed from the visual arts, prevents him from seeing that "both in writing and in reading it is the emotion that comes first": "whenever Mr Lubbock talks of form, it is as if something were interposed between us and the book as we know it." In Lubbock's case, this "alien substance" which imposes itself on "emotions which we feel naturally" is the result of a "method" that at least attempts to shake the reader out of his "passive expectation" and to guide him towards a better understanding of the "book itself" as it "endures" (*E III* 339–341). However, the risk here is to "pierce through the flesh" of a work of art, to "look at the skeleton," thereby forgetting "life itself" (*E III* 342).[32]

When the contemporary critic appears to see the work of art as an autonomous artefact, Woolf indeed describes him as being dangerously immune to life: "But it is evident that Mr Hamilton does not like life [...]. He has found life troublesome, and [...] rather unnecessary; for, after all, there are books" (*E III* 45). Her recurring use of the words "anatomy" and "dissection" builds an image of criticism as a science that danger-ously misses the point:

> There is the complication, the major knot, and the explication; the inductive and the deductive methods; the kinetic and the static; the direct and the indirect with sub-divisions of the same; connotation, annotation, personal equation, and denotation; logical sequence and chronological succession – all parts of the frog and all capable of fur-ther dissection. [...] Still, as Mr Hamilton uneasily perceives now and

then, you may dissect your frog, but you cannot make it hop; there is, unfortunately, such a thing as life.

(ibid.)

In a similar way, although Woolf's judgement is less harsh, Lubbock's Röntgen X rays "dissolve" the "flesh" of fiction – here allegorised as a woman assaulted by the patriarchal critic as scientist. Her "finery," her "smile and witchery," together with "the umbrellas and brown paper parcels which she has collected along her long and toilsome journey, dissolve and disappear; the skeleton alone remains."[33] Because there is "something satisfactory in bone—one can grasp it" (*E III* 341), Woolf's contemporaries persist in using their "industrious pen" to "dessicate [...] the living tissues of literature into a network of little bones" (*E IV* 237).

Woolf's profound mistrust of all types of self-appointed experts was, therefore, not merely a condemnation of male arrogance. Coleridge, she reminds us in a review that reads as another comparison "pitting" the past against the present, had a critical "method"; but he had no desire to be "exhaustive, comprehensive, and monumental"; his "inconclusive ideas" were not tied up in "unreal symmetry"; his art as a critic was "not the power of imposing anything from the outside" but of "bring[ing] to light what was already there beforehand" (*E II* 222–223). Likewise, her dubiousness around literary theory is not merely the result of a wish to pursue literature and criticism outside academic boundaries, nor is it a rejection of "novelty" if novelty means a keen attention to modern life, culture and art. Her argument in this matter follows the logic that underlies her essays on modern literature, a logic grounded in a sense of historicity – "the consciousness of history and of being historical" (Jameson 2012: 28) – and of historicism.[34] Woolf's famous essay on "Modern Fiction" is the obvious example here.[35] Woolf begins by sharing a commonly held view – "it is difficult not to take it for granted that the modern practice of the art [of fiction] is somehow an improvement upon the old" – asserting once more a contemporary situation that might drive readers, writers and critics to look backwards. But in the next sentence, she dismisses the analogy between literature and technological progress that the word "improvement" brings to mind:

> It is doubtful whether in the course of the centuries, though we have learnt much about making machines, we have learnt anything about making literature. We do not come to write better; all that we can be said to do is to keep moving, now a little in this direction, now in that, but with a circular tendency should the whole course of the track be viewed from a sufficiently lofty pinnacle.

What "scarcely holds good beyond the first glance," according to Woolf, is the nineteenth-century ideology of progress applied to general history or indeed to the history of literature, which does not mean that this history follows no course. Its shifting direction, however, can only be grasped from the vantage point of historical distance. Where "we" are now, Woolf suggests, is impossible to perceive

> we seem to see ourselves on the flat, in the crowd, half-blind with dust, [...]. It is for the historian of literature to decide; for him to say if we are now beginning or ending or standing in the middle of a great period of prose fiction, for down in the plain little is visible.
>
> (*E IV* 157–158)

Where Woolf's contemporaries need to go is as uneasy to discern, since they are "still in the thick of battle," she explains in the first version of this essay. Nonetheless, they need to "strive and press on" towards the "heights reached by others" (*E III* 31), in their time, with their own tools, so that "life" does not escape them, for "without life nothing else is worth while." Just as the "materialists" in Woolf's famous essay – Wells, Bennett and Galsworthy – have "come down with [their] magnificent apparatus for catching life just an inch or two on the wrong side," modern critics use the "magnificent apparatus" of science to see the bones of an art that they kill in the process (*E IV* 159).

The "life" that escapes those critics, also called "spirit," "truth" or "reality" (*E IV* 159), is what their tools exclude or ignore whenever they omit one dimension of art, or, on the contrary, single out another. In this respect, the difference between nineteenth- and twentieth-century men of letters and scholars is one of cultural context. Canon Alfred Ainger – a "typical product of his age" – gave "undue prominence [...] to moral excellence in literature" (*E I* 85); Sir Walter Raleigh never managed to make his students love literature because he had "no generous measure of the gifts of a writer" (*E IV* 344); Edmund Gosse lacks the "enthusiasm" that is "the life-blood of criticism" (*E III* 116). Lubbock does not realise that "emotion is our material" (*E III* 341); contemporary literary history forgets the common reader and the writer by addressing an audience of teachers, and university students who only learn how to "keep [...] the ranks" (*E V* 222). Woolf's "life" brings up the "fallible human being" absent in "most books of criticism" (*E III* 117), or the attention bestowed on the "sound of the sea and the red of the rose; [...] music, imagery, and a voice speaking from the heart" (*E V* 223). It includes the domestic, political or social influences to which an artist is not immune, as she suggests in "American Fiction" in 1925: "Where the land itself is so different, and the society so different, the literature must needs differ, and differ more and more widely as time goes by, from those of other countries" (*E IV* 277). At other times, it will touch on the polemics of contemporary life and of a world at war as in "The Leaning Tower." "Life," in Woolf's critical essays, is thus the same manifold metaphoric notion that she uses as a reader of history books, biographies, poems and fictions. What the contemporary critic misses is what the materialist novelist fails to see, or what the male academic literary historian feigns to ignore when he prompts his students to "strid[e] through the centuries from one pinnacle of accomplishment to the next," so much so that they forget

> all the hubbub that once surged around the base; how Keats lived in a street and had a neighbour and his neighbour had a family – [...] how Oxford Street ran turbulent with men and women while De Quincey walked with Ann.

> (*E I* 159)

As Claire Joubert explains, life is a "major Woolfian concept that enables her to decongeal Victorian values, and to think and enact at the same time the historical continuity of literature, of the subject, and of society." But it is also a poetic and critical concept "synonymous with the modern" (Joubert 2005: 44).[36] To record "life" in art, and art as "life," Woolf concludes in "The Art of Fiction," requires the English critic to be "bold," less "domestic" and "less assiduous to protect the rights of what it pleases him to call life" (*E IV* 603); that he should accept critical rules and values that can only be provisional, since we "frame our questions differently at different times" (*E IV* 159). Above all, to record life in art and art as life rests on the critic's awareness, Woolf explains in "How It Strikes a Contemporary," of "his position at the table" and on his determination to "scan the horizon; see the past in relation of the future; and so prepare for the masterpieces to come" (*E IV* 240–241). For Woolf, therefore, the question was never to take position in a battle of "camp opposed to camp" (*E V* 222), period to period, discipline to discipline, high- to low-brows, but to create, as a writer and a critic, from the reality of the present, while being acutely conscious, as Mark Goldman's puts it, of "the place in time of [her] own contemporaneity" (Goldman 1976: 13).[37]

A Modernism of Her Own: Historical "Difference"

To Woolf, therefore, criticism was bound to be rooted in history, not in the sense of the traditional temporality of literary history but as the shared perception, in the present, of those "differences" that necessarily underpin any writer's attempt to represent "life as it is": the shifts in historical and social scale, in influences and education, the way the "accent," now, "falls differently from of old" (*E IV* 160), the "rearrangement[s]" in attitudes and manners – these "scenes, thoughts, and apparently fortuitous groupings and incongruous things that impinge upon us with so keen a sense of novelty" (*E IV* 238). To acknowledge, assess and represent those differences and their various configurations was the common task of writers, readers, critics and literary historians, a task which, Woolf considered, required a keen sense of historicity, a constant preoccupation with the forces at stake – economic, institutional, social, ideological – along with the unwriting of those historical orthodoxies and critical assumptions that she saw as barriers to change. Her goal was never the nostalgic reconstruction of, or reconnection with, the "pastness" of the past, nor was it to "preserve the stores, to guard the treasures, of past civilization, and then to bind the present with the past" (Coleridge 1976: 43). Her aim was rather to bind the present with the future, to find the "different song" (*TG* 140) that would contribute to bridge the "gulf" between the "dying world, and the world that is struggling to be born" (*E VI* 276).

Woolf's political and democratic ambition as a writer-critic wishing to empower the reader into a process of creative criticism has often been examined; so has her dialogical method as an essayist. However, the historical-critical dialectic that underlies her agenda and the critical method that derives from it have been more rarely discussed. And yet, I would argue that this very dialectic sheds a new conceptual light on her critical thought and on the apparent contradictions evoked in the introduction to this chapter. The interconnectedness between Woolf's criticism and her historical consciousness takes on three essential dimensions, all related to her aspirations as a cultural innovator. Her constant awareness of her own situatedness as an artist, a critic and an observer of history in the making is the first of these dimensions: to "investigate literature with a view to answering certain questions about ourselves" was the objective she set for herself (*D II* 265). Committed to the burning cultural issues of the present and engaged with the historical urgencies that were bound to intersect with the course of her planned work, Woolf then never failed to contextualise the interrogations, current literary fashions and dominant discourses that she responded to, along with her own statements and tentative theories. This method implied the foregrounding of historical references and elements of contexts, along with her own critical tools and views, in a way that acknowledged their provisional dimension: critics, Woolf kept demanding, need to "declare the standard which they had in mind" (*E III* 271). As a result, Woolf's critical writings imply what Jerome McGann calls a "double act of observation," one that " 'reflects'—and reflects upon—those individual and social forms of human life which are available to the artist's observation, and which are themselves a part of his process of observation" (McGann 1983: 12). In this respect, the "we" that keeps recurring in her essays and the common ground that it designates cannot be separated from the specific and fluctuating circumstances underlying their structure as acts of enunciation. By "specific," I refer here to the stories of social, political, cultural or educational change within which she and her readers were situated. As to the idea of changing contexts, it underlies Woolf's historiographical essays in criticism whenever she tries to assess the present situation by comparing it to the past. Thus, in 1910, "a change there was," and "human relations [...] shifted" so that the Edwardian writer should not have continued to use literary conventions that were "good" only for another "age and generation" (*E III* 422; 431). But the "now" – 1924 – that Woolf described in "Character and Fiction" was not the "now" that she explored in "The Leaning Tower" 16 years later:

> To-day we hear the gunfire in the Channel. We turn on the wireless; we hear an airman telling us how this very afternoon he shot down a raider; [...]. Scott never saw the sailors drowning at Trafalgar; Jane Austen never heard the cannon roar at Waterloo.
>
> (*E VI* 261)

One should not understate these fluctuations between different moments of enunciation and present experiences. Conversely, Woolf herself never referred to these chosen temporal references as infallible landmarks: they were part of her "hazard[ed] assertions" and she knew them to be "disputable" and "arbitrary" (*E III* 421–422) as any historiographer who does not deny that he or she has a story to tell, and that, as Reinhart Koselleck (2004: 3) would later explain: "the more a particular time is experienced as a new temporality, as 'modernity,' the more the demands made on the future increase."

Her insistence on the present in relation to the future is thus the driving force under her critical perception, representation and reconstruction of the literary past, and the second modality of the interconnectedness mentioned earlier: from an always situated "now," Woolf looked backwards in an act of prefiguration, and forward in an act of anticipation. "Modern Fiction," "Character in Fiction," "How It Strikes a Contemporary" and "The Leaning Tower" strikingly follow this backward and forward pattern. They begin with an assessment of the present moment and end on the celebration of future possibilities in the form of a performative address, whether to the imagined "art of fiction com[ing] alive and standing in our midst, [...] her youth [...] renewed and her sovereignty assured" (*E IV* 164), to "the greater writer who is not yet born" (*E III* 359), or to the "commoners and outsiders" that will teach themselves "how to write, how to preserve and how to create" (*E VI* 278). The present moment as Woolf, herself, and her contemporaries recorded and felt it is contrasted to past experiences and masterpieces: "differences" and "resemblances" are duly noted, the aim being, again, to grasp the specificities of the present before moving forward, not to indulge into "some imperious need to anchor our stability upon [the] security" of past generations (*E IV* 239): "much though we admire the dead, we prefer life as it is" (*E IV* 238). Shaped by her training in general history, by the epistemological tools and questions that she kept remodelling and addressing as a reviewer and an essayist, Woolf's historicism was, therefore, never removed from the "historical experience of time," whether individual or collective: in Koselleck's words again, by "differentiating past and future, or (in anthropological terms) experience and expectation," she grasped "something as historical time" (Koselleck 2004: 4), an ongoing "process" – with "comparison," another of her chief critical concepts – nourished by ongoing conversations between a literary past that serves as the laboratory of the present – not as a "history [...] that shall enforce our prejudices" (*E V* 573). Inseparable from her sense of historicity, Woolf's "historicism" thus undercuts the conception of modernist criticism as a formalist activity eschewing most historical approaches; but it also challenges a conception of Woolf as a "postmodernist critic," at least whenever this conception separates her persona as a critic from the historiographer that she also was. All the more so as the historiographer, in Woolf's case, is also a storyteller, or to put it in less blunt terms, a writer who constructs her own understanding of literary history and criticism for pragmatic and political reasons,[38] adopting the empowering selective method of Michel de Certeau's poacher, building personal networks of affiliations and affinities: with the romantic poets who were able to judge "the whole"; with artist-critics such as "Lamb, Arnold and Sainte-Beuve" who had "a lively enough passion for the artist's view to be in sympathy with the different forms of it" (*E II* 67) or with Leslie Stephen's (1955: 31) vision of literary history as "an account of one strand [...] in a very complex tissue" and "connected with the intellectual and social development."[39]

The third dimension of Woolf's enacted historical-critical dialectic thus takes the form of the unwriting and rewriting process examined in the first part of this book. What Woolf challenges and complicates along her career as a reviewer and essayist, is the history of criticism itself, one that traditionally relies on homogeneous periods, clear turning points and sharp polarisations. This is not to say that her work eschews continuities and contrasts, but that these very continuities and contrasts are reshuffled within a multilayered, diachronic as much as synchronic, narrative. This underlying story invites us first to replace linear unfolding by meaningful overlaps and genealogies, thereby anticipating the histories of literature and culture that present each "age" as diverse. In the words of Melba Cuddy-Keane (2018: 29), Woolf proposes a "complex model [of literary history] that neither denies nor reifies change." Nor is it built on strictly defined historical periods, critical camps or literary classifications. In her essays, the past and the present become loose categories in which her contemporaries may waver between tradition – in the sense of a nostalgic attachment to the past – and modernity, while some of their predecessors are found to have raised enduring questions. Usual historical contrasts and divisions – between critics and writers, writers and readers, or between the different schools of criticism – are replaced by a multilayered, flexible story line reflecting ongoing conversations between past and present writers, critics, readers and literary masterpieces. Acknowledging that "no age can have been more rich than ours in writers determined to give expression to the differences that separate them from the past" (*E IV* 238), Woolf analyses every literary work on the grounds of these differences, thus anticipating Jerome McGann's definition of the paradox fundamental to all works of art which is best revealed through a historical method of criticism: that such works transcend their age and speak to alien cultures because they are so completely true to themselves, because they are time and place specific, because they are—from our point of view—different.

By actually seeking to "clarify and promote" this difference instead of maintaining "older ideas in continuities and processive traditions" that serve more reactionary, "cooptive powers" (McGann 1983: 2), Woolf engages in successive conversations between situated interlocutors, discourses and texts that resist undebated cultural or institutional power.

If the word, and the notion, of "difference" recurs throughout Woolf's essays in criticism, it does not only serve the project of a "historical" form of criticism. In its insistence on contextualisation and comparison, the reading method that Woolf adopts for herself and proposes to her audience is also pragmatic, meta-critical, political and poetical. Along with "Hours in a Library" (1916) and "An Essay in Criticism" (1927), "How Should One Read a Book" (1926) is a revealing example of a writing process reflecting these four dimensions while resorting to the "heuristic" value of "different regimes of historicity" (Hartog 2017: xv).[40] The essay first begins in its original version as a talk addressed to 60 girls at Hayes Court School in Kent on January 30, 1926; it was then revised for the *Yale Review*'s more academic audience in October 1926, before ending six years later with the article published in *CR II*. As Beth Daugherty explains, these successive revisions take into consideration Woolf's different audiences, their imagined background and questions while underlining the various postures and "voices" that Woolf chose accordingly (Daugherty 1997: 159–175). The second and third "stories" that this essay recounts no longer depend on external circumstances (material culture, editorial choices, varying audiences) but on the double question introduced by its title: how should one read a book and enjoy the "freedom" that a library allows, without resorting to cumbersome authorities – in Woolf's words "How are we to bring order into this multitudinous chaos and so get the deepest and widest pleasure from what we read?" (*E V* 573) – how then should we "refresh and exercise our own creative powers" to "pass judgment upon these multitudinous impressions" (*E V* 576; 579). The last story, in the form of its conclusion, links a personal past experience – "I have sometimes dreamt, at least, that when the Day of Judgment dawns on the great conquerors and lawyers and statesmen come to receive their reward [...]" – to a witty, if not ironic, utopian dream:

the Almighty will turn to Peter and will say, not with a certain envy when He sees us coming with our books under our arms, 'Look, these need no reward. We have nothing to give them here. They have loved reading.'

(*E V* 582)

Each of these stories has its own "regime of historicity" depending on external circumstances or individual experience, on a critical method and a set political purpose: to read for one's own pleasure, to read as a critic, to teach the common reader-student how to read outside of lecture rooms, finally, to talk about books in such a way, Bell and Ohmann aptly suggest, "that they matter, not in literary history, but in our lives" (Bell and Ohmann 1989: 57).[41] In "How Should One Read a Book" as in all Woolf's essays in criticism, the common reader is an embodied being, located in one of those "sanctuaries" – a room of his or her own, a library – where "authorities," "laws" and "conventions" have no place, looking freely for a place to begin in the midst of books "written in all languages by men and women of all tempers, races, and ages" (*E V* 572). The beginning of his or her journey has its own purpose, method and temporality: to keep an "open mind," to renounce any form of prejudice, to "try to become" the author so as to find what he or she is offering before appreciating the "mastery" of each by turning to some "great" models and assessing differences: of "person," of represented "world," and of "perspective" (*E V* 572–573). This first stage requires one to indulge in the time of exploration – to "make your own experiment with the dangers and difficulties of words" – of memory – "recall, then some event that has left a distinct impression on you" – and of comparison (574). The other part of the journey has another aim or destination but relies on a similar essential "process" of comparison:

> 'we only have to compare' [...] if we are to get the whole pleasure from a book, by another. We must pass judgment upon these multitudinous impressions; [...]. But not directly. Wait for the dust of reading to settle; for the conflict of the questioning to die down; walk, walk, walk, talk, pull the dead petals from a rose, or fall asleep.
>
> (579)

The time has now come to "judge," "to compare each book with the greatest of its time," and as "time goes on perhaps we can train our taste, perhaps we can submit it to some control." An active process of "discrimination" opens onto the work of giving "names" and framing "rules" as we engage in conversations with artist and critics "laden with questions and suggestions won honestly in the course" (*E V* 581).

In this essay composed of embedded stories and temporalities, Woolf proposes a timeline that entwines the threads of the literary past, of successive reading experiences and of comparative valuation processes with "life itself," always considered a welcome interference. The reader is offered a pedagogical and critical method requiring the acceptance of momentaneous chaos and the challenging of self-training for the sake of a different future. This method implies a repeated back and forth movement in time, and the assessment of differences and contradictions that traditional normative literary histories tend to dismiss. As they read new and old books, good and bad books side by side, Woolf's audiences are invited to face the present, and, in the wake of Katharine Hilbery in *Night and Day* as she looks at her grandfather's portrait again and again, to bring to their ancestors their "own perplexities," the "doubts, questionings, and despondencies" that "would be more welcome to [them] than homage" (*ND* 335). Altogether, readers, students and aspiring authors become investigators, writers who unwrite and rewrite, critics who "reconsider [their opinions] and test them" while embracing inconclusiveness as a strategy (*E III* 442). As criticism and historiography interact, the questions of interpretation, standards, value and institutional formations remain unrestricted, while otherness, estrangement and contrasts are assumed to be mediated, rather than radical. Past works survive in the present whenever their literary "permanence" – another of Woolf's favourite words – is linked with their openness to different readings and reconfigurations, and to that not very distant future which it pleases us to call "immortality" (*E IV* 236). The active transmission of culture, outside of lecturing institutions, along with the elaboration of an inclusive, democratic literary praxis, replaces nostalgic commemoration and the "anxiety of influence."[42] In the end, the literary past becomes a laboratory of the modern and of the future.

Notes

1 Woolf (*L I* 190).
2 The reference is to "A Professor of Life" (1926): "Once make the fatal distinction between life and letters, once exalt life and find literature an occupation for old maids and inevitably, if one is Walter Raleigh, one becomes discontented with mere praise" (*E IV* 345).
3 Rosenberg mentions the following exceptions: her own work on *Woolf and Samuel Johnson* (1995); Alison Booth's *Greatness Engendered* (1992); Juliet Dusinberre's *Virginia Woolf's Renaissance* (1997); Alice Fox's *Virginia Woolf and the Literature of the English Renaissance* (1990); Beverly Ann Schlack's *Continuing Presences: Virginia Woolf's Use of Literary Allusions* (1979); Perry Meisel's *The Absent Father* (1980). For full references, see the Bibliography.
4 Unless specified otherwise, references to "How It Strikes a Contemporary," initially published in the *TLS* in April 1923, are to the revised version of the essay for *The Common Reader*, vol. I (*E IV* 233–242).
5 On Woolf and the nineteenth-century domestic novel, see Emily Blair (2007); on Woolf and George Eliot, see Alison Booth (1992); on Woolf and Walter Pater, see Perry Meisel (1980).
6 See, for example, the titles of the essays collected in "Part II: Woolf and Literary History" of *Virginia Woolf and the Essay* (Rosenberg and Dubino 1997): "Entering Woolf's Renaissance Imaginary: A Second Look at the Second Common Reader"; "Virginia Woolf's Reviews of the Romantic Poets"; "'The Burning Ground of the Present': Woolf and Her Contemporaries"; "A Modernism of Her Own: Virginia Woolf's *TLS* Reviews and Eliotic Modernism." I am also indebted to Cuddy-Keane's (2003: 100–106; 146–166) pages on Woolf's literary histories, their various functions and forms, in *Virginia Woolf, the Intellectual, and the Public Sphere*.

7   Collini acknowledges the "conventional" aspect of his selection and the absence of other women than Queenie Leavis. He justifies his choice by referring to the "established intellectual and personal filiation that binds" these critics (he also explores the work of Basil Willey, L.C. Knights and Richard Hoggart) and to their legacy. And yet, one might want to argue that what he says of T.S. Eliot, which did not prevent the poet-critic from being acclaimed as such, could easily be applied to Virginia Woolf: "indeed, Eliot, notoriously, did not write books: he wrote essays, lectures, and reviews, and then made books out of a selection of these shorter forms" (Collini 2019: 23; 33).

8   In her Ph.D. Thesis on Virginia Woolf's Literary Criticism, Yvonne Nicole Richter mentions some of the critics who, from the 1940s onwards, have rejected Woolf's method and style on account of their impressionism: the Canadian scholar Solomon Fishman, for example, who assumed in 1943 that "Impressionism afforded her the freedom which would have been denied by a rigorous analytical method"; he also considered that her criticism "operated by intuition without the mediation of a method" ("Virginia Woolf on the Novel." *Sewanee Review* 51/2 (1943): 321–340). American writer and critic Mark Schorer is another example. The same year he asserted in the *Yale Review* that

> Woolf approached her reading, in her criticism, as she approached the whole of experience in her novels: with aggressive curiosity, a refined sensibility, but an exaggerated sense of the relevance of impression [...]. What is lacking, finally, is the sense of value.
>
> (*Yale Review* 32/2 [Winter 1943]: 377–381; 380; quoted in Richter [2009: 36])

9   This is an idea shared by Jane de Gay (2006: 2): "Woolf's route towards innovation came not through rejecting the literary past but through drawing upon it."

10   The widely acclaimed American scholar and critic Joel Elias Spingarn (1875–1939) had written his doctoral thesis on "A History of Literary Criticism in the Renaissance" (1899). The lecture mentioned here was later regarded as the earliest manifesto of "The New Criticism."

11   René Wellek (1941: 1) considers that Thomas Warton's *History of English Poetry*, published in 1774–1781, was the first history of English literature the form of which would determine "the whole future of English Literary History."

12   On literary history in the eighteenth century, see René Wellek (1941) and April London (2010).

13   In England, the *Modern Language Review*, *The Year's Work in English Studies* and the *Review of English Studies* appeared between 1905 and 1925.

14   Among representative examples of this evolution, one can mention "The Great Writers Series" established by Eric S. Robertson in 1887, and *The Cambridge History of English Literature* whose first volume was published in 1907.

15   On this subject, see Ted Underwood (2013).

16   "How It Strikes a Contemporary" (*E IV* 236).

17   On this subject, see Mary Waters (2004), Solveig Robinson (2003), Bellamy et al. (2000).

18   On Woolf's engagement in the cultural debates of her time, notably the new academic and institutional identity of the study of English, see Cuddy-Keane

(2003: 68–80): and more particularly the pages on Woolf's indirect knowledge of these controversies and harshly critical responses to them.

19 Arthur Symons (1865–1945), English editor, poet, critic and translator, in "Mr Symons's Essays" (1916).

20 George Moore (1852–1933), in "Winged Phrases" (1919).

21 Alfred Ainger (1837–1904), English biographer and critic, in "A Nineteenth-Century Critic" (1906).

22 See "Patmore's Criticism" (1921).

23 William Ernest Henley (1849–1903), English poet, writer, critic and editor, in "Henley's Criticism" (1921).

24 Woolf is alluding here to George Bradshaw's *Railway Time-Tables, Monthly Railway Guide* or *Continental Railway Guide*. In "Romance" (1917).

25 Walter Raleigh (1861–1922), Professor of English Literature, poet and critic, author of *The English Novel* (1894), in "A Professor of Life" (1926).

26 Clayton Hamilton (1881–1946), American critic, member of the Academy of Arts and Letters, author of *Materials and Methods of Fiction* (1908), in "The Anatomy of Fiction" (*E III* 43–47).

27 T.S. Eliot, *"Professionalism, Or...?" (The Egoist, 5/4, 1918: 61)*. On Woolf and the Leavises, see Eleanor McNees (1997).

28 Augustine Birrell (1850–1933), British chief secretary for Ireland (1907–1916), president of the Board of Education (1905–1907), man of letters, essayist, author of *Essays About Men, Women, and Books* (1895); *William Hazlitt* (1902); *Andrew Marvell* (1905). His *Collected Essays* (1899) comprise *Obiter Dicta*; *Res Judicatae*; *Essays About Men, Women, and Books*.

29 Queenie Leavis's review of *Three Guineas* was published in *Scrutiny* in September 1938.

30 Alice Meynell (1847–1922), British writer, editor, critic and suffragist. Published in 1917, *Hearts of Controversy* is a collection of critical essays on Tennyson Dickens, Swinburne, Charlotte and Emily Brontë, Charmain and the Augustan Age.

31 Nick Greene, the "undying" character of the writer-critic in *Orlando* (ageless, everlasting and perennial), is the butt of Woolf's satire on the male critic's arrogance, scornful treatment of his contemporaries, conservativeness and immunity to change.

32 Percy Lubbock (1879–1965), English man of letters, critic and biographer. *The Craft of Fiction* was published in 1921.

33 Wilhelm Conrad Röntgen (1845–1923) was a German physicist who won the first Nobel Prize in Physics in 1901 for his discovery of X-rays, or Röntgen rays, in 1895.

34 In *A Singular Modernity*, Fredric Jameson also assumes that

> it is the present's responsibility for its own self-definition of its own mission that makes it in its own historical period in its own right and that requires the relationship to the future as much as it involves taking a position on the past.
>
> (Jameson 2012: 28)

I argue that this dialectic between past, present and future is at the core of Woolf's historicism.

35 The revised version of Woolf's 1921 essay "Modern Novels" – originally published in 1921 in the *TLS* (*E II* 30–36) – appeared in the first volume of

The Common Reader in 1925 (*E IV* 157–165). In the following lines, I will use quotations referring to the two texts.

36 In an article where she analyses F.R. Leavis's positions on English as a national language and as an academic discipline, Claire Joubert (2005: 27–54) compares Leavis's criticism to Woolf's and Joyce's: "Woolf, comme Leavis, fait de 'life' un concept majeur qui lui sert à dégeler les valeurs victoriennes et à penser et effectuer à la fois le continu historique de la littérature, du sujet et de la société." *My translation.*

37 See Mark Goldman, *The Reader's Art, Virginia Woolf as Literary Critic* (1976).

38 I use here the word "pragmatic" as referring to a critical practice grounded in experience, both inferential and analytical, envisioning literature both as an aesthetic object and a situated discourse with its interactional dimension and political effects.

39 On Woolf and the Romantic poets, see Edward A. Hungerford's "Virginia Woolf's Reviews of the Romantic Poets" (Hungerford 1997: 97–115); on Woolf and Leslie Stephen, see Hill (1998: 351–362).

40 See Beth Rigel Daugherty, "Readin', Writin', and Revisin': Virginia Woolf's 'How Should One Read a Book'" (1997: 159–175).

41 See Barbara Currier Bell and Carol Ohmann, "Virginia Woolf's Criticism: A Polemical Preface" (1989: 48–60).

42 The reference is obviously to Harold Bloom, *The Anxiety of Influence: A Theory of Poetry* (1997).

6 Literary History as a Laboratory
Practices of Knowledge

It is one brain, after all, literature; and it wants change and relief. The text book writers cut it up all wrong.[1]

"Most histories of literature," René Wellek and Austin Warren wrote in *Theory of Literature* (1956), "are either social histories, or histories of thought as illustrated in literature, or impressions and judgments on specific work arranged in specific order." They either "treat literature as mere documents for the illustration of national or social history" or "recognize that literature is first and foremost an art, but appear unable to write history" (Wellek and Warren 252). This opening assessment in their chapter on "literary history" might explain why Wellek's own history of English literary historiography, published one year earlier, closed at the end of the eighteenth century, before most histories of literature became "social histories or histories of thought as illustrated in literature, in the nineteenth century" (ibid.). According to the two scholars, Leslie Stephen "regarded literature as a 'particular function of the social organism,' a kind of 'by-product' of social change"; W.J. Courthope looked for the unity of his subject – English Poetry – "in the life of a nation as a whole"; Edmund Gosse's books were "a series of critical remarks on authors and some of their works, chronologically arranged in sequence."[2] As to George Saintsbury's appreciative criticism in the wake of Walter Pater, he never wrote an actual "history" (Wellek and Warren 1956: 253). The list of such prestigious examples, Wellek and Warren argue, "could be extended almost indefinitely," even to French and German critics: late nineteenth- and early twentieth-century histories of literature failed to establish a process of actual historical evolution; nor did they clearly engage such essential concepts as "change," "periods," "movements," "norms," "genres" or the nature of "literary relationships" between works of art and authors (Wellek and Warren 258–269).

If we accept this vision of literary history with its chief notional requirements, then Woolf reviewed very few and wrote none, at least in a form that would have grounded literary culture in nineteenth-century conceptions of historical development, historical contrasts, period style

DOI: 10.4324/9780429331787-9

and national tradition. And yet, when most of her contemporaries, except for Lytton Strachey and Ford Madox Ford,[3] had abandoned literary history to university lecturers and scholars, Woolf provided alternative forms of literary history anchored in the pragmatics of experience and interlocution, and grounded in the fruitful tension between the learning and unlearning of pre-existing models of literary knowledge.[4] Strikingly, when we contrast them with her contemporaries' approach to the history of literature, Woolf's "literary histories" seem to take the well-trodden path of more traditional narratives as they work through, rather than abandon, what Herbert Grabes (2001: 8) calls the "a-priori notions of history." Conversely, if we compare them with her predecessors' histories of literature, Woolf's historiographical essays in criticism read like experiential ventures and open fields of enquiry. In those reconfigured sites of experimentation and free conversation, the common reader and the critic collaborate as both apprentices and researchers; experimentation and provisional conclusions challenge theoretical certainties; innovators are indeed also inheritors. The purpose is not to offer a globalised meta-history of literature nor is it to supply "topics for Ph.D. dissertations, articles, and books" and write criticism to "produce more criticism" (Perkins 1992: 65).[5] In fact, what T.S. Eliot, F.R. Leavis and William Empson did with poetry, Woolf did mostly with the novel, a genre that, as the next chapter (Chapter 7) will show, she constantly associated with "life itself," modernity and the female gender. But she also addressed questions of "genre," "origins," "narrative," "periodisation," "immanent change," "literary classifications" and "contextualism" in ways that, she explained, require "rules," "discipline" and "method" along with a knowledge of the past that never excludes individual pleasure and wanderings.

In this chapter, therefore, I would like to take Woolf at face value – "I shall write a history of English literature, I think, in those days" (*D III* 297) – and read some her literary-historical endeavours as the work of a modernist "literary historian," one who needed to negotiate the dialectical tensions inherent in her status as a woman of letters in a context of competing epistemologies. Thus, rather than insisting on how Woolf's diverse, incomplete and scattered attempts at literary history paved the way for, or were written in the wake of, her feminist, "revisionist" literary histories in *A Room of One's Own* and *Orlando* – which they obviously did and were[6] – I propose to look at her critical work on the essay as a genre, then at "Phases of Fiction" and "Anon" and "The Reader" as historiographical models of "creative criticism" (*E II* 122) that have contributed in an underrated way to the ideal that German scholar Herbert Grabes (2001: 25; 30) envisioned in his 2001 article on "Literary History and Cultural History": they draw our attention to the "Other" of culture (what it "excludes or marginalises" within "historically changing limits"); they "reinvigorate the collective memory of the literary works of the past and their alternative worldmaking through a particular history of literary discourse"; they offer new literary-historical solutions that reconfigure the space of literary theory while incorporating the imprint of the long lineage to which they belong and from which they spring.

The Essay, Literary History and the Functions of Genre

In the literary histories of Woolf's past, "genre" mattered as a principle of classification, if only because those histories focused on one particular "form," or would use literary "kinds" as a structuring principle. In nineteenth-century Britain, however, and contrary to what happened in Germany and in France, critics and literary historians rarely defined the notion theoretically. Walter Raleigh's *The English Novel* (1894) had little to say about the development of the "many forms" displayed by "literary artistry" over the centuries, except that the success of some of them is "conditioned by the taste of the public" – the evolution of the literary marketplace indeed meant new relationships between publishers, writers and readers – and the "decline" of others (Raleigh 110; 140–141). In the preface to his *History of Nineteenth-Century Literature* (1896), George Saintsbury refers to the "progress of distinct literary kinds," but the "various kinds" that he keeps mentioning remain as vague as the expression itself (Saintsbury vii). In fact, many nineteenth-century men of letters shared Leslie's Stephen almost Darwinian formulation, in *English Literature and Society in the Eighteenth Century* (1904), that "in every form of artistic production [...] schools arise; each of which seems to embody some kind of principle, and develops and afterwards decays, according to some mysterious law," which could be that the "environment has become uncongenial" (Stephen 1955: 20–21). The late Victorians and Edwardians, Steven Monte explains, tended to examine genre from both an aesthetic and organic perspective as a reaction against prescriptive neo classical taxonomies. By associating genres with Zeitgeist, with nineteenth-century historicism, and, from the 1860s onwards, with biological metaphors, they revisited the "triad of literary genres – fiction (narrative), poetry (lyric) and plays (dramatic) – [...] discernible in Renaissance thought if not in Plato and Aristotle" (Monte 2013:481). For Ruskin, the decay of certain literary forms was mainly caused by moral decline; in *Shakespeare's Predecessors in the English Drama* (1884), John Addington Symonds considered that the "rules of triple progression" of Greek dramatic art followed the "law of growth which may be traced in all continuous products of the human spirit" (Symonds 7–8) and that they paved the way for the three stages of the development of English drama – "preparation"; "maturity"; "decadence and dissipation."[7] As to Woolf's father, to give a third representative example, he saw "changes" in the "intellectual development [and] the social and political state of the nation" as the chief cause of the rise and decline of most art forms (Stephen 1955: 24).[8]

Although they would often refer to this triadic vision of genre, nineteenth-century British and American writers, Steven Monte explains, tended "to avoid the kind of abstract theory associated with German philosophy, sometimes to the point where their theories of genre seem little more than justifications of their own aesthetic preferences" (Monte 493–494). And yet, these descriptive "theories" retrospectively appear more prescriptive than they claimed to be, a commendatory dimension mainly linked to the professionalisation of English studies over the period, and to the forms of institutional conservatism that went with it.[9] "Literary kinds" existed, the causes of their growth and disappearance could easily be explained, but these explanations seldom presupposed any thorough analysis of the way genres are cultural formations depending on "tradition, present interests, self-classifications of authors, views of contemporaries, and observed features of texts" (Perkins 1992: 81). Modernist criticism was, therefore, bound to eschew a literary category that appeared as the result of old historicism, positivistic scholarship and fallacious attempts at coherence.

In this context, Woolf's constantly renewed interest in old and new generic forms might look like a tribute to outdated models of literary history and criticism, or simply as a reference to the titles of the works she was reviewing – "Romance" (1917), "A Book of Essays," "Women Novelists" (1918) or "Henry James's Ghost Stories" (1921), to name a few. In "How Should One Read a Book," however, Woolf explains that "since books have classes—fiction, biography, poetry—we should separate them and take from each what it is right that each should give us" (*E V* 573). In other reviews and essays, she states that poetry, drama, biography, the romance or the novel are specific "shapes" – each of them being "the proper depository" (*E IV* 217) of "a peculiar substance" that cannot be expressed "with equal fitness" in another "form" (*E I* 25).[10] In her 37-year-long career as a critic, Virginia Woolf actually addressed the question of "genre" a considerable number of times, whether directly – in such texts as "The Decay of Essay Writing" (1905), "The Poetic Drama" (1906), "Romance" (1917), "Modern Novels" (1919), "A Talk About Memoirs" (1920), "The New Biography" (1927), "Poetry, Fiction and the Future" (1927) – or indirectly, in the course of critical "conversations" on reading, writing, literary history and the role of the critic.[11] The question thus seems to have interested her more than it did her contemporaries and those that came after her, and more than recent scholarship has acknowledged. This, perhaps, because although genre theory has a history dating back to Aristotle, its underlying principles along with other categories and notions such as "nation," "race," "age" and "style" imply a vision of literary knowledge that most critics have long rejected. For a feminist woman of letters to situate herself within a long tradition of male poetics, when the rejection of all rules, essences and generic strictures could appear to allow for more freedom and inclusion, is a choice worth examining. At a time when her contemporaries experimented with genres but rarely indulged in genre theory, Woolf's theoretical and historiographical approach to "genre" in general, and to the "essay" in particular, is symptomatic of her method as a critic and historiographer transforming apparent paradoxes into fruitful tensions and empowering reflections.[12]

The title of Woolf's early published essay, "The Decay of Essay Writing" (1905), flags one of these apparent contradictions. Woolf had planned to call it "A Plague of Essays" but discovered as she was sent the proofs that the editors had changed the title – "which means nothing" – and cut its contents "by a good half" (*L I* 180–181). While the original title would have inscribed Woolf's practice and conception of the genre in her contemporaries' embattled discourse on the threatening overabundance of reviewers and practitioners of the form, the idea of "decay" carries the trace of a more Victorian approach to the development of "genres." On first examination, however, this signed essay and Woolf's later review of Ernest Rhys's *Modern English Essays 1870 to 1920* (1922) in "The Modern Essay" bear the hallmark of Woolf's forefathers. First, Woolf's genealogy of great essayists from Montaigne, Charles Lamb, Francis Bacon, Matthew Arnold, Robert Louis Stevenson, Samuel Butler, Addison, Leslie Stephen to Max Beerbohm includes no women, except for Vernon Lee whose work she alludes to only rapidly. As she writes herself into a tradition of male poetics and critical discourses in the first phase of her career, Woolf does not clearly depart from the expected canon – "the very great of old" (*E I* 26).[13] When she does, her argument relies on some of the chief ingredients of former critical and historiographical approaches. The essay, Woolf easily acknowledges, regularly submits to "change" and has a "history"; the form "admits variety" and a retrospective look on its recent evolution shows evidence of "progress" (*E IV* 216). She also seems to agree with Rhys (1922: v) that the "the modern essay attained its majority" with the later Victorian essayists "who sustained the tradition of the great essay in an earlier period," such as De Quincey, Carlyle, Addison, Steele and Charles Lamb. Apparently borrowing from the mode of appreciative criticism rather than leading her readers towards a theoretical approach, Woolf keeps distinguishing "good writing from the bad" in a way that first reads as subjective, or at least as one that shows a penchant for the work of the long tradition of eighteenth- and nineteenth-century gentleman essayists (*E IV* 223). However, as Caroline Pollentier has shown, Woolf's apparent allegiance to the past is palimpsestuous in its form and polemic in its intent (Pollentier 2011: 36–41).[14]

In fact, if the essay has a "history," Woolf rejects any teleological version of its development. What matters, she repeats, is not the "past" of the genre, but its "present" that only the knowledge of the past can enlighten (*E IV* 216). Refusing to impose a linear plot on a succession of periods, she unwrites the long-dominant concept of "historical contrast," a method of "boundary-drawing" underlain by the "premise that literature's power to cultivate readers depends on vividly particularizing and differentiating vanished eras" and according to which one century or age is subsumed under the name of one or two exemplary writers (Underwood 2013: 3). The "age" Woolf takes an interest in is actually "this age" (*E I* 25); the contrast she focuses on is not so much the difference between the "ancients" like Homer, Alexander the Great, Epaminondas and the moderns of whom Montaigne "is the first" (*E IV* 76), as the opposition between novelty and modernity:

> fresh and amusing shapes must be given to the old commodities—for we really have nothing so new to say that it will not fit into one of the familiar forms. So we confine ourselves to no one literary medium; we try to be new by being old;
>
> (*E I* 25)[15]

Rewriting here Ernest Rhys's image of fashion in his introduction – "a vagabond and a free spirit," the essay "ostensibly wears the fashion of its time—hat and coat and collar" (Rhys ix) – Woolf associates change and temporality in a way that anticipates her 1910 review of *Modes and Manners of the Nineteenth Century*:

> If there are thus an infinite variety of fashions in the external shapes of our wares, there are a certain number—naturally not so many—of wares that are new in substance and in form which we have either invented or very much developed.[16]

Although the historian and the critic should take into consideration the new rhythms of daily life, they should not, Woolf suggests, mistake the "devices" concocted by "some ingenious youth" with the modernity of literary invention – by definition always a reinvention (*E I* 24–25). Form should be fused with substance, not replace it.

Unlike most of her predecessors, Woolf does not establish any direct links between the "changes" that she examines and physical milieu, spiritual atmosphere or social circumstances. The shifting conditions that she sees as affecting the essay writer are instead cultural forces such as the spread of education; the diversification and price of the new media; the possibility to read "at all hours of the day and fall in the night" because "the literary productions of friends come by post, by van, by messenger" (*E I* 24); the increasing demands "for the light middle not exceeding fifteen hundred words" (*E IV* 222). Besides, Woolf's exploration of historical shifts in material culture goes along with other concretely palpable evolutions, as the sustained metaphor associating the consumption of books with bodily needs suggests. Thus, when Woolf explains that the function of the essay is to provide individual "pleasure," the capitalist subtext that appears in the vision of the British public – a "monster" that needs feeding and whose "stale palate" should constantly be "tickle[d]" (*E I* 24) – is coupled with a more positive image of individual and collective satisfaction: "Everything in an essay must be subdued to that end. It should lay us under a spell with its first word, and we should only wake, refreshed, with its last." But "so great a feat is seldom accomplished," she adds, "though the fault may well be as much on the reader's side as on the writer's. Habit and lethargy have dulled his palate" (*E IV* 216).

As she explores the essay's history and specificity, Woolf thus begins by emphasising its essential mission in relation to the reader's needs. The list of what an essay "must" do – to feed us with the "honest truth" (*E I* 27), to "blow" knowledge into us and "lay us under a spell with its first word," to share with the reader an idea to "lap us about and draw its curtain across the world" (*E IV* 216) – comes along with the list of what it "should" rule out: insincerity, the lack of "an obstinate conviction" (*E IV* 224), the temptation of exhaustivity and "literal truth-telling" (*E IV* 217).[17] But another inventory accompanies these two prescriptive statements, this time implying the common reader's participation in the valuation process of the essayist's art: "We must compare them; we must bring out the quality. We must point to this and say it is good because it is exact, truthful, and imaginative" (*E IV* 224). Woolf's approach to the essay as a genre thus relies on a series of connected concepts – "change," "pleasure," "truth," "personality" or "soul" – that progressively build an organic theory of the essay. This programmatic theory combines empiricism, experimentation and pragmatism while never confusing the essay's loose generic strictures with an absence of controlling principle. First, the essay's history, just as "life itself," does not follow a linear plot since continuity and change cannot be anticipated; within this Woolfian history, tradition takes the form of an ongoing conversation between writers and readers that can either lead to a shared "feast" or to more unpalatable "feats." The "truth" of an essay, then, does not lie in the choice of its subject matter, style and format, but in the writer's capacity to reach "permanent value" by using the "self" which, "while it is essential to literature, is also its most dangerous antagonist" (*E IV* 221). Only by knowing how to write can he move beyond this paradox and offer his reader both knowledge and pleasure. As to the notions of "personality" or "intimacy" – themselves inextricably linked with Woolf's focus on biography and subjectivity as chief ingredients of literary modernity – they constitute the "peculiar substance" of the essay (*E I* 25). In "Montaigne," this essential substance takes on the feminine figure of an allegorical "soul" – the essayist's indomitable self – whose "vagaries, [...] map, weight, colour, and circumference" give us access to "its confusion, its variety, its imperfection" (*E IV* 71).

The organic dimension of Woolf's theory, therefore, cannot be dissociated from "life itself," whether the notion is associated with the author's writing itself, with reading, or with the life that "wells up and alters and adds up" when an essayist like Max Beerbohm possesses his art "to perfection," showing "that indescribable inequality, stir, and final expressiveness which belong to life and to life alone" (*E IV* 221). "Even things in a book-case change if they are alive," Woolf explains in "The Decay of Essay Writing." Only when essayists "revive" old genres and "affect an archaic accent" instead of acknowledging change – which, again, is not synonymous with novelty – does life escape them: they have indeed confused craftsmanship with the more "mechanical" art of "penmanship" (*E I* 25–26). To encapsulate the "complex and infinitely mysterious" dimension of "human nature" within its formal limits (*E IV* 76), the essay, therefore, needs to give free rein to what constitutes life itself: movement, change and the freedom that eschews all forms of conformism. In this respect, Montaigne, Woolf believes, is "this great master of the art of life" (*E IV* 73). His intense and pleasurable quest for the truth of his own soul reads as an ode to his representation of life's protean dimension:

> It is life that emerges more and more clearly as [Montaigne's] essays reach not their end, but their suspension in full career. It is life that becomes more and more absorbing as death draws near, one's self, one's soul, every fact of existence.
>
> (*E IV* 77)

So defined, Woolf's organic conception of the essay dialectically plays with her use of an apparently prescriptive, if not essentialist, lexis. Since "movement and change are the essence of our being" and "conformity is death," she explains in "Montaigne," "we" – whether essayists or their readers – should feel free to "say what comes into our heads, repeat ourselves, contradict ourselves, fling out the wildest nonsense." This freedom, however, needs to be "controlled," not so much by "public opinion" or "Divine guidance" as by this "monitor" or "invisible censor within" which guides us towards truth and authenticity, "for nothing matters," Woolf states quite unexpectedly, "except life; and, of course, order" (*E IV* 75). The latter maxim-like statement becomes clearer, though, when read alongside passages in other essays when Woolf articulates the link between modern profusion and fragmentation, and the search for the unseen "order" underlying it, or between the private experience of an emotion and the necessity of organising principles.[18] Under Woolf's pen, therefore, the words "order," "principles," "rules" and "laws" retain their aesthetic and ethical connotations while losing their connection with the ideas of binding discipline and imposed stability. In the case of the essay, the principles that need to "control" its "essentially egoistical" dimension (*E I* 25) echo, in her mind, the obligation the essayist has to others and to himself as he needs to govern his soul, without hindering its "freedom to explore and experiment" (*E IV* 75). Similarly, if the essay needs to be "pure," this "purity" – interestingly associated with water and wine – is the antonym of "dullness, deadness, and deposits of extraneous matter"; it results from the triumph of style and from "the spirit of personality" (*E IV* 221) without excluding forms of generic hybridity, or the presence of an unruly "I."

Woolf's conception of the essay, and by extension, of other literary kinds, simultaneously looks back in time while anticipating recent critical

views on the subject, contrasting, therefore, with the modern resistance, from the 1920s to the 1980s, to the ideological values associated
with genre theory – among them, the denial of creativity, singularity
and autonomy. First, her implicit debt to the Romantics should be
remembered. Shaped by the experiential and conceptual notion of "life
itself," Woolf's approach to genre recalls the organic metaphors commonly used during the Romantic age in that they establish an analogy
between the literary artefact and physical organisms, the natural world
and even the cosmos. Although her personal imagery rather borrows
from the rhythms of modern daily life, the opposition she establishes,
in "The Decay of Essay Writing," between genuine inspiration and penmanship echoes Coleridge's (1849: 65) way of contrasting "mechanic"
form – "when on any material we impress a pre-determined form" – and
"innate" organic form that "shapes as it developes, itself from within."
Conversely, Coleridge's idea that the "fullness" of a form's development
"is one and the same with the perfection of its outward form" seems
to anticipate Woolf's vision of the "magic of writing" as enabling the
"essayist's knowledge" to be fused by the substance of his work (*E IV*
216).[19] William Hazlitt's (1889: 2–3) lecture on the periodical essayists
also comes to mind: he praises Montaigne – the first "of his kind" – for
his "naked simplicity and force" and associates the form and substance of
the familiar essay with its choice of the "experimental" method over the
"dogmatic one." More generally, there is something definitely Romantic
in Woolf's insistence that each literary kind should provide the reader
with a specific form of pleasure and increase in sensation.[20]

Beyond intertextual allusions and genealogical affinities, Woolf appears
to have shared with the Romantics the belief that literary "kinds" and
"shapes" need to be recognised, exploited artistically, examined empir-
ically and theoretically while embracing a notion of literariness that
required the concept of "genre" but transcended it at the same time.
In a context of historical and aesthetic revolutions, but also when an
increasingly urban reader was craving for instant gratification, Woolf re-
discovered the power of genre and exploited it in a way that anticipated
far more recent critical views on the subject such as Adena Rosmarin's in
The Power of Genre (1985), Thomas Beebee's in *The Ideology of Genre*
(1994) or John Frow's in *The Performance of Genre* (2013).[21] In fact, her
essays on literary shapes use the word "function" to encapsulate her own
conception of the "power" and "performance" of genre as a dynamic
process that "generates effect of reality and truth, authority and plausi-
bility" (Frow 2). Thus, the first function of "genre," according to Woolf,
is to lift up texts and writers to a different status in a cultural hierarchy
that tends to ignore or undervalue them. In this respect, a constantly
renewable definition of all genres is all the more required, as the present state of the form tends to offer an undefined, if not chaotic, vision
of their purpose and principles. What Woolf does with the "Modern
Essay," therefore, she will apply to "Modern Fiction" (1925), "The

New Biography" (1927) and "Modern Letters" (1930), assuming that although theories "are dangerous things," "we must risk one" whenever we are about to discuss our "modern tendencies" (*E VI* 260). Indeed, the second goal of a genre "theory," Woolf suggests, is to enlighten the present – which cannot be achieved without a comparison with prior traditions and, therefore, without some knowledge of literary history. The third function of genre is pragmatic in the linguistic sense of the word. Woolf explains in "Montaigne" that "communication is health; communication is truth; communication is happiness." If "to share is our duty" (*E IV* 76), then awareness of genre establishes a common ground – or "code of manners" – "which writers and readers accept as a prelude to the more exciting intercourse of friendship" (*E III* 434). Woolf's art of conversation, and how genre structures it, thus anticipates Jauss's theory of reception and his well-known concept of the horizon of expectation.[22] It also anticipates the now widely accepted idea in literary criticism that "all acts of communication can be modeled in terms of genre, insofar as they are partly dependent on codes and conventions" (Duff 2000: 16). But Woolf adds an ethical and democratic dimension to this transfer of attention from the point of production (the writer) to the point of reception (the reader). The dynamic pedagogy that underlies her conception of genre implies a form of conversation that can guide the reader from an impression of confusing chaos towards the perception of "order," and then towards the possibility of critical assessment from which he or she is never excluded. This common ground, however, is also the soil in which the expressive function of art – and of genre – needs to take root. Misunderstandings arise when "writers are attempting what they cannot achieve" and use a form to contain a meaning which is strange to it (*E IV* 429). Thus, genre provides both readers and writers with constraining, yet also empowering, historical and aesthetic tools. From the tension between the conventions of form and a writer's creativity, the essential dialogue of singularity with permanence can emerge and be assessed.

"Phases of Fiction" – Phases of Reading

The conception of "Phases of Fiction" has a long and revealing history. Woolf evokes a future "book on criticism" – "some theory about fiction" but not a "matter of 'development'" – for the first time in November and December 1925 (*D III* 47; 50), at a moment when her husband, Leslie Stephen, and George Rylands were planning a series to be called *The Hogarth Lectures on Literature*. She worked at this "book [she] hate[d]" intermittently (*D III* 227), often feeling burdened by the task, and finished the first draft before going to Cambridge in October 1928 for her own "lecture" on "Women and fiction." Her notebooks and diary show that her research kept getting mixed up with her exploration of women, fiction and historiography and continued for years after the American literary journal *The Bookman: A Magazine of Literature and Life* finally published what had become a signed essay in three installments (April, May, June 1929).[23] The introduction to the April issue praised the author's work as might be expected, while discreetly dismissing its critical reach in a typically gendered way (*The Bookman*'s readership was distinctly middle class and masculine):

> Mrs Woolf has been thinking about her craft of novelist, letting her eye and mind run over the great examples of the art in which, as the author of *Mrs Dalloway*, *To the Lighthouse*, *Orlando*, etc., she has won such distinction. The result is a survey of fiction at once profound and charming.[24]

"Charming" was probably not the appreciation Woolf was looking for, although she was never satisfied with her "unwritten" book. In July 1934, she revised the first "truth telling chapter" (*D IV* 229); three months later, she tried "a new method" for it: "to be phases of the readers mind: different situations. Part 2. To be a dialogue, in a hotel on the Mediterranean: each chapter to correspond with the period. Thus to rob it of formality" (*D IV* 250). Ironically, on February 9, 1932, J.J. Thompson, Master of Trinity College since 1918, sent a letter informing Woolf that the University Council had decided to ask her to deliver the Ford Clarke Lectures the next year, five decades after her father's inauguration of this academic ritual in 1883. The daughter of the Victorian gentleman would have been the first woman to receive such a "great honour," but Leslie's "poor little Ginny" nonetheless declined: "how could I write six lectures [...] without giving up a year to criticism; without becoming a functionary; without sealing my lips when it comes to tilting at Universities" (*D IV* 79). A few days later, however, "the devil whispered" in her ear, along with her sister, Vanessa Bell, and Alice Ritchie who were pressuring her to accept the council's proposition. Woolf hesitated all the more as she had "six lectures written in Phases of Fiction; I could furbish them up & deliver the Clark lectures & win the esteem of my sex, with a few week's work." But then, what about "freedom," and being "a time serving pot hunter"? Above all, to "re-cast" her essay for the occasion – "L. says since the middle 4 were published in America I could not do this without complete re-writing" – would imply that she "should be impregnated with the lecturing manner: its jocosity, its emphasis" (*D IV* 79–80).

In the end, Woolf delivered no lectures at Trinity College; as to the reason why she was not among the very few women included in the *Hogarth Series on Literature*, we can assume that it had to do with the dilemma expressed in her diary.[25] *The Bookman*'s readers were indeed neither Cambridge students, nor did they have anything to do with the intended audience of a Hogarth *Series* whose published writers were mostly male academics occupying recognised positions in the academic world. Arthur Quiller-Couch, then editor of the famous *The Oxford Book of English Verse, 1250–1900* (1900), wrote the introductory volume of the Series in 1927; the same year, his *Lecture on Lectures* was followed by F.R. Lucas's *Tragedy*, Allardyce Nicoll's *Studies in Shakespeare* and Harold Nicolson's *The Development of English Biography*; a year later appeared H.J. Grierson's *Lyrical Poetry*, Edwin Muir's *The Structure of the Novel* and *Phases of English Poetry*, a volume written by Herbert Read that replaced Woolf's own essay, originally announced as No 7—*Phases in the Novel*.[26] The authors mentioned here had neither difficulty nor reluctance to use the "lecturing" format and the "emphatic," if not prescriptive, tone that Woolf wanted to avoid. They also generally complied with the traditional categories and developmental mode of academic literary histories.[27] Edwin Muir's definition of his method in the first chapter of *The Structure of the Novel* is here a case in point:

> I shall divide the novel into a few rough and ready but easily recognisable classes; I shall consider not merely one kind of structure but several, discover if possible the laws which operate each, and find an aesthetic justification for those laws.
>
> (Muir 1928: 7)

We have no trace of Woolf's response to these publications, some of which dealt with two of her favourite subjects, fiction and poetry, but we may find it ironical, in view of her opinion on the new critics of the time, that Herbert Read should have used the word "phases" in his own title and conferred upon it an odd geometrical significance throughout the book:

> The Phases through which we have traced the development of English poetry might be illustrated by a series of diagrams: in the first the poet coincides with his circle; in the second he is a point within the circle; in the third he is a point on the circumference; and finally he is a point outside the circle. [...] The four phases complete a cycle, beginning with the world as poet and ending with the poet as world.
>
> (Read 1928: 130–131)[28]

Compared with Read's, Woolf's "phases" can seem indeed more "charming" – or less conceptual – than the critical practice consisting in equating theory with "classification" – classification by "chronology" and "subject matter" – or with anything that manages to sound both "scientific and trim," an expression used by E.M. Forster in his introduction to *Aspects of the Novel* (Forster 1927: 27).[29] As a matter of fact, Woolf's undefined "phases" echo the haziness of her friend's "aspects" in his own theory of the genre: they do not refer to a distinct period of time or stage in a process of development, nor do they imply an exploration of "schools and influences and fashions" (Forster 40).[30] A nineteenth-century scholar might find it easier to associate them with Francis William Newman's religious autobiography *Phases of Faith: Or,*

Passages from the History of My Creed (1850) – a book that the Woolfs happened to have in their personal library – than with any chapters of literary history.[31] From the start, Woolf announces that her "phases of fiction" – The Truth-Tellers, The Romantics, The Character-Mongers and Comedians, The Psychologists, The Satirists and Fantastics, The Poets – will have a length and a principle of organisation of their own, resulting from the "attempt to record the impressions made upon the mind by reading a certain number of novels in succession." The "succession" in question has nothing to do with the progression of a literary-historical survey: the reader's mind is "allowed to read what it like[s]," only "for interest and pleasure" (*E V* 40–41). In her analysis of the essay, Anne E. Fernald (1997: 194; 197) shows how Woolf's "most sustained theory" of fiction "dismisses any other scale of judgment as irrelevant." Woolf, she explains, turns what characterises "most of our reading, into a virtue" while transforming the usual organising principle of development into one of "contrast." Fernald also convincingly explores the contradictory association in "Phases of Fiction" between reading and pleasure, along with the "haphasardness" of the movements of a reader's mind and body as he or she circulates in a library. I share her conclusion that Woolf here "creates a map of discovery, suggesting much about what is yet unknown as it traces the uncertain boundaries of what is" (210). However, I would like to put forward the theoretical thrust proposed in Woolf's project, first by comparing Woolf's essays with some of her predecessors' and contemporaries' literary histories of the novel, then by examining her unscholarly practice as a mode of historiographical performative revisionism.

"The more I read of other peoples criticism the more I trifle; can't decide," Woolf confided to her diary in May 1921. She was then thinking of a way to "shape" her "Reading Book" – to be *CR* (*D II* 120) – trying to find its "main line," as she would write two years later, along with a form that would neither be the "inartistic method" of the collection of essays, nor "too artistic" and, therefore, artificial (*D II* 261). In a sense and in all her literary-historical essays, Woolf kept pitting questions of "line," "method," critical posture and disciplinary boundaries against her "own individuality" and the need to "get them into a current of life" (ibid.). In this respect, to determine the theory underlying "Phases of Fiction" requires more critical skills than to determine what it is not. Read against the grain of most late nineteenth- and early twentieth-century criticism, Woolf's 50-page essay appears to differ from the various genres of literary history. It does not read as a series of lectures arranged chronologically nor as a social and cultural history of the novel in the wake of Leslie Stephen's *English Literature and Society in the Eighteenth Century* (1904). Her unfinished book does not explore solely national culture since it figures Melville, Proust, Dostoevsky, Maupassant and Henry James, nor does it take the reader teleologically from the origins of the genre to its possible future within the common framework of an "advent

narrative."[32] It is not a treasury of excellence either – Woolf says herself that W.E. Norris was "an industrious writer" now belonging to the
long list of "forgotten novelists" (*E V* 44) – and does not offer to rewrite
the canon or to recover the voices of "the Obscure." Searching for traditional forms of contextualism, historicism, source- and fact-hunting will
be fruitless, so that the critic might wonder, in a Woolfian way: "How
should one read [Phases of Fiction]?"

This essay should first be read as symptomatic of a moment in Britain's
cultural life when the novel as a genre had become an essential preoccupation for Woolf and her contemporaries. In the words of Katherine
Mansfield reviewing *Night and Day* in 1919:

> there is at present day no form of writing which is more eagerly,
> more widely discussed than the novel. What is its fate to be? We
> are told on excellent authority that it is dying; and on equally good
> authority that only now it begins to live.
>
> (Mansfield 1919: 79)

In July 1922, Woolf had discussed Percy Lubbock's *The Craft of Fiction*
in her *TLS* essay "On Re-reading Novels" (*E III* 336–345); a year later
she compared Lubbock's "false [...] doctrine" to her "tunneling process" in *Mrs Dalloway* (*D II* 272), a clear proof, Woolf thought, that the
critic was wrong.[33] On December 1, 1923, her reply to Arnold Bennett's
(1923: 88) criticism of her characters in *Jacob's Room* – a book too clever
for them "to vitally survive in the mind, because the author has been
obsessed with details of cleverness and originality" – appeared as "Mr
Bennett and Mrs Brown" in the *Nation & Athenaeum* (*E III* 384–389).[34]
In August 1924, she feared that John Middleton Murry's own assessment
of the "younger generation of novelists," including herself, might apply
to *Mrs Dalloway*:

> Character, atmosphere, an attitude to life, a quality of perception—
> these things have interested a D.H. Lawrence, a Katherine Mansfield,
> a Virginia Woolf; but the old mechanism of story not at all. None of
> them has solved the problem of the novel; neither did Marcel Proust,
> nor has Mr Joyce or Miss Richardson solved it.
>
> (Middleton Murry 1923: 109)[35]

But while Murry considered that the genre had "reached a kind of
impasse" (ibid.), Woolf, along with Forster, Ford Madox Ford and other
modernists, had no doubt that "the novel ha[d] become indispensable to
the understanding of life" (Ford 8). Therefore, she needed to situate herself in a genealogy of debates that had begun in the eighteenth century
and that continued to be grounded in the ideological oppositions between
growth and decay; highbrow or lowbrow culture. These debates resulted,
above all, in the often-pessimistic sense that no formalistic considerations

could encapsulate the novel's complexity as a genre. In this sense, "Phases of Fiction" belongs to its time while enabling Woolf to find a path of her own beyond the seemingly unbridgeable oppositions between literature, theory, aesthetic criticism and historical development.

The first two pages of the essay bear the striking marks of such an attempt: they unwrite scholarly claims such as Walter Raleigh's in his preface to *The English Novel* (1894): Woolf's goal is overtly not "critical and historical" and she will not "furnish studies of the work of the chief English novelists before Scott, connected by certain general lines of reasoning and speculation on the nature and development of the novel" (Raleigh 1894: vi). She will not begin at the beginning when the "spirit" of fiction – in Raleigh's case, of "the romance" – "has been born"; she will not provide an anatomy of the genre since its origins, nor speak of "revivals," "definitions," "merits and influence," "movements" or "style."[36] On first examination, Woolf's introductory remarks echo Forster's "sympathies" for "the untidy and harassed people who are scribbling away at their books," as she herself comments in a review of her friend's book (*E IV* 458). Just as Forster distrusted "pseudo-scholars," "period of periods" and "classification by chronology" (Forster 8–11), Woolf is "suspicious of fixed labels and settled hierarchies" (*E V* 42). Her association, inside one chapter, of authors belonging to different generations – Swift and Trollope in "The Truth-Tellers," Radcliffe and Stevenson in "The Romantics," for example – seems to nod to Forster's own pairing of her "fantasist's" art and Laurence Sterne's (Forster 19).[37] However, in spite of the two writer-critics' rejection of "the scholar's attitude" (*E IV* 457), of their belief in the centrality of character in fiction, and of their shared trust in the common reader's capacity to judge – "the final test of a novel will be our affection for it" (Forster 23) – Forster's way of assembling "the parts of fiction" and of "comment[ing] upon their use and nature" does not totally convince Woolf (*E IV* 459). She regrets that he should "theorise" about fiction only "incidentally": "he has in his 'mind's eye' something [...] which he calls 'life' in which his comparison of novelists and their works is grounded," but his vision of "life" implies the "humane as opposed to the aesthetic." Because Forster does not analyse the connection between what he calls "life" and "plot," "character" or "story," "we are back in the old bog; nobody knows anything about the laws of fiction; or what its relation is to life; or to what effects it can lend itself. We can only trust our instincts." Forster's book is "wise and brilliant," Woolf admits, and yet it says "almost nothing [...] about words" and the "the medium in which a novelist works" (*E IV* 460–462). Woolf, therefore, does not blame Forster for his rejection of any form of historicism, nor for having his own point of view – she sees "where he stands." However, she considers that he has not defined fiction "firmly" and "severely" enough, using "rules" that would have conferred "dignity" to his subject by reminding us that fiction is "a work of art." Strikingly enough, the reader of "Phases of Fiction" may fail to notice those very "laws" and "critical equipment" that Woolf finds missing in Forster's book (*E IV* 462–463). Indeed, Woolf's own "theory" of fiction first reads as a subtle reshuffling of the chief ingredients of nineteenth-century literary histories, as if, again, she needed to unwrite and rewrite simultaneously the very tradition that used to "admit" most literary genres (but not fiction) "to a place in civilised society" in order to clear the ground for her own voice (*E IV* 460).

Woolf's choice of the word "phase" leads the reader to expect a study of genre involving different stages in a developmental process, but no such process is explored. She chooses chapter headings that may appear to organise past and present examples of fiction into familiar categories, but whether generic, generational or chronological, these categories are constantly blurred: within and between her "phases," the essayist undercuts expectations as to temporal linearity and traditional classification. "The Truth-Tellers" thus begins with Defoe who is then followed by W.E. Norris, Maupassant, Swift and Trollope; Walter Scott offers the first quotation of "The Romantics" before Woolf turns to Stevenson, then to Ann Radcliffe; in "The Character-Mongers and Comedians" – an unexpected title for fiction writers – Dickens appears prior to Jane Austen whose *Pride and Prejudice* is then compared with George Eliot's *Silas Marner*; "The Psychologists" draws links between, in order of appearance, Henry James, Marcel Proust and Dostoevsky. The unity of the phase named "The Satirists and Fantastics" appears still more random: it begins with an allusion to Voltaire and Anatole France then focuses on Thomas Love Peacock's *Crochet Castle* before moving backwards in time with Laurence Sterne's *Tristram Shandy*; as to "The Poets," the section includes some of Woolf's favourite novelists: Dostoevsky again, Tolstoy, Emily Brontë, Thomas Hardy, Marcel Proust, Meredith and Melville. In fact, only "The Character-Mongers and Comedians" figures British authors belonging to the same century: the other sections assemble writers from different historical periods or cultural eras.

In this essay, therefore, Woolf does not consider time as her "enemy." Contrary to Forster, she indeed "contemplate[s] its stream" (Forster 1927: 9; 14) but reframes and redefines the categories with which traditional literary history used to associate temporality. Far from erasing the concept of "literary development" – she admits, in her conclusion, that "prose itself is still in its infancy, and capable, no doubt, of infinite change and development" (*E V* 79) – she orientates it towards the future. However, the absence, in her essay, of a proper beginning and ending suggests that her understanding of time and change does not rely on the ideas of "origin," "growth" or "influence" achieved by an author's position on a timeline. In the end, "development" is not the development of a genre, but "the growth and development of feelings, which is the novelist's aim"; chapters and sequence belong to him who "copies the order of the day, observes the sequence of ordinary things even if such fidelity entails chapters of description and hours of research" (81).

Similarly, the metaphor of reading as a journey does not impose a teleological plot on the studied material, but rather the sense of an individual and collective trajectory and spatiality: "even though the time at our disposal has been short," Woolf writes, "we have travelled, in reading these few books, a great distance emotionally," and a sense of "the vastness of fiction and the width of its range" has been "gained" (80). At a time when, Ted Underwood explains, "a strongly contrastive, periodized model of cultivation ha[d] shaped literary study even more deeply and enduringly than it shaped the discipline of history itself," Woolf does not dramatise "the vertiginous gulfs between eras" so as to homogenise each age (Underwood 4–5), but rather insists on periodic overlaps, perpetual transformation and affinities crossing time and space—boundaries that the discipline of English was still trying, in 1929, to keep safe and solid. As any literary historian, she groups individual writers, chronicles prominent examples, but outside a sense of chronology or evolution: instead, she focuses on what their writing and "worldmaking" achieves in the reader's mind and body (Grabes 2001: 20).

And so the changes that Woolf mentions throughout the essay do not refer to historical events or abrupt contextual transformations, but to the novelists' art – changes in perspective, mood, manners, idiom, point of view – and to the readers' desire for novelty. Since novels "make us live imaginatively, with the whole of the body as well as the mind," Woolf explains, they "produce in us the physical sensations of heat and cold, noise and silence, one reason perhaps why we desire change and why our reactions to them vary so much at different times" (55). Associated with the notion of "desire" and the reader's varying "appetites," change – this essential historiographical category – once more becomes one of the essayist's chief critical tools[38]: "desires, appetites, however we may come by them, fill in [some design that has been traced upon our minds], scoring now in this direction, now in that"; one appetite – whether for truth, "for music, for shadow, for space," for broader understanding – "leads on all the others in turn"; and when "One desire [has] run its course, another leaps forward to take up the burden" (44). Woolf's "phases" of fiction, therefore, deconstruct the model of the series of lectures and of the period survey while being embedded in a redefined course of time, where temporality and timelessness, diachronicity and synchronicity are combined. Connected with "life itself," this multilayered temporality implies past contexts, a sense of our own time and of "the time to come" (84); it incorporates the influence of history on the reader, the writer and his or her characters, the experiential time of reading, the time of comparing and writing; last but not least, it finds echoes in the way each author's "sentence" shapes itself, "shrinks and wraps itself firmly round the meaning," or "runs like a knife, in and out, cutting a shape clear" (58). Thus, what "appears" in Woolf's phases – according to the Greek origin of the word "phanein" – cannot be separated from the "aisthetikos" of fiction: this imaginary experience of a singular fictional world aesthetically conveyed and grabbed by the senses before our reasoning mind tries to make sense of it.

The different phases explored in Woolf's essay also reflect the history of fiction's "fertility" (83) and its capacity to satisfy appetites that are bound to change as time goes by. Because of our changing expectations, the "phases of fiction" can never be "complete," nor can our desires receive "full satisfaction." On the contrary, reading excites them; they well up and make us inarticulately aware of a dozen different novels that wait just below the horizon: hence the "futility at present of any theory of 'the future of fiction'" (79). Whether Woolf has produced a theory of the past and present of the genre in the course of her essay is arguable. At any rate, the disclaimer in her introduction, an example of counter-academic discourse describing the following pages as an "attempt," far from the "universal" and "more learned" language of the critic and historian, signals the contrary. However, Woolf's unwritten, incomplete book has enacted her poetic, ethic and political drive away from the patriarchal authority of lectures, textbooks and the New Criticism, and towards the emancipation of the reader-as-critic. In this respect, "Phases of Fiction" should be read along with "Hours in a Library" (1916), "How Should One Read a Book" (1926) and "Reading" (1919) as a forceful example of Woolf's "transactional theory of reading" and of the way it builds a democratic community of readers (Cuddy-Keane 2003: 119).[39] First, Woolf's essay unwrites the nineteenth-century academic vision of literary history which was generally accompanied, according to April London, by "restrictive attitudes to readers deemed inexperienced, naïve, or innately limited" (London 6). Then, and as Caroline Pollentier has shown in her analysis of the essay, it also anticipates recent theories of co-creative imagination as world-making, notably Nelson Goodman's *Ways of World Making* (1978), Thomas Pavel's *Fictional Worlds* (1986) or Ruth Ronen's *Possible Worlds in Literary Theory*.[40] Strikingly, the capacity of Woolf's common reader to inhabit one of these worlds not only temporally but also spatially – to "trace his course through literature with great exactness" and to "think himself, from time to time, in possession of a whole world as inhabitable as the real world" (*E IV* 41) – will later be explored by Mikhail Bakhtin and Paul Ricœur among others.[41] Woolf, it seems, did not "miss the centre" of what writers and readers have in mind when they immerse themselves in fiction, and despite her so-called limited, personal and erratic record of reading, she has foregrounded the endless "process of creation" (*E IV* 41).

Woolf's critical method in "Phases of Fiction" is adapted to this process: it relies on the chief ingredients evoked in earlier chapters of this book: a sense of historicity embedded in phenomenological experience, a multilayered vision of time and change, an exploration of "life" in connection with the specificities of the novel as a genre. A pedagogical, empowering act towards both reader and writer, Woolf's reading "course" has an unfolding of its own: only "in looking back at the few novels that we have glanced at here" have we learnt to see and to feel "the whole [that] is exposed to view" (82). As literary history, therefore, "Phases of Fiction" fills in some of the essential prerequisites of the genre: it has a subject, an organising principle (although this principle de-homogenises the usual eighteenth- and nineteenth-century cultural periodisation), and an explanatory principle: the reader's need for change and fiction's capacity to "follow life" in its various, ever-changing shapes and guises. According to Robert Grabes's (2001: 21–22) definition of literary history as a history of discourse, Woolf's essay "pays attention to those individual works that have introduced new kinds of arrangements or have substantially changed existing ones" while insisting on "the relationship between a particular work and other literary works and genres." As a telling example of Woolf's historiographical and modernist art of the essay, it functions both as a revisionist history keeping score of the tools, practices and critical courses that it exposes and questions, and as a counter literary history that refuses closure, systematism, ostentatious formalism and authority as the central ingredient of the knowledge it passes on.

"Anon" and "The Reader"

How to Begin Again or the Power of Narrative

Virginia Woolf began the conception of her last historiographical project on September 12, 1940 in Rodmell, thinking that she would call the first two chapters "Reading at Random" and "Turning the Page." Two days before, a bomb had wrecked her house on Mecklenburgh Square in London. In the preceding months, the Germans had entered Paris, the Battle of Britain had started over England, Hitler had asked England to capitulate, Woolf had attended her first air-raid meetings, and imagined, several times, that "This, I thought yesterday, might be my last walk" (*D V* 298). And yet, in January of the year before she committed suicide, she composed "The Leaning Tower" and began *Between the Acts*; over the course of the summer, she also sent in the proofs of *Roger Fry*, resumed her work on her play-novel, kept reading the Romantics (Shelley, Coleridge, Macaulay) while looking for a "new critical method—something swifter and lighter and more colloquial and yet intense: more to the point and less composed; more fluid and following the flight; than my C.R. essays" (*D V* 298).[42] In November, thinking of her "common history book," she regained some energy: "having this moment finished The Pageant—or Poynst Hall?—(begun perhaps April 1938) my thoughts turn well up, to write the first chapter of the next book (nameless). Anon, it will be called" (*D V* 340). That was only a few days after a bomb had dropped on the river Ouse, flooding the marshes and meadows surrounding it. Hermione Lee reports how Woolf oddly loved the sight: from then on, "Deluge" and "island" became among her favourite words (Lee 1997:

747). The spectacle of nature had become a form of consolation: "Hills & fields; I can't stop looking. October Blooms; brown plough; & and the fading & the freshening of the marsh" (*D V* 329).

A same attention to close surroundings, natural elements and history in the making characterises the first page of "Anon," from the "matted boughs" of a perennial English forest where "innumerable birds sang" to the environment in which the anonymous poet lived his "roaming life," "crossing the fields, mounting the hills, lying under the hawthorn to listen to the nightingale" (*E VI* 581). The subject of Woolf's history book – the birth of Anon as a communal, unprinted author and with him, of English culture – obviously required it. Besides, Woolf's notes for "Reading at Random" suggest that she wanted "to begin with English country before E^th^" and to evoke "the effect of country upon writers" and to always relate her subject to both time and geography (*NFRR* 373). In fact, the numerous correspondences between her two draft chapters and her own circumstances constitute a poignant subtext, especially if one remembers how different her emotions were when, in April 1931, she wrote to Ethel Smyth: "A vast vista of intense and peaceful work stretches before me – a whole book on English lit; some stories: biographies: this is as I spin" (*L IV* 321). In her Rodmell home, nine years later, Woolf felt that she lived on her own private island: she experienced the "queer [...] contraction of life to a village radius" (*D V* 329), sensed the isolation of her friends and of herself, but also heard the reassuring silence around her when no sounds of air raids came breaking it. In *Between the Acts*, Woolf had used the image of the island as a country, a separate territory and an illusory protection: "This is a pageant, all may see / Drawn from our island history / England am I" (*BA* 70). "Anon" begins with a quotation from G.M. Trevelyan's *History of England* (1926) that pictures Britain as "an island" where, once upon a time, "the untamed forest was king" (*E VI* 581). Strikingly, the image of the island also appears in Woolf's letters and diaries whenever she mentions this particular project. On September 17, 1940, after a trip to the local Public Library where she wanted to find "a history of English literature," she writes: "Turned me against all literary criticism. [...] Our island is a deserted island" (*D V* 321–322). A month later, she evokes "our lovely free autumn island" on which she can peacefully "read Dante, & for [her] trip thro' English lit[erature] book" (*E V* 329).

I have already suggested that Woolf's acute awareness, from 1935 onwards, of the threat weighing on England and on all its citizens pervades her fiction and essays. In "Anon" and "The Reader," this awareness does not fuel the controlled anger and satiric thrust that characterise *Three Guineas*. Here, the coalescence of nostalgia with a utopian dream of cultural unity brings to mind Michel de Certeau's definition of historiography as both a "labour of death" – one that "denies loss by appropriating to the present the privilege of recapitulating the past as form of knowledge" – and a "labour against death" (de Certeau 1988a:

5). In this respect, the voice of Anon emerging from the silence echoes Woolf's own voice and feeling of loss in the last months of her life: "No audience. No private stimulus, only this outer roar" (*L VI* 460). Her protective, although sometimes stifling, "island" had thus become the only place where she could still make her voice heard, by going, once more, "through English literature, like a string through cheese, or rather like some industrious insect, eating its way from book to book, from Chaucer to Lawrence" (*D IV* 63).[43] Now at least, she felt detached "from the hierarchy, the patriarchy," and could "walk over the marsh saying, I am I: and must follow that furrow, not copy another. That is the only justification for my writing, living" (*D V* 347).

Although very different from the voice of her other critical and historiographical essays, Woolf's voice in "Anon" and "The Reader," however, is still the voice of a fighting innovator, looking for a new critical method, torn between what "the flight of the mind" can conceive – a "sketch" – and the finished work (*D V* 298). It springs from her dissatisfaction with the "exhausted air" of the literary criticism practised by her "contemporaries" (*D V* 322).[44] But it also results from a constantly renewed wish to find the best format for her subject: "Keep to time sequence. Pass from criticism to biography. Lives of people. No 'periods': No text book. [...] The Life of a Book" (*NFRR* 373). Her voice thus strikingly resounds with the echoes of her favourite historians, when their craft did not eschew the art of the storyteller: Michelet and Macaulay, and perhaps also Hakluyt whom she had enjoyed reading.[45] If not "Elizabethan," the "style" of "Anon" and "The Reader" is indeed "long-winded," almost romantic in its picturesque descriptions of surroundings, at any rate poetic in its use of imagery, sound-patterns, anaphoras and syntactic rhythm:

> Anon sang because spring has come; or winter is gone; because he loves; because he is hungry, or lustful; or merry; or because he adores some God. Anon is sometimes man; sometimes woman. He is the common voice singing out of doors, He has no house. He lives a roaming life crossing the fields, mounting the hills, lying under the hawthorn to listen to the nightingale.
>
> (*E VI* 581–582)

To follow the vestiges of this "homo narrans," Woolf thus chose to fuse mûthos (oral narrative in Greek), with history as story and poetics in the making.[46]

According to Melba Cuddy-Keane (1997: 71), Woolf's chronological narrative of "the changing methods of production and consumption of the literary text" is more conventional in its writing than Woolf's other alternative historiographical projects. One could indeed argue that Woolf's story of the birth and the death of Anon, followed by the emergence of the individual reader, is a tribute to what David Perkins (1992: 29–33) describes as the "readable and popular, yet informed and intelligent," nineteenth-century models of literary histories with their "omissions and emphases," their "structure of cause and effect," their heroic plot grafted upon the author's "desires," whether "conscious and unconscious," and their resort to "metaphors of origins, emergence from obscurity, neglect and recognition, conflict, hegemony, succession, displacement, decline and so forth." By resorting to the linear covering of more than one period of English literary history – from the Anglo-Saxons to the Renaissance and after – Woolf can also appear to re-establish the prestige of national teleological narratives grounded in the exploration of continuities and changes. Then the constant shifts, in her two draft chapters, from the preterit tense to the present, along with a way of "presenting pictures to the imagination" (Macaulay 1828a: 188) anchored in the sensorial experiences of the story's protagonists and readers remind us of her early interests in the modes and principles of romantic historiography: "By shutting out a chimney or a factory," Woolf writes, "we can still see what Anon saw" (*E VI* 582). As always, however, beyond this palimpsestuous tribute that half covers its tracks, Woolf's allegiance to the past takes the form of a counter-discourse. Not only are former historiographical narratives given a "supplement" (*AR* 35), they are in various ways transformed and undermined. Unlike most nineteenth- and early-twentieth literary histories, hers begins with the prehistory of Britain before the Norman Conquest. It gives shape to its swamps, forests, folk-tunes, pagan Gods and incomprehensible words before the advent of the written text.[47] In Woolf's narrative, Chaucer does not come first, nor does Beowulf; instead, the "common" voice of an anonymous singer, "sometimes man; sometimes woman," breaks the silence, letting the audience join in the chorus: " 'Terly, terlow' they sang." Whether brutal or more gradual adaptations to circumstances, changes are not determined by the logic of cause and effect but by the current of life itself: "Anon sang because spring has come; or winter is gone; because he loves; because he is hungry, or lustful; or merry; or because he adores some God" (*E VI* 581–582). No heroes figure in this alternative advent narrative: "Anon's words were as uncouth to the master and mistress as to us"; the simple singer was often "despised" or merely "tolerated." Yet, he "gave voice to the old stories," accompanied the rituals and beliefs of the people and encouraged various forms of "connection" between the commoners (583). As to the reader, his "life" begins with the diminished "acuteness" of his hearing and sight before his "sense of words and their associations is developed" (600). This history then does not rely on a chronology shaped by dates and clear-cut periods. Nor is the birth of Anon and of the reader a cycle in a decline and fall historiographical paradigm either: although linear, Woolf's conception of time is once more thickly layered, a "reservoir" of individual and collective gestures, acts and dreams that all give her readers a sense of time as flux. Her narrative keeps moving backwards and forwards as it compares and contrasts works belonging to different generations. Besides, if "it was the printing press that finally was to kill Anon," "it was the press also that preserved him" (583); loss, therefore, equals transformation as much as death. Last but not least, in her own "theatre of memory," the authors of the canon – Malory, Chaucer, Spenser, Sir Philip Sidney, Marlowe, Kyd, Bacon, Shakespeare – are surrounded by the anonymous founders of the English language and culture and by the outsiders who wrote against "the established" (582). Similarly, to the familiar facts of mainstream historiography Woolf adds the newly assembled material of what Raphael Samuel has since called "unofficial" forms of knowledge – ethnographic observations, ancient wisdoms, the interrelations between the arts and, obviously, oral trad- ition as "it wells up from those lower depths – history's nether-world – where memory and myth intermingle, and the imaginary rubs shoulders with the real" (Samuel 3; 5).

In these remarkably dense chapters, Woolf thus weaves the threads of several narratives: the history of the means of production and the recep- tion of a literary work, that of the construction of a cultural past through oral literature, the recording of an audience's, and then, of a reader's cog- nitive and emotional experience, the development of the material cultures of the past, of the English language, and of the influences – material and psychological – affecting an artist's productions. All these narratives are embedded in a "current of life" while anticipating more recent approaches to historiography. "Part-anthropological, part-social, part- psychological," as Hermione Lee puts it (Lee 1997: 750), Woolf's reading of literary history is here again the work of a cultural innovator who knows not only that culture is "a site of forms of ideological and political contestations in which dominant, residual and emergent forces coexist," but also that "what we encounter in literary discourse is overwhelmingly particular and even wholly individual" (Grabes 5; 18). In this respect, "Anon" and "The Reader" testify to what Elena Gualtieri describes as Woolf's gradual shift of focus, in the 1930s – one that we have already observed in Part I of this book – "from exceptional individualities and characters who cannot be assimilated to anything other than themselves to figures who are so embedded in communal textures that their contours become indistinguishable from the historical background" (Gualtieri 45). In December 1939, Woolf was "gulping up" Freud's *The Future of an Illusion* (1928) along with *Civilisation and Its Discontent* (1930), finding both works "upsetting": "If we're all instinct, the unconscious, whats all this about civilisation, the whole man, freedom &c?" (*D V* 250). A year later, she bought Eileen Power's *Medieval People* (1924) in which the economic historian and medievalist spoke about "the lives of ordinary people," arguing that "the past may be made to live again for the general reader more effectively by personifying it than by presenting it in the form of learned treatises" (Power v). She also read *Patterns of Culture* (1934), the work of American anthropologist Ruth Benedict.[48] In *Three Guineas*, she had already urged her readers "never [to] cease from thinking—what is this 'civilization' in which we find ourselves?" (*TG* 145); in *Between the Acts*, Miss La Trobe's struggles to bring "Civilization" to her audience "with the very limited means at her disposal" (*BA* 163). And if she never uses the word "civilization" in "Anon" or "The Reader," her writing nevertheless enacts a powerful intervention in what she considered to be the fossilised field of literary history. By centring her history on anonymity and orality, she anticipates the work of Lawrence Stone in "The Revival of Narrative" (1979), of Richard Bauman in *Story, Performance and Event* (1986) and of John D. Niles who claims, in *Homo Narrans* (1999), that "oral narrative is and for a long time has been the chief basis of culture itself [...] for it is chiefly through storytelling that people possess a past" (Niles 2).

A unique "variety of historicist experience," to follow on Cuddy-Keane's phrase in her 1997 essay, the first two draft chapters of Woolf's last unwritten common history book also have much in common with her previous historiographical essays. First, they need to be read in context, both from a specific moment of history and from Woolf's life as a citizen and a female intellectual adopting the double vantage point of the insider, and of the outsider, unwriting dominant historiographical models. In this regard, her pages describing how Latimer, around 1549, chose to "see England itself at this moment in its reality" and took the risk to unveil the "truth" of its condition to the King even if it "br[ought] him to the faggot" epitomise with eloquence the way she fuses documentary record with political ambition (*E VI* 586–587). Then the tensions that characterise her own history – between an inward- and an outward-oriented discourse, between changes and permanence, breaking points and unseen connections, between the apparent spontaneity of a seamless narrative and the intense research that gave birth to it – are all recognisable signs of her method. Embedding her narrative in a meta-critical approach, Woolf keeps reminding us that as a historiographer, she "suggests, debates, theorizes about, and presents the ways in which historians grapple with 'truth', subjectivity, ethics and otherness in their practice and approach" (De Groot 2016: 7). In this particular case, however, Woolf's negotiation with her heritage moves beyond the recovery of the voices of the obscure. In "Anon," she strives to build a cultural bridge between the origins of vernacular culture and the utopian project of healing the scars of a community that needed to hold together in the face of a terrifying future. To heal those scars, Woolf exposes them while uncovering the mechanisms of individualisation, differentiation and division – a semantic field that is omnipresent in "Anon" and "The Reader" – that fracture personal and collective identities. The estrangement of a community from its collective memory and instincts, the separation of the reader from the writer, the erasure of the once heard voices from the recordings of official history all illustrate the personal and collective fear of loss and disconnection. But as she weaves those threads, Woolf offers us a counter-history of collaboration by mapping the literary geography of the roads, tracks and interrelations that testify to cultural forms of collaboration. What

Anon sang and how it affected the commoners, Thomas Malory managed to continue by "bringing to the surface the old hidden world," before Shakespeare, and others. In Malory's pages "we hear the voice of Anon murmuring still" (*E VI* 584). In "Anon" and "The Reader," the power of story and history makes their voices and ours resound in the silence of past centuries: the playwright has been "replaced by the man who writes a book," the audience "by the reader. Anon is dead. [...] Now the reader is completely in being" (*E VI* 599; 601).

Notes

1 *Virginia Woolf's Letters*, vol. 4, to Vita Sackville West, January 8, 1928, 4.
2 On Woolf's Knowledge of Gosse's and Courthope's work, see "Edmund Gosse" (*E V* 248–257) and "Tchekhov on Pope" (*E VI* 549–554). The references are to Leslie Stephen, *English Literature and Society in the Eighteenth Century* (1955: 14; 22) and to W.J. Courthope, *A History of English Poetry* (1895: xv).
3 See Lytton Strachey, *Landmarks in French Literature* (1912) and Ford Madox Ford: *The English Novel: From the Earliest Days to the Death of Joseph Conrad* (1930) and *The March of Literature from Confucius' Day to Our Own* (1938). Published in 1932, F.R Leavis's *New Bearings in English Poetry* was, as its subtitle indicates, a *Study of the Contemporary Situation*; his *The Great Tradition* (1948) was a book of criticism more than a literary history of the novel. T.S. Eliot's critical reconstruction of "tradition" never led him to write a "literary history" in the sense defined by Wellek and Warren. As to I.A. Richards, his *Principles of Literary Criticism* (1925) never refer once to "literary history," as expected.
4 See, for example, in the early decades of the twentieth century, George Saintsbury's *A History of Elizabethan Literature* (1891); Hugh Walker's *The Literature of the Victorian Era* (1910), *A History of Nineteenth Century Literature* (1896), *The English Essay and Essayists* (1915) and *The English Satire and Satirists* (1925). A research in the catalogues of the British Library indicates that George Watson (a Cambridge professor and specialist of literary criticism) was right when he claimed in 1962 that "there is no such thing as a historical school of criticism in twentieth-century English, if by 'school' we mean anything coherent or reasonably homogeneous" (Watson 1962: 223).
5 On the contrast between Woolf's work and the "strong propensity within the Modernist period toward overarching historical narratives," whether cyclical or not, and "universal explanations," see Melba Cuddy-Keane (1997: 64).
6 In *Virginia Woolf: Feminism and the Reader* (2006), Fernald builds "a feminist theory of intertextuality" that enables her to compare and contrast Woolf's "active, revisionist form of literary history" to Eliot's conception of tradition ("Tradition and the Individual Talent": 1919), to Harold Bloom's *Anxiety of Influence* (1973) and to the "strict historicism" endorsed by Margaret Ezell in *Writing Women's Literary History* (1993). She contends that Woolf's revisionist literary theory relies on a "resistant" method that "reaches outside the realm of the literary" and "speaks to the major literary theorists of the twentieth century" (Fernald 3–5).

7 John Addington Symonds (1840–1993) was an English poet, a literary critic, a Renaissance scholar and one of Leslie's Stephen's closest friends. In 1925, Woolf reviewed his daughter Margaret Vaughan's life of her father, *Out of the Past*, published the same year, and wrote: "[Mrs Vaughan's] father was not a great writer; nor indeed was he primarily interested in literature" (*E IV* 13). Among his most famous books are *A History of The Renaissance in Italy* (1875–1876) and *Shakespeare's Predecessors in the English Drama* (1884).

8 Using terms and expressions such as "species," "survival" or "rise and decline," Stephen, like a number of his contemporaries, explains in the same chapter that literary schools "may resemble the animal species," and that the

> development of new literary types [...] implies a compromise between the two conditions which in literature correspond to conservatism and radical-ism. The conservative work is apt to become a mere survival: while the radical may include much that has the crudity of an imperfect application of new principles.
>
> (Stephen 1955: 19; 23)

9 On this subject, see Steven Monte, "Theories of Genre" (2013: 502–505).

10 As most of her British predecessors and contemporaries, Woolf preferred the words "kind," "form," "class" or "shape" and "variety" to "genre," a noun borrowing from Modern French "genre."

11 I'm referring here to Woolf's idea, if not theory, of conversation as the necessary "intercourse" in which the "writers of England and the readers of England" "must be forever engaged" (*E III* 499); as a mode of criticism inherited from Samuel Johnson – yet the only one "worth having at present"; as the proper tone and style for an essayist or as the "turn and turn about method" (*D II* 247).

12 The reviews and essays examined in the following pages are "The Decay of Essay Writing," an essay submitted as "A Plague of Essay" in *Academy & Literature* (February 25, 1905); "A Book of Essays," a review in the *TLS*, January 17, 1918, of *If the Germans Conquered England and Other Essays* (1917) by Robert Lynd; "The Modern Essay," a review of *Modern English Essays 1870 to 1920* (5 vols., ed. Ernest Rhys, 1922) written for the *TLS*, November 30, 1922, and revised for *CR I*; "Montaigne," an essay in the *TLS* (January 31, 1924) based on *Essays of Montaigne* (5 vols., 1923) and also revised for *CR I*.

13 In the five volumes edited by Rhys and figuring more than a hundred English and American essayists, only four are women: Alice Meynell, Vernon Lee, Grace Rhys and Vida D. Scudder.

14 I am particularly indebted here to Caroline Pollentier's Ph.D. Thesis on Woolf's essays and ordinary life, and more particularly her pages on "The Decay of Essay-Writing," "The Modern Essay." My angle of analysis, how-ever, consists in exploring Woolf's "theory" of the essay as an example of her theory of genre, and as typical of her approach as a modernist literary his-torian (Pollentier 2011). On Woolf and the practice of essay writing, see also Brosnan (1997), Rosenberg and Dubino (1997), Gualtieri (2000), Cuddy-Keane (2003), Koutsantoni (2009), Saloman (2012), Bernard (2015) and Reynier (2018).

15 On this reversal of categories and the use of tradition as Woolf's tool to dis-criminate between the contemporary and the modern, see Pollentier (83–87).

On the way Woolf sees Montaigne as having "reversed the hierarchy of values typical of the Edwardian essay by placing the simplicity of direct expression at a far higher level of achievement than the sophistication of style or 'good writing'," see Gualtieri (50).

16 See Part I, Chapter 1 of this book.

17 In "The Decay of Essay Writing," "Modern Essays" and "Montaigne," Woolf uses the modal verbs "should" and "must" at least 50 times.

18 In "The Moment: Summer Night" (1938), Woolf wonders at the elements composing a past or present moment of being, this sought-for truth underlying the unseen order of our perceptions (*E VI* 509–514); in the revised version of "On Re-reading Novels" (1938), she asks: "Is there not something beyond emotion, something which though it is inspired by emotion, tranquillises it, orders it, composes it? – that which Mr. Lubbock calls form, which, for simplicity's sake, we will call art?" (*E VI* 427); in "American Fiction" (1925) Woolf explains that because the American people "are equally diversified into fragments of many nationalities," then a "new art" and "the control of a new tradition" are needed in order "to describe, to unify, to make order out of all these severed parts" (*E IV* 278).

19 The much-commented passage, in Wordsworth preface, about "the great National Events which are daily taking place, and the encreasing accumulation of men in the cities, where the uniformity of their occupations for extraordinary incident which the rapid communication of intelligence hourly gratifies" strikingly anticipates Woolf's evocation of the activities of writing and reading in her own contemporary world (Wordsworth 1802: x).

20 See, for example, how the poet and essayist Leigh Hunt (1784–1859), for Woolf another model of the romantic poet-critic – she describes him in her diary as "our spiritual grandfather" (*D II* 130) – speaks of the necessity to "enhance the experience of a literary text."

21 On this subject, see David Duff (2009).

22 Montaigne, in his essays, speaks of this form of discussion or conversation as "la conference." The Latin origin of the word implies the notion of comparison ("conferre"), the idea of shared experiences and thoughts, and the art of communication. Thus defined, and as the ancient art of dialogue used to do, the "conférence," or "conversation," in Charles Cotton's translation, Montaigne explains, "apprend et exerce d'un coup" (Montaigne, "De l'art de conférer," 1827: 197): "it teaches and exercises at once" (Montaigne 1877: 183).

23 On Woolf's 94 contributions to *The Bookman*, a journal associated with the cause of New Humanism, see Yuzu Uchida (2010: 223–236).

24 Quoted by Stuart N. Clarke (*E V* 85).

25 The first Series of the *Hogarth Lectures on Literature* counted 15 volumes. Rose Macaulay wrote N° 14: *Some Religious Elements in English Literature* (1931); Jean Stewart, who was Faculty Lecturer in French at Cambridge, wrote N° 15: *Poetry in France and England* (1931).

26 Arthur Thomas Quiller-Couch (1863–1944), editor of the famous *The Oxford Book of English Verse, 1250–1900* (1900) and of *On the Art of Writing* (1913–1914), was a novelist, literary critic and lecturer at Cambridge; F.R. Lucas (1894–1967), Fellow of King's College, Cambridge, was an English classical scholar, literary critic, poet, novelist and playwright, and a sharp opponent of the New Critics; H.J.C. Grieson (1866–1960) was Professor of

Rhetoric and English Literature at the University of Aberdeen and Edinburgh, and a specialist of English poetry in the seventeenth century; Edwin Muir (1887–1959) was a Scottish poet, novelist, essayist and translator, author of *Transition: Essays on Contemporary Literature* (1926); Sir Herbert Read (1893–1968) was a prolific English art historian, poet, philosopher and literary critic. In 1955, he was appointed Norton Professor of English at Harvard University.

27 Two examples here: Jean Stewart divides her lectures in five chapters entitled The Renaissance, The Late Renaissance, The Augustan Age, The Romantic Movement, After Romanticism; H.J.C. Grierson subsumes poetic movements and periods under the names of canonical writers: Blake, Wordsworth and Coleridge; Scott, Byron, Shelley and Keats; Tennyson, Browning and Some Others; Arnold and the Pre-Raphaelite Group; The Nineties.

28 Read entitled his chapters: "The Beginnings of Poetry," "Poetry and Humanism," "Poetry and Realism," "Poetry and Nature," "Pure Poetry," "Modern Poetry."

29 In these introductory pages, Forster makes the same kind of disparagingly witty remarks on Clayton Hamilton, without giving the name of the author of *Materials and Methods of Fiction*, as Woolf had in "The Anatomy of Fiction." Published in 1927, *Aspects of Fiction* was about to become the most widely book of criticism for 25 years.

30 On the meaning of Forster's "aspects," see S.P. Rosenbaum (1998: 89). The elements of the novel that Forster examines are "The Story," "People," "Plot," "Fantasy," "Prophecy," "Pattern" and "Rhythm."

31 Francis William Newman (1805–1897) was the younger brother of Cardinal Newman, an English classical scholar, religious liberal and moral philosopher who described himself as a rebel and was suspicious of all types of doctrinaires. In *Phases of Faith*, Newman uses "the historical form" to expose the "progress of his creed" and his "successive convictions" (Newman 1850: iv). His "phases" are both chronological and experiential. Woolf might have been interested, among other passages, by his conclusion on the necessity to approach God's world as "learners" and for "any spiritual church" to be guided by an "inward power" that "fears no truth, but rejoices in being corrected, intellectually as well as morally," so that it will "not be liable to be 'carried to and fro' by shifting winds of doctrine" (Newman 1850: 233).

32 On the definition of "advent narrative," "whether it entails the becoming of a literary form—'the rise of the novel'—or the coming to consciousness of a literary subject (be it character, narrator or reader)," see Daniel Brewer's "Writing Literary History Belatedly" (2005: 59).

33 On November 16, 1927, she returned to the subject in a letter to E.M. Forster:

> No; Percy Lubbock doesn't 'altogether satisfy' me. But I don't agree with you that he's a critic of genius. An able and painstaking pedant I should call him; who doesn't know what art is; so, though his method of judging novels as works of art interests me, his judgments don't.
>
> (*L III* 437)

34 Bennett's short essay, "Is the Novel Decaying?," appeared in *Cassell's Weekly* on March 28, 1923 (*The Author's Craft and Other Writings of Arnold Bennett*, ed. Samuel Hynes, Lincoln: University of Nebraska Press, 1968, 87–89, p. 88). Wool refers to his commentary in her Diary, vol. 2, 248.

35 Woolf's diary entry, dated August 2, 1924 reads: "If only I could get [Mrs Dalloway] into my vein & work it thoroughly deeply easily, instead of hacking out this miserable 200 words a day, and then, as the manuscript grows, I have the old fear. I shall read it & find it pale. I shall prove the truth of Murry's saying, that there's no way of going on after Jacob's Room" (*D IV* 306).

36 All these words can be found in Raleigh's Table of Contents (ix–xii).

37 "[Virginia Woolf] and Sterne are both fantasists. They start with a little object, take a flutter from it, and settle on it again. They combine a humorous appreciation of the muddle of life with a keen sense of its beauty" (Forster 19).

38 Woolf uses the word "change" 15 times in her essay, and the word "desire" 23 times.

39 On this subject, see also Beth Carole Rosenberg (2000), Anne E. Fernald (2006), Catherine Bernard (2011).

40 "Grounded in the reader's desire to believe' rather than in the authors intention to represent reality," Pollentier explains, Woolf's fictional worlds are redefined according to "their imaginative potentialities." Each of these worlds affords a "space of available experience" which acts as a "common denominator between writing and reading" (Pollentier 206). *My translation.*

41 One can find about 60 occurrences of "world" in "Phases of Fiction."

42 In the same journal entry, dated June 22, 1940, Woolf compares Coleridge's and Shelley's art to the British poets of the "Leaning Tower" generation:

> And I read my Shelley at night. How delicate and pure and musical and uncorrupt he and Coleridge read, after the Left Wing group. How lightly and firmly they put down their feet and how they sing; and how they compact; and fuse and deepen.
>
> (*D V* 298)

43 The letter to Ethel Smyth mentioned here movingly anticipates Woolf's shortened life: "This is a programme," she wrote "considering my slowness, & how I get slower, thicker, more intolerant of the fling & the rash, to last out my 20 years, if I have them" (*L IV* 63).

44 In August 1940, Woolf read books by F.L. Lucas – a "pure Cambridge: clean as a breadknife, and as sharp" (*L V* 357), which, she wrote in her diary a month later, "check[ed] with her impulse to write her own book" (*D V* 321). She might have been interested here in his critical work on Greek and Elizabethan tragedy, for example, *Seneca and Elizabethan Tragedy* (1922), and *Tragedy in Relation to Aristotle's 'Poetics'* (1927). As to G.M. Trevelyan's book that Woolf began in October of the same year, she considered that it "provides a service like Roman roads, but avoids the 'forests & and will of the wisps'" (*D V* 333).

45 See Diary (*II* 271): "I used to read it & dream of those obscure adventurers, & no doubt practised their style in my copy books." On the voice of the storyteller, see Gillian Beer (1996: 3), and Christine Reynier who compares Anon's anonymous and universal voice to that of Walter Benjamin's storyteller: "Indeed, what goes into the storyteller's story is not only his own individual experience but also the other's experience as well as the listener's. The storyteller's is therefore a human and a universal experience" (Reynier 2018: 157).

46 See here John D. Niles, *Homo Narrans: The Poetics and Anthropology of Oral Literature* (1999).

47 In *A Short History of Literature* (1940) that Woolf read for her own project, Ifor Evans begins with a chapter entitled "Before the Conquest" and considers that "the Angles and Saxons and Jutes [...] made English history possible." Very quickly, however, he focuses on the manuscripts on which the literature of the Anglo-Saxon period was recorded (Evans 13).

48 In *Patterns of Culture*, Benedict focuses on the Pueblo cultures of the American southwest, the Native American cultures of the Great Plains, the Kwakiutl of the Pacific Northwest (based on the fieldwork of her mentor Boas), the Pueblo of New Mexico (among whom she had direct experience), the nations of the Great Plains, the culture of New Guinea. She argues that

> the desire to grasp the meaning of a culture as a whole compels us to consider descriptions of standardized behaviour merely as a stepping-stone leading to other problems. We must understand the individual as living in his culture; and the culture as lived by individuals. The interest in these sociopsychological problems is not in any way opposed to the historical approach.
>
> (Benedict 1955: x)

7 Virginia Woolf, Fiction and the "Woman Question"

> but now I am a woman again – as I always am when I write.

"The Great Problem of the True Nature of Woman"

Woolf had just come back from a visit to her husband's mother when she wrote in a journal entry dated May 31, 1929, about "one of these little journeys which seem to have last[ed] 600 years. I was in a queer mood, thinking myself very old: but now I am a woman again—as I always am when I write." Did she feel that the visit to the 76-year-old lady had changed her for a few hours because "Everything looks a little strange & symbolical when one comes back"? Was the "woman" writer she could return to the same person as the wife and daughter-in-law who was wondering about old age, "human nature" and the "beauty" of the "sea flowing in & out the bay that very afternoon"? Or was relieved to no longer appear as this "stranger" – "not a woman, but an elderly woman" – whom she had discovered in the eyes of her oculist that same day (*D III* 230–231)? Because Woolf, like Orlando and her contemporaries, knew that she "had a great variety of selves to call upon" (*O* 294), we might also wonder whether the "woman" she could be again was not another name for her "fictitious" and "famous" self, a happier persona who had finalised the "revision of 'Women & Fiction'" two weeks earlier – a "brilliant essay," she thought (*D III* 222–223).[1] The "but" in the quotation reminds us of a similar "but" which unexpectedly materialises in the beginning of Woolf's feminist essay: "But, you may say, we asked you to speak about women and fiction—what, has that got to do with a room of one's own?" (*AR* 3). With other connectives and repeated words such as "difference," "influence," "truth" and "woman," "but" belongs to the specific Woolfian lexis that Judith Allen examines in "But [...] I had said 'but' too often. Why 'but'?" (2012). "But," Allen suggests, enables Woolf to "counter [the] stifling of ideas, imagination, and creativity," to perform "the crossing of boundaries." More fundamentally, "these words convey the multifarious constructs that we designate as 'meanings'" while pushing the readers to come their own conclusions (Allen 2012: 3–7).

DOI: 10.4324/9780429331787-10

"But," one might want to argue, if "woman" is a mere word, inces-santly revitalised according to contexts and personal interpretations, what about "women," those individuals existing in the past or the present but missing in history books? To probe into the question of "woman" as Woolf inherited it, addressed it and transformed it, one must start with the way Woolf uses the word: even "crude," Woolf explains in *Three Guineas*, definitions "must serve" (*TG* 170). Woolf's women are more often "daughters of educated men" than "women of the working-class" (*TG* 97). "Doctors and biologists" identify them by their sex (*AR* 21); collectively, they can be called a "class," a "race" or a "tribe" when Woolf borrows this terminology from many of her predecessors and a few of her contemporaries. When looked at individually, "a woman" can be "ordinary" or "eccentric"; she might be associated with, and even defined by, her occupation, profession or "gender role," as we have learnt to say. But her singularity never seems to protect her from the disparaging comparison with this other "species" – men. Whether called "Mary Beton, Mary Seton, Mary Carmichael or by any name you please—it is not a matter of any importance," this unique, yet rep-resentative, woman can thus be intercepted by the beadle on the turf of a university college where she should not have found herself: "he was the beadle; I was a woman. This was the turf; there was the path" (*AR* 4–5). "She spoke. He was dumb. She was woman; he was dog," Woolf's biographer will later explain in *Flush*, as if neither Elizabeth Barrett Browning nor her spaniel could escape a category that satiric-ally, yet ontologically, unites them and separates them at the same time: "Thus closely united, thus immensely divided, they gazed at each other" (*F* 19). In Woolf's texts, the notion (in the linguistic sense of the term) of "woman" appears precisely whenever "a woman" or "women" become an object of study for "those gentlemen who specialize in woman and her effect on whatever it may be—politics, children, wages, morality—numerous and learned as they are" (*AR* 24). But when history, science, ideology or literature tries to define "woman" or the nature of "woman-hood," the female object of their studies and theories still eludes them. Whether they, or anyone for that matter, ponder on the woman who "must have money and a room of her own if she is to write fiction," or on the woman who "wrote so many poems without singing them, the reflection leaves the great problem of the true nature of woman [...] unsolved" (*AR* 38; 3).

If labels "kill and constrict" (*TG* 211) and "categories" are heuristic tools meant to replace dogmas by insoluble questions, then, as it has now become clear, Woolf's feminism cannot be homogenised. Beyond the obvious misinterpretations and ideological dismissals, the polemic reception of her feminism in the 1920s and 1930s already pointed to contradictions and ambivalence. Although unfair, the Leavises' class-attacks against her art and feminism, for example, raised the issue of her inherited privileges and her claimed status as a marginal. Similarly, even if the critical tradition that underscored her modernist aesthetics at the expense of her politics has long been challenged, this emphasis might also appear as a consequence of her vexed relationship with feminist militancy.[2] Nevertheless, today, Woolf's feminism appears "as all-pervasive and multifarious," susceptible to be reinterpreted by each generation. In the words of Anna Snaith,

> as usual, most feminist methodologies brought to bear on Woolf's writing are anticipated by Woolf herself: the recovery of lost texts by women, the destabilizing of gender categories, the foregrounding of women's histories, the subversion of dominant narrative strategies, the exposure and resistance to the material and psychological circumstances of women's oppression.
>
> (2007: 6)

Which does not mean that we should not bring before the author of *A Room of One's Own, Orlando* and *Three Guineas* some of the questions that she so frequently raised in her conversations with her predecessors and contemporaries, whether male or female. Woolf herself, who feared that she might "settle into a figure" (*D IV* 85), overtly demanded from the common reader what she demanded from herself: self-reflexive questioning and the search for answers, however perplexing and "doomed to failure" they might be.[3]

To the question of how we can evaluate Woolf's political feminism today, Naomi Black has provided her own convincing answer, one that suggests deep coherence whilst avoiding easy consensus. Choosing *Three Guineas* as Woolf's most controversial and overtly feminist text, she assesses its "apparent limits" as symptomatic of its author's feminism in general, pitting against one another the "very long list of specific changes for women that Woolf demanded" and the issues she did not address for obvious contextual reasons, or for more personal ones: divorce, birth control, abortion, child care and more generally "the risks as well as the possibilities attached to female embodiment," along with "the link between individual and group action" and the under-representation of lower class women (Black 181; 185). Alex Zwerdling (1986) and Laura Marcus (2000) have also recounted how Woolf's feminism was, from the start, "attacked or championed according to the political exigencies of the moment" (Zwerdling 210). While, for example, some of Woolf's contemporaries saw her feminism as "extreme," J.B. Bachelor could write in 1968 that "feminism proper is aesthetically unacceptable to Virginia Woolf."[4] Today, Woolf's "contradictoriness" tends to be understood as part of her legacy for a still increasing number of readers.[5] As Derek Ryan and Stella Bolaki write in their introduction to *Contradictory Woolf* (2012), "Woolf's writing constantly refuses settled readings or closed meanings, revealing and reveling precisely in its potential or actual, subtle or forceful, contradictions" (Ryan and Bolaki 2012: ix).

If we turn to Woolf as one of the foremothers, if not *the* foremother, of feminist literary historiography, a similar impression of contradictoriness appears. One might want to begin with what Woolf does not speak about, or only incidentally: the sensationalist female Victorian writers and their fallen heroines, for example, or the "new" women of the decadent fin de siècle such as George Egerton, Sarah Grand and Charlotte Mew. Then, if "Anon is sometimes man; sometimes woman," as she acknowledged twice, in *A Room of One's Own* and in her last essay drafts (*E VI* 580),[6] the pronoun that refers to "him" or "her" is always masculine, just as the reader in her essays is always a "he." From a twenty-first century perspective, we might have wanted otherwise, as if Woolf could have continued, as a critic, with the playful, yet ideologically potent, difficulty *Orlando's* narrator struggles with when his character changes sex: "but in future we must, for convention's sake, say 'her' for 'his,' and 'she' for 'he' " (*O* 133). And if Woolf was so intent on recovering the women lost to history and literary history, why didn't a greater number of her essays in criticism pay tribute to the "obscure" work of women historians, biographers and critics, three "masculine" domains and genres that she contributed to modernise and feminise while conversing almost exclusively with their male practitioners?

In their *Companion to Women's Historical Writing* (2005), Spongberg, Caine and Curthoys argue that "various forms of female biography can be read as counter-narrative to the masculinist historical tradition, a narrative that questioned the authority and historicity of male-authored texts and masculine understandings of the nature of history itself" (174). They mention published British works that "pre-empt[ed] the modernisation of biography by almost a century" (238) such as Mary Hays' six-volume *Female Biography, or Memoirs of Illustrious and Celebrated Women, of all Ages and Countries* (1803), the three-volume *The Growth of Literature* (1932, 1936, 1940) by English philologist Nora Kershaw and her husband Hector Munro Chadwick; Lucy Hutchinson's *Memoirs of the Life of Colonel Hutchinson* (1806), Catherine Macaulay's eight-volume *History of England from the Accession of James I, to That of the Brunswick Line* (1763–1783), Lucy Aikin's *Memoirs of the Court of Queen Elizabeth* (1818), of *James I* (1822) and of *Charles I* (1833), or Gertrude Bell's *The Thousand and One Churches* (1909). These names and titles do not appear, or very incidentally, in Woolf's essays on biography, except for the Duchess of Newcastle, an eccentric and "memorable figure" who is the subject of one of *CR I*'s essays in 1925 (*E IV* 81).[7] As to the European tradition of female essayists, a genre that Woolf was so eager to revisit and which has since been co-opted by women writers and critics as a "feminised space,"[8] Woolf appears to ignore it, or, at any rate, to minimise the importance of female essayists such as Eliza Haywood (editor of *The Female Spectator* between 1744 and 1746), Charlotte Lennox and her *Lady's Museum* in the mid-eighteenth century, Mary Russell Mitford, Harriet Martineau, Frances Power Cobbe,

Rebecca West or Alice Meynell. And yet, like her, those female writers negotiated private and more public definitions of their selves, and still represent "the missing piece to a larger history of the essay" (Spinner 2018: 1).[9]

Obviously, if it took almost one century for researchers to recover the voices of these women in cultural history, one cannot blame Woolf for not bringing them to the fore. Nonetheless, how she elaborated, whether consciously or unconsciously, a "selective tradition" of her own is a question worth asking. In *Writing Women's Literary History* (1996), the American Professor and feminist literary historian Margaret Ezell addresses the subject in a thought-provoking way by explicitly under-mining Woolf's feminist "model" of historiography in *A Room of One's Own*, along with the theoretical elaborators of this model from the 1970s onwards. The new feminist literary histories of Woolf and her followers, Ezell argues, share certain assumptions about female author-ship, the connections between genre and gender, and about modes of lit-erary production that she finds highly debatable on historicist grounds.[10] Since the 1990s, many scholars have indeed studied *A Room of One's Own* as the seminal text of Woolf's "active, revisionist form of literary history" (Fernald 2006: 3). Beth Carole Rosenberg speaks of "an alter-native history" (1995: 71), Gabrielle McIntire of "the work of a fem-inist historian, the first, with its contradictions, difference, différance, obscurity" (2008: 190) and Anne E. Fernald reaches the conclusion that this essay in "critical thinking" anticipates "a subsequent theory of reading: deconstructive, feminist, Bakhtinian" (Fernald 1994: 178). But for Margaret Ezell, to confuse Woolf with a historian – whether feminist or not – and to transform "the original conceptualization of an evolu-tionary pattern of female authorship" that Woolf proposes in *A Room* into a "theory of female creativity" is a critical problem (Ezell 22). Thus, Ezell challenges the theoretical assumptions that this pattern or model implies, among which

> the use of a linear cause and effect analysis, either to start in the past and work forward in time, looking for development and searching for patterns of influence, or to read backward, starting with the pre-sent and looking for predecessors, a sort of literary genealogy.
>
> (19)

She also points at the notions of "tradition" – implying "the existence of common ground and continuity in literary works" (19) – of "female literary family," "continuity" or "evolutionary pattern" all of which, she explains, refer us back to "a nineteenth-century model of narrative his-toriography" (22). Last but not least, Ezell problematises Woolf's legacy by questioning the constructed "tension," in women's literary history since 1929, "between concepts of the 'female' and 'feminism' based on androgyny, versus those based on 'difference'" (23).

It can be argued convincingly (and this is usually what the tradition of "feminist" scholarship that Ezell denounces does) that this so-called adherence to a nineteenth-century model of narrative historiography with its re-elaboration of the traditional concepts of "genealogy," "authorship," "periodization" and "literary influence," together with its "underlying assumptions about gender, genre, and historical progress" (Ezell 21; 15) is exactly the kind of historiographical discourse that Woolf satirised in *Orlando* and *A Room of One's Own*. Yet one might retort that the genealogy of "engendered greatness" that she refuses to produce at the beginning of *A Room*[11] – "a few remarks about Fanny Burney; a few more about Jane Austen; a tribute to the Brontës [...] some witticisms if possible about Miss Mitford; a respectful allusion to George Eliot a reference to Mrs Gaskell" – is a rather accurate account of how Woolf deals with literary history and its canonical female figures in most of her critical essays (*AR* 3). Seen in the light of Ezell's criticism, the opening lines of the revised version of Woolf's two lectures to the women of Girton and Newnham Colleges become a significant metonymy of Woolf's various historiographical narratives and their contradictory impulses. They also reflect and renew Woolf's implied conversations regarding history and literature with past and present authors, contemporary critics and herself.

There are, indeed, apparent contradictions and exclusions in Woolf's conception of historiography and her "re-written" feminist literary histories. Whilst they aim to unwrite the single master discourse of history, they also seem to maintain a traditional sense of the canon and of authorship. They reclaim the "lives of the obscure," but as far the nineteenth century is concerned, they erase the fin de siècle female avant-garde while neglecting foremothers less prestigious than Jane Austen, the Brontës or George Eliot. They are critical of "historians' histories," clearly adopt a "feminist" standpoint, but ignore the emergence of numerous female historians at the turn of the century. They resort to a sense of historical continuity, yet are inseparable from a form of fragmentation and Woolf's conception of essay writing. I contend that those apparent paradoxes will not be resolved from the vantage point of recent theoretical or philosophical approaches, even if these approaches were in part anticipated by Woolf. To address these seeming contradictions without ignoring Ezell's objections, I propose to follow Woolf's own method of critical analysis which I have adopted as mine, first by acknowledging the various phases of her thoughts on women and writing, then by measuring this method against the ways her predecessors engaged with "the woman question." I agree with Michael Whitworth's idea, in "Historicizing Woolf: Context Studies" (2013), that the aim here is not to recover the "precise meaning" of her theoretical assumptions but "those meanings that are nearly incomprehensible within our present frame of reference" – a process which permits to "restrict ambiguities and to dampen unwonted resonances" (Whitworth 7; 11).

The "Feminine Note" in Literary Criticism

"We frame our questions differently at different times," Woolf wrote in "Modern Fiction" (*E IV* 159). Her interest in reconciling women, art and self-assertion was undeniably a constant feature of her practice as a reviewer, an essayist and a fiction writer. But as with her interest in historiography, it was also influenced by her own fluctuating agenda, by the pragmatic link she could or could not establish between thought and action, and by the series of subject positions and personas that she felt she had to defend, or that her status as a woman writer interpellated her into. According to Elena Gualtieri, Woolf's early sense of "the lacunae or gaps" within the narratives of historiographic institutions and discourses led her to shift her focus gradually from the marginal figures of the "eccentrics," to the "obscure" and ultimately to "Anon," the anonymous poet and minstrel who might have been a woman (Gualtieri 2000: 18).[12] In "Woolf's Feminism, Feminism's Woolf" (2000), Laura Marcus also takes those "phases" into consideration when she explains how Woolf's participation in debates about women and creativity was "caught up in the sexual politics" of the 1920s, then of the 1930s. Thus, while Woolf's first writings addressed the questions of "difference" and of the place of women in literary history, she then contributed to a more socially oriented cultural debate in *A Room of One's Own*, before dramatising female exclusion by the patriarchy in a more radical way in *Three Guineas* (Marcus 2000: 212–216). The evolving pattern uncovered in Part I of this book adds another layer to these convincing remarks, since it understands the changes in Woolf's general approach to history and historiography as a reflection of Woolf's search for answers to the questions that she was faced with, first as a reader negotiating her Victorian heritage, then as a modernist writer rewriting "historians' histories," and later on as a cultural innovator whose aesthetic experiments were meant as a more overt political intervention in the public arena.

The women whom Woolf talks about in *Three Guineas*, whether ordinary citizens, militant writers, or daughters of educated men, seem indeed quite different from the writers of letters or the subjects of biographies that triggered her thoughts at the beginning of her career. And yet, the way Woolf addresses the question of women's creativity within a patriarchal culture shows her determination from the start, along with a hardly masked irritation that she frequently channelled into elaborate rhetoric. In her 1905 review of W.L. Courtney's *The Feminine Note in Fiction*,[13] Woolf acknowledges the author's merit but voices her frustration: Courtney "made a laborious attempt," but by refusing to assess the "virtues" and "failings" of the female writers under study, he did not assign them "their right place in literature." As to which characteristic are "essentially feminine and why," the book reaches the usual impasse (*E I* 15). That Woolf regrets the lack of "some definite verdict" might seem surprising in view of her own reticence to meet unsolvable problems with definitive judgments (ibid.). But Courtney's prose and method, she suggests, result from an upsetting combination of asserted convictions – "To me the modern history of novelistic literature seems to prove that there is such a thing as a distinctive feminine style in fiction" – and of absent facts or definitions: "Yet on such a topic all general propositions are apt to be fallacious, and only the broad tendencies are worth much consideration" (Courtney 1904: vii). In her short review, Woolf uses the same critical tools forged in her practice as a historiographical critic. The terms of the debate – here "feminine" and "woman" – need to be defined, she suggests; theories, in the sense of clear hypotheses, must be grounded in objective facts and a knowledge of literary history:

> women, we gather, are seldom artists, because they have a passion for detail which conflicts with the proper artistic proportion of their work. We would cite Sappho and Jane Austen as examples of two great women who combine exquisite detail with a supreme sense of artistic proportion.

The review also gives us a clear sense of how Woolf, on this subject more than others, feels the need to fight against stereotypes such as "the woman novelist is extinguishing the novel," or "women excel in 'close analytic miniature work'."[14] No wonder she finally dares to ask: "And will not the adequate critic of women be a woman?" (*E I* 16). And yet, Woolf will continue to respond to her male contemporaries, using rhetorical tactics and personas that she adapts according to her interlocutor and her evolving position in the world of English letters.[15]

In "Women Novelists," a 1918 review of *The Women Novelists* by Brimley Johnson, Woolf comes to the same conclusion about the necessity and impossibility of defining "feminine" writing: "As Mr Brimley Johnson again and again remarks, a woman's writing is always feminine, it cannot help being feminine; at its best it is most feminine: the only difficulty lies in defining what we mean by feminine."[16] Although Johnson appears less prejudiced than Courtney on the question, the reviewer remains "puzzled to state what his theory amounts to" (*E II* 316). Ten years before her lecture on "Women and Fiction," Woolf again uses the format of the review and her reactions as a reader to ask the questions that will later absorb her as a critic and literary historian:

> What, for example, was the origin of the extraordinary outburst in the eighteenth century of novel writing by women? Why did it begin then, and not in the time of the Elizabethan renaissance? Was the motive which finally determined them to write a desire to correct the current view of their sex expressed in so many volumes and for so many ages by male writers?

This time, however, Woolf states that "the question is not merely of literature, but to a large extent social history" (314). Without history as a reservoir of facts, along with biography and fiction as indispensable historical material, she considered that the effects of the repression experienced by women writers over time were bound to remain unearthed.[17] Noticeably, the vocabulary she uses in this review – and in fact, in all her other texts on "the woman question" and literature – recalls her lexis as a historiographer, with words such as "change," "influence" or "difference" being at the core of her reasoning. In this text, however, the idea of "difference" does not only refer to Woolf's method of assessment through comparison. Because Brimley Johnson implies that "feminine" fiction is bound to differ from its "masculine" counterpart without explicitly using the word "difference," Woolf takes up the issue – again, "a very difficult one" (316) – and uncovers the patriarchal premises underlying it. As with the notion of "women's influence" in *Three Guineas*, she lays the foundation stone of a cultural and sociological reflection on "difference" that is meant to restore complexity to a subject that had been, and still was in the 1920s, simplified for obvious ideological reasons. Similarly, when she explains that "no more than men" could nineteenth-century female novelists "free themselves from a more fundamental tyranny—the tyranny of sex itself" (315), she transforms the inherited debate on biological and psychological "differences" into a conversation on oppression that includes men in the shared role of the victim, while never making it evident whether she understands the notion of "sex" as most of her predecessors did, or if she uses it merely to undermine its traditional meaning. For her readers, therefore, the method that consists in unwriting and rewriting inherited debates is a demanding one, since Woolf requires from them that they pay close attention to her use of such contentious words as "sex" or "difference." Not because they are mere words, and therefore have no reference outside language, but because Woolf's use of them always implies contextualisation and meta-critical awareness that transform them into open-ended categories.

To borrow Woolf's famous expression, what "strikes a contemporary" when we read her "woman's essays"[18] is the apparent absence of any conspicuous change between the nineteenth-century and early-twentieth-century approaches to the question of women and literature that she registers. The weight of the Victorian heritage hardly shifted with women gaining the vote, and to "kill the angel in the house" required persistence and the elaboration of subtle rhetorical tools. Even in the 1920s, there indeed appears to have been a vast gulf between the Georgians' rejection of Victorian sexual ideology, Bloomsbury's revolutionary claims in matters of sex and intimacy, and the still conservative politics underlying most cultural arguments on the status of women intellectuals and artists.[19] In *Modernism, Sex, and Gender* (2019), Celia Marshik and Allison Pease remind us that H.D.'s "The Pool" is the first example of I.A. Richards's chapter on "Badness and Poetry" in *Principles of Literary*

Criticism (1925), that Ezra Pound called Amy Lowell "Amy-just-selling-the-goods," and that William Empson stated, in *Seven Types of Ambiguity* (1930), that some women writers "are almost out of reach of analysis" (Marshik and Pease 2019: 14–15). Many similar examples could be mentioned here, testifying to a long cultural inheritance embraced by her male contemporaries. For someone like Woolf, therefore, to write as an artist and a committed intellectual about "the Woman Question" was bound to imply the re-inscription of discursive structures that were still working as a language of oppression. In other words, to denounce these structures – the strain of which pervades all her reviews and essays on the subject – Woolf needed, again, to unearth their hidden premises before she could rethink and rewrite them entirely.

In *The Ends of History: Victorians and "The Woman Question"* (2013), Christina Crosby recalls that nineteenth-century thought was "indelibly marked by two inter-related features, a passion for 'history' and faith in historical explanations of all sorts, and a passion with 'women,' the ceaseless posing of 'the woman question'." Woolf and her female contemporaries had to negotiate this double heritage, along with the still pregnant idea that "women are the unhistorical other of history" (Crosby 2013: 1).[20] Strikingly, for the Victorians the woman "question" was both ontological and ideological, and a true question, that, when debated, would trigger a chain of arguments and responses over several decades. An example of these public grating exchanges across the generations is Olive Schreiner's answer, in *Woman and Labour* (1911), to George Henry Lewes's statement, in 1852, that

> If [women] turn their thoughts to literature, it is—when not purely an imitative act—always to solace by some intellectual activity the sorrow that in silence wastes their lives, and by a withdrawal of the intellect from the contemplation of their pain, or by the transmutation of their secret anxieties into types, they escape from that burden.

"The happy wife and busy mother," Lewes goes on explaining, "are only forced into literature by some hereditary organic tendency, stronger even than the domestic" (Lewes 1852: 43–44). Interestingly, as she eschews any biological analysis of women's aptitudes as artists – there is no "inherent connection in the human brain between the ovarian sex function and the art of fiction" – Schreiner also anticipates in her essay the link established by Woolf in a *Room of One's Own* between women's material circumstances, and the novel as a genre adapted to those circumstances:

> The fact is, that modern fiction being merely a description of human life in any of its phases, and being the only art that can be exercised without special training or special appliances, and produced in the moments stolen from the multifarious, brain-destroying occupations

which fill the average woman's life, they have been driven to find this outlet for their powers as the only one presenting itself.

(Schreiner 1911: 158)

Another inherited feature, in the first decades of the twentieth century, of the debates on the "woman question" is their enmeshment in a web of contradictions. Coventry Patmore's evocation of "the emancipated woman" in "The Social Position of Women" (1851), for example, hesitates as to how he should characterise and name her:

> She has often many attractive virtues; but whatever good she possesses, she remembers so well herself that she is apt to make others forget it. [...] She talks an immense deal about, and immensely admires art and poetry, artists and poets, but in her heart she believes them all to be lies and liars.
>
> (Patmore 1851: 525–527)

Because of her contradictions – once more emphasised by a series of "but" – the subject evades the essayist's attempts at definition. Read in the light of this short excerpt, Woolf's own "buts" suddenly sound as an ironic nod to her male predecessors as she turns the very idea of contradiction against them.[21] Unfortunately, contradiction created more victims among women writers than among their male counterparts. The authors of *The Woman Question: Literary Issues, 1837–1883* (1983) thus explain that the fundamental paradox at the core of the nineteenth-century world of letters took the form of a contradictory injunction. On the one hand, the period was "hailed as the age of the woman writer" and critics urged her to exert her "influence" to "widen the boundaries of literature by providing access to a new range of human experiences"; on the other hand, when such a woman gained popularity and literary status, she would be considered an economic and emotional threat, and her merits diminished, if not ridiculed, as a consequence (Helsinger et al. 1983: 3). To reconcile "true womanhood" with their new roles as successful artists, many Victorian female writers, therefore, continued, like their eighteenth-century female predecessors, to find a cause to justify their work – be it "the call of God, the pursuit of an elusive truth or a love of beauty so intense that it transcends personal ambition" (ibid. 9).

As a "Lady Novelist," critics required from a woman writer that she keep "strictly to the region within which she acquires her knowledge": should she accept such restraints, she "may never produce a fiction of the highest order" yet would be "in the right path to produce the best fiction of the class she is most likely to excel."[22] To write realistically within the limits of her experience as a woman would also prevent her from authoring those "Silly Novels by Lady Novelists," a "genus with many species determined by the particular quality of silliness that predominates in them,—the frothy, the prosy, the pious, or the pedantic" (Eliot 1887b:

157). Symptomatically, however, even when granted a place in literary history, she would be confined to the practices and talents prescribed by the sex binary and its prejudices. In her own "Lady Novelists" essay, George Eliot thus begins with the promising idea that since men cannot "express life otherwise than as they know it, and they can only know it profoundly by their own experience, the advent of female literature promises woman's view of life, women's experience—in other words, a new element." Yet a few paragraphs later, she explains that the "Masculine mind is characterized by the predominance of the intellect, and the Feminine by the predominance of the emotions" (Eliot 1887a: 10–11). Eliot's idea of the "new," therefore, precludes any real "change" in the sense that Woolf will propose two decades later. When writing poetry, then, Victorian female writers were celebrated as "poetesses" if their creative thrust appeared pure, feminine and in accordance with the aesthetics of self-renunciation. But whether they complied with the myths of the domestic angel or the pre-Raphaelite muse, or, on the contrary, embodied a more strong-headed version of womanhood, women's "otherness" led to "a process" of exclusion, Crosby explains, in which differences are manufactured only to construct "an imaginary unity of Englishmen then projected as the image of universal man" (Crosby 2013: 6).

As she makes clear in "The Feminine Note in Fiction" and "Women Novelists," reverberations of those debates appeared in the essays and literary histories of Woolf's male contemporaries. The necessity to uncover the ideological premises under these conversations, the terms of which had hardly changed from the Victorians to the modernists, explains, to a large extent, the salient features of her own critical writings on women and fiction: they rely on both the serious and playful, at any rate theoretically oriented, process of re-semioticisation of the usual terminology referring to both literary genre and gender. One useful comparison here is between George Lewes's (1852) essay "The Lady Novelist" in *The Westminster Review*, E.M. Forster's paper "the Feminine Note in Fiction" delivered to the Cambridge Apostles and The Bloomsbury Friday Club in December 1910,[23] and Woolf's own lecture on the same subject in 1928.[24] The titles of Lewes's and Forster's contributions to the question of "women and fiction" first inscribe their discourse in the series of arguments and responses mentioned earlier, as if this particular question was bound to be framed by similar terms – "feminine," the novelist as a "Lady" – and perspectives.[25] Lewes's approach, it should be noted, contrasts with most of his Victorian contemporaries' as he seems to assign to women a significant place in literary history. That women can be successful writers, he suggests, and that men should accept to share "their imperious dominion—Intelligence" is perhaps a painful "fact, yet it remains a fact" (Lewes 39). The actual question that the critic then raises – "What does the literature of women mean?" – anticipates Woolf's philosophy in *A Room of One's Own*. That "men and women have different organizations," Lewes writes, and "consequently different experiences," and that, therefore, "to know life, you must have both sides depicted" is an idea that Woolf will never disagree on (Lewes 40–41). The same can be said about Lewes's conviction that novels are women's "forte" and that "to write as men write, is the aim and besetting sin of women; to write as women, is the real office they have to perform" (42–43). In the second page of the essay, however, the "promises" that Lewes sees as a consequence of "the advent of female literature" give way to the same essentialist conception of the feminine and the masculine as in George Eliot's "The Lady Novelists." Far from providing any social or historical reasons explaining why female novelists feel bound to "imitate" men, for example, he reasserts that they are hampered by "nature and circumstance": "Hence we may be prepared to find women succeeding better in finesse of detail, in pathos and sentiment, while men generally succeed better in the construction of plots and the delineation of character" (43; 45).

In spite of a title that sounds behind the times, we can understand why Forster's 1910 lecture on the "feminine note in fiction" might have satisfied Woolf when it was delivered.[26] The same implicit "but," or contradictoriness, indeed characterises both his and Woolf's paper despite a difference in terms. "When you are reading," Forster suggests, "a book can tell you instinctively whether it is the work of a man or a woman." However, he later states that "the question of the feminine note is not really important in great literature. There personality dominates." Jane Austen, therefore, "is more an Austen than a Jane" (Forster 1910: 16; 19). Moving beyond the sex binary throughout most of his paper, Forster also acknowledges the importance of looking back to understand the present: "For think of the past," he says, when "women were mostly the servants or play things of men." Mentioning the "fear atmosphere" that used to lead to the production of literary and critical stereotypes as "the Chatelaine," the "Grande Dame" or "the Bluestocking," he also anticipates the moment when women writers will be freed from the dangers of "strident" self-consciousness: "what you mistake for the masculine or the feminine will disappear, and personality, and nothing besides personality will remain" (20).[27]

Almost two decades later, in her lecture to the female students of Newnham and Girton Colleges and in its final version as *A Room of One's Own*, Woolf will explore the timeline outlined by Forster, starting from the present, moving back in time, and then envisioning an inspiring future. She will use the "almost unlit corridors of history" as an indispensable field of knowledge (*E V* 28), obviously a most imperfect one, where to look for explanations – the words "causes" and "reason" are frequently used – to the present situation. While she never uses the expression, she will also associate the "feminine note in fiction" to character-presentation, having the same interest in subjectivity and personality as her modernist contemporary. To the "fear" experienced by her foremothers and mentioned by Forster, she adds "bitterness" and "anger" in the first two chapters of *A Room* and examines the social and psychological dimensions of these feelings, along with the often-neglected material aspects that accompany them. More urgently than her predecessor, however, Woolf embeds the terms of the debate within an implicit conversational pattern that first historicises and embodies these terms, before she interrogates and unwrites them so that they are never fuzzed by a hazy, impersonal inheritance. The anger of the narrator in *A Room* is thus triggered by "Professor von X" engaged in writing his monumental work entitled *The Mental, the Moral, and Physical Inferiority of the Female Sex* (*AR* 24). Anger then becomes a subject of investigation and self-discovery, a "disguised and complex" one: from books to their writers, to individuals and back to books, Woolf approaches it through the lens of psychology and history, looking for individual examples – "the Foreign Secretary," "The Judge," "Sir Austen chamberlain" (26) – to uncover collective mechanisms. From mutual acridity, she moves to the rarely examined question of courage and self-confidence, the lack of which in a male individual, she explains, leads to the defence of "some innate superiority" and to patriarchal domination. Exploring the privileges of all sorts of men – men of letters, clergymen, men of genius, common men parading the streets, men with or without a degree, and men who "have written about women" (*AR* 21) – she examines the effect of the social and ideological "environment" they have created upon women's lives. Answering mind-binding questions with both empirical and theoretical hypotheses, she delves into the unconscious and perennial logic of the two sexes' actions and reactions in a way that sheds new light on hackneyed clichés, disentangles the ideological threads of prejudice and reverses the constructed terms of gendered difference. Thus, anger, and, therefore, overwhelming emotionality, is first and foremost a symptom of men's irrational behaviour before it affects women: "But I had been angry because he was angry," the narrator of *A Room* explains. "Yet it seemed absurd, I thought, turning over the evening paper, that a man with all this power should be angry. Or is anger, I wondered, somehow, the familiar, the attendant sprite on power?" (26). In the following chapter of the essay, male "imagination" gives birth to a "very queer, composite being" – woman: "Imaginatively she is of the highest importance; practically she is completely insignificant." Ironically, this "odd monster that one made up by reading the historians first and the poets afterwards" is not the result of a woman's ill-used imagination threatening the world of facts, but an entirely subjective, almost grotesque, construction (*AR* 33–34).

In "Women and Fiction," Woolf forcefully hammers in the chief arguments of her demonstration with less rhetorical flourish than in the longer, written version of her talk, yet the very shortness of the text, I would argue, clarifies the essentials of Woolf's revisionist method in her other essays. The ambiguity of her title, Woolf writes, is "intentional," for in dealing with women as writers, as much elasticity as possible is desirable; it is necessary to leave oneself room to deal with other things besides their work, so much has that work been influenced by conditions that have nothing whatever to do with art.

(E V 28)

The room mentioned here is not the indispensable private place condensing the economic, psychological and artistic independence of women, but one that already contains, metaphorically, enough space for women writers and critics to bring in their actual "circumstances" rather than "their sex." Woolf's true interrogations differ from the rhetorical questions that often characterise those of her predecessors. In this essay, Woolf's "whys" indeed sound as some other "whys": the whys with which she began "Women Novelists" in 1918, but also those explored in Chapter 4 of this book, when Woolf was shown to answer the demands of historical causality in her own terms:

Why, we ask at once, was there no continuous writing done by women before the eighteenth century? Why did they then write almost as habitually as men, and in the course of that writing produce, one after another, some of the classics of English fiction? And why did their art then, and why to some extent does their art still, take the form of fiction?

(28)

Again, Woolf addresses these subjects both as the imperfect historiographer and the more experienced critic that she knows herself to be. As a historiographer, she asks for new materials and sources – memoirs, letters, historical records of "law and custom" – to propose a historical account that will provide an alternative to "historians' histories" and their "male line" (28–29). She then anchors her sketched literary history, from Sappho to the present, in a reconstructed social and material history, while attempting to recover the few "tangible remains" of a woman's day (33) – those details and subjective experiences that for a long time seemed incompatible with the scientific standards of truth. As a critic, she grounds her discourse in a theoretical framework the contours of which are transparently displayed: there will be no "clear answer" but further "fiction" – a word that can act as a disclaimer, or on the contrary as a justification for her resort to "fiction" whenever she needs to fill in the "strange spaces of silence that seem to separate one period of activity from another" (29). It is precisely this self-reflexive framework that enables Woolf to address old questions in new ways. When she writes that "the extraordinary woman depends on the ordinary woman," she answers Lewes's argument that "only exceptional women will [...] be found competent to the highest success in other departments" than fiction (Lewes 43). Not only is the myth of the exceptional woman debunked in its essentialist version, but the history of the ordinary woman becomes a narrative recording the changes that led to her emancipation as a woman and a writer: the changes in law, custom, attitudes, habits and states of mind that have "turned the English woman from a nondescript influence, fluctuating and vague, to a voter, a wage earner, a responsible citizen, has given her both in her life and in her art a turn toward the impersonal" (*E V* 33). Last but not least, as a critic and a writer who knows that thoughts are construed by language, Woolf finally addresses the question of female novelists and "the sentence" in a manner that reverses entirely old arguments about women's "natural" literary aptitudes or inabilities. It is not so much, she argues, that a woman novelist is "fit," or unfit, for certain modes of expression as the fact "that the very form of the sentence does not fit her. It is a sentence made by men; it is too loose, too heavy, too pompous for a woman's use." Woolf's ultimate freedom as an artist will, therefore, result from a talent that no male critic had envisioned – the talent and capacity of "altering and adapting the current sentence until she writes one that takes the natural shape of her thought without crushing or distorting it" (*E V* 32).[28]

By engaging with this history of change, past, present and future, Woolf thus broadens the range of meaning ascribed to sexual "diffe-rence," women's "influence" and "aptitudes," proposing in their stead a historiographical critique of social and cultural patriarchal structures. But while she situates herself outside the reductive terms of the dominant discourses of psychology and biology, she never detaches her process of conceptualisation from the complex and historicised "embodiment" of sexual difference. As Patricia Moran suggests in "What is a Woman? I Assure You, I Do Not Know" (2017), "Woolf set herself the challenge of embodying her critique of patriarchy in the form and texture of her writing"; the conventions and ideological discourses that she questions "develop out of long-standing assumptions about what is 'important,' even 'natural'; they thus become powerful ideological and institutional instruments that embody, transmit and authenticate patriarchal values and structures" (Moran 168–169). That Woolf never "disembodies sexual difference" while always moving beyond the gendered binary is an aspect of her essays that Derek Ryan has underlined in a persua-sive way in *Virginia Woolf and the Materiality of Theory* (2013: 63). Taking the example of the much-debated issue, among feminist critics, of androgyny, he shows how the notion is a "theoretically agile term" which does not imply the "transcendence of the mind over the body," but rather manages to reconcile the mind and the body, sex and gender, within a definition of subjectivity that can be irrevocably feminine and female, masculine and male according to the angle of analysis. Woolf's capacity for both social critique and abstract metaphors, her need for definitions and her resistance to labels, her alternative use of facts and fiction are essential features of what Ryan sees as her way of "theorising materiality" and "materializing theory" (Ryan 4). Strikingly, this double impulse informs her well-known creations of Mrs Brown in "Character in Fiction," of Judith Shakespeare and Mary Carmichael in *A Room of One's Own*, of Anon, and of Orlando as an immortal embodiment of the gendering of sex. Contrary to "Candour," "Honesty," "our Lady of Chastity," "Purity" and "Modesty" in the third chapter of Woolf's mock-biography (*O* 129; 134), those allegorical figures unwrite the moral didacticism and typological codifications of former feminine incarnations. Deployed in a palimpsestuous linguistic space that de-simplifies the link between representation and interpretation, they are powerful heuristic tools that indeed "materialize" Woolf's thoughts on the vexed relationship between sex and literature, genre and gender. As her position clarified in the enduring critical debates on the "Woman Question," Woolf thus imagined yet another process of allegorisation that exposed and denounced the gendering of mass culture and of the novel as feminine.

"That Fiction is a Lady": Un-gendering Genre and Gender

In a number of essays and reviews (including *A Room of One's Own*), Woolf makes the choice of gendering "fiction" ("she") rather than "the novel" (almost always referred to as "it") and disingenuously adopts a polemical persona while transforming discontent into parody. With its feminine construed attributes – such as "finery" or "smile and witchery" (*E III* 341) – "fiction" appears as a "lady" provoking the tyranny of male critics who claim to honour and praise her. It should be noted, however, that many of these critical pieces do not directly address the subject of women and fiction. In some, such as "The Anatomy of Fiction" (1919) or "What is a Novel?" (1927), the choice of "fiction" or "novel" seems to depend less on by Woolf's purposeful strategy than on the publishing context.[29] On a first reading, these texts show that Woolf's use of either term is no more precise than Lubbock's in *The Craft of Fiction* (1921) or Forster's in *Aspects of the Novel* (1927). In both books, "fiction" and the "novel" appear to be almost interchangeable terms, with fiction appearing simply as a larger "class" or "species of literature" composed of "prose novels," "stories" or "tales," to take up a definition in the *Oxford English Dictionary*. Last but not least, in Woolf's essays, fiction and the novel are both linked by her repeated refusal to define them by dogmatic statements or prescriptive rules. "When they write a novel," she implores in "What is a Novel?," "let [the novelists] define it. Let them say that they have written a chronicle, a document, a rhapsody, a fantasy, an argument, a narrative or a dream. For there is no such thing as 'a novel'" (*E IV* 416).

That just like "women," fiction or the novel are "unsolved problems" does not mean that the critic should renounce attempts to describe or analyse them. In Woolf's essays, "fiction" and the "novel" thus become discursive categories, always dependent on historical contexts, cultural practices and individual poetics. A rapid survey of her use of the two terms in *A Room of One's Own* also reveals how Woolf is inclined to reproduce the discursive paradigms that they refer to while at the same time complicating them. "Fiction" is included in the lecture's framing device, appearing in its introduction and its conclusion both as "an unsolved problem" and as a discursive mode, enabling Woolf to gain narrative agency and rhetorical persuasion: "Fiction is here likely to contain more truth than fact," she explains at the outset of her talk. "Therefore I propose, making use of all the liberties and licences of a novelist, to tell you the story of the two days that preceded my coming here" (4). Woolf's open use of fictionalisation as the only way of accessing some kind of truth, mixed with the ambiguous generic value of her statement – is she going to tell a true, i.e., biographical story or an invented one? – provocatively steers her audience to the old definition of fiction as opposed to truth and fact, a definition which she challenges from the start. Woolf goes on playing with words and situations, for example, when, evoking the October "mist" stealing over "the gardens and the river" around Fernham, she wishes that she could describe "lilacs hanging over garden walls, crocuses, tulips and other flowers of spring." Ironically assuming the voice of a generation of anonymous critics for whom "the truer the facts, the better the fiction," Woolf, or rather her fictional persona, allegorises fiction for the first time: "I dare not forfeit your respect and imperil the fair name of fiction by changing the season" she explains; in October, there are no "lilacs [...] hanging over garden walls, [and] tulips and other flowers of spring." Woolf seems to lay the blame on Rossetti: "perhaps the words of Christina Rossetti were partly responsible for the folly of the fancy." Obviously, though, she praises the Victorian poetess, poetry and fiction at the same time. In the end, the initial idea "that fiction must stick to facts, and the truer the facts the better the fiction" has become a debatable statement (*AR* 12–13).[30]

Indeed, facts are usually "disappointing" (32). You cannot find them when they are needed, and since history cannot provide the genuine researcher with some "authentic fact" on the subject of women and fiction in the Elizabethan age, Woolf needs to turn to fiction again. As she discusses the paradox of women's "highest importance" in literature and their absence from history, the word "fiction" acquires a different meaning. No longer a specific genre, it is now an "imaginative work" contrasting with "science" and "history" in its "attachment" to life and truth: "fiction is like a spider's web, attached ever so lightly perhaps, but still attached to life at all four corners" (34). The first example of this valued "attachment" offered by Woolf is Shakespeare's plays, but soon another binary appears. The representation of woman in the fiction written by men is opposed to the real women those men never wrote about – the "Mrs Martin[s]." These anonymous women should at long last be brought to life by thinking poetically and prosaically at one and the same moment, thus keeping in touch with fact [...]; but not losing sight of fiction either—that [Mrs Martin] is a vessel in which all sorts of spirits and forces are coursing and flashing perpetually.

(34)

But as literary history unfolds, the glorious days of fiction as a genre are waning, Woolf suggests in Chapter 4. When she deals with nineteenth-century literature, the word "fiction" is replaced by "the novel," a change that illustrates the new status of this newly dominant genre associated with "great names" in a period described as "that purely patriarchal society" where "it is the masculine values that prevail" (55–56). And although Woolf acknowledges that "the novel alone was young enough to be soft in [a woman's] hands," she nonetheless wonders whether "this most pliable of all forms is rightly shaped for her use" (58). As she reaches the end of her talk, Woolf is thus led to question the conditions of possibility for Mary Carmichael, her allegory of the past, present and future female writer, to become a modern novelist at the turn of the twentieth century, since all "novels, without meaning to, inevitably lie" when it comes to seeing women as they are (67). However, when Woolf's lecture draws to a close, "fiction" occupies centre-stage again. Directly addressing her audience of "young women," Woolf returns to her original question ("women and fiction") and makes a "fantastic" suggestion of her own for the future. This suggestion is put in the form of a utopian "fiction" and allegory:

Now my belief is that this poet who never wrote a word and was buried at the cross-roads still lives. She lives in you and in me, and in many other women who are not here tonight, for they are washing up the dishes and putting the children to bed. [...] I maintain that [Shakespeare's sister] would come if we worked for her.

(*AR* 86)

As expected then, "fiction" in *A Room of One's Own* appears to be a more "pliable" (to use a Woolfian adjective) category than the novel, a more flexible form. Maybe less expected, fiction also emerges as a discursive site haunted by a genealogy of debates, almost trapped, like women themselves, or rather their representation, in a binary system: fact and fiction, truth and imagination. As real and as imagined as Mrs Martin in the lecture, or Mrs Brown in Woolf's essay "Character and Fiction," fiction is a literary and critical obsession that comes from the past and becomes a pervading presence even when Woolf tries to imagine the future. Above all, as an allegorised form and idea, fiction seems to be more willing than the novel to resist the assertive male critics' assaults. And yet, "the lady still escapes him" (*E III* 388). Interestingly, according to Gordon Teskey in *Allegory and Violence* (1996), it is when "meaning" needs "a place to occur [...] which does not become meaning itself" that the "enlightening or witty analogy between two things" that we usually call allegory might take place (Teskey 18; 1).

"That fiction is a lady and a lady who has somehow got herself into trouble, is a thought that must often have struck her admirers" (*E IV* 457). It is also a thought that should surprise us no more than it did Woolf's readers who were probably used to the cliché and to the centuries of debate on the feminisation of the novel that such clichés implied. Woolf's use of the gendered allegory is nonetheless an intriguing rhetorical instrument. She introduces it in "Philosophy in Fiction," a 1918 review of several "tales" and "stories" by L.P. Jacks; in "Modern Novels," the essay published in 1919 in the *Times Literary Supplement* that she later revised and published in *CR I* under the title "Modern Fiction"; in "On Re-reading Novels" (1922), and in "Is Fiction an Art" (1927). The subject of these four prose pieces is "fiction" or "the novel." Each of them is polemical or at least engages Woolf in a quarrel, more than in a polite discussion, with her male predecessors or contemporaries: in order of appearance, the now obscure L.P. Jacks, the Edwardian novelists (Bennett, Wells and Galsworthy), Percy Lubbock, Walter Raleigh and E.M. Forster. Each of these writers is considered a personal interlocutor and a representative of his "class," whether as a male critic or a male fiction writer. In each case, Woolf stages stock-characters that seem to be performing recognisable gender-roles, although the setting varies from one allegory to the other. In "The Philosophy of Fiction," the "dusky draperies" of fiction (*E II* 208), along with the desire that this feminine vestment arouses in the common reader ("us"), create an unreasonable "child" or a "sultan" and send him back to the Islamic Golden Age of the *Arabian Nights* and the lures of Scheherazade (*E II* 211). In "Modern Novels," Woolf hopes that fiction as "English fiction" will soon "turn [...] its back upon [the Edwardian novelists], as politely as may be and [will] march [...], if only into the desert, [which would be] the better for its soul" (*E III* 32). When she then defines the task of the modern novelist and asserts that "the proper stuff of fiction doesn't exist," she again endows fiction – this time personified as "she" and "her" – with female attributes. Fiction is now a "lady" engaged in what could be a courtly love scenario: "All that fiction asks of us is that we should break and bully her, honour and love her, till she yields to our bidding, for so her youth is perpetually renewed and her sovereignty assured" (36). In "Modern Fiction," her 1925 revised version of the essay, Woolf's watered-down conclusion suppresses the image of fiction "yielding to our bidding," as if to ensure a more obvious balance between the image of fiction as an inaccessible sovereign, and the more disturbing allusion to abusive coercion:

> And if we can imagine the art of fiction come alive and standing in our midst, she would undoubtedly bid us break her and bully her, as well as honour and love her, for so her youth is renewed and her sovereignty assured.

Still, the paradox remains: the lady's integrity needs respect, and freedom from external control, but "we" – readers and critics – should help her get rid of "custom," "falsity and pretence," even if this should harm her a little (*E IV* 164).

The background, costumes and protagonists change again in "On Re-reading Novels." To suggest that Lubbock, in *The Craft of Fiction*, loses sight of the novel as life, Woolf imagines fiction in the guise of a Victorian, middle-class, "voluminous" yet ordinary lady "submitted" to "scientific examination." Science here appears as a method of investigation that is both radically new and radically dangerous: as mentioned earlier in this book, the scientist can only fully grasp his subject after she is dead. Lubbock's X-rays in Woolf's essay "dissolve" the respectable lady's "flesh," her "finery," her "smile and witchery," together with "the umbrellas and brown paper parcels which she has collected along her long and toilsome journey." Nothing is left of her but her "skeleton" (*E III* 341).

There is something inevitable here in the critic's hopelessness and incompetence, whether he belongs to the past, or to the generation of "New Critics" Woolf was so suspicious about. On the examination table, "fiction" is impossible to cure, like the female malady in the Victorian Age. You may "dissect" it like a "frog" – another allegory Woolf adopts in "The Anatomy of Fiction" – use "the inductive" or "deductive" method, "you cannot make it hop; there is, unfortunately, such a thing as life" (*E III* 44–45). Besides, like fiction and like Mrs Brown, life is "emotional" and "unamenable to discipline" (*E II* 341). And yet, seeing how often the lady "has [...] got herself into trouble [...], many gallant gentlemen have ridden to [fiction's] rescue, chief among them Sir Walter Raleigh and Mr Percy Lubbock" (*E IV* 457). Fortunately, E.M. Forster, Woolf suggests in "Is Fiction an Art?," is less "ceremonious" in his approach, showing more "intimacy" with the subject than his predecessors: "None more suggestive [than his book] has been written about the poor lady who, with mistaken chivalry perhaps, we still persist in calling the art of fiction" (*E IV* 467; 463). However, like many other critics who did not manage to "grasp [...] her firmly and define [...] her severely," Forster, according to Woolf, fails to "draw up" rules for fiction, a failure that prevents him from conferring "dignity and order upon [his] subject." For although "rules may be wrong, and must be broken," Woolf goes on explaining, "they have this advantage: [...] they prove that [fiction] is worthy of consideration." Unfortunately, Forster "is not going to theorise about fiction except incidentally; he doubts whether she is to be approached by a critic, and if so by what critical equipment" (460). As Rachel Bowlby remarks in her introduction to *A Woman's Essays* (1992),

> While characteristically claiming a need for rules, Woolf also jokingly genders the rule-makers and the rule-breakers, acknowledging too that the breaking occurs through the agency of a woman who insists on slipping away from the grasp of men's attempts to hold her in one place.
>
> (Bowlby xxx)

As they expose to ridicule common stereotypes, and with them, the genealogy of patriarchal discourses enacting them, Woolf's gendered allegories also re-inscribe the iconic power of "woman" to render intelligible this allegorical "other" that fiction is declared to be.[31] Woolf's four ladies are indeed figures of parody and satire that paradoxically uncover, while blurring it, the possible – yet finally ungraspable – identity of fiction, of woman and of their associative links. Like "woman," "fiction" thus appears as a discursive playground that is fraught with contradictory ideological postures: depending on contexts, and sometimes within the same context, she is a distant sovereign, a middle-class domestic woman or a concubine, a witch, yielding to or arousing the desires of her admirers whether they be chivalrous "knights," "gallant gentlemen," or ordinary critics and scientists. A passive victim or a disruptive force, fundamentally unruly yet asking for rules, she is never at the right distance, so that men rarely engage in an "animated conversation" with her. Refusing to fix either "woman" or "fiction" in their essentialised versions, Woolf contextualises the terms, juxtaposes a "variety" of images (*E IV* 458), and provocatively "questions [...] a reassuring association between femininity and stable values, substituting for the good woman or mother the promiscuous wench" (Bowlby 1992: xxx). This is when Woolf's allegories involve a disruptive form of inversion in the symbolic order of language and representation: to be "rescued," the lady-fiction needs more intimacy; she, herself, asks of us that we should "break her and bully her" (*E III* 36), and her "dusky draperies" are sometimes less "indecent" than the "brief, pointed" and pseudoscientific words of philosophy or criticism (*E II* 211).

However, it seems difficult for both fiction and woman to escape the dichotomies that trap them within the claustrophobic discourse of binarity: in Woolf's short allegorical narratives, ladies are opposed to gentlemen, submission to authority, intimacy to distance, passivity to agency, examination to conversation, life to science, the art of fiction to the practice of criticism. Momentarily, Woolf's prose is transformed into a battlefield, and Woolf's tone gets highly polemical: "Whatever stage we have reached we are still in the thick of battle" (*E III* 30). In a world where "fiction" as a genre and "woman" as a sex are usually belittled, Woolf ironically fights back, dissimulating her anger under the guise of parody. But she is also careful to move beyond confrontation by subtly reconfiguring the terms and by urging her readers to do the same. This is the case with the crucial yet ambivalent way the ideas of convention, hierarchy and values circulate in her texts. According to Emily Blair, in *Virginia Woolf and the Domestic Novel* (2007), the use of such notions in Woolf's essays betrays her "vexed entanglement" with "Victorian etiquette practices" and is a manifestation of her "tea-table tactics" whereby she "creates an analogy between the 'hostess' and the 'writer'" and prompts a male audience to cooperate" (Blair 41–42). But if for Woolf both "genre" and "gender" implied a "code of manners," the acceptance of "rules" and a form of "propriety," it does not mean that she unambiguously adopts nineteenth-century valorisation of such notions as order, stability and decorum.[32] Rules and conventions are indeed as dangerous as their absence: they are "the prelude to the more exciting intercourse of friendship." They "bring [...] order into our perceptions" (*E V* 580). Without them, no dialogic cooperation between writer and reader, author and critic, men and women is possible; yet they should be incessantly historicised, challenged, reconfigured, because they, like the labels and definitions we ascribe to genres and individuals, are essentially contingent.

Woolf's gendered allegories undoubtedly form a dangerously powerful rhetorical weapon. They suggest that her essayistic prose was wrongly praised for its "sensitive" and "exquisite" nature, or for its "sufficiency and freshness,"[33] and yet, Northrop Frye's reaction to her "fiction is a lady" trope suggests that Woolf was taking some risks here. In his review of Woolf's *The Moment and Other Essays* (1948), Frye openly criticises her "self-conscious delicacy of perception," and her "arch female cuteness and irritating female trick of avoiding the straight abstract line of argument in order to dither the metaphor" (Frye 81). With her gendered allegories, Woolf appeared to engage in a new war between the sexes, which, until *Three Guineas*, she had kept saying she wanted to avoid, and this, by letting a form of belligerence cover the voice of the common reader. She also took the risk of overestimating her audience's intelligence; last but not least, to reactivate old clichés could have led to their perpetuation. But I imagine Woolf thought it was worth it. Besides, risk is an idea she valued repeatedly, especially when "women" and "fiction" were concerned. It first enabled her to take position as a literary critic and historian outside the academy while increasing her reader's receptivity to the controversies on women and fiction that had started in the eighteenth century and culminated in the late nineteenth century. In her essays, Woolf implicitly answers a genealogy of writers: eighteenth-century essayists and critics preoccupied with the novel being "entirely engrossed by the ladies,"[34] with its opposition to the romance, its so-called feminisation around the 1740s or with the emergence of "domestic" fiction leading to its decline in the hierarchy of genres around the same period; their followers in the nineteenth- and twentieth centuries. By taking rhetorical and ideological risks Woolf found a way to raise her voice above the humdrum of other, more assertive, critical discourses. Doing so, she also produced a pragmatic counter-discourse grafted on the problematisation of utterance and the engagement of the common reader in alternative, more creative, forms knowledge. But beyond the well-known trope of "conversation" as a writing and reading method, what Woolf looked for here, I would suggest, is a form of discomfort related to allegory's way of encoding meaning. Indeed, although "genre" and "gender" – "fiction" and "woman" – enabled Woolf to refer her reader to a body of traditional thought and recognisable patterns, we are soon provoked as readers out of our potential passivity by the three fold effect of the poetics of allegory. As Teskey reminds us, "an allegory means something other than what it says and says something other than it means"; as such it is a "figure of deferral"; then, it always implies some kind of "rift between heterogeneous others" (Teskey 1996: 164), between the philosophical "categories of the material and the ideal," brought together by "force of meaning" (ibid. 1). Thus, by personifying "intractable conceptual dilemmas," allegory becomes a complex artistic transaction. It "opens a schism in consciousness—between a life and a mystery, between the real and the ideal": it renders an analogy visible, yet allows its truth to escape. Last but not least, when it figures, as it so often does, the appropriation of a female body by a male embodied or abstract figure, it implies a form of epistemological violence, a hidden process of "capture" whereby female materiality is submitted to masculine desire, while simultaneously "being raised up from its logical place, which is beneath the lowest species, into the realm of abstractions" (Teskey 22).

Woolf will continue to denounce this epistemological violence along the years, returning its performative value against the patriarchal system that gave birth to it: if men could protect "culture and intellectual liberty" instead of waging wars, she explains in *Three Guineas*, then

> 'culture,' that amorphous bundle, swaddled up as she now is in insincerity, emitting half truths from her timid lips, sweetening and diluting her message with whatever sugar or water serves to swell the writer's fame or his master's purse, would regain her shape and become, as Milton, Keats and other great writers assure us that she is in reality, muscular, adventurous, free.
>
> (*TG* 176–177)

Notes

1 Woolf's article on "Women and Fiction" was to be read to student societies at the two women's colleges at Cambridge in October 1928, before being expanded and published a year later as *A Room of One's Own*.

2 On the evolution of Woolf's reception as a feminist and an artist, see Naomi Black (2004: 146–170), Anna Snaith (2007: 1–15), Patricia Moran (2017) and Laura Marcus (2000).

3 The reference is to *Three Guineas*, and to the long-unanswered, essential question raised by the essayist in the first page:

> But one does not like to leave so remarkable a letter as yours—a letter perhaps unique in the history of human correspondence, since when before has an educated man asked a woman how in her opinion war can be prevented? Therefore let us make the attempt; even if it is doomed to failure.
>
> (*TG* 89)

4 J.B. Bachelor, "Feminism in Virginia Woolf," in *Virginia Woolf: A Collection of Critical Essays* (1971); quoted in Marcus (2000: 127). The expression "extreme feminism" is borrowed from E.M. Forster's tribute to Woolf's life

and works two months after her death: "There is something old-fashioned about this extreme Feminism." It produced, according to Forster, "one of the most brilliant of her books—the charming and persuasive *A Room of One's Own*" but was also "responsible for the worst of her books—the cantankerous *Three Guineas*—and for her less successful streaks in *Orlando*" (Forster 1942: 23).

5 On the difference between contradiction and contradictoriness, see this book's introduction.

6 "Indeed, I would venture to guess that Anon, who wrote so many poems without singing them, was often a woman" (*AR* 38).

7 The index of the six volumes of Woolf's essays indicates that neither Nora Kershaw nor Lucy Aikin or Catherine Macaulay and Mary Hayes are mentioned. *The Letters of Gertrude Bell*, a volume that was part of Leonard and Virginia Woolf's library, appears in "Preferences" (1928) – "Gertrude Bell's letters interested me profoundly" – without further commentary (*E IV* 543). Of Lucy Hutchinson — the "pious Mrs Hutchinson" (*E I* 145) — whose *Fugitive Pieces* was published by The Hogarth Press in 1927, Woolf writes in "The New Biography" (1927): "the biographer, whether he was Izaak Walton or Mrs Hutchinson [...] told a tale of battle and victory" (*E IV* 474). As to the Duchess of Newcastle, "her language was coarse," her "philosophies [...] futile, and her plays intolerable, and her verses mainly dull." Yet, Woolf considered that the "vast bulk" of her work was "leavened by a vein of authentic fire." It is mainly her "erratic and lovable personality" which seems to have fascinated her, along with the circumstances that made it possible for her to write (*E IV* 81–91; 87).

8 In a very personal essay on the essay, Rachel Blau DuPlessis claims Woolf as her foremother and evokes the "feminized space" of the essay in very Woolfian terms:

> the essay embodies, and can claim, a feminized space: of interruption, of beginning again and again, of fragmentation, of discontinuities. But most in its distrust of system, its playful skepticism about generalization. And interest in the small, the odd, the quirky, the by-the-side, the thing changeable, the viewer changeable too. Skepticism even about one's own self-interested positions.
>
> (2006: 43)

9 In the third part of *Three Guineas*, Woolf explains that "once more we will have recourse to Victorian biography because it is only in the Victorian age that biography becomes rich and representative" (*TG* 204).

10 Ezell mentions, among others, Ellen Moers in *Literary Women* (1976); Sandra Gilbert and Susan Gubar in *The Mad Woman in the Attic* (1979); Elaine Showalter in A *Literature of Their Own* (1999) and many of the essays collected in Mary Eagleton's *Feminist Theory* (1986).

11 I borrow the expression from Alison Booth's *Virginia Woolf and George Eliot: Greatness Engendered* (1992).

12 I also borrow from Elena Gualtieri's *Virginia Woolf's Essays: Sketching the Past* (2000) the idea that we need to read Woolf not simply as one of those "exceptional" figures she was herself so fascinated with, but "against a background embedded in communal textures" (45).

13 William Leonard Courtney (1850–1928), English author, philosopher and journalist, former tutor in Philosophy at New College, Oxford, also published

The Metaphysics of John Stuart Mill (1879), *Studies in Philosophy* (1882) and *Constructive Ethics* (1886). *The Feminine Note in Fiction* is a 300-page long book, containing chapters on, among others, the fiction of Mrs Humphry Ward, Margaret Louisa Woods, Ethel Voynich and the letters of Dorothy Osborne, Fanny Burney and Margaret Fuller.

14 Courtney's actual words on the subject are:

> Recently complaints have been heard that the novel as a work of art is disappearing and giving place to monographs on given subjects, or else individual studies of character. If the complaint be true—and in some respects it obviously is true—the reason is that more and more in our modern age novels are written by women for women.
>
> (1904: xii)

15 One of the most famous "conversations" of the kind is reported in "The Intellectual Status of Women" (1920), a "letter" in which Woolf reacts in a highly ironical, if not sarcastic, way to Affable Hawk's (Desmond MacCarthy) endorsement of Arnold Bennett's view that women are inferior to men in intellectual power:

> That Mr Bennett can name fifty of the male sex that can be [Sappho's] superior is therefore a welcome surprise, and if he will publish their names I promise, as an act of submission which is so dear to my sex, not only to buy their works but, so far as my faculties allow, to learn them by heart.
>
> (*AWE* 34)

16 In his study of *The Women Novelists*, Johnson has two chapters on Fanny Burney, three on Jane Austen, three on Charlotte Brontë and another significantly named "The Great Four: Burney, Austen, Brontë, George Eliot" (Johnson 1918: vii–viii).

17 In "Men and Women," her 1920 review of Léonie Villard's *La Femme Anglaise au XIXème siècle et son Évolution d'après le Roman Anglais Contemporain*, Woolf praises the author for using "fiction as her material," for being "concrete and definite," and describing "change in the nineteenth century" in a convincing way (*E III* 192–194).

18 This expression is a reference to Rachel Bowlby in her 1992 edition of *Virginia Woolf: A Woman's Essays*.

19 On this subject see Jessie Wolfe, *Bloomsbury, Modernism, and the Reinvention of Intimacy* (2011).

20 Crosby very convincingly argues in her introduction that in the nineteenth century, history "produced a man's truth, the truth of a necessarily historical Humanity, which in turn requires that 'women' be outside history, above, below, or beyond properly historical and political life." History, therefore, becomes "an epistemological and an ontological principle, the determining condition of all life and therefore all knowledge." It is "first a displacement and then a reconfirmation, at a more profound, more abstract level, of man itself" (Crosby 2013: 1–2).

21 Woolf concludes "The Feminine Note in Fiction" with a delightful example of this kind of irony: "Mr Courtney has given us material for many questions such as these, but his book has done nothing to prevent them from still remaining questions" (*E I* 16).

22 See "Female Novelists," *London Review*, 1 (1860: 137–138; 137). Quoted by Helsinger et al. (1983: 53).

23 This lecture was delivered to the Cambridge Apostles, and then to the mixed audience of the Bloomsbury Friday Club in June 1910. In her article on "Forster and Woman" (2007), Jane Goldman reminds her readers that Woolf was one of the founders of this Club; she explains that Forster showed "great sensitivity to the gender of his audience in providing two versions of his paper, one addressed exclusively to his exclusively male Cambridge colleagues, the other to the mixed company of Bloomsbury" (Goldman 2007: 121–123).

24 Woolf's draft paper was published as "Women and Fiction" in the American monthly *Forum* in March 1929 before it was revised and completed as *A Room of One's Own*.

25 British Poet Laureate Alfred Austin (1835–1913) addressed the issue of "the feminine note" in poetry during a meeting of the members of the Leicester Literary and Philosophical Society in 1895. As a report in *Transactions of the Leicester Literary and Philosophical Society*, vol. III suggests, he understood the "note" in question as "the personal and domestic note, the note of pity and suffering, and the sentimental note, or notes of romantic love." Interestingly, Austin does not see the feminine note in poetry as belonging to the female sex. Yet, his thoughts are in line with the traditional "gendering" of genre – whether fiction or lyric poetry (Leicester: George Gibbons, 1895, 459–460).

26 An entry of Forster's Diary dated December 11, 1910 reads: "Miss Stephen said the paper was the best there had been, which pleases me." Quoted in Peter Stansky's *On or About December 1910* (1997: 150).

27 See *A Room of One's Own* (75):

> Here I came to the books by living writers, and there paused and wondered if this fact were not at the root of something that had long puzzled me. No age can ever have been as stridently sex-conscious as our own; those innumerable books by men about women in the British Museum are a proof of it.

28 See here George Lewes (1852: 42):

> Woman, by her greater affectionateness, her greater range and depth of emotional experience, is well fitted to give expression to the emotional facts of life, and demands a place in literature corresponding with that she occupies in society; and that literature must be greatly benefited thereby, follows from the definition we have given of literature.

29 As mentioned previously, "The Art of Fiction" is a review of *Materials and Methods of Fiction* by Clayton Hamilton published in the *Athenaeum* in 1919; "What is a Novel," published in the *Weekly Dispatch* in 1927, was initially a contribution to a symposium in *The Highway*, the journal of the Worker's Educational Association, on the question "What is a Good Novel?"

30 The reference here is to Christina Rossetti's "A Birthday."

31 It has often been argued that because allegory works by literalising lexical effects, and because the gender of abstract nouns in Latin is feminine, then most allegories are feminine personifications (in Latin, fictio – onis is indeed a feminine noun). However, there are masculine allegories in Greek (Phobos,

Thanatos, Ploutos and Demos) and in Latin (Amor and Furor). Moreover, literary history suggests that depending on contexts and authors, the use of feminine allegories might be accompanied "by an engagement of the trope of personification with actual female agency," if not by a "self-conscious proto-feminist" or feminist purpose. On this subject see Quilligan (2010: 165).

32 See Woolf in "Character in Fiction":

> At the moment we are suffering, not from decay, but from having no code of manners which writers and readers accept as a prelude to the more exciting intercourse of friendship. The literary convention of the time is so artificial [...] that, naturally the feeble are tempted to outrage, and the strong are led to destroy the very foundations and rules of literary society.
>
> (*E III* 434)

33 Lord David Cecil's words reported by Leïla Brosnan in *Reading Virginia Woolf's Essays and Journalism* (Brosnan 1999: 96).

34 A comment found in the *Monthly Review* 48 (1773: 154) and quoted by Katherine Binhammer and Jeanne Wood in *Women and Literary History* (2003: 116).

8 Our Perfect and Imperfect Mothers
Woolf's Nineteenth-Century Counter-Narratives

Virginia Stephen was not born on the 25th January 1882,

but was born many thousands of years ago;

and had from the very first to encounter

instincts already acquired by thousands of ancestresses in the past.[1]

Virginia Woolf "Practising"

In July 1859, George Lewes wrote a laudatory essay on the novels of Jane Austen for the *Blackwood's Edinburgh Magazine*. In this 15-page text, which begins with an assessment of Austen's place in literary history and ends with memorable quotations from *Pride and Prejudice* and *Emma*, Lewes deplores the contrast between Austen's "great excellence and real success" and her near invisibility to critics for almost two generations. In spite of the novelist's excellent "attainments," he remarks, "her name is not even now a household word." And yet, "she is an artist of high rank, in the most rigorous sense of the word"; her "pictures of English life" are "exquisite," and her "dramatic instinct [...] makes the construction of her stories admirable." As a matter of fact, Lewes finds Fielding "immeasurably inferior to her" in this "department of art"; as to Shakespeare, like him Miss Austen "makes her very noodles inexhaustibly amusing, yet accurately real." Neither Miss Burney "who is no longer read, nor much worth reading," nor Charlotte Brontë "who, we fear, will soon cease to find readers," compare with her. As a "Lady novelist" (the expression is never used but often implied), her excellence is "unobtrusive": her "eloquent blood spoke through her modest cheek" and she "never publicly avowed her authorship, although she spoke freely of it in private." Of course, there are limitations to her genius, and Lewes again resorts to those "buts" his readers must have been accustomed to whenever the subject of women and fiction was discussed: Miss Austen is "exquisitely and inexhaustibly humorous; but when she speaks in her own person, she is apt to be commonplace, and even prosing"; her place "is among great artists, but it is not high among them. She sits in the House of

DOI: 10.4324/9780429331787-11

Peers, but it is as a simple Baron." This is "because she never stirs the deeper emotions," and she "never fills the soul with a noble aspiration, or brightens it with a fine idea" (Lewes 1859: 444–457). In spite of these negative comments, shared by many of Lewes's contemporaries and subsequent generations of critics, the assessment differs here from George Saintsbury's three pages on the author of *Pride and Prejudice* in his *History of Nineteenth-Century Literature* (1896b), to cite a significant example: Saintsbury agrees with Lewes in praising Austen for her "perfections": she " 'set the clock,' so to speak, of pure novel writing," moving away from "violent and romantic adventure," "popular or passing fashions, amusements, politics" towards the most strikingly ordinary life. But his short critical comment is more straightforwardly essentialist than his predecessors: "there is something feminine about her method," in particular her use of "an exceedingly nice and delicate analysis of motive and temperament." Austen, Saintsbury writes, "crystallise[s] the special talent and gift of an entire sex into a literary method." He nonetheless wonders at her pervading irony – "by no means a frequent feminine gift; and as women do not often possess it in any degree, so they do not as a rule enjoy it" (Saintsbury 1896b: 130–131).

When, on July 15, 1922, Woolf wrote "Jane Austen Practising" for the *New Statesman*, she infused the opening paragraphs of her signed review with her own irony – this "infrequent" gift among women.[2] In the parodic tone that she would use in *Orlando* each time a new "age" and its "spirit" were introduced in the narrative's blurred chronology, or in the passage when "he," having become a woman, the course of time appears suspended, Woolf pays a tribute to her foremother resounding with anterior voices:

> The summer of 1922, remarkable for public reasons in many ways, was privately remarkable for the coldness of its nights. Six blankets and a quilt? A rug and a cold bottle? All over England men and women went to bed with such words upon their lips. And then, between two and three in the morning, they woke up with a start. Something serious had happened.

Introduced by the reviewer, enters Jane Austen, adorned with the guises of her youth, discovered anew as if her reputation had not "accumulat[ed] on top of us like the same quilts and blankets" for almost twenty years. In a few sentences, a small patriarchal world gathers on a stage created by Woolf, its male protagonists ready to perform their roles in a typically Austenian comedic scene: "the voices of the elderly and distinguished, of the clergy and the squirearchy, have drowned in unison praising and petting, capping quotations, telling anecdotes, raking up little facts." In her foremother's manner, Woolf's satiric thrust relies here on the burlesque contrast between the theatricality of situations – "it was stifling. It was portentous" – and the prosaic depiction of an overdue awakening.

As Austen's famous gossip-mongers – usually female characters – a few gentlemen, and the institutions they stand for, are shown gaggling away as they engage in a flimsy conversation with little logic and less interest: "she is the most perfect artist in English literature. And one of her cousins had his head cut off in the French Revolution. Did she ever go fox-hunting? No, but she nursed Miss Gibson through the measles" (*E III* 331–332).

At long last, Woolf suggests, we can read Austen by ourselves, before "she was the great Austen of mythology." The reviewer will therefore guide us along well-trodden paths while inviting us to abandon the parochial thinking these paths habitually encourage: what matters thus is not the fact that "Austen was personally attractive" (Lewes 1859: 445), but that as a girl of seventeen she wrote in a country parsonage. Woolf's biographical account of Austen's youth is an animated scene in the midst of which the future novelist scribbled her first stories to entertain relatives – in "some private corner of the common parlour where she was allowed to write without interruption." Quoting from Austen's early works, the reviewer imagines the young woman as a writer, interrupted by her siblings, her pen scratching the paper, "faster than she could spell" (333), as she chose her fictional "territory" upon the "map of human nature" without an ounce of "anger at the snub" that she undoubtedly received (333–334). As many of her male predecessors, Woolf does not hesitate to speak her truth regarding Austen's defects: "and, after all, she was a limited, tart, rather conventional woman for all her genius" (334). But whether those words are actually hers or the weaving, in free indirect speech, of prior hackneyed assessments, it cannot be easily known. After all, Woolf begins her review by reporting the collective voice of critical nonsense. Thus, that Jane Austen "never trespassed beyond her boundaries" is not proof of submissive femininity but of her control over her art. These boundaries do not imply that the young girl never thought of "mountains and castles," nor should they prevent the reader from knowing about her romantic passion for English History and the Queen of Scots. More importantly, Woolf's reading of Austen's *Juvenilia* uncovers the singular quality of the young author's laughter, a reminder of her transgressive potential: "The girl of seventeen is laughing, in her corner, at the world" (333). As she recreates the scene of Jane Austen practising, Woolf finally renders the past in its detailed materiality vividly present for our imagination while insisting that we should pay attention to the rhythm of the novelist's sentences and to the "tune beneath her breath" (334).

As Anne Maria Reus has remarked in *Virginia Woolf's Rewriting of Victorian Women Writers' Lives* (2018),[3] Woolf's reviews and essays on Jane Austen almost always developed as a response to the exemplary woman writer who emerges from official family biographies.[4] Read chronologically, Reus argues, those responses nonetheless appear to change over the course of Woolf's career, from the "initial rejection of this perfect predecessor, who was frequently used by Victorian men to control subsequent women writers," to Woolf's version of Austen in the 1920s as "a complex and sophisticated writer and role model," the lost proto-modernist and predecessor of all women's writing (Reus 2018: 40). I agree that Woolf's various discussions of Austen's merits "circle [...] around the problem of gender and femininity, but never directly addresses it." I also believe that those conversations encourage us to look back at Lewes's (1859) essay and Leslie Stephen's 1885 *Dictionary of National Biography* entry on Austen. Read alongside these two texts, "Jane Austen Practising" indeed appears to recycle the Victorian critical trope that associates faultless femininity with true genius. However, I doubt that Woolf is aligning in her review with Charlotte Brontë's resistance to Austen, or with her father's sceptical appraisal of her merits as a novelist.[5] Once more, Woolf's comments sound like an ironic nod to the criticism of her male predecessors; additionally, it casts a shadow of doubt on the origin of many of the previous examinations of Austen's art and the difficulty that a female critic in the nineteenth- and early-twentieth centuries might have responding to their entangled threads. Woolf's opening metaphor in this text actually suggests that it always requires "a frightful effort [...] to shake off all these clothes" (*E III* 332).

As readers engaged with the critical appraisals of Woolf's foremother's, we too must grapple with the uneasy task of disentangling similarly entwined threads. In "Jane Austen," a 1913 review of the novelist's *Life and Letters* written for the *TLS*, Woolf thus comments, "Jane Austen was never a revelation to the young, a stern comrade, a brilliant and extravagantly admired friend, a writer whose sentences sang in one's brain and were half absorbed into one's blood." But this depreciative judgement is undercut by the reviewer's next sentence: "And directly one has set down any of the above phrases one is conscious of the irony with which she [Austen] could have disclaimed any such wish or intention" (*E II* 11). It is "plain that life sowed [Austen] a great deal that was smug; commonplace; and, in a bad sense of the word, artificial," Woolf then suggests, which explains why "characters such as the characters as Elinor Dashwood and Fanny Price bore us frankly." But Austen's circumstances, more than her sex, can explain her "conservative spirit." Also true, Woolf remarks, is Austen's awareness of her "own limitations"; but instead of praising this awareness as a mark of feminine distinction, she considers it in a way that breaks with the traditional assumption of women's inborn insufficiencies: Austen's talent, she suggests, could have enticed her "to run almost of the risks" of invention (*E II* 11). One might argue here that the idea of "risk taking" reflects back on Woolf's own literary experimentations and how she regularly felt that she could be misunderstood or misread. Conversely, we can consider the impossibility for women to take any "risk" in the early-nineteenth century, a fact that Woolf could not have ignored. What I hear in the word "risk," however, is the possibility of "agency" – the ability for any young girl and woman to aspire and achieve beyond sociocultural constraints – that anticipates recent feminist debates and will be further discussed at the end of this chapter.

Framed in the context of Austen's reception, Woolf's own dialogue with the novelist is typical of her critical method. It looks back and forward in a thought-provoking way, keeping track of former discourses and the ideological resistances that need to be undermined to hold a perspective that differs from the dominant culture. As it brings into play both externally imposed and self-regulatory norms, this "dialogue" musters more than two voices, sometimes as numerous and encumbering as the layers of blankets and quilts at the beginning of "Jane Austen Practising." As such, it prompts us to take into consideration the contexts of utterance and the power relations that complicate all forms of dialogue. But as it focuses on the literary creativity of female writers, this conversation also stages in a particularly conspicuous way the gendered positions, ascribed to them by others, of the reviewer and of the writer under review. As Woolf explains in the fourth chapter of *A Room of One's Own,* since such an opinion as "female novelists should only aspire to excellence by courageously acknowledging the limitations of their sex" can be asserted in "August 1928," then "it would have needed a very stalwart young woman in 1828 to disregard all those snubs and chidings and promises of prizes" (*AR* 57).[6] Woolf thus inescapably shared with her female predecessors the "common experience" of being "impeded by the extreme conventionality of the other sex" (*E VI* 483) and having to negotiate with "influences" that she knew were extremely difficult to escape.

Thus, what appears with ever greater clarity in this study of Woolf's "thinking back through her mothers," is Woolf herself practising, mustering the counter-mechanisms that she developed from an early age as a female artist, critic and historiographer. Most of these mechanisms have been explored in the previous chapters of this book, and many, like satirical distance, the palimpsestuous rewriting of former discourses or the use of narrative as a powerful revisionist tool, look back to Woolf's female predecessors as they, themselves, needed to negotiate a place and a voice of their own in the world of English letters. In this respect, these mechanisms remind us that only writers occupying a secure and established position in the world have the privilege of evading questions of strategy and rhetorical tactics. But beyond the unavoidable debates on Woolf's and her forebears' struggle with the "Angel in the House," I am interested in the way these counter-mechanisms, taken this time altogether, also bring forth the question of the generative power of Woolf's feminist literary histories. Following the insights opened up by Barbara Herrnstein Smith in *Contingencies of Value: Alternative Perspectives for Critical Theory* (1988), Madelyn Detloff has recently shown, in *The Value of Virginia Woolf* (2016), how this enduring power is grafted on a reading method that incites a collective "process of reflection, contestation, and remaking" (Detloff 2016: 3). Thirteen years earlier in *Virginia Woolf, the Intellectual, and the Public Sphere* (2003),

Melba Cuddy-Keane had reached a similar conclusion in her chapter on Woolf's "theory and pedagogy of reading." Describing Woolf's reading practice as a "feminist development of 'countermechanisms'" relying on "a contextual placement of texts and reception in relation to the assumptions and attitudes, social configurations, and material conditions of each time," Cuddy-Keane explained how these counter-mechanisms could take the readers "beyond confrontations of differing values to an analysis of how value operates" (Cuddy-Keane 2003: 177). In her wake, Detloff grounds her demonstration in the idea that "the endurance of Woolf's work is due in part to its complexity," and that an invaluable aspect of this work is its "capacity to change us – not because of what it says or means, but because of the habits of mind that it cultivates as we experience it" (Detloff 12).

Interestingly, where the two American scholars see the empowering dynamic of Woolf's counter-narratives, Margaret Ezell saw the elaboration of a problematic "model" imported into British and American women's studies without the careful scrutiny that its theoretical assumptions would have required. "Hailed as the new feminist literary history," this model, she argues, is essentialist, linear and "'evolutionary' in nature," moving from "imitation of male forms with an internalization of patriarchal values, to protest against standards (the feminine phase), arriving finally at 'self-discovery' (the feminist phase) in which the turning inward frees the individual from constantly defining one's self in opposition" (Ezell 1996: 64). Since it was imported into British and American women's studies, the "evolutionary pattern of female authorship proposed by Woolf in *A Room of One's Own*" has become, with such writers as Showalter, Gilbert and Gubar, or Ellen Moers, "a theory of female creativity" grounded in debatable assumptions: among them, the ideas that any women's history imply the quest for some origin (in Woolf's case, the nineteenth-century female novelist), that the future will mean "progress," or that "anger" is the "only positive signal to a female consciousness" (Ezell 25).[7] In other words, Ezell indirectly pictures Woolf as the founder of an "orthodox" school of criticism, and while the "founder" might be absolved, her followers should know better (Ezell 6). As suggested earlier in this book, Margaret Ezell's critique of Woolf's "model" in *Writing Women's Literary History* is a forceful one: the epistemological and methodological questions that it raised almost three decades ago cannot be easily dismissed as outdated. Besides, Ezell's dialogue with Woolf, envisioned here as the foremother of Anglo-American feminist criticism, is quite Woolfian in its method. Firstly, Ezell uses the tools of both historicism and critical theory in order to undermine some of Woolf's theoretical arguments. Her aim is then to uncover a genealogy of discourses that expand on Woolf's legacy but that fail to engage with the revisions that this legacy inescapably requires. Last but not least, Ezell's enquiry proposes a methodology that Woolf would have agreed with entirely: "what is needed now is a consideration of our historiography and a reconsideration of the patterns of inquiry which will determine the future direction of women's literary history" (Ezell 12).

Since 1993 and the publication of Ezell's *Writing Women's Literary History*, numerous commentaries of Woolf's most influential feminist work have opened up new paths for interpretation. While Quentin Bell had dismissed the relevance of his aunt's "meditations upon aggression and affection" to the "world of practical politics" in his *Bloomsbury* (Bell 1968: 71), a generation of feminist critics have studied *A Room of One's Own* as a theoretical and political project, while acknowledging that its value needs to be historicised and reassessed ongoingly. Evoking the construction, in *A Room*, of a "double linear narrative" – first, the increasing restriction and limitation of women's lives since the sixteenth century, caused by the hardening of gender roles, and second, the emancipatory counter-narrative of the emergence of "women's writing" – Melba Cuddy-Keane thus agrees with Ezell that "a problem" with such a metanarrative is that it inevitably runs the risk of "reinscribing the same kind of exclusionary history that characterized the patriarchal model." If, however, we "adopt Woolf's own reading practice" and "approach this work as a historically located text, written at a particular time for a specific audience," then the performative value of Woolf's teleological history will appear in the construction of an "empowering past" and the "enabling [of] a progressive future" (Cuddy-Keane 2003: 164). Commenting on *A Room's* assimilation into mainstream feminism[8] – Naomi Black underlines, in *Virginia Woolf as Feminist* (2004), the social and material dimension of Woolf's demonstration while suggesting that her "conviction that women are different than men" leads to the debatable assertion that "women's own developing literary tradition will remain distinct and ought to produce a new sort of novel, written differently and based on everyday experience" (Black 2004: 114–115). In her introduction to the 2015 edition of *A Room of One's Own* and *Three Guineas*, to take another significant example, Anna Snaith insists on Woolf's "radical redefinition of a historiography focused on elite, male culture" in the context of the 1920s while also addressing Margaret Ezell's concern that this historiography perpetuated the "myth that the history of women's writing starts in the eighteenth century and that the early modern woman writer is a doomed, crazed individual." Snaith's answer here consists in recalling that Woolf's issue was "recovery rather than production," and that she urged the women in her audience "to participate in the recuperative project" (Snaith 2015: xix).

Without ignoring Ezell's remarks, and with them, the conflicting aspects of Woolf's polemic manifest for the emancipation of women's creativity, I would like to add "a supplement" to a very rich field of scholarship (*AR* 37). Like Woolf's own various "supplements" to "historians' histories," mine builds on ongoing questions and conversations, and on the theoretical assumptions that the previous chapters of this book have put forward regarding Woolf's critical approach to historiography and gender.

Looking at Woolf's feminist literary history in *A Room* not as a prescriptive model – the word "model" implying a form of replication rather than the idea of critical recreation or reappropriation – but again as an open-ended "pattern of inquiry" and practice of meaning, I would like to examine those "habits of the mind" described by Detloff and the way they are encapsulated in Woolf's feminist historiographical narrative. I believe that it is precisely Woolf's mode of criticism in this emblematic text that has over time generated the fruitful chains of assessments and responses that I have found necessary to mention in this book, as they testify both to her intellectual freedom and to the interpretative freedom that she made possible. In this respect, "Virginia Woolf practising" seems to me a more interesting subject of exploration than *Virginia Woolf Icon*, this "powerful and powerfully contested cultural [figure] whose name, face, and authority are persistently claimed or disclaimed in debates about art, politics, sexuality, gender, class, the 'canon,' fashion, feminism, race, and anger."[9]

A "Pattern of Inquiry" for Future Generations

A Room of One's Own begins with the well-known question – "women and fiction—what has that got to do with a room of one's own?" – and includes more than a hundred others. Some of them sound anecdotal, a way for the lecturer-as-narrator to break the rhythm of her dense demonstration: "Still an hour remained before luncheon, and what was one to do? Stroll on the meadows? Sit by the river?" (*AR* 6). Others are more puzzling and trigger long reflections, in turn raising other questions: "Shall we lay the blame on the war? When the guns fired in August 1914, did the faces of men and women show so plain in each other's eyes that romance was killed?" (12). A third category of queries formulates clearly the ways to reach an answer, as in the passage where the narrator, wondering about the luncheon parties in the past and their equivalent in the present, observes by a Manx cat on the lawn of the college library – "as if it too questioned the universe":

> But what was lacking, what was different, I asked myself, listening to the talk? And to answer that question I had to think myself out of the room, back into the past, before the war indeed, and to set before my eyes the model of another luncheon party held in rooms not very far distant from these; but different. Everything was different.[10]

For the first time, the narrator introduces the word "model" along with the ideas of the open air, the past and comparison as necessary nutrients for a thinking mind. When the reservoirs of individual or collective memory cannot provide the inquisitor with the needed resources, a "model," in the sense of a significant but malleable example, notion or theory, is thus required.[11] Later on, as she looks on the shelves of the library in search of the historical facts that would help her bring to life the Elizabethan woman, the narrator deplores that "that nothing is known about women before the eighteenth century. I have no model in my mind to turn about this way and that" (*AR* 35).

As suggested earlier, the absence of documentation concerning women's writings "before the eighteenth century" is one of Ezell's points of contention with Woolf. But whether the remark refers us to what was actually missing in the historiography of the narrator's time, or to the beginning of her own history of literature as she construes is, I would argue, not as essential as what it implies: the researched "facts lie somewhere," "scattered" in documents that need one day to be collected and made into "a book." The essential role of history is acknowledged, and with it the task of the historian. Confronted with the hidden truths of an absent past, he or she will search for material, investigate them by means of old or new methodologies and bring into focus whatever insights he has gained in the process. When faced with missing information, he – this time Woolf's generic male historian – can be tempted to be as assertive as the "bishop" who "declared that it was impossible for a woman, past, present, or to come, to have the genius of Shakespeare" (35); she – the feminist female historiographer – will recover lost stories and disregarded voices in order to "light a torch in that vast chamber where nobody has yet been" (*AR* 63). As Michel de Certeau explains, the writing of history is thus always a "making" of history, a "procedure" grafted on "a modus operandi" that fabricates "scenarios" capable of organising practices into a currently "intelligible discourse" (de Certeau 1988a: 6). Because "There exists a historicity of history, implying the movement which links interpretative practice to social praxis," we obviously need to contextualise Woolf's "scenarios" in *A Room of One's Own*. Thus, from a twenty-first-century perspective, her famous pages on the contrast between the lack of historical facts on the "woman question" before the eighteenth century and the multiplication of theories and discourses on "womanhood" might appear as a sign of the times. However, if one reads these pages alongside French historian Michelle Perrot's introduction to her 2006 book, "*My*" *history of women* ("*Mon*" *histoire des femmes*), one is struck by how Woolf's words still resound in the present. Recounting briefly her story as an adolescent, later on as a participant in the events of May 1968, a feminist militant and a Professor at the Sorbonne, Perrot directly addresses the paradox uncovered by Woolf in *A Room*, one that still besets researchers in her discipline: "The prolixity of the discourse on women contrasts with the absence of precise and detailed information concerning them" (Perrot 7).[12] That a living female academic should begin her history by "present determinations" (de Certeau 1988a: 11) and, more importantly, by inserting her story within the long history of women's silencing is a testimony to Woolf's transhistoric legacy – this ability, evoked by Dominick LaCapra, "to pose problems that call for renewed thought in different contexts over time" (LaCapra 2004: 18). Obviously, Perrot's "I" is not the fictionalised and problematised "I" speaking in *A Room*, one that frequently shifts positions and displays itself in a plurality of personas. But Perrot's "I" is definitely the "I" of the historian as historiographer and storyteller, registering herself in history while assessing the bearing of the past on the future.

The female lecturer looking for a way to answer the question the female students of Newnham and Girton colleges had asked in 1928 is also a situated subject, always anchoring her thoughts in the here and now of her personal circumstances. She speaks from the present, these thoughts being "the work of a moment." As she changes locations, from the banks of a river to the streets of London and the British Museum, she records the dialectic movement of her position as an outsider provisionally invited "inside" institutions that used to exclude women – and sometimes still do – and as a woman who now has the "liberty" to entertain ideas that send her "audaciously trespassing" (*AR* 5). Throughout her narrative, Woolf thus brings into play the in-betweenness of her position in time, space and culture, anticipating once more de Certeau: the described "real" written in *A Room* originates from "the determinations of a place," and "the effective relations that appear to characterize this space of writing" depend on "a power established from elsewhere, a mastery of techniques dealing with social strategies, a play with symbols and references that represent public authority. [...] Placed next to power, based upon it, yet held at a critical distance" (de Certeau 1988a: 10). Since to "rewrite history" is to add a "supplement to it," and not to erase previous historical discourses, then the idea of historiography as the process by which the past as a written text should be continually revised is also brought to the fore right from the beginning of Woolf's essay. So is the "modus operandi" that leads all historians to choose a "name" for their work – Woolf imagines that, for a history of women, this name should be "inconspicuous" so that "women might figure there" (*AR* 35) – and to decide on the point of inaugural rupture where his or her investigations stop. As always, Woolf's inquiry into the past is regularly interrupted by observations and experiences grounded in the "now": "it was now evening"; "this college where we are now sitting"; "the scene was now changed"; and "perhaps now it would be better to give up seeking for the truth" (*AR* 11; 15; 20; 32). "Silly and absurd though comparisons are" (11), the narrator will continue to read the past through the lens of present interrogations and experiences and assess the present by comparing it to the past. In search of the reasons that might explain the enduring invisibility of women and women's writings, she unearths the mechanisms of patriarchal "influence," those economic, sociological and psychological "forces" that historians usually refer to as "causes"[13] and which have led to women's exclusion from the spheres of power. Using the lives and experiences of the subjective, yet representative, Mary Beton, Mary Seton and Mary Carmichael, Woolf thus documents women's economic dependence, limited access to education and the professions, along with the psychological effects of hierarchical dynamics. In this respect, she writes in the wake of a fourth Mary, the proto-feminist Wollstonecraft whose conclusion in *A Vindication of the Rights of Women* (1792) was that "from the tyranny of man, I firmly believe, the greater number of female follies proceed" (Wollstonecraft 1792: 193).[14] In *A Room*, the "female follies" that Woolf's foremother tried to account for in her own polemical essay give way to a study of the familiar "fact of anger" as "the attendant sprite on power" (*AR* 25–27). Modern psychology and "Freudian theory" (*AR* 24) offer an alternative to the patriarchal discourses on the essential difference between the sexes by enabling Woolf to deconstruct this very difference, as she uncovers the existence of ancestral male anger.

Since Wollstonecraft's time, the situation of women has evolved. Yet at the beginning of her exploration of male writings about women – Milton's, Oscar Browning's, Samuel Butler's and La Bruyère's, among others – the narrator notices no radical transformations. "Everything was different," yet "nothing was changed" (*AR* 9), except for a few anecdotal alterations in her own situation: a change in the atmosphere, in her whereabouts, or the direction of the wind over London one evening, as it "lashed the houses and rattled the hoardings," heralding, perhaps, another type of change (31). But change takes some time, and for a while the narrator continues to wander back and forth in the chronology of literary history: from Shakespeare's plays to Greek tragedies, to Jane Austen, Joanna Baillie and Mary Russell Mitford in only three pages (32–35). Suddenly, though, her chronicle takes a new turn:

> towards the end of the eighteenth century a change came about which, if I were rewriting history, I should describe more fully and think of greater importance than the Crusades or the Wars of the Roses. The middle-class woman began to write.
>
> (49)

The narrative registers a breaking point: a "divide" is acknowledged, retrospectively envisioned and constructed. From the account of women's struggles against misogyny and patriarchy, Woolf moves to a story of gradual empowerment and possibilities. As a historiographer, she engages here with "the labor of division," this "self-motivated" act of "breakage" described by de Certeau. She maps a new trajectory by selecting what "matters" to her and, in the sense that the French historian gives to the word, generates her own "myth" (de Certeau 1888a: 14):

> For if *Pride and Prejudice matters*, and *Middlemarch* and *Villette* and *Wuthering Heights* matter, then it matters far more than I can prove in an hour's discourse that women generally, and not merely the lonely aristocrat shut up in her country house among her folios and her flatterers, took to writing.
>
> (*AR* 49)[15]

The chosen breaking point – middle-class women beginning to earn a living by writing – provides the first brick to the edifice of a teleological history. If, indeed, one reads *A Room of One's Own* as the sole example of Woolf's feminist counter-narrative, as many feminist scholars have done, then, obviously, Woolf becomes the contestable historian of the rise of the female novel, in the nineteenth century, with the "unstated notion of evolutionary progress built into it" (Ezell 1996: 23). In this case, and in view of her ongoing critique of nineteenth-century teleologies and hegemonic discourses, Woolf's contradictoriness becomes ever more puzzling. But we might also want to remember that the first volume of the *Common Reader* begins with "The Pastons and Chaucer" (1925) and that its main reading line, if any, is not the novel; again, the opening essay of the second volume (1932) is "The Strange Elizabethans." Besides, while most of Woolf's essays on modern literature focus on the Edwardian/ Georgian "divide," around 1910, "Anon" is the history of literature before the Anglo-Saxons. If we choose to adopt a critical standpoint, we should therefore blame Woolf for her inconsistency, rather than for the prescriptive value of her historiographical "models."

If, on the other hand, we want to assess the historiographical and political value of this moment of "great importance" situated at the turn of the eighteenth century – in this text and more generally in Woolf's whole oeuvre – then we need to bear in mind the way she weaves deftly the threads of her historiographical practice with those of theoretical self-reflexivity. A close scrutiny of the passage that frames the narrator's "breakage" statement invites us first to examine its context, in the sense, this time, of what comes before and what after in the unfolding of the narrator's argument. As it happens, the account of the advent of the nineteenth-century novelist is preceded and followed by a consideration of Aphra Behn, with whom, she has just stated, "we turn a very important corner on the road," leaving behind "those solitary great ladies who wrote without audience or criticism." Mrs Behn was "a middle-class woman" and "all women together ought to let flowers fall upon [her] tomb [...] for it was she who earned them the right to speak their minds" (*AR* 48–50). Aphra Behn thus appears as the embodiment of another turning point. Yet with this reference, Woolf replaces chronological linearity with genealogy and its thickly layered temporality: unlike Michel Foucault's genealogist in "Nietzsche, Genealogy, History," though, she does not "dispel the chimera of an origin" (Foucault 1984: 80) but displaces it to prove her point. This new point of departure, at any rate, will highlight what "historians' histories" have left out of the picture. There is therefore no "monstrous finality" here (Foucault 76), since inherited dominant discourses are undermined and the future is an open horizon. In fact, the notion of an "origin" matters less, I would suggest, than the search for, and tribute to, Woolf's foremothers, whether anonymous or not: for "masterpieces are not single and solitary births; they are the outcome of many years of thinking in common, of thinking by the body of the people." Woolf's move from the obscure Lady eccentrics to the "experience of the mass [...] behind the single voice" has undoubtedly a highly symbolic thrust (*AR* 50). As Anna Snaith points out, "what seems to us commonplace was, in the context of the 1920s, a radical redefinition of a historiography focused on elite, male culture" (Snaith 2015: xix).

The second point that I would like to make concerns another aspect of what I understand as Woolf's feminist counter-discourse. In light of her knowledge of the ideology hidden behind any form of teleology, I would suggest that her own use of the nineteenth-century belief in "progress" – a word that, interestingly, she never uses in *A Room* – is not only the sign of a utopian gesture towards the future, but also a powerful way of using the tools of the "masters" against them, in favour of the female subjects they continue to ignore. If progress is possible, such progress will be inscribed in the narrator's historical elaboration without, however, producing another "whig interpretation of history," this process of "ratification if not glorification of the present" described by Butterfield, implying some providential plot regardless of individual agency (Butterfield 1931: v). In fact, Woolf does not speak of progress but freedom: the "freedom of the mind" (19) and the "freedom to think of things in themselves" (30). She explains that "freedom and fullness of expression are of the essence of the art" (58). But "intellectual freedom depends on material things. Poetry depends on intellectual freedom. And women have always been poor" (81). In its inescapably logical formulation, Woolf's syllogism justifies the frequent shifts, in her text, from the considerations of the past to future possibilities. On the one hand, entire categories of subjects were deprived of essential liberties; on the other hand, freedom is a collective and individual "habit" that requires "courage" (*AR* 86). Woolf thus writes into her "teleological history" of emancipation the very ideas of agency and risk – the risk, among others, of being "thought a monster" when one is a woman and publishes something with one's name (*AR* 44). Each risk bravely taken contributes to the emancipation of future generations. The possibility of emancipation for women in general and women writers in particular begins "now" but its completion is projected onto the future – when Shakespeare's sister, in another century or two, "will be born" (*AR* 86).

"The teleological narrative of *A Room of Own*," Melba Cuddy-Keane explains, "is best understood as 'a piece of business' being 'transacted between writer and reader'—the business, in this case, being to encourage and empower the women in the audience by inscribing them as the culminating point in a progressive narrative." Cuddy-Keane considers here Woolf's project in its pragmatic and performative dimensions: its "historical success," she continues, "can be seen in the way it has supplied an effective model [...] for the task of constructing an empowering past and enabling a progressive future" (Cuddy-Keane 2003: 164). I would like to add to this assessment the idea that the generative power of Woolf's history also lies in the way it deliberately unwrites and rewrites the very historiographical tools that it uses to illustrate its own argument, opening new theoretical paths for feminist criticism. In this respect, *A Room* can be read both as a counter-discourse and an alternative feminist discourse. To begin with, its "essentialist" dimension – womanhood is not fundamentally deconstructed by its author – raises a question that Anglo-American second- and third-wave feminism have been struggling with for a long time: if there are no "women" as embodied subjects or as those "objects" of patriarchal discourse that come under the same designation, no commitment in the name of "women" is possible, and Woolf's utopian gesture away from the "little separate lives that we live as individuals" and towards "common life which is the real life" is doomed to failure (*AR* 86). In this respect, I am tempted to read *A Room* in the light of the following statement by Jane Gallop in *The Daughter's Seduction: Feminism and Psychoanalysis* (1982):

> 'Never one without the other,' knowingly, lucidly to exercise and criticize power is to dephallicize, to assume the phallus and unveil that assumption as presumption, as fraud. A constantly double discourse is necessary, one that asserts and then questions. Who is capable of such duplicity? 'Perhaps a woman.'
>
> (Gallop 1982: 122)

But I also read this text for its art of questioning and the manner it exhibits the process of its own "making." As it exposes pre-existing knowledge and discourses, making its way through or around them, Woolf's history of women writers' emancipation requires of the readers that they not only excavate the relationships between texts and contexts, but also that they negotiate with language itself. Thus, just as Woolf hijacks – or, at least, diverts from its nineteenth-century conception – the idea of teleological progress, she complicates the very terms and concepts attached to dominant cultural discourses. Thereby, she "offers a model of how women can read their history out the male-dominated cultural text" (Gättens 1995: 12). With "influence," for example, Woolf lays the groundwork for a counter-discourse that will gain full power in *Three Guineas*, as I suggest in Chapter 4. In *A Room*, she explores its multifaceted meaning through the lens of ideology – "his was the power and the money and the influence" (*AR* 26); psychology; material culture when she evokes "the influences of the common sitting room" (51); female agency when she concludes on the "influence" that her female audience "can exert upon the future" (83). When she speaks of "change," Woolf anticipates *Orlando* and its multilayered temporality anchored in both individual and collective experience. As to "tradition," this construction of man-made "archades" and "domes" and "built sentences" which used to have no place for her foremothers (58), she lays the foundations of a new edifice, "shaped by women for women" (Marcus 2000: 218). In so doing, she symbolically breaks the line of British primogeniture and patriarchal transmission while registering women in an alternative history of transmission – one that replaces the ideas of reverence, duty and fixed conventions by an act of democratic incorporation.

Woolf's linguistic reflection on the ever-shifting meaning of words in "Craftsmanship" thus finds in this essay a more political outlet. For the writer and the reader, to combine "old words in new orders so that they survive [...], so that they tell the truth" (*E VI* 95) is to acknowledge that any chosen tool or expression is already interpretative before it has been used. Again, her historiographical work is indissociable from her poetic work. In this respect, one cannot reify or homogenise the past on which she provides a critical overview while uncovering its unrecorded dimensions: instead, *A Room* proposes that we examine this typically Woolfian, and incomparably modern, combination of dialogism, powerful emplotment and epistemological doubt. If Woolf's "new historiography" appears as a "model" here, in the sense of what can only be reproduced with critical distance or self-reflexivity, it is in the way that it situates itself at the intersection of representation and intervention, of prefiguration and anticipation, reading and writing, factuality and fictionality, plurivocality and historicity – the "ands" in my sentence emphasising the performative power of a dialectical approach that eschews all sense of hegemony or closure. In the words of Dominick LaCapra in *History in Transit: Experience, Identity, Critical Theory* (2004), "the transitional condition of history requires a continual rethinking of what counts as history in the dual sense of historical processes and historiographical attempts to account for this." This transitional condition, however, does not imply "either relativistic skepticism or an overall teleology for history or historiography but a willingness to rethink goals and assumptions, including the very meaning of temporality, as a structural feature of historicity itself" (LaCapra 2004: 2). As she indeed rethinks the goals and assumptions of history as a written text, Woolf unwrites and rewrites the meanings of temporality, experience and identity – this "constellation of more or less changing subject positions" – while giving a new importance to the "experiential" sources the American historian refers to when he speaks of the personal and collective "identity" of "nondominant groups" (ibid. 5–6).

But beyond the quality of openness that its entwined historiographical and theoretical threads confer to it, *A Room of One's Own* is also a text that derives power from its literary creations – these allegories and metaphors which nurture our capacity to think, understand and, hopefully, change. No critic, scholar or common reader can forget about Woolf's forceful embodiment of her "difficult questions" (*AR* 59) in the visual and pedagogical shapes that enable her to resemioticise prior conceits and concepts. With Judith Shakespeare, she links the question of artistic genius with the social and material conditions of its possibility. The "rooms" in which female writers can or cannot write speak literally and metaphorically of freedom and its relation to the politics of space and place.[16] Her elaboration of androgyny is a palimpsestuous text that rewrites the sex binary and opens up the path for creative transcendence.[17] These pedagogic heuristic tools are still the objects of thought-provoking debates and conversations. But because Woolf's endlessly reinterpreted feminist history is first and foremost a historiographical and critical study of difference, I would like to end this section by looking at Woolf's pattern of enquiry and practice of meaning as reflected in another powerful allegory. "Women have served all these centuries as looking-glasses possessing the magic and delicious power of reflecting the figure of man at twice its natural size," Woolf explains in the second chapter of her essay. "Without that power probably the earth would still be swamp and jungle" (*AR* 28). There is no "Lady in the Looking-Glass" here, as in Woolf's 1929 short fiction.[18] As she unwrites the eighteenth- and nineteenth-century genealogy of texts that represent mirrors as sites of female vanity, anxieties and desires framed by cultural norms and imposition, Woolf proposes that we should rather look at men looking at themselves, faced with their own fear of disappearance: "Take [the looking glass away] and man may die" (*AR* 28).

"We Think through Our Mothers if We Are Women"[19]

Caught in the reflection of Woolf's looking-glass in *A Room*, and once men have left the scene, one can imagine the shadows of other "ladies" and female characters: Elizabeth Gaskell and "The Poor Clare" (1856), Vernon Lee's haunting presences in her *Fantastic Stories* (1890), Katherine Mansfield's "Little Governess" (1915), all unveiling a certain continuum of preoccupations and affiliations across the Victorian/Modernist divide. With other women writers, they form what Susan Wolstenholme calls a "symbolic community" in *Gothic (Re)Visions: Writing Women as Readers* (1993) – one that is not characterised "by a position of marginality, [...] nor by a common bond of directly accessible experience, but rather by the symbolic exchange among the group itself" (xiii).[20] In the large female "community" that Woolf's work contributed to through a process of selective inclusion, and that the following generations of readers and critics continue to uncover, one can find the women writers Woolf frequently paid tribute to, those she rarely mentioned, and the female forebears with whom she engaged in somewhat more distant conversations. In *A Room of One's Own*, these "mothers" are numerous; in the following order of appearance: Fanny Burney, Jane Austen, the Brontës, Miss Mitford, George Eliot, Elizabeth Gaskell, Christina Rossetti, Rebecca West, George Sand, Lady Winchilsea, Margaret Cavendish, Aphra Behn and Sappho. And although comparisons can be "silly" – but Woolf perfectly knew that they are not – there are significantly more women here and in the whole corpus of Woolf's essays than in the literary histories of Walter Raleigh, George Saintsbury or Hugh Walker read together.[21] In *The Common Reader* I and II, however, only

Margaret Cavendish, Jane Austen, the Brontës, George Eliot, Elizabeth Barrett Browning, Christina Rossetti and Miss Mitford focus on an entire review or essay. In "Phases of Fiction," Jane Austen is the first and last female writer to be cited, and the other female novelists – Ann Radcliffe, George Eliot and Emily Brontë – are clearly outnumbered by their male forebears and contemporaries. Sometimes the tribute paid by Woolf to her foremothers is short but indubitable: in this same text, Emily Brontë's *Wuthering Heights* is examined alongside the novels of Herman Melville, Tolstoy and Proust and receives one of Woolf's highest accolades:

> By a master stroke of vision, rarer in prose than in poetry, people and scenery and atmosphere all in keeping. And what is still rarer and more impressive, through that atmosphere we seem to catch sight of larger men and women, of other symbols and significance.
>
> (*E V* 78)

Sometimes the "tribute" is short and dismissive: in her 1908 review of Vernon Lee's *The Sentimental Traveller*, published the same year, Woolf writes,

> Her method then, so far as the portrait of the place is concerned, is purely impressionist, for if she were to concentrate her mind upon seeing any object as exactly as it can be seen there would be no time for these egotistical diversions. And who but pedants and antiquaries want to know when a palace was built, or exactly what style its architecture?
>
> (*E I* 157)

At other times, there is no tribute at all: except for Dorothy Richardson in Woolf's review "The Tunnel" (*E III* 10–12), Woolf's modernist female contemporaries – Katherine Mansfield and May Sinclair, for example – do not appear in the essays collected by Andrew McNeillie and Stuart M. Clarke.[22] But to be fair, Woolf did not publish any articles on the novels of D.H. Lawrence or James Joyce either. In "The Claim of the Living," a review in the *TLS* of *A Novelist on Novels* by W.L. George (1918), she explains the reason why Mr George's selection of "promising contemporary novelists" (Mr Beresford, Mr Cannan, Mr Forster, Mr Lawrence, Mr Compton Mackenzie, Mr Onions and Mr Swinnerton), is "fairly representative, but certainly if our income depended upon passing an examination in their works we should be sweeping the streets tomorrow," not because they are not worth reading, but because "our knowledge is perfectly haphazard and nebulous. To discuss the point of view, the growth, nature and development of any of those writers in the same spirit that we discuss the dead proves impossible" (*E II* 256–257). Considering the number of times that Woolf refers to Henry James and Marcel Proust in other reviews or essays, we might think that her remark is here tainted with bad faith: after all, James died in 1916, and Proust in 1922.[23] Yet, we saw how before the 1930s Woolf frequently invoked the lack of "historical distance" to justify her critical method, insisting that critics and readers could not understand the present and prepare for the future without first "considering the masterpieces of the past" (*E IV* 239).

"But if we ask for masterpieces, where are we to look?," Woolf wonders in "How It Strikes a Contemporary" (*E IV* 237). In the course of her career as a critic and fiction writer, Woolf looked almost everywhere, lighting her torch in the "Elizabethan Lumber Room" and the forest where the voice of Anon resounded, on the literary scenes of Britain, France, America and Russia, and through the centuries, weaving the threads of her enduring affinities and partialities. With the Renaissance, Juliet Dusinberre argues in *Virginia Woolf's Renaissance: Woman Reader or Common Reader* (1997) that Woolf "connected herself with a life which included her own rebirth as writer and reader through the recovery of female forebears."[24] In her introduction, Dusinberre strikingly unwrites, so to speak, Margaret Ezell's perception of Woolf's absent foremothers by opposing the Renaissance "tradition" that Woolf revised with another tradition, closer to her in time, yet much more difficult to negotiate: "the sixteenth and seventeenth centuries represented for Virginia Woolf a key aspect of her revolt against the nineteenth century" (Dusinberre 1997: 3). Indeed, even if Woolf was certain that Judith Shakespeare, had she existed, was doomed to die tragically, the relative freedom of *Orlando's* female characters among the Elizabethans is relatively at odds with Woolf's description of the female condition in the Victorian age: "Now [...] the woman's right hand was invariably passed through the man's left and her fingers were firmly gripped by his" (*O* 231). Woolf's direct lineage was Victorian, male or female, and this vexed heritage remained the chief reservoir of perpetually renewed conversations. As to the female tradition that she "poached" upon and revised, it has been shown before how the "four names" of her time, acclaimed by most critics and literary historians, occupy centre stage in her work. In this respect, Woolf did not recover the lives of her "obscure" nineteenth-century female forebears; she instead remapped a pre-existing canon.[25]

The story of how Woolf thought back through her mother's began to be written in the 1990s and is far from complete. Given the nature and generic breadth of her writings, the appraisal of this heritage resembles her own work, composed of monographs centring on her dialogue with one particular author – George Eliot in Alison Booth's *Greatness Engendered* (1992) – with the practitioners of one particular genre – as in Emily Blair's *Virginia Woolf and the Nineteenth-Century Domestic Novel* (2007) – or with a group of female authors examined through the lens of Woolf's approach to biography, in Anne Maria Reuss's Ph.D. The dialogues within this other "symbolic community" of scholars and Woolf specialists build on several converging views that all take on board her contradictoriness. Like Eliot, Booth suggests, Woolf "thought within a certain feminist tradition that affirms a supposed feminine selflessness as it rejects masculine self-assertion that has conventionally fuelled notions of greatness" (Booth 3). As a result, Woolf was more "lenient" with "great" women Victorian writers than with the minor ones, with a preference for the "distinctly feminine writer" who "seized a masculine artistic freedom" (Booth 1992: 73). Yet, she found that it was fatal to write like a man. Another aspect of Woolf's "vexed dualism and essentialism" appears to be the way she "glorified the effects of oppression" and "the-suffering-woman-behind-the-book," a vision of women's literature that she inherited from Leslie Stephen, Booth argues, and that often remained blind to the "ambition and love of homage" of her female forebears (Booth 3; 61). According to Emily Blair, Woolf defended "her own position by defining with authority the field of women writers." She valued the "extraordinary women writers," usually single and childless, while diminishing the merits of writers such as George Eliot or Margaret Oliphant with a "productive publishing career" (Blair 2007: 17; 14). For Reus, Woolf's "ideal woman writer," like the fictional Judith Shakespeare, is obscure and awaiting recovery, but without any biographical and literary history: she can be reshaped and adapted to Woolf's purpose, and, like "the unknowable Miss Willatt in 'Memoirs of a Novelist,'" her literary and personal shortcomings are forgiven because she provides endless cause for speculation" (Reus 2018: 34).

In the mirror framed by these various forceful analyses, Woolf's vexed relation to the Victorians in general and her Victorian foremothers in particular appears again, and with it an image of Woolf herself, in the changing clothes of her contradictions, if not paradoxes. A comprehensive reading of Woolf's critical and fictional writings, I would argue, does not suppress the tensions examined by my predecessors. Part of the power of Woolf's work depends on these tensions, which themselves are born from Woolf's singular modernity and the alternative and various versions of her fragmented, incomplete literary histories. First, Woolf's view of a writer could indeed vary over time, depending on the evolution of her poetic and political project: what Anne Maria Reus shows with Jane Austen can be applied, for example, to Woolf's appraisal of George Eliot. Next, Woolf's "cameras" are pointed at "every character from every angle," which implies, as she herself explained in "The New Biography," that we should "admit contradictory versions of the same face" (*E VI* 186). Another difficulty in assessing the unwritten history of Woolf's nineteenth-century "mothers" lies in what I have described as her palimpsestuous practice with regard to texts and language: her own discourse can be misleading, close as it occasionally is to the nineteenth-century rhetorical tropes and ideological constructs that she seems to adopt at the very moment when she unwrites them. Thus, when Woolf writes in "Aurora Leigh" that Elizabeth Barrett Browning "could no more conceal herself than she could control herself" (*E V* 261), she appears to perpetuate the Victorian ideology of selfless femininity along with the problematic distinction between Victorian poets – the male, accomplished practitioners of the genre – and Victorian poetesses, whose art is lesser. However, Woolf's 1931 signed essay in *The Yale Review* mainly reads as a counter-narrative to previous histories of English literature, their "pageant of English writers" being described as embalmed in critical orthodoxies that say very little of anybody's genius. As she examines her foremother's life and art, Woolf thus contrasts the "immortality" that simultaneously relies on the cultural construction of mortiferous legends with a vision of Barrett Browning that breathes with life and energy (*E V* 257–258). Woolf states that life had done "damage" to her as a poet and therefore "impinged" upon her art "more than life should" – "she was triply imprisoned by sex, health and her father in her bed room in Wimpole Street" (261–262). She then mentions the "speed and energy, forthrightness and self-confidence" that "hold us enthralled," and how *Aurora Leigh* "remains with all its imperfections a book that still lives and can still be read" (259; 267). More importantly, Woolf assesses the "courage" (267) with which Browning engaged in an impossible task: "to poach upon a novelist's preserve," "deal with modern life in poetry" and "give us the sense of life in general" (264; 266).

As Woolf entwines in her appraisal of her nineteenth-century foremothers the relation between a "woman's art and a woman's life" (*E V* 261), she always brings to the fore the patriarchal system that impeded their talents and that they had to brave. But until the late 1930s, her own art and voice were constrained by the formats of the review and the essay. She, too, had to catch "the Angel in the House" by "the throat" and do "her best to kill her," which she does with her pen in her 1933 biography of Barrett Browning's spaniel dog, taking "the inkpot and [finging] it" at the phantom that used to haunt every Victorian home (*E VI* 480–481). With *Flush: A Biography*, Woolf unexpectedly extracts from a celebrated story of love and artistic collaboration a pedestrian experience of domesticity and alterity. Her indirect portrayal of Elizabeth Barrett Browning as a daughter, lover, wife and poet is framed by the character's status as an ordinary woman, and by the point of view of an unexpected focaliser, the dog himself. In *Flush*, Woolf takes the risk of writing a "fantasy" that could only be considered by her peers as marginal literature, in spite of the book's immense popularity, or precisely because of it. In this respect, Woolf anticipated Deleuze and Guattari's concept of "minor literature" – a literature that constantly defies and rewrites dominant discourses.[26] As Ruth Hoberman explains in *Modernizing Lives: Experiments in English Biography* (1987), *Flush* is about "biographical invisibility," the invisibility of usually unseen subjects: the dog and its undefinable status as a subject (Hoberman 1987: 60), and the female poet, looked at from the defamiliarising gaze of her pet. In this formal tour de force grafted on the inscription (through internal focalisation) of an impossible subject, Woolf unwrites Victorian biography while interlacing the threads of historiography, genre and gender across the binaries of the public and private spheres, everyday life and history in the making. She is at the same time a social observer aware of the broad historical landscape and local details, a Lockean chronicler of life reconciling eighteenth-century empiricism, phenomenology and historiography[27]; and a historian "in transit" anticipating the "experiential turn" of history in the 1990s by recapturing the voices that official histories do not record (LaCapra 2004: 3). In the process, Woolf also deconstructs the Victorian hierarchies of sex, class and race, while collapsing the ancestral divide between man and woman, man and animal.[28] In the symbolical space thus created, new encounters take place, and cognitive sympathies for past figures are made possible: with Flush and Elizabeth Barrett Browning, Woolf transmutes cultural heritage into the promise of innovation.

With its exclusions and revisions, the "canon" of Woolf's nineteenth-century foremothers reads her as much as she reads them. Sometimes the writings of her female predecessors seem to cohere under her pen: she sees them as a community of "ancestresses" with whom she shares "instincts," anxieties and desires. Most of the time, though, she writes about her female forebears as singular artists and unique talents: "Jane Austen can have had nothing in common with George Eliot," Woolf writes in "Women Novelists" and "George Eliot was the direct opposite of Emily Brontë" (*E V* 30). In the latter scenario, Woolf compares her female predecessors with their own forebears and contemporaries; more importantly, she frees them from prior assumptions and critical judgements, which she nonetheless registers in her texts as the still-present testimonies of the patriarchal enemy. Thus, Emily Brontë was to the Victorians a perplexing rebel; to Virginia Woolf she is a poet: "Wuthering Heights again is steeped in poetry [...]. The characters of Catherine and Heathcliff are perfectly natural; they contain all the poetry that Emily Brontë herself feels without effort" (*E V* 78). Christina Rossetti was the Victorians' muse; with Tennyson she continues to sing "passionately" about the "coming of their loves" (*AR* 12), but in "I am Christina Rossetti," Woolf unwrites the burdensome assessments that have prevented the poet's readers to hear her true voice. In a direct address to her foremother, Woolf raises her own voice and Rossetti's above George Saintsbury's, Walter Raleigh's, Matthew Arnold's, and above the cacophonic humdrum of "the refluent sea-music school; the line-irregularity school; and the school that bids one not to criticize but cry." At last, she can quote the poet's lines and praise her genius: "Modest as you were, still you were drastic, sure of your gift and convinced of your vision. A firm hand pruned your lines; a sharp ear tested their music. Nothing soft, otiose, irrelevant cumbered your pages" (*E V* 558–559).

"We tend to underestimate the extent to which the cultural tradition is not only a selection but also an interpretation," Raymond Williams explains in *The Long Revolution*. Woolf obviously saw her predecessors through the lens of her own "particular contemporary values" (Williams 2001: 67). She shaped her literary inheritance according to contingent criteria of her own, leaving in obscurity, or semi-darkness, some of her foremothers. In a chapter entitled "A Gap in Your Library, Madam,"[29] Anne Maria Reus shows how Woolf's history of women's writings largely fails to acknowledge the second generation of Victorian professional writers such as Mary Augusta Ward and Margaret Oliphant. She underlines Woolf's "unease" with the commercial engagement of her popular foremothers (Reus 159–201). Reus's conclusion can be extended to the overtly feminist authors of the fin-de-siècle whose "anger" "tamper[ed] with the integrity of their art" (*AR* 56). Thus,

> unfortunately for her fame as a writer, it was into debate and politics, and not into thought and literature, that [Olive Schreiner] was impelled, chiefly by her passionate interest in sex questions. She was driven to teach, to dream and to prophesy.
>
> (*E IV 5*)

In Woolf's eyes, and although they did not compare in terms of talents and achievements, neither the author of *The Story of an African Farm* (1883) nor Charlotte Brontë had mastered the "first great lesson": "to write as a woman, but as a woman who has forgotten that she is a woman" (*AR* 70). As to the mid-Victorians, whose world Woolf wanted to keep in the far distance, they remain a pervasive absence in Woolf's nineteenth-century revised canon. Although she was one of the most important female novelists in her generation, Elizabeth Gaskell, for example, is probably the Victorian figure the least mentioned in Woolf's letters, diary and essays. And yet, in *Virginia Woolf and The Nineteenth-Century Domestic Novel*, Emily Blair considers that both the author of *North and South* and Woolf deployed "the domestic as a [disruptive] aesthetic category" (Blair 2007: 73). Like Woolf, Gaskell was interested in the fictional recording of obscure lives and in the exploration of new forms of inscription for the female, social, individual and artistic subject. She wrote extensively: novels, short stories, letters and a biography – *The Life of Charlotte Brontë* (1857) – that Woolf quotes abundantly. But the "modest, capable woman" embodied for Woolf the mid-Victorians' flaws: their incapacity "to concentrate," she explains in "Mrs Gaskell": "able by nature to spin sentence after sentence melodiously, they seem to have left out nothing that they knew how to say" (*E I 341*).

In Lieu of Conclusion

"The partiality, the inevitable imperfection of contemporary criticism," Woolf confesses in "Notes on D.H. Lawrence," can best be "guarded against, perhaps, by making in the first place a full confession of one's disabilities, so far as it is possible to distinguish them" (*E VI 464*).

All Woolf's female predecessors are "imperfect" mothers – an adjective that she relished – Jane Austen included. But all are assessed with the same scrutiny, and at times cruelty, as their male contemporaries, and all belong to Woolf's celebrated community of imperfect talents. If Woolf's nineteenth century is one of the laboratories of her invention of the modern, a poetic and political battlefield and the place from which she negotiates the present and her own presence, this laboratory is an open, communal territory. It is not construed as a positivist episteme, but as cultural history embedded in historicity. It involves several layers of time: searching in the writings of her foremothers for "life itself" as it survives in the present, Woolf confronts the common reader with the "real nature of the choice[s]" she is making (Williams 2001: 67) while urging him/her to look at what "lie[s] in the twilight of the future" (*AR* 59). In the process, she leaves room for the unthought and unrecorded while raising simple, essential questions. How to resist the voice of admonition when one is a woman? How do material circumstances affect one's access to professional authorship? How should we negotiate our heritage? What is the price of maternity and economic dependence? Will the "Angel in the House" ever cease to haunt our rooms and minds?

The answers remain to be written: "I am not one and simple, but complex and many," says Rhoda in *The Waves*. "What am I? [...] This? No, I am that" (*TW* 42). But for "Judith Shakespeare" to come, the narrator of *A Room of One's Own* replies, we should "work [...] for her," and "so to work, even in poverty and obscurity, is worth while" (*AR* 86). "It is the imperfect artists who never manage to say the whole thing in their books who wield the power of personality over us," adds the essayist in "Personalities" (*E VI* 440). They

> have something elusive, enigmatic, impersonal about them. They rise slowly to their heights; and there they shine. They do not win fame directly, nor are they exposed to the alternations of praise and blame which rise from the passions and prejudices of our hearts. In ransacking their drawers we shall find out little about them. All has been distilled into their books.
>
> (*E VI* 440)

Joining the historian Miss Merridew in "The Journal of Mistress Joan Martyn" and Miss La Trobe in *Between the Acts*, Woolf the imperfect historian as storyteller and artist as historiographer concludes:

> Let us think in offices; in omnibuses; while we are standing in the crowd watching Coronations and Lord Mayor's Shows; let us think as we pass the Cenotaph; and in Whitehall; in the gallery of the House of Commons; in the Law Courts; let us think at baptisms and marriages and funerals. Let us never cease from thinking – what is this "civilization" in which we find ourselves?
>
> (*TG* 143–144)

Notes

1 Virginia Woolf, "A Sketch of the Past" (*MB* 82).

2 The reviewed book was Austen's *Love and Friendship and Other Early Works*, printed for the first time from the original manuscripts, with a preface by G.K. Chesterton (1922).

3 To my knowledge, Reus's Ph.D., submitted at the University of Leeds for the degree of Doctor of Philosophy, has not been published. I would like here to acknowledge my debt to this most stimulating work on a subject very close to mine, although Reus explores Woolf's relation to her nineteenth-century foremothers from the vantage point of biography.

4 In 1913, the book Woolf reviewed for her "Jane Austen," published in the *TLS*, was *Jane Austen. Her Life and Letters. A Family Record. With a Portrait by William Austen-Leigh* (1913), and *Old Friends and New Faces, by Sybil G. Brinton* (1913); "Jane Austen and the Geese," published in the *TLS* in October 28, 1920, was a review of *Personal Aspects of Jane Austen*, by Mary-Augusta Austen-Leigh; as to the "Jane Austen" that Woolf incorporated in 1925 in the first volume of *The Common Reader*, the essay drew upon, with variants, "Jane Austen at Sixty" (1923) and the other three reviews mentioned above.

5 See here Brontë's famous comment, quoted by Elizabeth Gaskell in *The Life of Charlotte Bronte* (1857): "Can there be a great artist without poetry? [...] Miss Austen being, as you say, without 'sentiment,' without poetry, maybe is sensible, real (more real than true), but she cannot be great" (Gaskell 2009: 273–275); see also Leslie Stephen, "Austen, Jane" (*Dictionary of National Biography Archive*, 1885): http://oxforddnb.com/view/olddnb/904 [accessed June, 2019].

6 The quotation comes from Desmond MacCarthy's review of *Another Country*, written by the Russian-born novelist Helene du Coudray (1928). Strikingly, the original comment includes a comparison between Jane Austen and Virginia Woolf: "Jane Austen and, in our time, Mrs Virginia Woolf, have demonstrated how gratefully this gesture can be accomplished." Woolf found MacCarthy's remark "condescending" (*D III* 195).

7 On this subject see Ellen Moers, *Literary Women: The Great Writers* (1976); Elaine Showalter, *A Literature of Their Own: British Women Novelists from Brontë to Lessing* (1999 (1977)); Sandra M. Gilbert and Susan Gubar, *The Madwoman in the Attic: The Woman Writer and the Nineteenth-Century Literary Imagination* (1979).

8 Naomi Black reminds us here of Woolf's fear concerning the reception of *A Room* expressed in her diary, on October 23, 1929: "Also I shall be attacked for a feminist & hinted at for a sapphist" (*D III* 262).

9 The reference is to Brenda Silver's *Virginia Woolf Icon* (1999: 3).

10 Anna Snaith suggests that the Manx cat, "a breed of tailless cat indigenous to Isle of man" might "symbolize women's silenced or missing histories" (Snaith 2015: 256, note 9).

11 Quoting from "Thoughts on Peace in an Air Raid" –

> Therefore if we are to compensate the young man for the loss of his glory and of his gun, we must give him access to the creative feelings. We must make happiness. We must free him from the machine. We must bring him out of his prison into the open air.

(*E VI* 245)

– Detloff analyses the recurrent motif of the "open air" in Woolf's texts as "signifying liberation from the constraints of parochial thinking, acquisitive materialism, and moribund allegiance to tradition for tradition's sake" (Detloff 2016: 10–11).

12 French historian Michelle Perrot is a pioneer in the emergence of women's history and gender studies in France. With Georges Duby, she edited in 1990–1991 *Histoire des femmes en Occident* (Paris: Plon). She is also the author of *The Bedroom: An Intimate History* (Yale University Press, 2018). To my knowledge, *"Mon" histoire des femmes* has not been translated into English. The original quotation reads: "La prolixité du discours sur les femmes contraste avec l'absence d'informations précises et circonstanciées."

13 On this subject, see Chapter 4 of this book.

14 Woolf had paid a tribute to Wollstonecraft in "Four Figures": "she had been in revolt all her life—against tyranny, against law, against convention" (*E V* 473). Published in *The Common Reader II* (1925), this series of articles contained biographical sketches and appraisals of four eighteenth-century figures: William Cowper, Beau Brummell, Mary Wollstonecraft and Dorothy Wordsworth.

15 In his pages on "History as myth," de Certeau explains that history is "neither the legend to which popularization reduces it, nor the criteriology that would make of it merely the critical analysis of its procedures. It plays between them, on the margin that separates these two reductions." It therefore tells "the tale of this relation of exclusion and fascination, of domination or of communication with *other* (a position filled in turn by a neighboring place or the future)," thus allowing "our society to tell its own story thanks to history" (de Certeau 1988a: 44–46).

16 On this subject, see Anna Snaith, and Michael Whitworth, *Locating Woolf: the Politics of Space and Place* (2007).

17 On this subject, see Derek Ryan's introduction to *Virginia Woolf and the Materiality of Theory* (2013).

18 See "The Lady in the Looking-Glass: A Reflection" (*CSF* 215–219). According to Susan Dick, the earlier typescript of the story is dated May 28, 1929.

19 *A Room of One's Own* (57).

20 On this question, see Anne Besnault-Levita, "Mirrors of the Self and the Tradition of the Female Gothic: Scenes of Hauntings and Apparitions in Victorian and Modernist Fiction" (2018).

21 See Walter Raleigh's *The English Novel: A Short Sketch of Its History from the Earliest Times to the Appearance of Waverley* (1894); George Saintsbury's *A History of Nineteenth-Century Literature* (1896); Hugh Walker and Mrs Hugh Walker's *Outlines of Victorian Literature* (1913).

22 Katherine Mansfield is the most revealing example here. On their complicated relationship and how Woolf was "haunted" by their rivalry and "failed living friendship" 15 years after Mansfield's death, see Hermione Lee's chapter "Katherine" (Lee 1997: 386–401; 398).

23 Woolf was as harshly critical of D.H. Lawrence's and James Joyce's writings as of some of her female forbears' and contemporaries'. Lawrence, she wrote, "has moments of greatness" (*E IV* 237) but "spoilt his early works" (*E III* 433). Joyce was "the most notable young writer" (*E III* 33), but *Ulysses* is "a memorable catastrophe" (*E III* 356). More importantly, in Woolf's mind they both "partly spoil their books for women readers by their display of

self-conscious virility; and Mr Hemingway, but much less violently, follows suit" (*E IV* 454).

24 On Woolf and the Renaissance, see also Alice Fox, *Virginia Woolf and the Literature of the English Renaissance* (1990); Sally Greene, *Virginia Woolf: Reading the Renaissance* (1999).

25 In the words of Melba Cuddy-Keane, Woolf "celebrates masterpieces while she denounces canons" (2003: 177).

26 On the notion of "minor literature," see Gilles Deleuze and Felix Guattari, "What is a minor literature," *Kafka: Toward a Minor Literature* (Paris: Les Éditions de Minuit, 1975), trans. Dana Poland, Réda Bensmaïa, Minneapolis: University of Minnesota Press, 1986, 16–27.

27 On this subject, see Stephen Davies, *Empiricism and History* (2003).

28 On *Flush* and the Victorian binaries, see Derek Ryan (2013).

29 A reference to a passage in *Three Guineas* which reads

> This time let us turn to the lives not of men but of women in the nineteenth century—to the lives of professional women. But there would seem to be a gap in your library, Madam. There are no lives of professional women in the nineteenth century.
>
> (*TG* 156)

Bibliography

Acheson, James. Ed. 2017. *Virginia Woolf*. London: Palgrave.

Agamben, Giorgio. 2009 (2008). "What is the Contemporary." In *What is an Apparatus and Other Essays*. Trans. David Kishik. Stanford (CA): Stanford University Press, 39–54.

Allen, Judith. 2012. "But… I Had Said 'but' too Often." Why 'but'?" In *Contradictory Woolf: Selected Papers from the Twenty-First International Conference on Virginia Woolf*. Eds. Derek Ryan, and Stella Bolaki. Clemson (SC): Clemson University Digital Press, 1–10.

———. 2013. "Feminist Politics: 'Repetition' and 'Burning' in *Three Guineas*: Making It New." In *Virginia Woolf in Context*. Eds. Bryony Randall, and Jane Goldman. Cambridge: Cambridge University Press, 193–205.

Andres, Sophia. 1996. "The Unhistoric in History: George Eliot's Challenge to Victorian Historiography." *Clio* 26/1: 79–95.

Armstrong, Tim. 1998. *Modernism, Technology and the Body: A Cultural Study*. Cambridge: Cambridge University Press.

Arnold, Matthew. 1863. "The Bishop and the Philosopher." In *Lectures and Essays in Criticism*. Ed. Robert Henry Super. Ann Arbor (MI): The University of Michigan Press, 40–55.

Ash, Timothy Garton. 2009. *History of the Present: Essays, Sketches, and Dispatches from Europe in the 1990s*. New York (NY): Vintage Books.

Augustine, Saint. 1838. *The Confessions of St Augustine*. Oxford: J. H. Parker.

Austin, Alfred. 1895. "The Feminine Note in Poetry." *Transactions of the Leicester Literary and Philosophical Society*, vol. III. Leicester: George Gibbons, 459–460.

Ayers, David. 1999. *English Literature of the Twenties*. Edinburgh: Edinburgh University Press.

Bambach, Charles Robert. 1995. *Heidegger, Dilthey and the Crisis of Historicism*. Ithaca (NY): Cornell University Press.

Banfield, Ann. 2007. *The Phantom Table: Woolf, Fry, Russell and the Epistemology of Modernism*. Cambridge: Cambridge University Press.

Bauman, Richard. 1986. *Story, Performance and Event: Contextual Studies of Oral Narratives*. Bloomington (IN): Indiana University Press.

Beebee, Thomas Oliver. 1994. *The Ideology of Genre: A Comparative Study of Generic Instability*. University Park (PA): Pennsylvania State University Press.

Beer, Gillian. 1996. *Virginia Woolf: The Common Ground*. Ann Arbor (MI): The University of Michigan Press.

Bell, Barbara Currier, and Carol Ohmann. 1989 (1975). "Virginia Woolf's Criticism: A Polemical Preface." In *Feminist Literary Criticism: Explorations in Theory*. Ed. Josephine Donovan. Lexington (KY): The University Press of Kentucky, 48–60.

Bell, Philip Michael Hett. 2007 (1986). *The Origins of the Second World War in Europe*. Abingdon: Routledge.

Bell, Quentin. 1974 (1968). *Bloomsbury*. London: Omega.

Bellamy, Joan, Anne Laurence, and Gillian Perry, Eds. 2000. *Women, Scholarship and Criticism: Gender and Knowledge. 1790–1900*. Manchester: Manchester University Press.

Benedict, Ruth. 1955 (1935). *Patterns of Culture*. London: Routledge & Kegan Paul.

Bennett, Arnold. 1968 (1923). "Is the Novel Decaying?" In *The Author's Craft and Other Critical Writings of Arnold Bennett*. Ed. Samuel Hynes. Lincoln (NE): University of Nebraska Press, 87–89.

———. 1975 (1929). "The Queen of the Highbrows." In *Virginia Woolf: The Critical Heritage*. Eds. Robin Majumdar, and Allen McLaurin. London and New York (NY): Routledge, 258–260.

Bentley, Michael. 1997. "Introduction: Approaches to Modernity: Western Historiography since the Enlightenment." In *Companion to Historiography*. Ed. Michael Bentley. London and New York (NY): Routledge, 395–506.

———. 2005 (1999). *Modern Historiography: An Introduction*. London: Routledge.

———. 2006. *Modernizing England's Past: English Historiography in the Age of Modernism: 1870–1970*. Cambridge: Cambridge University Press.

Bernard, Catherine. 1999. "'Capricious Friendships with the Unknown and the Vanished': A Reading of Some of Virginia Woolf's Essays." *Études Britanniques Contemporaines*, Special Issue for the Société d'Études Woolfiennes/Autumn: 123–134.

———. Ed. 2011. *Woolf as Reader, Woolf as Critic or The Art of Reading in the Present*. Montpellier: Presses Universitaires de la Méditerranée.

———. 2015. *"Préface" to Virginia Woolf: Essais Choisis*. Paris: Gallimard, 7–32.

Besnault-Levita, Anne. 2018. "Mirrors of the Self and the Tradition of the Female Gothic: Scenes of Hauntings and Apparitions in Victorian and Modernist Fiction." *Journal of the Short Story in English* 70/Spring: 23–40.

Besnault-Levita, Anne, and Anne-Florence Gillard Estrada, Eds. 2018. *Beyond the Victorian/Modernist Divide: Remapping the Turn-of-the-Century Break in Literature and the Visual Arts*. New York (NY) and London: Routledge.

Bignami, Marialuisa, Francesca Orestano, and Alessandro Vescovi, Eds. 2011. *History and Narration: Looking Back from the Twentieth Century*. Newcastle upon Tyne: Cambridge Scholars Publishing.

Binhammer, Katherine, and Jeanne Wood. 2003. *Women and Literary History: "For There She Was."* Newark (NJ): University of Delaware Press.

Bishop, Edward. 1989. *A Virginia Woolf Chronology*. Basingstoke: Palgrave Macmillan.

Blaas, P. B. M. 1978. *Continuity and Anachronism: Parliamentary and Constitutional Development in Whig Historiography and in the Anti-Whig Reaction Between 1890 and 1930*. The Hague: Martinus Nijhoff.

Black, Naomi. 2004. *Virginia Woolf as Feminist*. Ithaca and London: Cornell University Press.

Blair, Emily. 2007. *Virginia Woolf and the Nineteenth-Century Domestic Novel.* Albany (NY): State University of New York.

Blakeney-Williams, Louise. 2002. *Modernism and the Ideology of History: Literature, Politics, and the Past.* Cambridge: Cambridge University Press.

Blau DuPlessis, Rachel. 1985. *Writing Beyond the Ending: Narratives Strategies of Twentieth-Century Women Writers.* Bloomington (IN): Indiana University Press.

———. 2006. "f-Words: An Essay on the Essay." In *Blue Studios: Poetry and Its Cultural Work.* Tuscaloosa (AL): The University of Alabama Press, 34–47.

Bloch, Marc. 2004 (1954). *The Historian's Craft.* Trans. Peter Putman. Manchester: Manchester University Press.

Bloom, Harold. 1997 (1973). *The Anxiety of Influence: A Theory of Poetry.* Oxford: Oxford University Press.

Booth, Alison. 1992. *Greatness Engendered: George Eliot and Virginia Woolf.* Ithaca (NY): Cornell University Press.

Bourdieu, Pierre. 1993. "The Field of Cultural Production, or: The Economic World Reversed." In *The Field of Cultural Production: Essays on Art and Literature.* New York (NY): Columbia University Press, 29–73.

Bowlby, Rachel. 1992. "Introduction: A More Than Maternal Tie." In *A Woman's Essays.* Ed. Rachel Bowlby. London: Penguin Books, ix–xxxiii.

Brady, Ciaran. 2013. *James Anthony Froude: The Intellectual Biography of a Victorian Prophet.* Oxford: Oxford University Press.

Brake, Laurel. 1994. *Subjugated Knowledges: Journalism, Gender, and Literature in the Nineteenth Century.* New York (NY): New York University Press.

Braudel, Fernand. 1980 (1969). *On History.* Trans. Sarah Matthews. Chicago (IL): The University of Chicago Press.

Brewer, Daniel. 2005. "Writing Literary History Belatedly." In *REAL – Yearbook of Research in English and American Literature*, vol. 21. Ed. Herbert Grabes. Tübingen: Narr, 57–78.

Briggs, Julia. 2005. *Virginia Woolf: An Inner Life.* London: Penguin Books.

Bronner, Stephen Eric. 2012. *Modernism at the Barricades: Aesthetics, Politics, Utopia.* New York (NY): Columbia University Press.

Brosnan, Leïla. 1999 (1997). *Reading Virginia Woolf's Essays and Journalism: Breaking the Surface of Silence.* Edinburgh: Edinburgh University Press.

Brown, Marshall, Ed. 1995. *The Uses of Literary History.* Durham and London: Duke University Press.

Buckle, Henry Thomas. 1857. *History of Civilisation in England*, vol. I. London: John W. Parker and Son.

Bürger, Peter. 1984 (1974). *Theory of the Avant-Garde.* Trans. Michael Shaw. Minneapolis (MN): University of Minnesota Press.

Burke, Peter. (1979) 1998. "Introduction: Concepts of Continuity and Change in History." In *The New Cambridge Modern History*, vol. 13. Cambridge: Cambridge University Press, 1–14.

Burns, Christy. 1994. "Re-Dressing Feminist Identities: Tensions between Essential and Constructed Selves in Virginia Woolf's Orlando." *Twentieth Century Literature* 40/3: 342–364.

Bury, John Bagnell. 1903. *An Inaugural Lecture Delivered in the Divinity School.* Cambridge: Cambridge University Press.

Butler, Judith. 1999 (1990). *Gender Trouble.* New York (NY): Routledge.

Butterfield, Herbert. 1965 (1931). *The Whig Interpretation of History*. New York (NY), London: W. W. Norton.

Carlyle, Thomas. 2002 (1830). *"History."* In *Historical Essays*. Ed. Chris Vanden Bossche. Berkeley (CA): University of California Press, 3–13.

———. 1899 (1831). "Characteristics." In *Critical and Miscellaneous Essays in Five Volumes*, vol. III. London: Chapman and Hall, 1–43.

———. 1899 (1832). "On Biography." In *Critical and Miscellaneous Essays in Five Volumes*, vol. III. London: Chapman and Hall, 44–61.

———. 1899 (1833). "On History Again." In *Critical and Miscellaneous Essays in Five Volumes*, vol. III. Cambridge: Cambridge University Press, 167–176.

———. 1845. "Introduction." *Cromwell's Letters and Speeches*, vol. 1. Part 1. New York (NY): Wiley and Putnam, 3–12.

Carr, David. 1991 (1986). *Time, Narrative and History*. Bloomington (IN): Indiana University Press.

Carr, Edward Hallett. 2018 (1961). *What is History?* London: Penguin Classics.

Cassirer, Ernst. 1950. *The Problem of Knowledge: Philosophy, Science and History since Hegel*. Trans. William H. Woglom, and Charles W. Hendel. New Haven (CT): Yale University Press.

———. 1951. *The Philosophy of the Enlightenment*. Trans. Fritz Carl Koelln, and James P. Pettegrove. Princeton (NJ): Princeton University Press.

Caughie, Pamela. 1991. *Virginia Woolf and Postmodernism: Literature in Quest Literature in Quest & Question of Itself*. Urbana (IL): University of Illinois.

de Certeau, Michel. 1988a (1975). *The Writing of History*. Trans. Tom Conley. New York (NY): Columbia University Press.

———. 1988b (1984). "Reading as Poaching." In *The Practice of Everyday Life*. Trans. Steven Randall. Berkeley (CA): University of California Press, 165–176.

———. 1989. *Heterologies*. New York (NY): Columbia University Press.

Chase, Karen. 1989. "'Bad, Was My Commentary'—Propriety, Madness, Independence in Feminist Literary History." In *Victorian Connections*. Ed. Jerome John MacGann. Charlottesville (VA): University of Virginia Press, 11–87.

Cohen, Ralph. 1991. "Genre Theory, Literary History, and Historical Change." In *Theoretical Issues in Literary History*. Ed. David Perkins. Cambridge (MA): Harvard University Press, 85–113.

Coleridge, Samuel Taylor. 1849. *Notes and Lectures Upon Shakespeare and Some of the Old Poets and Dramatists* vol.I. Ed. Sarah Coleridge. London: William Pickering.

———. 1921. *The Poems of Samuel Taylor Coleridge, Including Poems and Versions of Poems Herein Published for the First Time*. Ed. Ernest Hartley Coleridge. London and New York (NY): Humphrey Milford.

———. 1976, *The Collected Works of Samuel Taylor Coleridge, Vol. 10, On the Constitution of the Church and State*. Ed. John Colmer. London: Routledge & Kegan Paul; Princeton (NJ): Princeton University Press.

Collingwood, Robin George. 1924. *Speculum Mentis, or The Map of Knowledge*. Oxford: Clarendon Press.

———. 1999 (1934). "History as the Understanding of the Present." In *The Principles of History, and Other Writings in Philosophy of History*. Eds. William Herbert Dray, and W. J. (Jan) Van der Dussen. Oxford: Oxford University Press, 140–142.

———. 1935. *The Historical Imagination: An Inaugural Lecture, Delivered before the University of Oxford on 28 October 1935*. Oxford: Clarendon Press.

Collini, Stefan. 2019. *The Nostalgic Imagination: History in Literary Criticism*. Oxford: Oxford University Press.

Coste, Bénédicte, Catherine Delyfer, and Christine Reynier, Eds. 2017. *Reconnecting Aestheticism and Modernism: Continuations, Revisions, Speculations*. Abingdon: Routledge.

Courthope, William John. 1895. *A History of English Poetry*, vol. I. London and New York (NY): Macmillan.

Courtney, William Leonard. 1904. *The Feminine Note in Fiction*. London: Chapman & Hall.

Crosby, Christina. 2013 (1991). *The Ends of History: Victorians and "The Woman Question."* Abingdon: Routledge.

Cuddy-Keane, Melba. 1996. "The Rhetoric of Feminist Conversation: Virginia Woolf and the Trope of the Twist." In *Ambiguous Discourse: Feminist Narratology and British Women Writers*. Ed. Kathy Meisei. Chapel Hill (NC): University of North Carolina, 137–161.

———. 1997. "Virginia Woolf and the Varieties of Historicist Experience." In *Virginia Woolf and the Essay*. Eds. Beth Carole Rosenberg, and Jeanne Dubino. New York (NY): St. Martin's Press, 59–77.

———. 2003. *Virginia Woolf, the Intellectual, and the Public Sphere*. Cambridge: Cambridge University Press.

———. 2018. "Crossing the Victorian/Modernist Divide: From Multiple Histories to Flexible Futures." In *Beyond the Victorian/Modernist Divide: Remapping the Turn-of-the-Century Break in Literature and the Visual Arts*. Eds. Anne Besnault-Levita, and Anne-Florence Gillard-Estrada. New York (NY) and London: Routledge, 40–54.

Culler, Arthur Dwight. 1985. *The Victorian Mirror of History*. New Haven (CT) and London: Yale University Press.

Cunningham, Valentine. 1988. *British Writers of the Thirties*. Oxford: Oxford University Press.

Cuthell, Edith. 1905. *Wilhelmina Margravine of Bayreuth*, vol. 1. London: Chapman & Hall.

Daileader, Celia R. Caputi. 2013. "Othello's Sister: Racial Hermaphroditism and Appropriation in Virginia Woolf's *Orlando*." *Studies in the Novel* 45/1 (Spring): 56–79.

Dale, Peter Allen. 1977. *The Victorian Critic and the Idea of History*. Cambridge (MA): Harvard University Press.

Daugherty, Beth Rigel. 1997. "'Readin', Writin', and Revisin': Virginia Woolf's 'How Should One Read a Book'." In *Virginia Woolf and the Essay*. Eds. Beth Carole Rosenberg, and Jeanne Dubino. New York (NY): St. Martin's Press, 159–175.

Davies, Stephen. 2003. *Empiricism and History*. Basingstoke: Palgrave Macmillan.

Davis, Thomas Saverance. 2016. *The Extinct Scene: Late Modernism and Everyday Life*. New York (NY): Columbia University Press.

———. 2008. Distressed Histories: Late Modernism and Everyday Life, 1929–1945. A Dissertation. Notre Dame (IN).

Dawidowicz, Lucy Schildkret. 1997 (1981). *The Holocaust and the Historians*. Cambridge (MA): Harvard University Press.

Dekker, Thomas. 1608. *The Great Frost: Cold Doings in London, Except it Be at the Lotterie. With Newes Out of the Country. A Familiar Talk betwene a Country-Man and a Citizen Touching This Terrible Frost and the Great Lotterie, and the Effects of Them*. London: Henry Gosson.

Detloff, Madelyn. 2016. *The Value of Virginia Woolf*. New York (NY): Cambridge University Press.

DiBattista, Maria. 2000. "Virginia Woolf." In *The Cambridge History of Literary Criticism, Vol. VII, Modernism and New Criticism*. Eds. Arthur Walton Litz, Louis Menand, and Lawrence Rainey. Oxford: Oxford University Press, 122–137.

Dickstein, Morris. 1992. *Double Agent: The Critic and Society*. Oxford: Oxford University Press.

Didi-Huberman, Georges. 2018 (2002). *The Surviving Image: Phantoms of Time and Time of Phantoms*. Trans. Harvey Mendelsohn. Philadelphia (PA): Pennsylvania University Press.

Dillon, Sarah. 2005. "Re-inscribing De Quincey's Palimpsest: The Significance of the Palimpsest in Contemporary Literary and Cultural Studies." *Textual Practice* 19/3: 243–263.

Dowling, Linda. 1996. *The Vulgarization of Art: The Victorians and Aesthetic Democracy*. Charlottesville (VA) and London: University Press of Virginia.

Dubino, Jeanne. 1997. "Virginia Woolf: From Book Reviewer to Literary Critic, 1904–1918." In *Virginia Woolf and the Essay*. Eds. Beth Carole Rosenberg, and Jeanne Dubino. New York (NY): St. Martin's Press, 25–40.

Dubino, Jeanne, Ed. 2010. *Virginia Woolf and the Literary Market Place*. New York (NY) and Basingstoke: Palgrave Macmillan.

Duff, David. 2000. *Modern Genre Theory*. London: Routledge.

———. 2009. *Romanticism and the Uses of Genre*. Oxford: Oxford University Press.

Dusinberre, Juliet. 1997. *Virginia Woolf's Renaissance: Woman Reader or Common Reader*. Iowa City (IA): University of Iowa Press.

Eagleton, Mary, Ed. 1986. *Feminist Literary Theory*. Oxford: Basil Blackwell.

Eliot, George. 1887a. "The Lady Novelists." In *Essays and Reviews of George Eliot*. Boston (MA): Aldine Book Publishing, 7–24.

———. 1887b. "Silly Novels by Lady Novelists." In *Essays and Reviews of George Eliot*. Boston (MA): Aldine Book Publishing, 157–183.

Eliot, Thomas Stearns. 1928 (1920). *The Sacred Wood: Essays on Poetry and Criticism*. London: Methuen.

Ellis, Steve. 2007. *Virginia Woolf and the Victorians*. Cambridge: Cambridge University Press.

Esty, Jed. 2004. *A Shrinking Island: Modernism and National Culture in England*. Princeton (NJ) and Oxford: Princeton University Press.

Eysteinsson, Astradur. 1990. *The Concept of Modernism*. Ithaca (NY): Cornell University Press.

Ezell, Margaret. 1996 (1993). *Writing Women's Literary History*. Baltimore (MD): The Johns Hopkins University Press.

Felski, Rita. 1995. *The Gender of Modernity*. Boston: Harvard University Press.

Fermanis, Porscha, and John Regan. 2014. *Rethinking British Romantic History, 1770–1845*. Oxford: Oxford University Press.

Fernald, Anne E. 1994. "*A Room of One's Own*: Personal Criticism and the Essay." *Twentieth Century Literature* 40/2: 165–189.

———. 1997. "Pleasure and Belief in 'Phases of Fiction'." In *Virginia Woolf and the Essay*. Eds. Beth Carole Rosenberg, and Jeanne Dubino. New York (NY): St. Martin's Press, 193–214.

———. 2006. *Virginia Woolf: Feminism and the Reader*. New York (NY): Palgrave Macmillan.

Fischel, Oskar, and Max Von Boehn. 1909. *Modes & Manners of the Nineteenth Century as Represented in the Pictures and Engravings of the Time: 1790–1817*. London: J.M. Dent & Co.

Forster, Edward Morgan. 2001 (1910). *The Feminine Note in Literature*. London: Cecil Woolf.

———. 1944 (1927). *Aspects of the Novel*. London: Edward Arnold.

———. 1939. "The 1939 State." *New Statesman & Nation*, June 10, 1939, 888–889.

———. 1942. *Virginia Woolf*. Cambridge: Cambridge University Press.

Foucault, Michel. 1984 (1971). "Nietzsche, Genealogy, History." In *The Foucault Reader*. Ed. Paul Rabinow. New York (NY): Pantheon, 76–100.

———. 1972. *The Archeology of Knowledge*. Trans. Alan Mark Sheridan-Smith. New York (NY): Harper and Row.

———. 1980. *Power/Knowledge: Selected Interviews and Other Writings*. Ed. Colin Gordon. New York (NY): Pantheon.

———. 1990. *The History of Sexuality. Vol. 1: An Introduction*. Trans. Robert Hurley. New York (NY): Vintage Books.

Fox, Alice. 1990. *Virginia Woolf and the Literature of the English Renaissance*. Oxford: Clarendon Press.

Froude, James Anthony. 1867. "The Science of History." In *Short Studies on Great Subjects*. London: Longmans, Green and Co, 1–25.

———. 1895. *English Seamen in the Sixteenth Century. Lectures Delivered at Oxford, Easter Terms, 1893–4*. New York (NY): C. Scribner's Sons.

Froula, Christine. 2007. *Virginia Woolf and the Bloomsbury Avant-Garde: War, Civilization, Modernity*. New York (NY): Columbia University Press.

Frow, John. 2015 (2013). *The Performance of Genre*. London: Routledge.

Frye, Northrop. 2010 (1948). "Virginia Woolf." In *Northrop Frye on Twentieth Century Literature*. Ed. Glen Robert Gill. Toronto: University of Toronto Press, 80–81.

Gallop, Jane. 1982. *The Daughter's Seduction: Feminism and Psychoanalysis*. Ithaca (NY) and New York (NY): Cornell University Press.

Gaskell, Elizabeth. 2009 (1857). *The Life of Charlotte Brontë*. Oxford: Oxford University Press.

Gättens, Marie-Luise. 1995. *Women Writers and Fascism: Reconstructing History*. Gainsville (FL): University Press of Florida.

de Gay, Jane. 2006. *Virginia Woolf's Novels and the Literary Past*. Edinburgh: Edinburgh University Press.

———. 2007. "Virginia Woolf's Feminist Historiography in Orlando." *Critical Survey* 19/1: 62–72.

Genette, Gérard. 1997 (1982). *Palimpsests: Literature in the Second Degree*. Trans. Channa Newman, and Claude Doubinsky, Lincoln (NE): University of Nebraska Press.

Gilbert, Sandra, and Susan Gubar. 2000 (1979). *The Madwoman in the Attic: The Woman Writer the Nineteenth-Century Literary Imagination*. New Haven (CT): Yale University Press.

Goldman, Jane. 2007. "Forster and Women." In *The Cambridge Companion to E. M. Forster*. Ed. David Bradshaw. Cambridge: Cambridge University Press, 120–137.

Goldman, Mark. 1976. *The Reader's Art, Virginia Woolf as Literary Critic*. The Hague, Paris: Mouton.

Goodman, Nelson. 2013 (1978). *Ways of Worldmaking*. Indianapolis (IN) and Cambridge: Hackett Publishing.

Grabes, Herbert. 2001. "Literary History and Cultural History." In *Literary History, Cultural History: Force-Fields and Tensions*. Ed. Herbert Grabes. Göttingen: Gunter Narr, 1–34.

Grabes, Herbert, Ed. 2005. *Literature, Literary History, and Cultural Memory*. Göttingen: Gunter Narr.

Greene, Sally, Ed. 1999. *Virginia Woolf: Reading the Renaissance*. Athens (OH): Ohio University Press.

Grierson, Herbert John. 1928. *Lyrical Poetry*. London: The Hogarth Press.

de Groot, Jerome. 2016. *Remaking History: The Past in Contemporary Historical Fictions*. London and New York (NY): Routledge.

Gualtieri, Elena. 2000. *Virginia Woolf's Essays: Sketching the Past*. Basingstoke: Palgrave.

Guy, Josephine M., and Ian Small. 1993. *Politics and Values in English Studies: A Discipline in Crisis?* Cambridge: Cambridge University Press.

Habib, M. A. Rafey, Ed. 2013. *The Cambridge History of Literary Criticism, Vol. VI, The Nineteenth Century, 1830–1914*. Cambridge: Cambridge University Press.

Harrison, Antony. 1998. *Victorian Poets and the Politics of Culture: Discourse and Ideology*. Charlottesville (VA) and London: University Press of Virginia.

Hartog, François. 2017 (2012). *Regimes of Historicity: Presentism and Experiences of Time*. Trans. Saskia Brown. New York (NY): Columbia University Press.

Hazlitt, William. 1889. *Essays of William Hazlitt*. Ed. Frank Carr. London: W. J. Gage.

———. 1845 (1819). "On the Periodical Essayists." In *Lectures on the English Comic Writers*. New York (NY): Wiley and Putnam, 106–123.

———. 1825. *The Spirit of the Age; or, Contemporary Portraits*. London: Colburn.

———. 1889. *Essays of William Hazlitt*. Ed. Frank Carr. London: W. J. Gage.

Helsinger K. Elizabeth, Robin Lauterbach Sheets, and William R. Veeder. 1983. "The Woman Question: Literary Issues, 1837–1883." Vol. III of *The Woman Question: Society and Literature in Britain and America, 1837–1883*. New York (NY) and London: Garland Publishing.

Herrnstein Smith, Barbara. 1988. *Contingencies of Value: Alternative Perspectives for Critical Theory*. Cambridge (MA): Harvard University Press.

Hewitson, Mark. 2014. *History and Causality*. Basingstoke: Palgrave Macmillan.

Heyck, Thomas William. 1982. *The Transformation of Intellectual Life in Victorian England*. Beckenham: Croom Helm.

Hill, Katherine. 1998. "Virginia Woolf and Leslie Stephen: History and Literary Revolution." *Publications of the Modern Language Association of America (PMLA)* 96/3 (May): 351–362.

Himmelfarb, Gertrude, Ed. 2007. *The Spirit of the Age: Victorian Essays*. New Haven (CT) and London: Yale University Press.

Hoberman, Ruth. 1987. *Modernizing Lives: Experiments in English Biography, 1918–1939*. Carbondale (IL): Southern Illinois University Press.

Holland, Katherine. 2013. "Late Victorian and Modern Feminist Intertexts: The Strachey Women in *A Room of One's Own* and *Three Guineas*." *Tulsa Studies in Women's Literature* 32/1 (Spring): 75–98.

Holtby, Winifred. 1978 (1932). *Virginia Woolf: A Critical Memoir*. New York (NY): Arden Library.

Homans, Margaret. 2013. "Woolf and the Victorians." In *Virginia Woolf in Context*. Eds. Bryony Randall, and Jane Goldman. Cambridge: Cambridge University Press, 410–422.

Hotho-Jackson, Sabine. 1991. "Virginia Woolf on History: Between Tradition and Modernity." *Forum of Modern Language Studies* 27/4: 293–313.

Hume, David. 1904 (1741–1742). *Essays, Moral, Political and Literary*. London: Grant Richards.

Hungerford, Edward A. 1997. "Virginia Woolf's Reviews of the Romantic Poets." In *Virginia Woolf and the Essay*. Eds. Beth Carole Rosenberg, and Jeanne Dubino. New York (NY): St. Martin's Press, 97–115.

Huyssen, Andreas. 1986. *After the Great Divide: Modernism, Mass Culture, Postmodernism*. Bloomington (IN): Indiana University Press.

Hynes, Samuel. 1992 (1976). *The Auden Generation: Literature and Politics in England in the 1930s*. London: Pimlico Open Library.

Ifor, Evans. 1951 (1940). *A Short History of Literature*. Harmondsworth: Penguin Books.

Iggers, Georg Gerson. 2005 (1997). *Historiography in the Twentieth Century: From Scientific Objectivity to the Postmodern Challenge*. Middleton (WI): Wesleyan University Press.

Jablonka, Ivan. 2018. *History Is a Contemporary Literature: Manifesto for the Social Sciences*. Trans. Nathan J. Bracher. Ithaca (NY): Cornell University Press.

James, William. 1994 (1906–1907). *Pragmatism: A New Name for Some Old Ways of Thinking*. New York (NY): Longmans.

Jameson, Fredric. 1993. *The Political Unconscious*. London: Routledge.

———. 2012 (2002). *A Singular Modernity*. London: Verso.

Jameson, Storm. 1939. *Civil Journey*. London: Cassell.

Johnson, Reginald Brimley. 1918. *The Women Novelists*. London: William Collins Sons & Co.

Jones, Clara. 2017. *Virginia Woolf: Ambivalent Activist*. Edinburgh: Edinburgh University Press.

Joubert, Claire. 1999. "Literary Unknowing: Virginia Woolf's Essays in Fiction." In *Théorie et création littéraire*. Ed. Jean-Pierre Durix. Dijon: Presses Universitaires de Dijon, 145–159.

———. 2005. "L'Anglais de F. R. Leavis et l'acritique littéraire." In *La Critique, le critique*. Rennes: Presses Universitaires de Rennes, 27–54.

Joyce, Simon. 2004. "On or About 1901: The Bloomsbury Group Looks Back at the Victorians." *Victorian Studies* 46/4 (Summer): 631–654.

Kaplan, Carola M., and Ann B. Simpson, Eds. 1996. *Seeing Double: Revisioning Edwardian and Modernist Literature*. New York (NY): St. Martin's Press.

Kaufmann, Michael. 1997. "A Modernism of One's Own: Virginia Woolf's *TLS* Reviews and Eliotic Modernism." In *Virginia Woolf and the Essay*. Eds. Carole Rosenberg Beth, and Jeanne Dubino. New York (NY): St. Martin's Press, 137–155.

Keen, Suzanne. 1998. *Victorian Renovations of the Novel: Narrative Annexes and the Boundaries of Representation*. Cambridge: Cambridge University Press.

Klein, Kathleen Gregory. 1983. "A Common Sitting Room: Virginia Woolf's Critique of Women Writers." In *Virginia Woolf: Centennials Essays*. Eds. Elaine K. Ginsberg, and Laura Moss. New York (NY): Whitson Publishing, 231–248.

Koppen, Randi S. 2009. *Virginia Woolf and Literary Modernity*. Edinburgh: Edinburgh University Press.

Kore Schröder, Linda. 2008. "Who's Afraid of Rosamond Merridew: Reading Medieval History in 'The Journal of Mistress Joan Martyn'." *The Journal of the Short Story in English* 50/Spring: 103–119.

Koselleck, Reinhart. 2004 (1979). *Futures Past: On the Semantics of Historical Time*. Trans. Keith Tribe. New York (NY): Columbia University Press.

Koutsantoni, Katerina. 2009. *Virginia Woolf's "Common Reader."* Farnham: Ashgate.

LaCapra, Dominick. 1985. *Rethinking Intellectual History*. Ithaca (NY): Cornell University Press.

———. 1987. *History, Politics and the Novel*. Ithaca (NY): Cornell University Press.

———. 2004. *History in Transit: Experience, Identity, Critical Theory*. Ithaca (NY): Cornell University Press.

Lair, Jules Auguste. 1902. *Louise de La Vallière et la jeunesse de Louis XIV*. Paris: Plon.

Landow, George Paul. 2015. *Victorian Types, Victorian Shadows: Biblical Typology in Victorian Literature, Art and Thought*. Abingdon: Routledge.

Lassner, Phyllis. 1998. *British Women Writers of World War II*. Basingstoke: Palgrave Macmillan.

Leavis, Queenie. 2003 (1975). "Review." In *Virginia Woolf: The Critical Heritage*. Eds. Robin Majumdar, and Allen McLaurin. London and New York (NY): Routledge, 409–419.

Lecercle, Jean-Jacques. 1999. *Interpretation as Pragmatics*. London: Macmillan Press.

Lee, Hermione. 1997. *Virginia Woolf*. London: Vintage.

Leitch, Vincent B. 1992. *Cultural Criticism, Literary Theory, Poststructuralism*. New York (NY): Columbia Press.

Levenback, Karen L. 1999. Virginia Woolf and the Great War. Syracuse: Syracuse University Press.

Levenson, Michael Harry. 1991. *Modernism and the Fate of Individuality: Character and Novelistic Form from Conrad to Woolf*. Cambridge: Cambridge University Press.

Levine, Philippa. 1986. *The Amateur and the Professional: Antiquarians, Historians and Archaeologists in Victorian England, 1838–1886*. Cambridge: Cambridge University Press.

Lewes, George Henry. 2016 (1852). "The Lady Novelists." In *A Victorian Art of Fiction: Essays on the Novel in British Periodicals, 1851–1869*. Ed. John Charles Olmsted. Abingdon: Routledge, 37–52.

———. 2016 (1859). "The Novels of Jane Austen." In *A Victorian Art of Fiction: Essays on the Novel in British Periodicals, 1851–1869*. Ed. John Charles Olmsted. Abingdon: Routledge, 441–457.

Lewis, Wyndham. 1931. *Hitler*. London: Chatto & Windus.

Lilenfeld, Jane. 2003. "Introduction: Virginia Woolf and Literary History." In *Virginia Woolf and Literary History. Woolf Studies Annual 9*. Eds. Jane Lilenfeld, Lisa Low, and Jeffrey Oxford. New York (NY): Pace University Press, 85–116.

Locke, John. 1888 (1689). "Of Identity and Diversity." In *An Essay Concerning Human Understanding*. London: Ward, Lock & Co, 241–256.

London, April. 2010. *Literary History Writing, 1770–1820*. Basingstoke: Palgrave Macmillan.

Longdon-Davies, John. 1927. *A Short History of Women*. New York (NY): The Viking Press.

Longenbach, James. 1987. *Modernist Poetics of History: Pound, Eliot and the Sense of Past*. Princeton (NJ): Princeton University Press.

Lounsberry, Barbara. 2018. *Virginia Woolf: The War Without, The War Within: Her Final Diaries & the Diaries She Read*. Gainesville (FL): University Press of Florida.

Lubbock, Percy. 1921. *The Craft of Fiction*. London: Jonathan Cape.

Lucas, Frank Laurence. 1927. *Tragedy*. London: The Hogarth Press.

Lucas, John. 1997. *The Radical Twenties: Aspects of Writing, Politics and Culture*. Nottingham: Five Leaves Publications.

Lukacs, George. 1962. *The Historical Novel*. London: Merlin Press.

Macaulay, Thomas Babington. 1865 (1824). "On Mitford's History of Greece." In *Lord Macaulay's Miscellaneous Writings*, vol. 1. London: Longman, Green, 69–82.

———. 1841 (1828a). "History." In *Critical and Miscellaneous Essays*, vol. 1. Philadelphia (PA): Carey and Hart, 153–195.

———. 1841 (1828b). "Hallam's Constitutional History." In *Critical and Miscellaneous Essays*, vol. 1. Philadelphia (PA): Carey and Hart, 196–282.

———. 1875 (1848). *The Works of Lord Macaulay. History of England*, vol. 1. New York (NY): Longmans, Green.

Macfie, Alexander Lyon, Ed. 2015. *The Fiction of History*. Abingdon: Routledge.

Machosky, Brenda, Ed. 2010. *Thinking Allegory Otherwise*. Stanford (CA): Stanford University Press.

Madge, Charles, and Tom Harrisson. 1938. *Britain by Mass Observation*. London: Penguin Books.

Madox Ford, Ford. 1930 (1929). *The English Novel: From the Earliest Days to the Death of Joseph Conrad*. London: Constable.

Maitzen, Rohan Amanda. 1998. *Gender, Genre, and Victorian Historical Writing*. New York and London: Taylor & Francis.

Majumdar, Robin, and Allen McLaurin, Eds. 2003 (1975). *Virginia Woolf: The Critical Heritage*. London and New York (NY): Routledge.

de Man, Paul. 1970. "Literary History and Literary Modernity." *Daedalus, Theory in Humanistic Studies* 99/2 (Spring): 384–404.

———. 1983. *Blindness and Insight*. Minneapolis (MN): University of Minnesota Press.

Mansfield, Katherine. 2003 (1919). "A Ship Comes into Harbour." In *Virginia Woolf: The Critical Heritage*. Eds. Robin Majumbar, and Allen McLaurin. London and New York (NY): Routledge, 79–81.

Marcus, Jane. 1981. "Thinking Back Through our Mothers." In *New Feminist Essays on Virginia Woolf*. Ed. Jane Marcus. London: Macmillan, 1–30.

Marcus, Laura. 2000. "Woolf's Feminism and Feminism's Woolf." In *The Cambridge Companion to Virginia Woolf*. Eds. Sue Roe, and Susan Sellers. Cambridge: Cambridge University Press, 209–244.

Marcus, Laura, Michèle Mendelssohn, and Kirsten E. Shepherd-Barr, Eds. 2016. *Late Victorian into Modern*. Oxford: Oxford University Press.

Markus, Julia. 2005. *James Anthony Froude: The Last Undiscovered Great Victorian*. New York (NY): Scribner.

Marshik, Celia, and Allison Pease. 2019. *Modernism, Sex and Gender*. London: Bloomsbury.

Maxwell, Claire, and Peter Aggleton. 2013. "Introduction." In *Privilege, Agency and Affect—Understanding the Production and Effects of Action*. Basingstoke: Palgrave Macmillan.

McGann, Jerome. 1983. *The Romantic Ideology: A Critical Investigation*. Chicago: The University of Chicago Press.

McIntire, Gabrielle. 2008. *Modernism, Memory, and Desire: T. S. Eliot and Virginia Woolf*. Cambridge: Cambridge University Press.

McNees, Eleanor. 1997. "Colonizing Virginia Woolf: *Scrutiny* and Contemporary Cultural Views." In *Virginia Woolf and the Essay*. Eds. Beth Carole Rosenberg, and Jeanne Dubino. New York (NY): St. Martin's Press, 41–58.

McNeillie, Andrew. 2001–2002. "Woolf's America." *The Dublin Review*, 5/2 (Winter): 41–55. https://thedublinreview.com/article/virginia-woolfs-america/ [accessed June 2020].

McWhirter, David. 1988. "The Novel, the Play, and the Book: *Between the Acts* and the Tragicomedy of History." *Papers on Language and Literature* 24: 423–435.

Meinecke, Friedrich. 1972 (1936). *Historicism: The Rise of a New Historical Outlook*. Trans. John Edwards Anderson. London: Routledge & Kegan Paul.

Meisel, Perry. 1980. *The Absent Father: Virginia Woolf and Walter Pater*. New Haven (CT) and London: Yale University Press.

Melman, Billie. 2001. "Changing the Subject: Women's History and Historiography 1900–2000." In *Women in Twentieth-Century Britain: Social, Cultural and Political Change*. Ed. Ina Zweiniger-Bargielowska. Harlow: Longman, 16–35.

Menand, Louis, and Lawrence Rainey. 2000. "Introduction" to *The Cambridge History of Literary Criticism, Vol. VII, Modernism and New Criticism*. Eds. Arthur Walton Litz, Louis Menand, and Lawrence Rainey. Oxford: Oxford University Press, 1–16.

Middleton Murry, John. 2013 (1923). "Romance." In *Virginia Woolf: The Critical Heritage*. Eds. Robin Majumbar, and Allen McLaurin. London and New York (NY): Routledge, 109.

Mill, John Stuart. 1986 (1831). "The Spirit of the Age." In *The Collected Works of John Stuart Mill, Volume XXII – Newspaper Writings December 1822 – July 1831, Part I*. Eds. Ann P. Robson, and John M. Robson. Toronto: University of Toronto Press, 20–21.

Miller, Andrew John. 2009. "Fables of Progression: Modernism, Modernity, Narrative." In *Modernism and Theory: A Critical Debate*. Ed. Stephen Ross. London: Routledge, 176–189.

Miller, Jane Eldridge. 1994. *Rebel Women: Feminism, Modernism and the Edwardian Novel*. London: Virago.

Mini, Piero V. 1991. "Lytton Strachey and the New History." In *Keynes, Bloomsbury and the General Theory*. New York (NY): St Martin's Press, 125–144.

Miracky, James. 2003. *Regenerating the Novel: Genre and Gender in Woolf, Forster, Sinclair and Lawrence*. New York (NY): Routledge.

Moers, Ellen. 1976. *Literary Women: The Great Writers*. Garden City (NY): Doubleday.

Moi, Toril. 1985. *Sexual/Textual Politics: Feminist Literary Theory*, London: Methuen.

Montaigne, Michel de. 1827. *Essais de Montaigne*. Tome V, livre III. Paris: Rapilly.

————. 1877. "Of the Art of Conference." *The Essays of Montaigne*. vol. III. Ed. William Carew Hazlitt. Trans. Charles Cotton. London: Reeves & Turner.

Monte, Stephen. 2013. "Theories of Genre." In *The Cambridge History of Literary Criticism, Vol. VI, The Nineteenth Century, 1830–1914*. Ed. Rafey Habib. Cambridge: Cambridge University Press, 481–505.

Montefiori, Janet. 2003. *Men and Women Writers of the 1930s: The Dangerous Flood of History*. London and New York (NY): Routledge.

Moran, Patricia. 2017. "'What is a Woman? I Assure You, I Do Not Know': Woolf and Feminism in the 1920s." In *Virginia Woolf*. Ed. James Acheson. London: Palgrave, 165–179.

Muir, Edwin. 1928. *The Structure of the Novel*. London: The Hogarth Press.

Mumby, Frank Arthur. 1909. *The Girlhood of Queen Elizabeth, 1533–1603. A Narrative in Contemporary Letters*. London: Constable.

Namier, Lewis Bernstein. 1939. *In the Margin of History*. London: Macmillan.

Newman, Francis William. 1850. *Phases of Faith; or Passages from the History of My Creed*. London: John Chapman.

Nicoll, Allardyce. 1927. *Studies in Shakespeare*. London: The Hogarth Press.

Nicolson, Harold. 1927. *The Development of English Biography*. London: The Hogarth Press.

Niles, John D. 1999. *Homo Narrans: The Poetics and Anthropology of Oral Literature*. Philadelphia (PA): University of Pennsylvania Press.

North, Michael. 2013. *Novelty: A Study of the New*. Chicago (IL): The University of Chicago Press.

Olmsted, John Charles, Ed. 2016 (1979). *A Victorian Art of Fiction: Essays on the Novel in British Periodicals, 1851–1869*. Abingdon: Routledge.

O'Malley, Seamus. 2015. *Making History New: Modernism and Historical Narrative*. Oxford: Oxford University Press.

Orestano, Francesca. 2011. "Virginia Woolf's *Between the Acts*: History, Herstory, 'History in the Raw'." In *History and Narration: Looking Back from the Twentieth Century*. Ed. Marialuisa Bignami. Cambridge: Cambridge Scholars Publishing, 85–107.

Parkin-Gounelas, Ruth. 1991. *Fictions of the Female Self: Charlotte Brontë, Olive Schreiner and Katherine Mansfield*. New York (NY): St Martin's Press.

Pater, Walter. 1928 (1873). *The Renaissance: Studies in Art and Poetry*. London: Jonathan Cape.

Patmore, Coventry. 1851. "The Social Position of Women." *North British Review*, 14: 515–540.

Paul, Janis M. 1987. *The Victorian Heritage of Virginia Woolf: The External World in Her Novels*. Norman (OK): Pilgrim.

Pavel, Thomas. 1986. *Fictional Worlds*. Cambridge (MA): Harvard University Press.

Pawlowski, Merry. 2001. *Virginia Woolf and Fascism: Resisting the Dictators' Seduction*. Basingstoke: Palgrave.

Peach, Linden. 2000. *Virginia Woolf and New Historicism*. London: Macmillan.

Perkins, David, Ed. 1991. *Theoretical Issues in Literary History*. Cambridge (MA): Harvard University Press.

————. 1992. *Is Literary History Possible?* Baltimore (MD): The Johns Hopkins University Press.

Perrot, Michelle. 2008 (2006). *"Mon" histoire des femmes*. Paris: Seuil.

Phillips, Mark Salber. 2000. "Historical Distance and the Historiography of Eighteenth-Century Britain." In *History, Religion and Culture: British Intellectual History, 1750–1950*. Eds. Collini Stephen, Richard Whatmore, and Brian Young. Cambridge: Cambridge University Press, 31–47.

————. 2013a. *On Historical Distance*. New Haven (CT): Yale University Press.

————. 2013b. "Introduction." In *Rethinking Historical Distance. Re-enactment History*. Eds. Mark Salber Phillips, Barbara Caine, and Julia Adeney Thomas. Basingstoke: Palgrave Macmillan, 1–18.

Pollentier, Caroline. 2011. L'Invention de la communauté: esthétique et politique de l'ordinaire dans les essais de Virginia Woolf. Ph.D. Thesis. Paris: University René Diderot, VII.

Power, Eileen. 1966 (1924). *Medieval People*. New York (NY): Barnes and Noble.

Pykett, Lyn. 1995. *Engendering Fictions: The English Novel in the Early Twentieth Century*. London: E. Arnold.

Quilligan, Maureen. 2010. "Allegory and Female Agency." In *Thinking Allegory Otherwise*. Ed. Brenda Machosky. Stanford (CA): Stanford University Press, 163–187.

De Quincey, Thomas. 1998. "Suspiria de Profundis." In *Thomas De Quincey: Confessions of An English Opium Eater and Other Writings*. Ed. Grevel Lindop. Oxford: Oxford University Press, 87–182.

Rabaté, Jean-Michel, Ed. 2015. *1922: Literature, Culture, Politics*. Cambridge: Cambridge University Press.

Raleigh, Walter. 1894. *The English Novel: A Short Sketch of Its History from the Earliest Times to the Appearance of* Waverley. London: John Murray.

Randall, Bryony. 2013. "Woolf and Modernism." In *Virginia Woolf in Context*. Eds. Bryony Randall, and Jane Goldman. Cambridge: Cambridge University Press, 28–39.

Randall, Bryony, and Jane Goldman, Eds. 2013. *Virginia Woolf in Context*. Cambridge: Cambridge University Press.

Read, Herbert. 1928. *Phases of English Poetry*. London: The Hogarth Press.

Reed, John R. 1989. *Victorian Will*. Athens: Ohio University Press.

Reus, Anne Maria. 2018. Virginia Woolf's Rewriting of Victorian Women Writer's Lives. Ph.D. Thesis. Leeds Trinity University.

Reviron-Piégay, Floriane. 2013. "*Eminent Victorians:* Outrageous Strachey? The Indecent Exposure of Victorian Characters and Mores." *Études Britanniques Contemporaines* 45: https://journals.openedition.org/ebc/638 [accessed June 2020].

Reynier, Christine. 2009. *Virginia Woolf's Ethics of the Short Story*. Basingstoke: Palgrave Macmillan.

————. 2018. *Virginia Woolf's Good Housekeeping Essays*. Abingdon: Routledge.

Rhys, Ernest. 1922. *Modern English Essays*, vol. 1. London: Dent.

Rich, Adrienne. 1979. "When We Dead Awaken: Writing as Re-Vision." In *On Lies, Secrets and Silences: Selected Prose, 1966–1978*. New York (NY): Norton, 33–49.

Richter, Yvonne Nicole. 2009. A Critic in Her Own Right: Taking Virginia Woolf's Literary Criticism Seriously. Ph.D. Thesis. Georgia State University. https://scholarworks.gsu.edu/english_theses/56 [accessed July 2019].

Rigney, Ann. 2001. *Imperfect Histories: The Elusive Past and the Legacy of Romantic Historicism*. Ithaca (NY): Cornell University Press.

Robinson, Solveig, Ed. 2003. *A Serious Occupation: Literary Criticism by Victorian Women Writers*. Peterborough: Broadview Press.

Roe, Sue, and Susan Sellers, Eds. 2000. *The Cambridge Companion to Virginia Woolf*. Cambridge: Cambridge University Press.

Roessel, David. 1992. "The Significance of Constantinople in Orlando." *Papers on Language and Literature* 28/4: 398–416.

Ronen, Ruth. 1994. *Possible Worlds in Literary Theory*. Cambridge: Cambridge University Press.

Rosenbaum, S. P. 2003 (1987). *Georgian Bloomsbury: The Early History of the Bloomsbury Group, 1910–1914*. London: Palgrave Macmillan.

———. Ed. 1995. *The Bloomsbury Group: A Collection of Memoirs and Commentary*. Toronto: University of Toronto Press.

———. 1998. *Aspects of Bloomsbury: Studies in Modern English Literary and Intellectual History*. Basingstoke: Palgrave Macmillan.

———. 2014. *The Bloomsbury Group Memoir Club*. Ed. James M. Haule. Basingstoke: Palgrave Macmillan.

Rosenberg, Beth Carole. 1995. *Virginia Woolf and Samuel Johnson: Common Readers*. New York (NY): St. Martin's Press.

———. 2000. "Virginia Woolf's Postmodern Literary History." *Modern Language Notes* 115/5 (January): 1112–1130.

Rosenberg, Beth Carole, and Jeanne Dubino. 1997. *Virginia Woolf and the Essay*. New York (NY): St. Martin's Press.

Rosenfeld, Natania. 2000. *Outsiders Together: Virginia and Leonard Woolf*. Princeton (NJ): Princeton University Press.

Rosenthal, Edna. 2008. *Aristotle and Modernism: Aesthetic Affinities of T.S. Eliot, Wallace Stevens and Virginia Woolf*. Brighton: Sussex Academic Press.

Rosmarin, Adena. 1985. *The Power of Genre*. Minneapolis (MN): University of Minnesota Press.

Ross, Christine. 2012. *The Past is the Present; It's the Future Too: The Temporal Turn in Contemporary Art*. London: Bloomsbury Publishing.

Ross, Stephen. 2009. *Modernism and Theory: A Critical Debate*. London: Routledge.

Rousso, Henry. 2016. *The Latest Catastrophe: History, the Present and the Contemporary*. Trans. Jane Marie Todd. Chicago and London: The University of Chicago Press.

Ryan, Derek. 2013. *Virginia Woolf and the Materiality of Theory: Sex, Animal, Life*. Edinburgh: Edinburgh University Press.

Ryan, Derek, and Stella Bolaki, Eds. 2012. *Contradictory Woolf: Selected Papers from the Twenty-First International Conference on Virginia Woolf*. Clemson (SC): Clemson University Digital Press.

Saintsbury, George. 1891. *A History of Elizabethan Literature*. London: Macmillan.

———. 1896a (1890). "The Kinds of Criticism" In *Essays in English Literature: 1780–1860*. London: Rivington, Percival & Co, ix–xxix.

———. 1896b. *A History of Nineteenth-Century Literature (1780–1895)*. London: Macmillan.

———. 1898. *A Short History of English Literature*. London: Macmillan.

Saloman, Randi. 2012. *Woolf's Essayism*. Edinburgh: Edinburgh University Press.

Samuel, Raphael. 2012 (1994). *Theatres of Memory: Past and Present in Contemporary Culture*. London: Verso.

Saunders, Max. 2010. *Self Impression: Life-Writing, Autobiografiction, and the Forms of Modern Literature*. Oxford: Oxford University Press.

Schlack, Beverly Ann. 1979. *Continuing Presences: Virginia Woolf's Use of Literary Allusion*. University Park (PA) and London: Pennsylvania State University Press.

Schreiner, Olive. 1985 (1911). *Woman and Labour*. London: Virago.

Seeley, John Robert. 1883. *The Expansion of England: Two Courses of Lectures*. London: Macmillan.

Showalter, Elaine. 1999 (1977). *A Literature of Their Own: British Women Novelists from Brontë to Lessing*. Princeton (NJ): Princeton University. Press.

Silver, Brenda R. 1979. " 'Anon' and 'The Reader': Virginia Woolf's Last Essays." *Twentieth Century Literature, Virginia Woolf Issue* 25/3–4 (Autumn–Winter): 356–441.

———. 1999. *Virginia Woolf Icon*. Chicago (IL): The University of Chicago Press.

Smith, James, Ed. 2019. *The Cambridge Companion to the British Literature of the 1930s*. Cambridge: Cambridge University Press.

Smyth, Ethel. 1933. *Female Pipings in Eden*. London: Peter Davis.

Snaith, Anna, Ed. 2007. *Palgrave Advances in Virginia Woolf's Studies*. London: Palgrave Macmillan.

———. 2015. "Introduction to *A Room of One's Own* and *Three Guineas*." Oxford: Oxford University Press, vii–xxxvi.

Snaith, Anna, and Michael Whitworth. 2007. *Locating Woolf: The Politics of Space and Place*. Basingstoke: Palgrave Macmillan.

Southgate, Beverley. 2015. *"A New Type of History": Fictional Proposals for Dealing with the Past*. Abingdon: Routledge.

Spender, Stephen. 1955. *Collected Poems, 1928–1953*. New York (NY): Random House.

Spingarn, Joel Elias. 1911. *The New Criticism: A Lecture*. New York (NY): The Columbia University Press.

Spinner, Jenny, Ed. 2018. *Of Women and the Essay: An Anthology from 1655 to 2000*. Athens: The University of Georgia Press.

Spiro, Mia. 2012. *Anti-Nazi Modernism: The Challenges of Resistance in 1930s Fiction*. Evanston (IL): Northwestern University Press.

Spiropoulou, Angeliki. 2010. *Virginia Woolf, Modernity and History: Constellations with Walter Benjamin*. Basingstoke: Palgrave Macmillan.

Spongberg, Mary, Ann Curthoys, and Barbara Caine. 2005. *A Companion to Women's Historical Writing*. Basingstoke: Palgrave Macmillan.

Stansky, Peter. 1997 (1996). *On Or about December 1910: Early Bloomsbury and Its Intimate World*. Cambridge (MA): Harvard University Press.

Stephen, Leslie, Ed. 1885. "Jane Austen." In *Dictionary of National Biography*, vol. II. London: Smith, Elder and Co., 259–260.

———. 1898. "National Biography" in *Studies of a Biographer*, vol. 1. London: Duckworth and Co., 259–260.

———. 1955 (1904). *English Literature and Society in the Eighteenth Century*. London: Gerald Duckworth.

Stone, Lawrence. 1979. "The Revival of Narrative: Reflections on a New Old History." *Past & Present* 85/November: 3–24.

Strachey, Lytton. 1964 (1909). "A History of Rome." In *Spectatorial Essays*. New York (NY): Harcourt, 13–17.

———. 1918. *Eminent Victorians*. London: Chatto and Windus.

Strachey, Ray (Rachel). 1978 (1928). *The Cause: A Short History of the Women's Movement*. London: Virago.

———. 1935. *Careers and Openings for Women: A Survey of Women's Employment and a Guide for Those Seeking Work*. London: Faber and Faber.

Strand, Anders Christian. 2017. "'Memory is a Streamstress': Media of Memory in Virginia Woolf's *Orlando*." In *Exploring Text, Media and Memory*. Eds. Lars Sætre, Patrizia Lombardo, and Sara Tanderup Linkis. Aarhus: Aarhus University Press, 171–194.

Sweet, Rosemary. 2004. *Antiquaries: The Discovery of the Past in Eighteenth-Century Britain*. London: Hambledon and London.

Symonds, John Addington. 1884. *Shakespeare's Predecessors in the English Drama*. London: Smith, Elder & Co.

Taine, Hippolyte. 1875–1893. *Les Origines de la France contemporaine*. 4 vols. Paris Hachette.

Teskey, Gordon. 1996. *Allegory and Violence*. Ithaca (NY): Cornell University Press.

Tosh, John. 1984. *The Pursuit of History: Aims, Methods and New Directions in the Study of Modern History*. London: Longman.

Trevelyan, George Macaulay. 1952 (1926). *History of England*. New York: Double Day.

Underwood, Ted. 2013. *Why Literary Periods Mattered. Historical Contrast and the Prestige of English Studies*. Stanford (CA): Stanford University Press.

Uchida, Yuzu. 2010. "Appropriating Virginia Woolf for the New Humanism: Seward Collins and *The Bookman*." In *Virginia Woolf and the Literary Market Place*. Ed. Jeanne Dubino. New York (NY) and Basingstoke: Palgrave Macmillan, 223–236.

Usher, Roland Greene. 1915. *A Critical Study of the Historical Method of Samuel Rawson Gardiner*. Washington (DC): University of Washington.

Walker, Hugh. 1910. *The Literature of the Victorian Era*. Cambridge: Cambridge University Press.

———. 1915. *The English Essay and Essayists*. London: J.M. Dent.

———. 1965 (1925). *English Satire and Satirists*. New York: Octagon Books.

Walker, Hugh, and Mrs Hugh Walker. 2011 (1913). *Outlines of Victorian Literature*. Cambridge: Cambridge University Press.

Wallace, Diane. 2003. "'History to the Defeated': Women Writers and the Historical Novel in the Thirties." *Critical Survey* 15/2: 76–92.

Waters, Mary. 2004. *British Women Writers and the Profession of Literary Criticism, 1789–1832*. Basingstoke: Palgrave Macmillan.

Watson, George. 1962. *The Literary Critics: A Study of English Descriptive Criticism*. Harmondsworth: Penguin Books.

Wellek, René. 1941. *The Rise of English Literary History*. Chapel Hill (NC): The University of Carolina Press.

———. 1970. "English Literary Historiography during the Nineteenth Century." In *Discriminations: Further Concepts of Criticism*. New Haven (CT) and London: Yale University Press, 143–163.

Wellek, René, and Austin Warren. 1956 (1942). "Literary History." In *Theory of Literature*. New York (NY): Harcourt, 252–272.

Westerman, Molly. 2008. Narrating Historians: Crises of Historical Authority in Twentieth Century. A Dissertation submitted to the University of North Carolina at Chapel Hill (NC). https://cdr.lib.unc.edu/indexablecontent/uuid:1f79fbe0-199a-40c0-b33e-834d436d3b5f [accessed October 2020].

Westman, Karin E. 1998. "Virginia Woolf in Dialogue with History's Audience." *Clio* 28/1: 1–27.

White, Hayden. 1992 (1966). "The Burden of History." *Tropics of Discourse: Essays in Cultural Criticism*. Baltimore and London: The Johns Hopkins University Press, 27–50.

———. 2010. *The Fiction of Narrative: Essays on History, Literature, and Theory, 1957–2007*. Baltimore (MD): The Johns Hopkins University Press.

Whitworth, Michael. 2013. "Historicizing Woolf: Context Studies." In *Virginia Woolf in Context*. Eds. Bryony Randall, and Jane Goldman. Cambridge: Cambridge University Press, 3–12.

Wilde, Oscar. 1965 (1895). *The Importance of Being Ernest. A Trivial Comedy for Serious People*. New York (NY): Avon.

Wiley, Catherine. 1995. "Making History Unrepeatable in Virginia Woolf's Between the Acts." *Clio* 25/1: 3–20.

Williams, Harold. 1918. *Modern English Writers: Being a Study of Imaginative Literature, 1890–1914*. London: Sidgwick and Jackson.

Williams, Raymond. 2001 (1961). *The Long Revolution*. Calgary: Broadview Press.

———.1996 (1989). *The Politics of Modernism: Against the New Conformists*. London: Verso.

———. 2002 (1995). *The Sociology of Culture*. Chicago (IL): The University of Chicago Press.

Wilson, Peter. 2003. *The International Theory of Leonard Woolf: A Study in Twentieth-Century Idealism*. Basingstoke: Palgrave Macmillan.

Wolfe, Jessie. 2011. *Bloomsbury, Modernism, and the Reinvention of Intimacy*. Cambridge: Cambridge University.

Wollstonecraft, Mary. 1988 (1792). *A Vindication of the Rights of Women*. Ed. Carol H. Poston. New York (NY), London: W. W. Norton.

Wolstenholme, Susan. 1993. *Gothic (Re)Visions: Writing Women as Readers*. Albany (NY): State University of New York Press.

Wood, Alice. 2015 (2013). *Virginia Woolf's Late Cultural Criticism: The Genesis of 'The Years', 'Three Guineas' and 'Between the Acts'*. London: Bloomsbury.

Woolf, Leonard, Ed. 1933. *The Intelligent Man's Guide for the Prevention of War*. London: The Camelot Press.

Woolf, Virginia. 1992 (1915). *The Voyage Out*. Oxford: Oxford University Press.

———. 1992 (1919). *Night and Day*. Oxford: Oxford University Press.

———. 1992 (1922). *Jacob's Room*. Oxford: Oxford University Press.

———. 2000 (1925). *Mrs Dalloway*. Oxford: Oxford University Press.

———. 1938 (1927). *To the Lighthouse*. London: J. M. Dent.

———. 1992 (1928). *Orlando: A Biography*. Oxford: Oxford University Press.

———. 2000 (1929; 1938). *A Room of One's Own. Three Guineas*. London: Penguin.

———. 2000 (1931). *The Waves*. St Ives: Wordsworth Classics.

———. 2009 (1933). *Flush: A Biography*. Oxford: Oxford University Press.

———. 1992 (1941). *Between the Acts*. Oxford: Oxford University Press.

———. 1975. *The Letters of Virginia Woolf, 1888–1912*, vol. I. Eds. Nigel Nicolson, and Joanne Trautmann. London: The Hogarth Press.

——. 1976. *The Letters of Virginia Woolf, 1912–1922*, vol. II. Eds. Nigel Nicolson, and Joanne Trautmann. London: The Hogarth Press.

——. 1977. *The Letters of Virginia Woolf, 1923–1928*, vol. III. Eds. Nigel Nicolson, and Joanne Trautmann. London: The Hogarth Press.

——. 1977. *The Diary of Virginia Woolf, 1915–1919*, vol. I. Ed. Anne Olivier Bell. San Diego (CA), London and New York (NY): Harcourt Brace Jovanovich.

——. 1978. *The Diary of Virginia Woolf, 1920–1924*, vol. II. Ed. Anne Olivier Bell. San Diego (CA), London and New York (NY): Harcourt Brace Jovanovich.

——. 1978. *The Letters of Virginia Woolf, 1928–1931*, vol. IV. Eds. Nigel Nicolson, and Joanne Trautmann. London: The Hogarth Press.

——. 1979. "'Anon' and 'The Reader': Virginia Woolf's Last Essays." *Twentieth Century Literature* 25/3–4 (Fall/Winter): 356–361.

——. 1979. *Letters of Virginia Woolf, 1932–1935*, vol. V. Eds. Nigel Nicolson, and Joanne Trautmann. London: The Hogarth Press.

——. 1980. *The Letters of Virginia Woolf, 1936–1941*, vol. VI. Eds. Nigel Nicolson, and Joanne Trautmann. London: The Hogarth Press.

——. 1980. *The Diary of Virginia Woolf, 1925–1930*, vol. III. Ed. Anne Olivier Bell. San Diego (CA), London and New York (NY): Harcourt Brace Jovanovich.

——. 1982. *The Diary of Virginia Woolf, 1931–1935*, vol. IV. Ed. Anne Olivier Bell. San Diego (CA), London and New York (NY): Harcourt Brace Jovanovich.

——. 1984. *The Diary of Virginia Woolf, 1936–1941*, vol. V. Ed. Anne Olivier Bell. San Diego (CA), London and New York (NY): Harcourt Brace Jovanovich.

——. 1992 (1990). *A Passionate Apprentice, The Early Journals: 1897–1909*. Ed. Mitchell A. Leaska. London: Hogarth Press.

——. 1991. *The Complete Shorter Fiction*. Ed. Susan Dick. London: Grafton Books.

——. 1992. *A Woman's Essays*. Ed. Rachel Bowlby. London: Penguin Books.

——. 2002. *Moments of Being*. Ed. Jeanne Schulkind. London: Pimlico.

Wordsworth, William. 1802 (1800). *Lyrical Ballads, with Other Poems*, vol. 1. Philadelphia (PA): James Humphreys.

Zemgulys, Andrea. 2008. *Modernism and the Locations of Literary Heritage*. Cambridge: Cambridge University Press.

Zoltán Boldizsár, Simon. 2019. *History in Times of Unprecedented Change: A Theory for the 21st Century*. London: Bloomsbury Academic.

Zwerdling, Alex. 1986. *Virginia Woolf and the Real World*. Berkeley (CA): University of California Press.

Index

Woolf, Virginia

Essays

Fiction